CW00336897

THE GOOD
Web Site
GUIDE 2002

THE GOOD
Web Site
GUIDE 2002

GRAHAM EDMONDS

ORION

First published in 2001 by Orion Media
An imprint of Orion Books Ltd
Orion House, 5 Upper St Martin's Lane,
London WC2H 9EA

A CIP catalogue record for this book is
available from the British Library.

ISBN 0 75283 811 3

Designed by Staziker Jones, Cardiff

Printed by Clays Ltd, St Ives plc

Introduction

So what's all the fuss about the Internet? What
use is the World Wide Web anyway? This book
will help you find out. Whether you are new to
the Internet or an old hand, this is a guide to
the best and most useful web sites, it's
designed to help you get the best out of
the Net.

I've assumed that you know how to log on,
and that you're now looking for the best sites
that suit your needs. Maybe you're not a
confident surfer or perhaps can't be bothered,
either way this book will save you the hassle.
It'll save you money too and help you get the
most out of the Internet.

This is the second edition of the Good Web
Site Guide. When writing the first there was a
great deal of optimism and hype around the
Internet and in the last year the bubble has
largely burst, with several high profile firms
going under and currently there's a lot of gloom
around its future. It's true that some of the hype
was unjustified, but then, so is the current
pessimism; like all these things, it will find its
level eventually.

In all over 60,000 copies of the first edition
of this book have been sold, which is tremendous and a big thank you if you were one of
those who supported us. This edition is fully

updated and we've added more than 1500 sites and many extra sections, the book has more than doubled in length. We've included new sections on web site design, architecture, charities, teenagers, chat and much more. Our publishers have managed to keep the price down to £3.99 too.

The idea behind the Good Web Site Guide is that we fully review the very best sites in each section or genre, then we look for those sites that offer something unique or have features that make them stand out and review those too. We also list alternatives, especially in the popular genres such as music, shopping or finance. We have visited thousands of web sites covering a bewildering range of topics, but we have concentrated on what's really useful and popular.

SO WHAT'S CHANGED IN A YEAR?

Generally, sites have improved in design and in ease of use, more thought and care is being taken, but with prices for professional web design escalating, the gap between the best sites and the amateur ones is widening. There has still been an explosion of new sites this year so thankfully there's lots of creativity out there.

Quality is another issue, the cost and time

you need to maintain a good site is sometimes so prohibitive that many sites don't seem to be updated as frequently as they should be, or they just die through lack of interest and funding.

It's also becoming obvious that there will be less free information in the future with more sites charging subscription fees for access to the information they hold. There's more pressure on sites to become more commercial now as shareholders and investors demand a return.

All this is sounding a bit gloomy isn't it? So here are fifty things you can do on the Net right now, today:

1. Be more aware of your finances (**www.thisismoney.com**)
2. Get the number of someone you've been meaning to call but haven't (**www.bt.com**)
3. Get a deal on a holiday (**www.a2btravel.co.uk**)
4. Go on a ramble (**www.onedayhikes.com**)
5. Learn to take better holiday snaps (**www.betterphoto.com**)
6. Find a pub (**www.goodguides.com**)
7. Buy a train ticket without queuing at the station (**www.thetrainline.co.uk**)
8. Go on a shopping spree (**www.shopsmart.co.uk**)
9. Get something gorgeous for the home (**www.bluedeco.co.uk**)

10. Look the part, buy a designer label cheaply (**www.intofashion.com**)
11. Buy some sexy lingerie (**www.rigbyandpeller.com**)
12. Sod the shopping and get someone to do it for you (**www.ybag.co.uk**)
13. Try some new food (**www.bluemango.co.uk**)
14. Buy an antique from an auction (**www.icollector.co.uk**)
15. Visit a New York art gallery (**www.moma.org**)
16. Then buy a poster or two (**www.artrepublic.com**)
17. Find out about MP3 and download some music (**www.real.com**)
18. Share it with others (**www.aimster.com**) – maybe not...
19. Have a laugh over misheard lyrics (**www.kissthisguy.com**)
20. Find out what films are on, when and where (**www.popcorn.co.uk**)
21. Buy your favourite star's gear (**www.asseenonscreen.com**)
22. E-mail a celebrity (**www.celebritymail.com**)
23. Improve your sports knowledge (**www.sports.com**)
24. Keep up with the news (**http://news.bbc.co.uk**)

25. Do the garden, virtually (**www.crocus.co.uk**)
26. Find out what plants grow well in your area (**http://fff.nhm.ac.uk/fff**)
27. Send some flowers (**www.clareflorist.co.uk**)
28. Get a new job (**www.stepstone.co.uk**)
29. and a new house (**www.propertyfinder.co.uk**)
30. Get some work done on the house and find someone to do it (**www.improveline.co.uk**)
31. Let your fingers do the walking (**www.yell.co.uk**)
32. Get on your bike (**www.cycleweb.co.uk**)
33. Donate a cup of food to the hungry (**www.thehungersite.com**)
34. Fix a date (**www.dateline.co.uk**)
35. Or just have a chat (**www.delphi.com**)
36. Get fit (**www.netfit.co.uk**)
37. Look something up (**www.xrefer.co.uk**)
38. Have a laugh (**www.funny.co.uk**)
39. See something sad (**www.losers.org**)
40. Find your horoscope (**www.easyscopes.com**)
41. View another part of the world (**www.cammcity.com**)
42. Watch an 'angry kid' film (**www.atomfilms.co.uk**)
43. Buy the right car for you (**www.autobytel.co.uk**)
44. Get the weather forecast (**www.met-office.gov.uk**)

45. Play a game (**www.gamehippo.com**)
46. Do a quiz (**www.thinks.com**)
47. Have a flutter (**www.willhill.com**)
48. Get free legal advice (**www.lawrights.co.uk**)
49. Re-home a pet (**www.giveusahome.co.uk**)
50. Take the kids out for the day
    (**www.kidsnet.co.uk**)

In the past year I've used the Net to shop, extensively buying CDs and minidiscs (**www.cdwow.com** and **www.101cd.co.uk**), clothes (**www.diesel.com**), shoes (**www.shoe-shop.com**), computer accessories (**www.whsmith.co.uk**), a Which? best buy washing machine from Value Direct (**www.valuedirect.co.uk**) and a handheld PC from PC World at **www.pcworld.co.uk**

My best Internet experience was organising a holiday to Sri Lanka dealing direct with local companies to arrange tours and for accomodation **www.aitkenspence.com**, **www.lankadirectory.com/happyshan** and **www.aseatica-tours.com**. We booked the flights via Flight Bookers (**www.e-bookers.co.uk**) and saved hundreds in the process. There were no hitches and the service was excellent throughout.

Using the Internet does not need to take over your life but it can generally enhance it. I can really indulge my interests, be informed and experience things I've not experienced before, and it's saved me time and money.

It is disappointing that there are relatively few really well designed web sites. Most sites are informative and do the job but really entertaining sites, those that make you want to go back for more, are rare. Surprisingly, few have that genuine 'wow' factor. The best are brilliant, here's my top ten of the best designed and most useful and user-friendly sites (in no particular order of merit):

www.eyestorm.com
www.go-fly.co.uk
www.google.co.uk
www.mapblast.com
www.metmuseum.org
www.netradio.com
www.scoot.co.uk
www.shopsmart.co.uk
www.skyscrapers.com
www.thetrainline.com

There are more, but these are examples of sites with a special something that makes you want to come back and use them again, whether it be great design or excellent service. Web site designers who want our loyalty should take note and make their own sites similarly impressive.

KEEPING SAFE

Some people are worried about using their credit card to shop on the Net. In theory it's safer than giving your credit card details over the phone, as information is encrypted. When on a secure line there should be a small padlock icon appearing on your toolbar, and the http:// prefix should change to https://. Providing you shop from UK sites you are fully covered by the same fair trade laws that cover every form of shopping in the UK, so buying from abroad could have some risks attached. If in doubt shop from reputable firms and known brand names.

There's also a great deal of concern about cookies. A cookie is the popular name for a file which holds some information about your machine and, only if you give it out, about you. They have a sinister reputation but they are a way for web site owners to monitor traffic and find out who is visiting their sites, in theory so they can tailor their content to their customers or provide a better service. If you're worried about them, you can easily delete them or set your computer to not receive them. However, many sites need them to function, especially shopping sites.

USING THE LIST

Ratings

ORIGIN UK
SPEED ✓✓✓✓✓
INFO ✓✓✓✓✓
VALUE ✓✓✓✓✓
EASE ✓✓✓✓✓

✓ = slow/poor ✓✓✓✓✓ = fast/good

Speed – Some sites take ages to download and use. This gives an indication of what you can expect from the site in question. During the course of preparing the book I visited each site at least 3 times. All the work was done on the same PC using the same service provider.

Info – This gives you a gauge of how much information is available, with respect to how much you are entitled to expect. It's also a measure of the number and quality of links they provide.

Value – Value for money. The more ✓s the better value you can expect. In some cases it's just not quantifiable, and has been omitted.

Ease – This is intended to give an indication of how easy the site is to use. Is it logical, easy to navigate or well signposted?

Origin – It's not always obvious where the site originates. This can be important, especially when you are buying from abroad. There may be restrictions or taxes that aren't obvious at the time. Also information that is shown as general may apply to one part of the world and not another. For instance gardening advice on a US site will not necessarily apply in the UK.

Remember, I don't pretend to be a judge and jury, my ratings are just my opinion – that of a customer and consumer. We've decided not to go ahead with our own site for now, as we want to devote the time to making this book the best on the market. However you will see parts of this book featured on some web sites such as **www.whsmith.co.uk**.

If you have any suggestions as to how we can improve it or have a site you think should be included in the 2003 edition then please e-mail me at **goodwebsiteguide@hotmail.com**.

W?WT – Symbol indicates a member of the *Which?* Trader Scheme. For more information see page 319 or visit their web site at **www.which.net**

TAX

Beware of foreign taxes as not all foreign retailers include taxes in their quoted price. The US, for instance, quotes pre-tax prices and tax varies from state to state. Be aware and always check before purchasing as shopping from a low tax region can save you pounds.

Acknowledgements

I'd just like to end in thanking a few important people:

Firstly Orion, especially the sales team and Jo Carpenter who did a great job with the first books and I know will with this one.

In particular to Deborah Gray for great patience and excellent advice – i.e.: 'good grief man have a rest!'

All my many friends and colleagues for their support and suggestions.

Anyone who bought the first books.

Lastly to Michaela for love, holidays and incurable shopping.

ADSL

Asymmetric Digital Subscriber Line (ADSL) is a technology for transmitting digital information at a high bandwidth on existing phone lines to homes and businesses. It enables you to access the Internet many times faster than with conventional phone lines. By Winter 2001 BT say that 70% of the UK will get access – slower than in other parts of the world.

www.adsluk.co.uk
ADSL ALL YOU NEED TO KNOW

ORIGIN	UK	Informative and regularly updated, find out all the
SPEED	✓✓✓	latest news and commentary as well as a good
INFO	✓✓✓✓✓	explanation of what you get for your money. Also
EASE	✓✓✓	check out **www.bigpipes.org.uk** which is a chat
		forum and newsletter with all the latest information
		on ADSL, the roll out and its use.

www.btopenworld.com
BRITISH TELECOM

ORIGIN	UK	Not much information, but you can find out
SPEED	✓✓✓	whether you are in line to get access to broadband
INFO	✓✓✓	and more or less when. You can also sign up for the
EASE	✓✓✓✓	newsletter.

Aircraft and Aviation

www.airlinks.org.uk
SEARCH ENGINE OF THE AIR

ORIGIN	US	Excellent, quick, easy-to-use search facility where
SPEED	✓✓✓✓	you can find either sites or photos. See also
INFO	✓✓✓✓	**www.aviation.uk.com** which has sites listed in some
EASE	✓✓✓✓	30 categories from aerobatics to weather.

www.flyer.co.uk
AVIATION IN THE UK

ORIGIN UK
SPEED ✓✓✓
INFO ✓✓✓✓✓
EASE ✓✓✓✓

News, views and information about the world of aviation from the *Flyer Magazine* site, there's a good section on aviation links, and how to buy and sell an aircraft, classified ads and even free Internet access.

www.aeroflight.co.uk
AVIATION ENTHUSIASTS

ORIGIN UK
SPEED ✓✓✓
INFO ✓✓✓✓
EASE ✓✓✓

An expanding site that attempts to offer an 'information stop' for all aviation enthusiasts. It has details on international air forces, a section on the media including specialist books and bookshops, as well as details of air shows and museums. The information hasn't been updated much so we're not sure about the long-term future of the site.

www.f4aviation.co.uk
AIR SCENE UK

ORIGIN UK
SPEED ✓✓✓
INFO ✓✓✓✓
EASE ✓✓✓✓

Provided by F4 aviation, a group of enthusiasts, this site has lots of information, nostalgia, links to related sites and personal flying accounts. It's also got an air show listing with reports and previews.

www.raf.mod.uk
ROYAL AIR FORCE

ORIGIN UK
SPEED ✓✓✓✓
INFO ✓✓✓✓
EASE ✓✓✓✓

This site features lots of information on the RAF, the history section is particularly good with data on the very first planes to the latest, with a good gallery of pictures to complement the information, although the time-line section isn't quite up-to-date at time of writing. You can also find out what the Red Arrows are up to, get career advice and technical information.

http://theaerodrome.com
WW1

ORIGIN UK
SPEED ✓✓
INFO ✓✓✓✓
EASE ✓✓✓✓

Devoted to the aircraft and aces of the First World War, this site offers lots of background information, personal experiences and details about the pilots who fought above the trenches.

www.wpafb.af.Mil/museum
US Air Force Museum

ORIGIN US
SPEED ✓✓✓
INFO ✓✓✓✓✓
EASE ✓✓✓✓

A superbly detailed site with masses of data on the aircraft and their history from the first planes to space flight, the archive section is particularly good with features on particular types of aircraft and weapons, and how they were developed.

www.thunder-and-lightnings.co.uk
British post war military aircraft

ORIGIN UK
SPEED ✓✓✓✓
INFO ✓✓✓✓
EASE ✓✓✓✓

You won't find Spitfires here, but you will learn about great British military planes produced since the war, each has a linked page which is very detailed. There's also a spotter's guide, links, events and a photo quiz. If you do want to know about Spitfires try the excellent site www.spitfiresociety.demon.co.uk.

www.geocities.com/capecanaveral/hangar/8780
The ugly aircraft survey

ORIGIN US
SPEED ✓✓✓
INFO ✓✓✓✓
EASE ✓✓✓✓

We couldn't resist this one, with its devotion to uncommon and ugly aircraft, each with a page devoted to why it existed in the first place. You can contribute to the annual survey too.

www.airdisaster.com
NO.1 AVIATION SAFETY RESOURCE

ORIGIN US
SPEED ✓✓✓
INFO ✓✓✓✓✓
EASE ✓✓✓✓

A rather macabre site that reviews each major air crash, and looks into the reasons behind what happened. It's not for the squeamish, but the cockpit voice recordings and eyewitness accounts make fascinating, if disturbing, reading. See also **www.aaib.gov.uk** for the Air Accident Investigation Branch which has a monthly bulletin with details of crashes and current investigations.

http://catalogue.janes.com/jawa.shtml
JANES DEFENCE INFORMATION

ORIGIN UK
SPEED ✓✓✓
INFO ✓✓✓✓✓
VALUE ✓✓✓
EASE ✓✓✓

Janes are the authority on military information, and you can download (with monthly updates) their All the World's Aircraft list for £905 annually, or buy it on CD-Rom for £825. For their homepage go to **www.janesonline.com**.

http://vrml.environs.com/ivan
VIRTUAL FLYING

ORIGIN UK
SPEED ✓✓
INFO ✓✓✓✓
EASE ✓✓✓

You need a good computer to get the best out of this, you download the software and then you're ready to fly – virtually. You can have a go in a lunar lander and a Harrier jump jet. Great fun, but you need a bit of patience.

www.gliderpilot.net
GLIDER PILOT NETWORK

ORIGIN UK
SPEED ✓✓✓✓
INFO ✓✓✓
EASE ✓✓✓✓

Weather, news, links and information on all forms of gliding, plus chat and classified adverts. There's also an online shop, which is hosted by Amazon.

Antiques and Collectibles

The Internet is a great place to learn about antiques, it's also full of specialist sites run by fanatical collectors. If you want to take the risk of buying over the Net then the best prices are found on the big auction sites such as Ebay and Icollector.

www.antiques.co.uk
FIND AND BUY ONLINE

ORIGIN	UK
SPEED	✓✓✓✓
INFO	✓✓✓✓
VALUE	✓✓
EASE	✓✓✓✓

An attractive and well-designed site, which is basically an online showroom dedicated to most aspects of art and antiques. The emphasis is on quality and experts vet all items. There's also a news and reviews section with interesting articles on the latest fashionable antiques.

www.antiquesbulletin.co.uk
INTERACTIVE WORLD OF ANTIQUES

ORIGIN	UK
SPEED	✓✓✓✓
INFO	✓✓✓✓✓
VALUE	✓✓✓
EASE	✓✓✓✓

A huge site with loads of information and links to more specialist sites and dealers. It aims to cover every aspect of antiques and does a great job, there are details on auctions, specialist articles on over 30 topics and advice on how to buy and sell. You can also buy and sell from the site.

www.antiquegems.net
ANTIQUE JEWELLERY

ORIGIN	UK
SPEED	✓✓✓
INFO	✓✓✓✓
VALUE	✓✓✓
EASE	✓✓✓✓

A fine site from a Birmingham dealer and restorer with a good selection of gems and jewellery as well as watches and a selection of bargains. You can't buy online but there's a contact service for the pieces that you're interested in.

www.invaluable.com
ANTIQUE NEWS

ORIGIN UK
SPEED ✓✓✓✓
INFO ✓✓✓✓✓
EASE ✓✓✓

Get the latest word on antiques, plus contact details and links to hundreds of dealers and auction houses world-wide. The links section is particularly good.

www.antiquesworld.co.uk
FOR EVERYONE WITH AN INTEREST IN ANTIQUES AND COLLECTIBLES

ORIGIN UK
SPEED ✓✓✓✓
INFO ✓✓✓✓✓
EASE ✓✓✓

Catch up on the latest news, obtain details on major and local fairs and events, book a course or indulge your interests by linking to a specialist online retailer or club. You can't buy from this site but the links and information are very good. For a site that simply lists antiques and collectors fairs in date order with links to organiser's web sites go to www.antiques-web.co.uk/fairs.html

www.dmgantiquefairs.com
FOR THE LARGEST ANTIQUES FAIRS

ORIGIN UK
SPEED ✓✓✓
INFO ✓✓✓✓
EASE ✓✓✓✓

DMG run the largest fairs in the UK. Their attractive site gives details of each fair, including dates, location and local tourist information.

www.collectiques.co.uk
COLLECTIBLES

ORIGIN UK
SPEED ✓✓✓✓
INFO ✓✓✓✓✓
EASE ✓✓✓✓

Despite its fairly naff name, Collectiques is a good resource if you're searching for information or that elusive piece for your collection. It covers an impressive array of areas of interest from toys to architectural antiques, it's easy-to-use and it's great for

background info and links too. See also
www.collectorcafe.com which is great for links,
articles and chat.

www.worldcollectorsnet.com
BY COLLECTORS FOR COLLECTORS

ORIGIN US	If there's a market for it, it's here. Collectibles in all
SPEED ✓✓✓✓	shapes and sizes, the latest news, links to official
INFO ✓✓✓	sites, price guides and a newsletter. You can buy, sell
VALUE ✓✓✓	or trade at the Swap Shop, but beware of shipping
EASE ✓✓✓✓	costs and use your common sense.

www.eppraisals.com
WHAT IS IT? WHAT'S IT WORTH?

ORIGIN US	An American site that gives online appraisals for
SPEED ✓✓✓✓	your antiques, first you have to sign up then you're
INFO ✓✓✓	ready to get your appraisal. You enter the details of
VALUE ✓✓✓	your object either online or you can send a picture
EASE ✓✓✓✓	by post. Each appraisal costs $20. See also Hugh
	Scully's World of Antiques at **www.qxl.com**

Ceramics

www.ukceramics.org
A CERAMICS SHOWCASE

ORIGIN UK	An excellent showcase site for new and established
SPEED ✓✓✓	artists. It has beautiful pictures of the ceramics with
INFO ✓✓✓	good biographical information. The site enables you
EASE ✓✓✓✓✓	to contact artists to buy their work.

www.studiopottery.com
THE POTTERY STUDIO

ORIGIN UK	Divided into 3 sections: pots, potters and potteries,
SPEED ✓✓✓✓	this site gives information on the history of studio
INFO ✓✓✓✓✓	pottery. It's a huge site with over 2,300 pages and
EASE ✓✓✓✓	it's continually being updated. Everything is cross-referenced with good explanations and photographs.

www.claricecliff.com
THE FIRST LADY OF CERAMIC DESIGN

ORIGIN UK	A must for fans of Clarice Cliff pottery. There is
SPEED ✓✓✓	information on auctions, biographical details,
INFO ✓✓✓✓✓	patterns, shapes; also a newsletter and forum for
VALUE ✓✓	related chat. The site offers reproductions and
EASE ✓✓✓✓	related merchandise for sale.

Apple Mac Users

The following sites specialise in Apple Mac technology and programs. See also the general sections on Computers, Software and Games which may also have relevant information.

www.apple.com or www.uk.euro.apple.com
HOME OF THE ORIGINAL

ORIGIN US	Get the latest information and advances in Apple
SPEED ✓✓✓	computers at this beautifully designed site. You can
INFO ✓✓✓✓	buy from the Applestore but don't expect huge
VALUE ✓✓✓	discounts, although they do offer finance deals.
EASE ✓✓✓✓	

www.mygate.com/st
Buy apples

ORIGIN UK	Beautifully designed site from a retailer specialising
SPEED ✓✓✓✓	in Apple computers, there's a lot of information, a
INFO ✓✓✓✓	great product range and there's free delivery for
VALUE ✓✓✓	orders over £50. They've also got a good reputation
EASE ✓✓✓✓	for service.

www.macwarehouse.co.uk
Great prices on Macs

ORIGIN UK	Part of the Microwarehouse group, they specialise in
SPEED ✓✓✓	mail order supply with a reputation for excellent
INFO ✓✓✓✓	service. Good prices and a wide range make this a
VALUE ✓✓✓✓	good first port of call if you need a new PC or an
EASE ✓✓✓	upgrade.

www.macintouch.com
The original Mac news and information site

ORIGIN US	If you have a Mac then this is the site for you. It has
SPEED ✓✓✓	lots of information, bug fixes and software to down-
INFO ✓✓✓✓✓	load, but it is a little overwhelming and it takes a
EASE ✓✓	while to get your bearings. Once you've done that,

for the Mac user this is invaluable. In the unlikely
event that you can't find what you're looking for
here try **www.macaddict.com** or the Mac News
network at **www.macnn.com**

www.ihateapple.com
If you really don't like Apple

ORIGIN US	An entertaining anti-Apple web site devoted to
SPEED ✓✓✓✓	'debunking' and exposing Apple faults – it's actually
INFO ✓✓✓✓	quite informative and funny too.
EASE ✓✓✓	

Games for Macs

Here are three great sites to help you if you feel restricted by having an Apple Mac.

www.macgamer.com
MAC GAMER MAG

ORIGIN US	An online magazine with all the usual features we've
SPEED ✓✓✓	come to expect: news, reviews, links and even a few
INFO ✓✓✓✓	giveaways. It's all neatly packaged on an attractive
EASE ✓✓✓	website.

www.macgamefiles.com
MAC GAME FILE LIBRARY

ORIGIN US	To quote them 'Macgamefiles.com is THE one-stop
SPEED ✓✓✓	source for Macintosh game files. The web site
INFO ✓✓✓✓✓	features lively libraries of Macintosh demos, share-
EASE ✓✓✓	ware, updaters, tools, add-ons, and more.' And
	they're right; it's a very good site with some really
	good games and useful stuff.

www.insidemacgames.com
IMG MAGAZINE

ORIGIN US	A magazine devoted to Mac games where you can
SPEED ✓✓✓	find the latest demos, updates for the games, loads
INFO ✓✓✓✓	of shareware games, news and reviews.
EASE ✓✓✓	

Architecture

www.greatbuildings.com
ARCHITECTURE ONLINE

ORIGIN US	This site shows over 1,000 buildings and features
SPEED ✓✓✓	hundreds of leading architects, with 3D models,
INFO ✓✓✓✓	photographic images and architectural drawings,
EASE ✓✓✓	commentaries, bibliographies and web links. It's all
	well packaged, easy-to-use and you can search by
	architect, building or location.

www.skyscrapers.com
SKYSCRAPERTASTIC!

ORIGIN US	This really entertaining and award-winning site has
SPEED ✓✓✓✓	over 10,000 images of skyscrapers and major build-
INFO ✓✓✓✓	ings from around the world, there are also features,
EASE ✓✓✓✓	chat and you can search by region as well as archi-
	tect or building.

www.wallpaper.com
WALLPAPER MAGAZINE

ORIGIN UK	This leading architecture and design magazine has
SPEED ✓✓✓	produced one of the most original web sites, with a
INFO ✓✓✓✓	real 'wow' factor. It's informative and interesting
EASE ✓✓✓	and the site reflects the feel of the magazine. It's not
	that easy to navigate but it looks great and the
	graphics are fun.

Art and the Arts

One of the best things about the Internet is the ability to show-case things that otherwise would be quite obscure or inaccessible. Working artists can show their wares to excellent effect, and we can now 'visit' some of the world's great galleries and museums, and view art before we buy. Here are the best sites for posters, online galleries, museums, cartoons, exhibitions, showcases for new talent and how to get the best clip-art for your own use.

Art – resources, shops, museums, galleries and exhibitions

www.artlex.com

THE VISUAL ARTS DICTIONARY

ORIGIN US	From abbozzo to zoomorphic, there are over 3,000
SPEED ✓✓✓	definitions of art-related terms with links to other
INFO ✓✓✓✓	sites and articles. It can be quite slow to use, and
EASE ✓✓✓	some of the links aren't reliable.

www.artcyclopedia.com

THE FINE ART SEARCH ENGINE

ORIGIN CANADA	A popular resource for finding out just about
SPEED ✓✓✓	anything to do with art, it's quick, nicely designed
INFO ✓✓✓✓✓	and informative. At time of writing they had
EASE ✓✓✓✓✓	indexed 700 leading arts sites, and offer more than

24,000 links directly to an estimated 80,000 works by 7,000 different artists. See also the economically designed **www.artincontext.com** and **www.artswire.org**

http://wwar.com
THE WORLD-WIDE ART RESOURCE

ORIGIN US
SPEED ✓✓✓
INFO ✓✓✓✓✓
EASE ✓✓✓✓✓

This is an effective search vehicle with links to artists, exhibitions, galleries and museums. There are four main sections,
1. Services – art news, e-postcards, classified ads, young artist's CVs.
2. Visual – links to museums, artists, galleries, jobs and suppliers; also to performing arts, antiques, films and architectural sites.
3. Artist Portfolios – where you can view, buy or show art.
4. Art News.

www.design-council.org.uk
PROMOTING THE EFFECTIVE USE OF DESIGN

ORIGIN UK
SPEED ✓✓✓
INFO ✓✓✓
EASE ✓✓✓✓

This site effectively promotes the work of The Design Council through access to their archives of articles on design and details of their work with government; also gives feedback on design issues.

www.artguide.org
THE ART LOVER'S GUIDE TO BRITAIN AND IRELAND

ORIGIN UK
SPEED ✓✓✓
INFO ✓✓✓✓
EASE ✓✓✓✓

Organised by artist, region, exhibition or museum with more than 4,500 listings in all. This site is easy to navigate with a good search engine and cross-referencing making it simple to find out about events in a particular region which is aided by annotated maps.

www.artplanet.com
THE INTERNET FINE ART DIRECTORY

ORIGIN US
SPEED ✓✓✓
INFO ✓✓✓
EASE ✓✓✓✓

Art Planet is a comprehensive online fine art directory, claiming over 11,000 entries. There are sections on artists, auction houses, galleries, libraries, museums, exhibitions, publishers, etc. Its main strength is a list of good links to other art sites; however, it is biased towards the USA.

www.thegallerychannel.com
WORLD'S MOST COMPREHENSIVE ARTS LISTING

ORIGIN UK
SPEED ✓✓
INFO ✓✓✓✓
EASE ✓✓✓✓

The Gallery Channel provides information on exhibitions, with online cross-referencing for over 16,000 artists, 13,000 exhibitions at 5,000 venues in the UK. The site is continually updating and there's always something new to look at, with plenty of articles, news and previews.

www.24hourmuseum.org.uk
OPEN ALL HOURS

ORIGIN UK
SPEED ✓✓✓✓
INFO ✓✓✓✓✓
EASE ✓✓✓✓

Run by the Campaign for Museums, this site aims to give high quality access to the UK's galleries, museums and heritage sites, and it succeeds. The graphics are clear, it's easy-to-use and really informative. There's a museum finder, links, a magazine and resources for research. See also the rather pretentious **www.artmuseum.net** which is supported by Intel.

www.artchive.com
MARK HARDEN'S ARTCHIVE

ORIGIN UK
SPEED ✓✓✓
INFO ✓✓✓✓✓
EASE ✓✓✓✓

Incredible, but seemingly the work of one art fanatic, this superb site not only has an excellent art encyclopedia, but also the latest art news and galleries with special online exhibitions. The quality of the pictures is outstanding but it does take a while to download, it's usually worth the wait though. There's also a section on theory and good links.

www.surrealism.co.uk
ONLINE GALLERY

ORIGIN UK
SPEED ✓✓✓✓
INFO ✓✓✓
EASE ✓✓✓✓

Not as way out as you'd expect, this site gives an overview of surrealism and features contemporary artists. The online gallery is OK without being that exciting, but as a showcase it works.

www.graffiti.org
THE WRITING ON THE WALL

ORIGIN UK
SPEED ✓✓✓✓
INFO ✓✓✓✓
EASE ✓✓✓✓

If you're fascinated by graffiti then here's the place to go, it's got a gallery of the best examples, history and links to other graffiti sites.

www.the-artists.org
20TH CENTURY ART

ORIGIN UK
SPEED ✓✓✓✓
INFO ✓✓✓✓
EASE ✓✓✓✓

This site is easy-to-use, with minimalist design and details of every major artist of the last century.

The major museums and galleries

www.tate.org.uk
THE ARCHETYPAL GALLERY SITE

ORIGIN UK
SPEED ✓✓
INFO ✓✓✓✓
VALUE ✓✓✓
EASE ✓✓✓✓

A real treat with good design and quality pictures, the site is divided into these sections:

1. One for each Tate gallery, including what's on and what's coming.
2. The collection, which can easily be browsed or searched by artist.
3. The shop sells art related merchandise.
4. A forum for art chat and a feedback feature.
5. Notes about the sponsors.
6. Future plans for the galleries.
7. Details about touring exhibitions.

www.nationalgallery.org.uk
THE NATIONAL COLLECTION OF WESTERN EUROPEAN PAINTING

ORIGIN UK
SPEED ✓✓
INFO ✓✓✓✓✓
EASE ✓✓✓✓✓

A very comprehensive site, similar in style to the Tate but without a shop. Divided into five major sections:

1. The collection – very good quality pictures with notes on each one.
2. What's on and when.
3. Information on the gallery – how to get there etc.
4. What's new and coming.
5. A good search facility.

For access to the all the Scottish National Galleries on a similar site, go to **www.natgalscot.ac.uk** who have a similarly informative and enjoyable site.

www.thebritishmuseum.ac.uk
ILLUMINATING NEW CULTURES

ORIGIN	UK
SPEED	✓✓✓✓
INFO	✓✓✓✓
VALUE	✓✓✓
EASE	✓✓✓✓

Whether you explore the world's cultures with interactive mapping, understand and educate yourself or just browse the collection, this is a beautifully illustrated site. The online shop stocks a selection of gifts and goods based on museum artefacts. Delivery in the UK is £3.95. They also arrange museum tours.

www.npg.org.uk
THE NATIONAL PORTRAIT GALLERY

ORIGIN	UK
SPEED	✓✓✓✓
INFO	✓✓✓✓✓
VALUE	✓✓
EASE	✓✓✓✓

With over 10,000 works on view, this is one of the biggest online galleries. It shows the most influential characters in British history portrayed by artists of their time. You can search by sitter or artist, and buy the print. The online shop offers options on print size, framing and delivery, including overseas.

www.royalacademy.org.uk
THE ROYAL ACADEMY

ORIGIN	UK
SPEED	✓✓✓✓
INFO	✓✓✓✓
EASE	✓✓✓✓

Another well-designed gallery site with all the information you need on the Royal Academy as well as ticket information and live waiting times for the exhibitions. There's support for schools, colleges and teachers, but at time of writing the collection section was being put together, so unavailable to view.

www.vam.ac.uk
VICTORIA & ALBERT MUSEUM

ORIGIN UK
SPEED ✓✓✓
INFO ✓✓✓✓✓
VALUE ✓✓
EASE ✓✓✓

The world's largest museum has a good-looking web site, if slightly irritating to use. There are six sections:

1. Infodome – has information about galleries, museums and services.
2. Explorer – about design and its uses as well as a virtual museum tour.
3. Programme – what's on.
4. Newsroom – info on the latest exhibitions.
5. Shopping – excellent store with nice range of gifts. Delivery is £5.95 for orders of less than £100.
6. Learning Zone – information for schools and how to get the best out of a visit to the museum.

www.moma.org
THE MUSEUM OF MODERN ART IN NEW YORK

ORIGIN US
SPEED ✓✓✓
INFO ✓✓✓✓✓
VALUE ✓✓
EASE ✓✓✓

This attractive site is split into six major areas:

1. The collection, with a selection of the best paintings.
2. What's on.
3. Education resources, for teachers and pupils.
4. Details on becoming a member.
5. Visiting information.
6. The online store which is excellent for the unusual.

You need to install Shockwave for features such as the audio commentary on the paintings. Do browse the store as some products on sale are exclusive; members get discounts on items sold in the store. Delivery to the UK is expensive.

www.metmuseum.org
THE METROPOLITAN MUSEUM OF ART IN NEW YORK

ORIGIN US
SPEED ✓✓✓✓
INFO ✓✓✓✓
VALUE ✓✓✓
EASE ✓✓✓✓

A beautiful and very stylish site, featuring lots of great ideas, with quality illustrations and photographs, you can view any one of 3,500 exhibits, become a member, or visit a special exhibition. The shop offers a great range of products, many exclusive, and there's a handy gift finder service. Delivery costs to the UK depend on how much you spend.

www.uffizi.firenze.it/welcome.html
THE UFFIZI GALLERY IN FLORENCE

ORIGIN ITALY
SPEED ✓✓✓
INFO ✓✓✓
EASE ✓✓✓✓

It's the quality of the images of the paintings that make this site stand out. They are superb and it's a shame that there are not more of them to view. Navigating is easy and quicker than most. There is also gallery information and a tour.

www.louvre.fr
FRANCE'S TREASURE HOUSE

ORIGIN FRANCE
SPEED ✓✓
INFO ✓✓✓✓
VALUE ✓
EASE ✓✓✓✓

Similar to the UK's National Gallery site:
1. You can take a virtual tour.
2. View the collection.
3. Learn about its history.
4. Check out the latest exhibitions and buy advance tickets.
5. The shop has interesting items and delivery to the UK is about £7.

www.guggenheim.org
VANGUARDS OF ARCHITECTURE AND CULTURE

ORIGIN US
SPEED ✓✓✓
INFO ✓✓✓✓
VALUE ✓✓
EASE ✓✓✓✓

There is the promise of a unique virtual museum, but while we wait, the other four; Berlin, Bilbao, Venice and New York can be visited here.

1. You can find out about exhibitions and collections, projects, tours, events and developmental programs.
2. Join. Membership entitles you to free entry and a store discount.
3. The store is stocked with a wonderful selection of unusual goods and gifts, and is not bad value. Delivery to the UK is around £20.

Sites featuring the top artists:
www.daliuniverse.com – Dali
www.thelowry.com – Lowry
www.marmottan.com – Monet
www.tamu.edu/mocl/picasso/works – Picasso
www.vangoghgallery.com – Van Gogh.

Clip–art

www.clipart.com
THE PLACE TO START IF YOU NEED CLIP-ART

ORIGIN US
SPEED ✓✓✓✓
INFO ✓✓
EASE ✓✓✓✓

Links to over 500 clip-art sites but using the very good search facility, you should quickly find the perfect image. Although huge, this site is low on information. Many linked sites have free art for use, otherwise cost varies enormously depending on what you want. You can also try the very similar **www.clipart.net** as well.

Cartoons

www.cartoonbank.com
WORLD'S LARGEST CARTOON DATABASE

ORIGIN US	Need to find a cartoon for a particular occasion?
SPEED ✓✓✓	Then there's a choice of over 20,000, mostly from
INFO ✓✓✓	*New Yorker* magazine. You can send e-cards,
EASE ✓✓✓✓	but they only supply products to the USA. For
	a massive set of links to cartoon and humorous
	sites then try the excellent Norwegian site
	www.cartoon-links.com

www.cartoon-factory.com
BUYING CARTOON CELS

ORIGIN UK	Buy cartoon cels, mainly from Disney and Warner
SPEED ✓✓✓✓	cartoons; you can search by subject or artist.
INFO ✓✓✓✓	Delivery is expensive, although they are flexible
VALUE ✓✓	about payment.
EASE ✓✓✓✓✓	

Buying art

www.artrepublic.co.uk
BOOKS, POSTERS AND WHAT'S ON WHERE

ORIGIN UK	A nicely designed, easy-to-use site, which features
SPEED ✓✓✓✓	three sections:
INFO ✓✓✓✓	1. Posters – choose from over 1,500 posters, use the
VALUE ✓✓✓	glossary of art terms or peruse artist's biographi-
EASE ✓✓✓✓✓	cal data. Free shipping worldwide.

2. Books – read reviews or select from over 30,000 books. Delivery costs £3 for anywhere.
3. What's on world-wide – details of the latest exhibitions, competitions and travel information for over 1,200 museums around the world.

Also trades as www.onlineposters.com

www.barewalls.com

INTERNET'S LARGEST ART PRINT AND POSTER STORE

ORIGIN US	This site backs its claim with a huge range, it's also
SPEED ✓✓✓✓	excellent for gifts and unusual prints and posters but
INFO ✓✓✓✓	be aware that the shipping costs are high – $25 for
VALUE ✓✓	the UK. There's also a gift voucher scheme.
EASE ✓✓✓✓✓	

www.postershop.co.uk

FINE ART PRINTS AND POSTERS

ORIGIN UK	There are over 20,000 prints and posters available
SPEED ✓✓✓✓	to buy, covering the work of over 100 artists.
INFO ✓✓✓✓	There's also a framing service and a good user-
VALUE ✓✓✓	friendly search facility where you can search by
EASE ✓✓✓✓✓	subject as well as artist. In the museum shop there's
	a range of art-related gifts to choose from. Delivery
	costs £5 for the UK.

www.totalposter.com

GET THE BIG PICTURE

ORIGIN UK	Excellent poster store, specialising in photographic
SPEED ✓✓✓	posters with a very wide selection. Extra services
INFO ✓✓✓✓	include: printing up your own photos to poster size,
VALUE ✓✓✓	plus pictures of recent key sporting and news events
EASE ✓✓✓	in their 'stop press' section. Delivery costs vary.

www.arthouse.uk.com

WATERCOLOURS ON THE WEB

ORIGIN UK	Learn about watercolour techniques, go on a course,
SPEED ✓✓✓✓	find out about exhibitions, where to find designers
INFO ✓✓✓✓	or book an artistic holiday. There are also several
VALUE ✓✓	galleries devoted to artists with work for sale and
EASE ✓✓✓✓	many pictures to view.

www.finedition.co.uk
FINE REPRODUCTIONS

ORIGIN	UK
SPEED	✓✓✓
INFO	✓✓✓
VALUE	✓✓
EASE	✓✓✓✓

If you're not a lottery winner and you fancy a Turner or a Constable in your home, this is the site for you. Fine Edition will faithfully reproduce your favourite painting for £150 and upwards.

www.eyestorm.com
BUYING CONTEMPORARY ART

ORIGIN	UK
SPEED	✓✓✓✓
INFO	✓✓✓
VALUE	✓✓✓
EASE	✓✓✓✓✓

A really attractive and well-designed site, which showcases contemporary art and photography, you can buy online as well. For another large selection see www.artandparcel.com or the excellent www.art4deco.com

Astrology

www.astrology.com
ALL ABOUT ASTROLOGY

ORIGIN	UK
SPEED	✓✓✓
INFO	✓✓✓✓✓
EASE	✓✓✓✓

A very comprehensive site offering free advice from the stars, you can buy a personalised reading and chart or just browse the more general horoscopes. You can find celebrity horoscopes too, and learn about the history and techniques of astrology. See also www.horoscope.co.uk home of *Horoscope Magazine*.

www.russellgrant.co.uk
RUSSELL GRANT

ORIGIN	UK
SPEED	✓✓✓✓
INFO	✓✓✓✓
VALUE	✓✓
EASE	✓✓✓✓

Now is your chance to buy a horoscope from a real celebrity, costs range from £3.99 upwards. This site has been expanded in the last year to include dream interpretations, tarot and other astrological resources as well as the various horoscopes.

www.astrologer.com

THAT BEING DISCUSSED IS ALSO ARISING

ORIGIN UK
SPEED ✓✓✓✓
INFO ✓✓✓✓
EASE ✓✓✓✓

No, we didn't get it either, but this site has links to all the major astrological sites such as the Astrological Association, several online journals and the Matrix software site from which you can download programs that help you work out your own charts.

www.easyscopes.com

ASTROLOGY SEARCH ENGINE

ORIGIN USA
SPEED ✓✓✓✓
INFO ✓✓✓✓✓
EASE ✓✓✓✓

Here you can get as many different free horoscopes as you can handle, the site contains direct links to the daily, weekly, monthly and yearly horoscopes for each zodiac sign. You just have to select your zodiac sign and you are presented with a large list of horoscopes to choose from. It's amazing how different they all are for the same sign!

You can also get horoscopes from:
www.sunsigns.co.uk
www.horoscopes4u.com
www.excite.co.uk/horoscopes
www.starsignz.co.uk

Auctions and Classified Advertisments

Before using these sites be sure that you are aware of the rules and regulations surrounding the bidding process, and what your rights are as a seller or purchaser. If they are not properly explained during the registration process, then use another site. They should also offer a returns policy as well as insurance cover.

Whilst there are plenty of bargains available, not all the products on offer are cheaper than the high street or specialist vendor, it's very much a case of buyer beware. Having said that, once you're used to it, it can be fun, and you can save a great deal of money.

www.ebay.co.uk
YOUR PERSONAL TRADING COMMUNITY

ORIGIN UK
SPEED ✓✓✓
INFO ✓✓✓✓
VALUE ✓✓✓
EASE ✓✓✓✓

With over 3 million items you are likely to find what you want here. The emphasis is on collectibles and it is strong on antiques of all sorts, although there's much much more. There is a 24-hour support facility and automatic insurance cover on all items up to £120. Previous clients have reviewed each person who has something to sell, that way you can check up on their reliability.

www.ebid.co.uk
AUCTIONS AND CHAT

ORIGIN UK
SPEED ✓✓✓
INFO ✓✓✓
VALUE ✓✓✓
EASE ✓✓✓✓

No longer claims to be the UK's finest online auction house, but there's over 100,000 lots and it is strong on design. The auctions can easily be accessed and browsed; its strengths are in computing, electronics and music. You can also chat online about any of the auctions with fellow bidders and sellers.

www.icollector.com

REDEFINING THE ART OF COLLECTING

ORIGIN US	An attractive site bringing together the wares of some
SPEED ✓✓✓	950 auction houses and dealers, icollector is an ambi-
INFO ✓✓✓✓	tious project that works well. The emphasis is on art,
VALUE ✓✓✓	antiques and collectibles. Be sure that the auction
EASE ✓✓✓✓	house you're dealing with ships outside the USA.

www.qxl.com

A PAN-EUROPEAN AUCTION COMMUNITY

ORIGIN UK/EUROPE	This wide-ranging site offers anything from airline tickets and holidays to cars, collectibles and elec-
SPEED ✓✓✓	tronics (in several languages). The quality of
INFO ✓✓✓✓	merchandise seems better than most sites. There's
VALUE ✓✓✓✓	also a link to Hugh Sculley's World of Antiques who
EASE ✓✓✓✓	specialize in online valuations.

www.firedup.com

WHERE EVERYTHING HAS ITS PRICE

ORIGIN UK	Much improved since its launch, Fired Up now has a
SPEED ✓✓✓✓	good layout and is easy-to-use, it still features events
INFO ✓✓✓✓	heavily but there's a good selection of other prod-
VALUE ✓✓✓✓	ucts and services too. Providing News International
EASE ✓✓✓✓	keeps backing it, it should keep improving. Another

site worth checking out is **www.CQout.com** it has
over 4,000 lots and a nice design.

www.sothebys.com

QUALITY ASSURED, BUT JUST FOR THE CONNOISSEURS

ORIGIN UK/US	You can bid in their online auctions, find out about
SPEED ✓✓✓	their normal auctions or enlist their help with one of
INFO ✓✓✓✓	the many extra services they offer. The emphasis
VALUE ✓✓	here is on high quality and the arts. They also have a
EASE ✓✓✓✓	bookshop and you can buy catalogues.

www.christies.com
FOR THOSE WITH DEEP WALLETS

ORIGIN UK
SPEED ✓✓
INFO ✓✓✓
EASE ✓✓✓

Christies have a slow site with info on their programme of auctions and on how to buy and sell through them, but you can't carry out transactions from the site. The LotFinder service searches their auctions for that special item – for a fee.

www.ad-mart.co.uk
AWARD WINNING

ORIGIN UK
SPEED ✓✓✓✓
INFO ✓✓✓✓
VALUE ✓✓✓✓
EASE ✓✓✓✓✓

Excellent design and ease of use makes this site stand out; there are fourteen sections, all the usual suspects plus personal ads, boating and pets. There's also a section for announcements of upcoming events such as auctions and car boot sales. See also **www.nettrader.co.uk** which is also really well designed and easy-to-use.

www.ixm.co.uk
EXCHANGE & MART

ORIGIN UK
SPEED ✓✓✓✓
INFO ✓✓✓✓
VALUE ✓✓✓✓
EASE ✓✓✓✓✓

Everything the paper has and more, great bargains on a massive range of goods found with good search facility, all packaged in a bright easy-to-use site. It is split into five major sections:
1. Motoring – including cars, vans, number plates and finance.
2. Home – including DIY and gardening.
3. Travel and holidays.
4. Products – for small businesses including computers.
5. Property.
You can place an ad, or get involved with their online auctions.

www.loot.com
FREE ADS ONLINE

ORIGIN	UK
SPEED	✓✓✓
INFO	✓✓✓✓
VALUE	✓✓✓✓
EASE	✓✓✓

Over 100,000 ads and over 3,000 auctioned items make *Loot* a great place to go for a bargain. It's an interesting site to browse with nine major sections covering the usual classified ad subjects supplemented by areas featuring jobs, accommodation and personals. Go to *Loot* café for a chat.

Books and Booksellers

Books were the first products to be sold in volume over the Internet, and their success has meant that there are many online booksellers, all boasting about the speed of their service and how many titles they can get. In the main, the basic service is the same wherever you go, just pick the bookshop that suits you.

www.bookbrain.co.uk
BEST PRICES FOR BOOKS

ORIGIN	UK
SPEED	✓✓✓✓
INFO	✓✓✓✓
VALUE	✓✓✓✓✓
EASE	✓✓✓✓

All you do is type in the title of the book and Bookbrain will search out the online store that is offering it the cheapest (including postage). You then click again to get taken to the store to buy the book – simple. Access also available via WAP phone. It's also worth checking out the American site **www.bestbookbuys.com**

www.amazon.co.uk
MORE THAN JUST A BOOKSTORE

ORIGIN UK
SPEED ✓✓✓✓
INFO ✓✓✓✓
VALUE ✓✓✓
EASE ✓✓✓✓

Amazon is the leading online bookseller and most online stores have followed their formula of combining value with recommendation. Amazon has spent much on providing a wider offering than just books and now has sections for music, gifts, games, software and DVD/video. It also offers an auction service and there's an excellent kids' section, which is aimed at parents. There are also zshops where Amazon act as a guarantor for the stores it recommends. For books, there are better prices elsewhere.

www.bol.com
THE EURO-BOOKSELLER

ORIGIN UK/EUROPE
SPEED ✓✓✓
INFO ✓✓✓✓✓
VALUE ✓✓✓
EASE ✓✓✓✓

Owned by Bertlesmann the German media giant, you can get access to books in seven European countries. Slightly dull, it appeals to the true book lover, with lots of recommendations but few offers. The 'books in the media' section provides day-by-day listing of books that were featured in TV programs, the press or on the radio. Like Amazon it has expanded to include music, video, DVD and games, and you can also download audio books.

www.waterstones.co.uk
ASK A BOOKSELLER

ORIGIN UK
SPEED ✓✓✓✓
INFO ✓✓✓✓
VALUE ✓✓✓
EASE ✓✓✓✓

An extension of the high street store, this site is less fussy than Amazon and easier to use. If you are not sure of the book you want you can 'ask a bookseller' and they will reply with a recommendation. You can also pre-order books that are yet to be published and download e-books which can be read on your PC. There's also an out-of-print book finder service.

www.bookshop.co.uk
THE INTERNET BOOKSHOP

ORIGIN	UK
SPEED	✓✓✓✓
INFO	✓✓✓✓
VALUE	✓✓✓✓
EASE	✓✓✓✓

Owned by W.H.Smith, this follows the usual Internet bookshop pattern, but it is slightly clearer with a variety of offers. Also sells videos, CDs and games, with links to other magazines and, unusually, stationery.

www.ottakars.co.uk
FREE DELIVERY TO STORE

ORIGIN	UK
SPEED	✓✓✓
INFO	✓✓✓✓
VALUE	✓✓✓✓
EASE	✓✓✓✓

Ottakars' site is clear and easy-to-use with some nice personal touches; it offers the usual mix of range, recommendation, offers, competitions and they offer a free collection from the local store. In fact, there's even a web page for each store giving information on the locale and events. **W?WT**

http://bookshop.blackwell.co.uk
BLACKWELLS

ORIGIN	UK
SPEED	✓✓✓
INFO	✓✓✓✓
VALUE	✓✓✓✓
EASE	✓✓✓✓

Blackwells are best known for academic and professional books, but their site offers much more, with the emphasis on recommendation and help finding the right book. **W?WT**
For more academic books, a good place to try is www.studentbookworld.com

www.borders.com
BORDERS

ORIGIN	US
SPEED	✓✓✓
INFO	✓✓✓✓
VALUE	✓✓✓
EASE	✓✓✓✓

A bookseller making successful in-roads into the UK offering a site that is heavily US-biased, but great for something different. Good offers on books, music and DVD, though shipping is comparatively expensive.

www.countrybookshop.co.uk
YOUR LOCAL BOOKSHOP

ORIGIN	UK
SPEED	✓✓✓✓
INFO	✓✓✓✓
VALUE	✓✓✓
EASE	✓✓✓✓✓

A small bookseller attempting to take on the corporate giants and largely succeeding if this site is anything to go by. It's very comprehensive and although it may not offer the cheapest books it's easier and more enjoyable to use than many sites. Another triumph of content and good design is at the Book Pl@ce **www.thebookplace.com** who offer the usual online bookshop but with the addition of three magazines devoted to books.

www.bn.com
THE WORLD'S BIGGEST BOOKSELLER

ORIGIN	US
SPEED	✓✓✓
INFO	✓✓✓✓✓
VALUE	✓✓✓✓
EASE	✓✓✓✓

Barnes and Noble's site boasts more books than any other online bookseller. In style it follows the other bookshops with an American bias. It has a good out-of-print service and links up with **www.bol.com** for foreign language books. You can also buy software, prints and posters as well as magazines and music. Unusual features include an e-book shop and their online university where you can take courses in anything from business to learning a language.

www.alphabetstreet.com
STREETS AHEAD

ORIGIN	UK
SPEED	✓✓✓
INFO	✓✓✓✓
VALUE	✓✓✓✓
EASE	✓✓✓✓

Part of the Streets Online group, this site follows the pattern for other bookshops. However, it offers free delivery in the UK making it one of the cheapest booksellers. It also offers a cash back loyalty scheme in conjunction with its other sites that sell music, games and DVDs.

www.bookpeople.co.uk
INCREDIBLE DISCOUNTS

ORIGIN UK	Offers a limited range of discounted books with up
SPEED ✓✓✓	to 75% off the r.r.p; strong on children's titles but
INFO ✓✓✓	low on recommendations. Some books vary from
VALUE ✓✓✓✓✓	shop editions – using cheaper paper or are paper-
EASE ✓✓✓✓	back editions. Delivery is free if you spend over £25,

plus point-based loyalty scheme. For more bargains try www.bookcloseouts.com

www.powells.com
MASSIVE

ORIGIN US	A huge and impressive site, which is well designed
SPEED ✓✓✓✓	and relatively easy-to-use, Powells seems to occupy
INFO ✓✓✓✓✓	most of Portland in Oregon and for once the cost of
VALUE ✓✓✓	shipping isn't prohibitive for UK customers. A good
EASE ✓✓✓✓	place to go if you're looking for something unusual.

www.abebooks.com
ADVANCED BOOK EXCHANGE

ORIGIN US	A network of independent booksellers from around
SPEED ✓✓✓✓	the world claiming access to 27 million books, just
INFO ✓✓✓✓	use the excellent search engine to find your book
EASE ✓✓✓✓	and they'll direct you to the nearest bookseller.

http://classics.mit.edu
THE CLASSICS ONLINE

ORIGIN US	A superb resource offering over 400 free books to
SPEED ✓✓✓✓	print or download, there's also a search facility and
INFO ✓✓✓✓✓	help with studying.
VALUE ✓✓✓✓✓	
EASE ✓✓✓✓	

www.bibliomania.com
WORLD LITERATURE ONLINE

ORIGIN	UK
SPEED	✓✓✓✓
INFO	✓✓✓✓✓
VALUE	✓✓✓✓✓
EASE	✓✓✓✓

A superb resource, Bibliomania has changed to a more commercial and attractive site. You can search the entire site for quotes or for a specific book, or get help with research or subscribe to the magazine. There are also plans for a shop and a tie in with a specialist publisher.

www.shakespeare.sk
COMPLETE WORKS

ORIGIN	US
SPEED	✓✓✓
INFO	✓✓✓✓
EASE	✓✓✓✓

This is a straightforward site featuring the complete writings of Shakespeare, including biographical details, and a glossary explaining the language of the time.

www.booklovers.co.uk
QUALITY SECOND HAND BOOKS

ORIGIN	UK
SPEED	✓✓✓✓
INFO	✓✓✓✓
VALUE	✓✓✓✓
EASE	✓✓✓✓

If you can't find the book you want, then this is worth a try. There is an excellent search facility or you can leave them a request. They give a quote if you want to sell a book or you can swap too. There's also an events listing for book fairs. If you can't find what you're looking for here it's worth checking out three very good sites www.justbooks.co.uk www.bookfinder.com or www.bibliofind.com who all have very fast search facilities. For antiquarian give www.shapero.com a try.

www.justbooks.co.uk
SECOND-HAND AND ANTIQUARIAN

ORIGIN UK
SPEED ✓✓✓
INFO ✓✓✓✓
VALUE ✓✓✓
EASE ✓✓✓✓

To quote: 'JustBooks is a leading Internet market-place in Europe for second-hand and antiquarian books. Here you will find more than 3.8 million titles offered by over 900 book dealers around the world, from paperbacks to rare, second-hand, out of print, antiquarian books or first editions.' This sums it up well, and it's a good, easy-to-use site too.

www.achuka.co.uk
CHILDREN'S BOOKS

ORIGIN UK
SPEED ✓✓
INFO ✓✓✓✓
EASE ✓✓

Achuka are specialists in children's books and offer a comprehensive listing of what's available from a fairly boring site. There's plenty of information on the latest news and awards as well as reviews, author interviews, a chat section and links to booksellers. See also the very traditional **www.childrensbookshop.com**

www.audiobooks.co.uk
THE TALKING BOOKSHOP

ORIGIN UK
SPEED ✓✓✓✓
INFO ✓✓✓✓
VALUE ✓✓✓
EASE ✓✓✓

Specialists in books on tape, they have around 6,000 titles in stock and can quickly get another 10,000. They also stock CDs but no MP3 yet. Search the site by author or reader, as well as by title. There are some offers, but most stock is at full price with delivery being £2 per order. Also uses **www.talkingbooks.co.uk** See also **www.isis-publishing.co.uk** who offer thousands of unabridged audio books, and more in the way of CDs, but for a really unusual audio experience go to **www.totallyword.com**

www.contentville.com
BRAIN FOOD BANK

ORIGIN US	Unusual in concept, the idea is that Contentville
SPEED ✓✓✓✓	store information on book and magazine content so
INFO ✓✓✓✓✓	that when you search for a particular subject you get
EASE ✓✓✓	a list of selected titles and articles which you may

buy or get free access to. Also includes e-books, dissertations, screenplays, study guides and speeches. It's not the easiest to get your head around but when it all clicks the site is invaluable for research and homework.

Book specialists

The following sites specialise in one form or genre of book:

www.stanfords.co.uk – excellent site from the UK's leading travel and map retailers.

www.crimeboss.com – crime comic books.

www.poetrysoc.com – a comprehensive site from the Poetry Society.

www.purefiction.com – features, links and advice for budding novelists.

www.specialistbooks.co.uk – medical, legal, business and science.

www.sportspages.com – sport books.

Cars

Whether you want to buy a car, check out your insurance or even arrange a service, it can all be done on the Net. If you want to hire a car see page 439.

Information and motoring organisations

www.dvla.gov.uk
DRIVER AND VEHICLE LICENSING AGENCY

ORIGIN UK
SPEED ✓✓✓
INFO ✓✓✓✓✓
VALUE ✓✓✓
EASE ✓✓✓

Excellent for the official line in motoring, the driver's section has details on penalty points, licence changes and medical issues. The vehicles section goes through all related forms and there's also a what's new page. It's clearly and concisely written throughout and information is easy to find.

www.smmt.co.uk
SOCIETY OF MOTOR MANUFACTURERS & TRADERS

ORIGIN UK
SPEED ✓✓✓
INFO ✓✓✓✓
EASE ✓✓✓✓

The SMMT support the British motor industry by campaigning and informing the trade and public alike. Here you can get information on topics like the motor show and the new tax regime based on exhaust emissions. There's also a good company car tax calculator on Lex Vehicle Leasing's site www.lvl.co.uk If you're scared of getting a company car now, it may be worth your while checking out the offers at **www.contracthireandleasing.com** who have a large number of options available.

www.theaa.co.uk
THE AA

ORIGIN UK	Now a more comprehensive motoring site with a
SPEED ✓✓✓✓	route planner, new and used car info, travel infor-
INFO ✓✓✓✓✓	mation, insurance quotes, bookshop and a car data
VALUE ✓✓✓	checking facility.
EASE ✓✓✓✓	

www.rac.co.uk
THE RAC

ORIGIN UK	A much clearer site than The AA's, with a very good
SPEED ✓✓✓	route planner and traffic news service. There's also
INFO ✓✓✓✓✓	information about buying a car, getting the best
VALUE ✓✓✓	finance and insurance deals and a small shop.
EASE ✓✓✓✓	

www.greenflag.co.uk
GREEN FLAG

ORIGIN UK	The usual route planner and car buying advice all
SPEED ✓✓✓✓	packaged on a nice looking and very green site,
INFO ✓✓✓	there's a particularly good section on European
EASE ✓✓✓✓	travel and motoring advice from Sue Baker.

TV-tie-in sites

www.topgear.beeb.com
TOP GEAR

ORIGIN UK	A functional site with a shopping guide and lots of
SPEED ✓✓✓	features and reviews. There's a Formula 1 section,
INFO ✓✓✓✓	links and a good search facility. Somehow you
EASE ✓✓✓✓	expect more in the way of features and articles and
	less advertising – the Beeb at its most commercial.

www.4car.co.uk
DRIVEN

ORIGIN UK
SPEED ✓✓✓
INFO ✓✓✓✓✓
EASE ✓✓✓✓

News, sport, reviews, advice, chat and games – it's all here, and you can find out what's been and is being featured on each of their main motoring programmes.

Traders, magazines and buying guides

www.parkers.co.uk
REDUCING THE GAMBLE

ORIGIN UK
SPEED ✓✓✓
INFO ✓✓✓✓✓
EASE ✓✓✓✓

The premier buying guide with a premier site, this covers all the information you'll need to select the right car for you. There are five sections: pricing – a complete list of cars from 1982 and what you should be paying; choosing – advice on the right car for you; buying – with details of used cars and finance deals; owning – insurance, warranties and advice on how to sell; and advice – legal, important contacts and chat. It can be quite slow at times.

www.autoexpress.co.uk
THE BEST MOTORING NEWS AND INFORMATION

ORIGIN UK
SPEED ✓✓
INFO ✓✓✓✓✓
EASE ✓✓✓✓

Massive database on cars, with motoring news and features on the latest models, you can check prices too. It also has classified ads and a great set of links. You have to register to get access to most of the information.

www.whatcar.co.uk
BRITAIN'S NUMBER 1 BUYER'S GUIDE

ORIGIN	UK
SPEED	✓✓✓
INFO	✓✓✓✓✓
VALUE	✓✓✓
EASE	✓✓✓✓

A neatly packaged, one-stop shop for cars with sections on buying, selling, news, features and road tests, the classified section has thousands of cars and an easy-to-use search facility.

www.carnet.co.uk
ONLINE CAR MAGAZINE

ORIGIN	UK
SPEED	✓✓✓✓
INFO	✓✓✓
EASE	✓✓✓✓

Car Net has the latest news and new car reviews as well as feature micro-sites and links to deals on cars and insurance, statistics (on over 6,000 cars) and postcards of the best cars. You can also subscribe to specialist newsletters and take the trivia challenge.

www.hoot-uk.com
IT'S A HOOT!

ORIGIN	UK
SPEED	✓✓✓
INFO	✓✓✓✓✓
EASE	✓✓✓✓

A fun, simple site with a marque-by-marque news listing and the latest headlines. There are also sections with car tests, some good writing and chat.

www.carkeys.co.uk
INFORMATION SERVICE STATION

ORIGIN	UK
SPEED	✓✓✓
INFO	✓✓✓✓✓
EASE	✓✓✓✓

A wide-ranging magazine-style site with lots of data on current and new models as well as launch reviews and motoring news.

www.testcar.com
TEST REPORTS

ORIGIN	UK
SPEED	✓✓✓
INFO	✓✓✓✓✓
EASE	✓✓✓✓

With test reports on a large number of cars and free Internet access, this site is very useful if you're not sure what to buy. It's also got classified ads and an irreverent column called Let's be Frank. See also the new car review site www.new-car-net.co.uk which is attractive and has a good car magazine. A good feature is that you can compare up to three car specifications at the same time.

www.motortrak.com
USED CAR SEARCH

ORIGIN	UK
SPEED	✓✓✓✓✓
INFO	✓✓✓
EASE	✓✓✓✓

A hi-tech site where, in theory, you can find the right used car just for you. Just follow the search guidelines and up pops your ideal car! It's easy-to-use and very fast – turn the sound off though.

www.autobytel.co.uk
WORLD'S LEADING INTERNET-BASED NEW AND USED CAR BUYING SERVICE

ORIGIN	US/UK
SPEED	✓✓✓✓
INFO	✓✓✓✓✓
VALUE	✓✓✓✓
EASE	✓✓✓

The easy way to buy a car online, just select the model you want then follow the online instructions. They will get quotes from local dealers and there are detailed descriptions and photos. There's also financial information and aftercare service.

www.carbusters.com
BUY WITH *Which?* MAGAZINE

ORIGIN	UK
SPEED	✓✓✓✓
INFO	✓✓✓✓✓
VALUE	✓✓✓✓
EASE	✓✓✓✓

Which? make it easy to buy a new car from Europe at a substantial discount. It's easy-to-use and there's lots of guidance and reassurance about the process. The only downside is that the model selection is quite limited. You are better off joining as a *Which?* member as the fees are much cheaper. **W?WT**

www.eurekar.com
SAVE MONEY BY IMPORTING FROM EUROPE

ORIGIN	UK
SPEED	✓✓✓
INFO	✓✓✓✓✓
VALUE	✓✓✓✓✓
EASE	✓✓✓

Eurekar is a venture set up by the ISP Totalise to import cheaper right-hand drive cars from Europe. They claim to save up to 40% off UK prices. The choice of cars is limited, but all are inspected by Green Flag and have a warranty. Totalise offer quotes inclusive of VAT, delivery and duties.

www.oneswoop.co.uk
SMART WAY TO BUY

ORIGIN	UK
SPEED	✓✓✓
INFO	✓✓✓✓✓
VALUE	✓✓✓✓✓
EASE	✓✓✓✓

A straightforward site that concentrates on making the process of importing and buying a car from Europe as painless as possible. You can choose a car through one of three methods: buy what's available quickly; have a bit more choice; or be really picky. There are also some good special offers and a finance section.

www.jamjar.com
DIRECT LINE

ORIGIN	UK
SPEED	✓✓✓✓
INFO	✓✓✓
VALUE	✓✓✓✓✓
EASE	✓✓✓

One of the most hyped sites for car buying, Jam Jar is a big investment for Direct Line Insurance and they want to make it work well. The design isn't that great though, but if you persevere there are some fantastic offers – they don't hang around long though, as far as we could tell some only lasted 24 hours!

For more car buying information and cars for sale try:

www.autolocate.co.uk – excellent for links, good new car guide and review section, also good for used cars.

www.autoseek.co.uk – chat and thousands of cars for sale, great for links.

www.autotrader.co.uk – claiming to be Britain's biggest car showroom with 200,000 listed. Nice, clear design.

www.carseller.co.uk – free advertising if selling and good links.

www.carsource.co.uk – great for data and online quotes, lots of cars for sale.

www.fish4cars.co.uk – over 150,000 cars on their database, plus hundreds of other vehicles. Comprehensive.

www.importanewcar.co.uk – good site if you fancy importing a car from Europe, they help you all the way and there's the potential to save wads of cash in the process.

www.showroom4cars.com – bright, brash and fast.

www.tins.co.uk – sophisticated and with a large selection of new and used cars, not always the cheapest though.

www.topmarques.co.uk – luxury vehicles only, some 6,000 for sale.

www.vanbuy.co.uk – vans and more vans of all shapes and sizes.

www.virgincars.com – good savings and speedy delivery, nice design and good features such as a car servicing service.

Car registrations

www.dvla.som.co.uk
CHERISHED AND PERSONALISED NUMBERS

ORIGIN	UK
SPEED	✓✓✓✓
INFO	✓✓✓✓
VALUE	✓✓
EASE	✓✓✓✓

Here's the first port of call if you want that special number plate. They sell by auction but there's plenty of help and you search for un-issued select registrations in both new and old styles. Order over the phone using their hotline.

For more sites try:
www.newreg.co.uk – the world's largest directory of registration marks.
www.alotofnumberplates.co.uk – good search engine, over 5 million combinations.
www.statreg.co.uk – lots of cheap plates.

Insurance

www.easycover.com
CAR INSURANCE

ORIGIN	UK
SPEED	✓✓✓
INFO	✓✓✓✓✓
VALUE	✓✓✓
EASE	✓✓✓

Quotes from a large number of insurance suppliers, you just fill in the form, and they get back to you with a quote. **www.insureyourmotor.com** specialises in travel and car insurance and you can get a quote online.
See also **www.theaa.co.uk**, **www.swinton.co.uk**, **www.sureterm.com** and **www.eaglestar.co.uk**

Looking after and repairing your car

www.service4cars.com
CAR SERVICING AT YOUR CONVENIENCE
This company works with car manufacturers and

ORIGIN UK
SPEED ✓✓✓✓
INFO ✓✓✓✓
EASE ✓✓✓✓

dealerships to bring you car servicing online. Once you've booked – either a premier or last minute service – they will contact you within an hour during normal working hours for you to take the car to the garage chosen. There are no booking fees to pay, and they'll even remind you when your next service is due.

www.ukmot.com
M.O.T.

ORIGIN UK
SPEED ✓✓✓✓
INFO ✓✓✓✓
EASE ✓✓✓✓

Find your nearest M.O.T. test centre, get facts about the test and what's actually supposed to be checked, there's also a reminder service.

www.haynes.co.uk
HAYNES MANUALS

ORIGIN UK
SPEED ✓✓✓✓
INFO ✓✓✓
VALUE ✓✓✓
EASE ✓✓✓✓

Unfortunately they've stopped the download service, so now you have to buy the books – there's almost 2,000 available so there should be one for you.

Specialist car sites

www.classicmotor.co.uk
FOR CLASSIC CARS

ORIGIN UK
SPEED ✓✓✓
INFO ✓✓✓✓✓
VALUE ✓✓✓✓
EASE ✓✓✓

By far the best classic car site, it's comprehensive, including clubs, classifieds and books; here you can buy anything from a car to a headlight bulb. It's not the easiest site to navigate though it has improved in the past year. See also **www.classic-car-directory.com** which is a well categorised links site.

www.pistonheads.com
BEST OF BRITISH MOTORING

ORIGIN UK	Pistonheads is a British site dedicated to the faster
SPEED ✓✓✓	side of motoring and is great for reviews of the latest
INFO ✓✓✓✓✓	cars and chat. It's passionate and very informative.
VALUE ✓✓✓	
EASE ✓✓✓	

www.krbaker.demon.co.uk/britcars
HISTORY OF BRITISH CARS TO 1960

ORIGIN UK	An amateur site with a good make-by-make history
SPEED ✓✓✓	of the British car industry, it includes a glossary and
INFO ✓✓✓	information on tax and other historical references.
EASE ✓✓✓✓	Unfortunately it's not well illustrated.

Learning to drive

www.driving.co.uk
BSM TUITION

ORIGIN UK	Official site of the British School of Motoring, with
SPEED ✓✓✓	mock theory tests, lots of advice on taking the test,
INFO ✓✓✓✓✓	what to do in an accident and funny stories to help
EASE ✓✓✓✓	relax you.

www.learners.co.uk
LEARNER'S DIRECTORY

ORIGIN UK	The point of this site is to help you find the right
SPEED ✓✓✓	driving school, just type in your postcode and the
INFO ✓✓✓✓	schools will be listed along with helpful additional
EASE ✓✓✓✓	information such as whether they have a female
	instructor or that they train for motorway driving.

www.2pass.co.uk
THEORY AND PRACTICAL TESTS

ORIGIN UK
SPEED ✓✓✓✓
INFO ✓✓✓✓✓
EASE ✓✓✓✓

A leaner driver's dream, this site helps with your tests in giving advice, giving mock exams and then once you've passed helps you get a car. There's also information on driving abroad, on motorbikes and driving automatics. There's also plenty of fun with top stories, even poems.

Car miscellaneous

www.kitcars.org
BUILD YOUR OWN

ORIGIN UK
SPEED ✓✓✓
INFO ✓✓✓✓✓
EASE ✓✓✓✓

The owner's rather engaging plea for funding aside, this site is excellent for links, information, pictures and classified ads for all things to do with kitcars.

www.autofashion.co.uk
ACCESSORIZE YOUR CAR

ORIGIN UK
SPEED ✓✓✓✓
INFO ✓✓✓✓
EASE ✓✓✓

An entertaining site where you can buy body kits and accessories for many makes of car, including custom made. See also Motech at www.motech.uk.com who specialise more in performance enhancement.

www.caraudiocentre.com
IN CAR AUDIO SYSTEMS

ORIGIN UK
SPEED ✓✓✓
INFO ✓✓✓✓
VALUE ✓✓✓✓
EASE ✓✓✓✓

Here you can get loads of advice and offers on a wide range of stereos with a price promise and low delivery costs. See also www.toade.com who have a highly interactive site and can also supply security, multi-media and navigation equipment on top of audio.

www.speed-trap.co.uk
THE SPEED TRAP BIBLE

ORIGIN	UK
SPEED	✓✓✓
INFO	✓✓✓✓✓
EASE	✓✓✓✓

While not condoning speeding, this site gives the low down on speed traps, the law and links to police forces. There's even data on the types of cameras used and advice on dealing with the courts and police.

Celebrities

Find your favourite celebrities and their web sites using these online directories.

www.celebritysearchengine.co.uk
THE CELEBRITY SEARCH ENGINE

ORIGIN	UK
SPEED	✓✓✓✓
INFO	✓✓✓✓
EASE	✓✓✓✓

Type in the name of the celebrity you're looking for and a list of sites appears. All sites are rated 1-10 and a short description is given as well as the link to the chosen site.

www.celebrityemail.com
E-MAIL THE STARS

ORIGIN	US
SPEED	✓✓✓✓
INFO	✓✓✓
EASE	✓✓✓

E-mail addresses to over 18,000 of the world's most famous people, it's quite biased towards Americans but give it a try anyway, you might get a reply.

www.hello-magazine.co.uk
THE WORLD IN PICTURES

ORIGIN	UK
SPEED	✓✓✓
INFO	✓✓✓✓
EASE	✓✓✓

Hello magazine's web site features pictures and articles from current and previous issues with loads of celebrities. You can't search by celebrity but you can have fun trawling through the pictures.

Charities

The Internet offers a great opportunity to give to your favourite charity or support a cause dear to your heart. There are so many that we're unable to list them all, but here are some top sites with directories to help you find the one you're looking for. For charity cards see page 200.

www.charitychoice.co.uk
ENCYCLOPAEDIA OF CHARITIES

ORIGIN	UK	A very useful and well-put together directory of
SPEED	✓✓✓✓	charities with a good search facility and a list in over
INFO	✓✓✓✓✓	30 categories, there's also the excellent Goodwill
EASE	✓✓✓	Gallery where you can post up a service or a dona-tion you're willing to give to charity.

www.caritasdata.co.uk
CHARITIES DIRECT

ORIGIN	UK	A support site for charities with information on how
SPEED	✓✓✓✓	to raise funds and run a charity, there's also a good
INFO	✓✓✓✓✓	directory of UK charities and you can rank them by
EASE	✓✓✓✓	expenditure, revenue and fund size.

www.charitycommission.gov.uk
THE CHARITY COMMISSION

ORIGIN	UK	The Charity Commission is here to give the public
SPEED	✓✓✓✓	confidence in the integrity of charities in England
INFO	✓✓✓✓✓	and Wales, and their site lists over 180,000 charities.
EASE	✓✓✓✓	There's also lots of advice for charities too.

See also:
www.charitychallenge.com – raise money for your chosen charity by taking an adventure holiday through Charity Challenge.

www.bcconnections.org.uk – businesses can find out how they can get involved in charity donations and charities can find out how they can get businesses involved in their work.

www.thehungersite.com – just one click and you'll donate a cup of food to the world hungry via registered sponsors, a brilliant idea and one that works – over 200 million cups have been donated to date.

Chat

There are literally thousands of chat sites and rooms on the web, covering many different topics. However, this is the area of the Net that people have the most concerns about. There have been loads of cases where some have been tricked into giving out personal information and even arranged unsuitable meetings. But at its best, a chat program is a great way to keep in contact with friends, especially if they live miles away. So chat wisely by following our top tips for keeping safe.

CHAT – OUR TOP TIPS

1. Be wary, just like you would be if you were visiting any new place.
2. Don't give your e-mail address out without making sure that only the person you're sending it to can read it.
3. People often pretend to be someone they're not when they're chatting; unless you know the person, assume that's the case with anyone you chat with.

4. Don't meet up with anyone you've met online –
   keep your online life separate. Chances are they'd
   be a let down anyway, even if they were genuine.
5. If you like the look of a chat room or site, but
   you're not sure about it, get a recommendation
   first.
6. If you want to meet up with friends online,
   arrange a time and place beforehand.
7. If you don't like someone, just block 'em.
8. Check out the excellent **www.chatdanger.com** for
   more info on how to chat safely.

The following are the major chat sites and programs.

www.aol.com
AOL INSTANT MESSENGER

ORIGIN US
SPEED ✓✓✓✓
INFO ✓✓✓✓
EASE ✓✓✓✓

One of the most popular, it's pretty safe and anyway
you can easily block people who are a nuisance, or
just set it up so that only friends can talk to you.
You can also decide how much information about
you other users can see.

www.delphi.com
DELPHI FORUMS

ORIGIN US
SPEED ✓✓✓✓
INFO ✓✓✓
EASE ✓✓✓

A forum is a place where people chat, rather like
sitting round a table. Delphi has loads covering
many topics and it's easy to get involved, or you can
even start your own forum if you like. It has to be
said that some are a bit weird though.

www.mirabilis.com
ICQ – I SEEK YOU

ORIGIN US
SPEED ✓✓✓✓
INFO ✓✓✓✓
EASE ✓✓✓✓

There are lots of chat rooms here. It's quick and easy-to-use combined with a mobile phone. There are lots of features such as games, money advice, music and lurve.

www.msn.com
MICROSOFT MSN MESSENGER

ORIGIN US
SPEED ✓✓✓✓
INFO ✓✓✓✓
EASE ✓✓✓✓

Easy-to-use but it can be confusing as Microsoft are so keen for you to use other parts of their massive site you'll often find yourself suddenly transferred. The best bet is to customise it so that there's no mistake.

www.mirc.com
IRC – INTERNET RELAY CHAT

ORIGIN US
SPEED ✓✓✓✓
INFO ✓✓✓
EASE ✓✓✓✓

A straightforward chat program and easy-to-use. It's now overtaken by the likes of MSN and AOL but some web sites may still use it.

www.hayseed.net/MOO/
MOO AND MUD

ORIGIN US
SPEED ✓✓✓✓
INFO ✓✓✓✓
EASE ✓✓✓✓

A MOO is a program that enables you to go to a place on a computer where you can talk to others; a MUD is a sort of MOO. Schools are getting into MOOs in a big way, find out all you need to know at this site – it's easy once you get your head round it – honest.

Chat sites for children

www.freezone.com
WHERE KIDS CONNECT

ORIGIN US
SPEED ✓✓✓✓
INFO ✓✓✓✓✓
EASE ✓✓✓✓

Lots more than just chat, there are games; quizzes, links and you can construct your own home page. You don't need to download a special program, but you do have to register to participate (they guarantee not to use your personal info). See also **www.cyberkids.com** and **www.cyberteens.com**

www.kids-space.com
ENCOURAGING GLOBAL FRIENDSHIP

ORIGIN US
SPEED ✓✓✓✓✓
INFO ✓✓✓✓
EASE ✓✓✓✓✓

An idealogically sound site with children participating from 142 countries at the same time of writing. Go to the Web Kids Village here you can join a club and chat with new friends world-wide. Alternatively, pick a pen pal, ask a question or read a story. All submissions are monitored by editors.

Children

There's been a massive explosion in the number of sites in this category. You can save pounds on children's clothes and toys by shopping over the net; it's easy and the service is often excellent as the sites are put together by people who really care. The Internet also offers another way to educate and entertain children. They are fascinated by it and quickly become experts. Listed here are some of the best sites anywhere. For ideas on days out with children see the British travel listings page 429 and for parenting concerns see page 274.

Shopping for children

Sadly, the excellent e-toys has been closed down, but here are some good stores who have the potential to take up the reins.

www.elc.co.uk
EARLY LEARNING CENTRE

ORIGIN UK	A well designed and user-friendly site which offers a
SPEED ✓✓✓	wide range of toys for the under-fives in particular.
INFO ✓✓✓✓✓	It's strong on character products and traditional toys
VALUE ✓✓✓	alike. Delivery costs £2.95 per order and you can
EASE ✓✓✓✓✓	expect it to arrive in 3 days.

www.toymania.com
RAVING TOY MANIAC

ORIGIN US	A toy magazine full of details and news on all the
SPEED ✓✓✓	latest toys along with an online shop. It's an enjoy-
INFO ✓✓✓✓✓	able site to browse, the selection is vast and it's a
VALUE ✓✓	good place to start if you're looking for something
EASE ✓✓✓✓	you can't get in the UK. Shipping costs depend on
	the weight of your order.

www.funstore.co.uk
ONLINE TOYS AND GAMES FOR THE UK

ORIGIN UK	Funstore has brand names as well as the more tradi-
SPEED ✓✓✓	tional toys. The site is split into ten sections with
INFO ✓✓✓✓	several hundred items available to buy, and they
VALUE ✓✓✓	have a personal shopper to help you find the perfect
EASE ✓✓✓✓	gift. Prices seem to be in line with or slightly below
	high street. Delivery is £2.95 per order and gift-
	wrap at £1 per item.

www.hamleys.co.uk
FINEST TOY STORE IN THE WORLD

ORIGIN UK
SPEED ✓✓✓✓
INFO ✓✓✓
VALUE ✓✓✓
EASE ✓✓✓✓

Hamley's has improved its site and you can search for toys by gender, price or age. There's also an ok selection of character areas within the store as well as the more traditional range, which is their main strength. Delivery starts at £3.95.

www.toysrus.co.uk
NOT JUST TOYS

ORIGIN UK/US
SPEED ✓✓✓
INFO ✓✓✓✓
VALUE ✓✓✓✓
EASE ✓✓✓✓

Good site with all the key brands and 'in' things you'd expect – you can even buy a mobile phone. Has links to key toy manufacturer's sites and sister sites called www.discounttoys.co.uk for great bargains and www.babiesrus.co.uk Delivery is £2.50 for the UK.

www.character-warehouse.com
PRE-SCHOOL CHARACTER

ORIGIN UK
SPEED ✓✓
INFO ✓✓✓✓
VALUE ✓✓✓
EASE ✓✓✓✓

A colourful and easy site to use specialising in character merchandise. You browse the site by character and they have masses to choose from, plus some excellent prices. Delivery costs from £3.99 for the UK.

www.dawson-and-son.com
FOR TRADITIONAL WOODEN TOYS

ORIGIN UK
SPEED ✓✓✓
INFO ✓✓✓
VALUE ✓✓
EASE ✓✓✓✓

Specialists in the art of making simple, traditional, wooden toys, Dawson and Son offer a wide range of beautifully made items from rattles to sophisticated games. Delivery depends on the value and weight of order.

www.krucialkids.com
ALL ABOARD THE KRUCIAL KIDS EXPRESS

ORIGIN UK
SPEED ✓✓✓
INFO ✓✓✓✓
VALUE ✓✓✓
EASE ✓✓✓✓

Annoying name, but not an annoying site. It specialises in developmental toys for children up to eight years old. Provides detailed information on the educational value of each of the 200 or so toys. The prices aren't bad either. Delivery is free if you spend over £60.

www.airfix.com
AIRFIX KITS

ORIGIN UK
SPEED ✓✓
INFO ✓✓✓✓
VALUE ✓✓✓
EASE ✓✓✓✓

Some 50 current kits are available to buy with illustrations and background info on the real thing, and an indication of how difficult they are to put together. There are also details of the modeller's club and parts replacement service. Delivery costs are dependent on the weight of the order.

www.thepartystore.co.uk
SELLING FUN

ORIGIN UK
SPEED ✓✓
INFO ✓✓✓✓
VALUE ✓✓✓
EASE ✓✓✓✓

Great site, not just for children, but there is an excellent kids' party section. They sell character outfits, themed tableware, masks, party boxes and all sorts of accessories. Delivery takes five working days and costs £2.95 but free if you spend £70 plus (a price hike, which is a shame).

www.jojomamanbebe.co.uk
FASHIONABLE MOTHERS AND THEIR CHILDREN

ORIGIN UK
SPEED ✓✓✓
INFO ✓✓✓✓
VALUE ✓✓✓
EASE ✓✓✓✓

Excellent for everything from maternity wear and designer children's clothes to gifts for newborn babies. Also sections on toys, maternity products and special offers. All the designs are tested and they aim to be comfortable as well as fashionable.

Delivery cost depends on how much you spend and the size of items bought. For babywear try **www.overthemoon-babywear.co.uk** who offer free postage in the UK, while for older children **www.tots2teens.co.uk** is a good bet.

www.urchin.co.uk
SHOPPING WITH BRATTITUDE

ORIGIN UK
SPEED ✓✓✓
INFO ✓✓✓✓
VALUE ✓✓✓
EASE ✓✓✓✓

Urchin has some 300 products available: cots and beds, bathtime accessories, bikes, clothes, for baby, travel goods, toys and things for the independent child who likes to personalise their own room. They boast a sense of style and good design, and they succeed. Also have a bargains section. Delivery is £3.95 per order with a next day surcharge of £3.

Things to do

www.mamamedia.com
THE PLACE FOR KIDS ON THE NET

ORIGIN US
SPEED ✓✓✓
INFO ✓✓✓✓
EASE ✓✓✓✓

This versatile site has everything a child and parent could want, there is an excellent selection of interactive games, puzzles and quizzes, combined with a great deal of wit and fun. Best of all it encourages children to communicate through the use of message boards, competitions and gets them voting on what's important to them. There's a superb section on what's good on the Net featuring some 2,000 sites.

www.rumpus.com
RUMPS KID'S FUNDATION

ORIGIN US	A superb New York site with excellent games and a
SPEED ✓✓✓✓	real understanding of how to make the Internet
INFO ✓✓✓✓✓	exciting for children, with fun characters, plenty of
EASE ✓✓✓✓✓	games and a kids' club. Unfortunately, it's very
	commercial with too many ads.

www.bonus.com
THE SUPER SITE FOR KIDS

ORIGIN US	Excellent graphics and masses of genuinely good
SPEED ✓✓✓	games make a visit to Bonus a treat for all ages.
INFO ✓✓✓✓✓	There are quizzes and puzzles, with sections offering
EASE ✓✓✓✓✓	a photo library, art resource and homework help.
	Access to the web is limited to a protected environ-ment.

www.kidsonline.co.uk
FOR KIDS BY KIDS

ORIGIN UK	Excellent graphics make this site stand out, and its
SPEED ✓✓	content is very good too; however it can be a little
INFO ✓✓✓	slow. Split into two sections for younger and older
EASE ✓✓✓✓	kids, there are reviews of favourite books, films and
	web sites as well as a smattering of games.

www.yucky.com
THE YUCKIEST SITE ON THE INTERNET

ORIGIN US	Find out how to turn milk into slime or how much
SPEED ✓✓✓✓	you know about worms – yucky lives up to its
INFO ✓✓✓✓✓	name. Essentially this is an excellent, fun site that
EASE ✓✓✓✓	helps kids learn science and biology. There are
	guides for parents on how to get the best out of the
	site and links to recommended sites.

www.wonka.com
THE WILD WORLD OF WONKA

ORIGIN	UK
SPEED	✓✓✓
INFO	✓✓✓✓✓
EASE	✓✓✓✓

Ingenious site sponsored by Nestlé with great illustrations and a fun approach, it has several sections all with lots of interactivity, as well as an online club. There's the Invention Room with lots of trivia, Planet Vermes which is about space, Loompaland takes you into the animal kingdom and so on. You can also send postcards and get involved in competitions.

www.switcheroozoo.com
MAKE NEW ANIMALS

ORIGIN	US
SPEED	✓✓✓
INFO	✓✓✓
EASE	✓✓✓

Over 6,500 combinations of animals can be made at this very entertaining web site, you need Shockwave and a decent PC for it to work effectively.

Other activity sites worth checking out:
http://web.ukonline.co.uk/conker – The Kids Ark – Join Captain Zeb gathering material on the world, strange animals, myths and facts – before it all disappears.
www.alfy.com – excellent for the very young, with lots of games and plenty of things to do and see.
www.animalgame.com – think of an animal, then see if the site can guess what it is.
www.ex.ac.uk/bugclub – bugs and creepy crawlies for all ages.
www.hotwheels.com/kids – a slow site from a model car maker that has some good features and games.
www.kiddonet.com – download the interactive play area for games and surfing in a safe environment.
www.kids.warnerbros.com/karaoke – lots to do at the excellent Warner Brothers site.

www.kidscom.com – play games and have safe chat – a bit boring.

www.kidsdomain.com – lots to see and do here from games and quizzes to safe surfing.

www.kidsfun.co.uk – an online colouring book is probably the best thing about it.

www.kidskorner.net – great use of cartoons to introduce and play games – stealthily educational.

www.kidsreads.com – an American site all about kids' books, with games and quizzes. Good for young Harry Potter fans.

www.missdorothy.com – a good, wide-ranging site with plenty to do and see, linked to the Brownies.

www.tukids.com – masses of games to download, many are free.

www.wiltiky.com – educational games for younger children in a well-designed site.

www.zeeks.com – a very good American kids' magazine site.

TV, book and character sites

www.citv.co.uk
CHILDREN'S ITV

ORIGIN UK	Keep up-to-date with your favourite programmes
SPEED ✓✓✓	and talk to the stars of the shows. There's lots to do
INFO ✓✓✓✓✓	here including chat with fellow fans, play games,
EASE ✓✓✓	find something to do, enter a competition, e-mail a
	friend and join the club.

www.cartoonnetwork.com.uk
ALL THE FAVOURITES FROM THE TV CHANNEL

ORIGIN UK/US	Features all the characters, news, events and games
SPEED ✓✓	from the world of 'toons. Hop into Sylvester and
INFO ✓✓✓✓	Tweety's mystery machine or visit Scooby Doo.
EASE ✓✓✓✓	While the graphics and sound effects are good, it
	can be slow.

www.nickjr.com
THE NICKELODEON CHANNEL

ORIGIN US	Ideal for under-eights, this has a good selection of
SPEED ✓✓✓	games and quizzes to play either with an adult or
INFO ✓✓✓	solo. The major characters get a feature each and
VALUE ✓✓	you can personalise the site. The Red Rocket Store
EASE ✓✓✓✓	has an excellent selection of merchandise, but
	beware of shipping costs.

www.sesamestreet.com
THE CHILDREN'S TELEVISION WORKSHOP

ORIGIN US	Split into five sections: Let Ernie show you Preschool
SPEED ✓✓✓	Playground; get tips from the Parents Toolbox; learn
INFO ✓✓✓✓	about history in Kids' City; give your baby a work-
VALUE ✓✓✓	out in the Baby Workshop; and meet the characters
EASE ✓✓✓✓	in Sesame Street Central. It's fun in parts, but quite
	worthy in tone. Another site dedicated to the very
	young is **www.funschool.com**

www.bbc.co.uk/cbbc
CHILDREN'S BBC

ORIGIN UK	Built around *Blue Peter*, *Live & Kicking* and
SPEED ✓✓✓	*Newsround*, you can catch up on the latest news,
INFO ✓✓✓✓	play games and find out about the stars of the
EASE ✓✓✓✓	programs. The web guide links to other recom-
	mended children's sites.

www.disney.com
WHERE THE MAGIC LIVES

ORIGIN US
SPEED ✓✓
INFO ✓✓✓✓
EASE ✓✓✓✓

Or more precisely where advertising lives, this site has an awful lot of adverts. It also has details on every aspect of the world of Disney, with some audio and video clips. In between the ads for other sites there are games, stories and competitions, but the whole thing is very slow. The British version www.disney.co.uk has much less advertising while retaining most of the goodies. For young children a Disney colouring book can be found at http://disney.go.com/kids/color/index.html

www.cooltoons.com
RUGRATS, STRESSED ERIC AND MORE

ORIGIN UK
SPEED ✓✓✓✓
INFO ✓✓✓
EASE ✓✓✓✓

Each character has their own section where you can find lots to do and see. There's also an eight-step guide on how to become an animator. The store has all the related merchandise.

www.foxkids.co.uk
Fox TV

ORIGIN UK
SPEED ✓✓✓
INFO ✓✓✓✓
EASE ✓✓✓✓

All the characters and shows are featured on this bright and entertaining site with added extras like a games section, competitions, a sports page and a magazine. There's also a shopping facility where you earn Brix by using the site, they can then be spent on goodies in the Boutik. The graphics can be a little temperamental.

www.aardman.com

HOME OF WALLACE AND GROMMIT

ORIGIN UK
SPEED ✓✓✓
INFO ✓✓✓✓
EASE ✓✓✓✓

This brilliant site takes a while to download but it's worth the wait. There's news on what the team are up to, links to their films, a shop and an inside story on how it all began.

Here's where the best children's characters hang out:
Action Man – www.actionman.com
Art Attack – www.artattack.co.uk
Barbie – www.barbie.com
Beano – www.beano.co.uk and www.dccomics.com
Bob the Builder – www.bobthebuilder.org
Danger Mouse – www.dangermouse.org
Dragonball Z – www.dragonballz.com
Goosebumps –
    http://place.scholastic.com/goosebumps/indexa.htm
Letter Land – www.letterland.com
Mr Men – www.mrmen.net
Paddington – www.paddingtonbear.co.uk
Pokemon – www.pokeland.yorks.net/ or
    www.pokemon.com or
    www.pokemone.yorks.net/
Roald Dahl – www.roalddahl.org or
    www.roalddahlclub.com
Teletubbies – www.teletubbies.com
Thomas the Tank Engine –
    www.thomasthetankengine.com
Tintin – www.tintin.be
Winnie the Pooh – www.winniethepooh.co.uk

Harry Potter

Harry Potter deserves a special mention and with loads of web sites springing up here are the official ones and the best unofficial ones as well. You might want to keep checking the Warner Brothers site for information on the film – www.warnerbros.com

www.bloomsbury.com/harrypotter
WHERE IT ALL BEGAN

ORIGIN US	You have to enter using a secret password known
SPEED ✓✓✓	only to witches and wizards everywhere then you
INFO ✓✓✓✓	get to find out all about the books, meet JK Rowling
EASE ✓✓✓✓	and join the Harry Potter club. 'Howlers and
	Owlers' – e-mail insults and compliments – is great,
	but don't worry if you're a Muggle, all is explained.

www.scholastic.com/harrypotter
HARRY AMERICAN STYLE

ORIGIN US	Here's wizard trivia, quizzes, screensavers, informa-
SPEED ✓✓✓	tion about the books and an interview with JK
INFO ✓✓✓✓	Rowling, all on a fairly boring web site.
EASE ✓✓✓✓	

www.dailyprophetnews.com
THE DAILY PROPHET NEWS

ORIGIN US	An unofficial newspaper featuring all that goes on in
SPEED ✓✓✓	the world of Harry Potter. There are articles, book
INFO ✓✓✓✓	reviews, features on wizard life and classified ads
EASE ✓✓✓✓	too.

www.fandom.com/harrypotter

HARRY POTTER FAN CLUB

ORIGIN US	Everything a fan could want. There's news on the
SPEED ✓✓✓	forthcoming books and film, articles, features and
INFO ✓✓✓✓	polls on all things Harry. The emphasis is on selling
EASE ✓✓✓✓	you Potter merchandise though so you have to put
	up with lots of adverts.

Search engines and site directories

www.yahooligans.com

THE WEB GUIDE FOR KIDS

ORIGIN US	Probably the most popular site for kids, yahooligans
SPEED ✓✓✓	offers parents safety and kids hours of fun. There
INFO ✓✓✓✓	are games, articles and features on the 'in' charac-
EASE ✓✓✓✓	ters, education resources and sections on sport,
	science, computing and TV. It has an American bias.

www.ajkids.com

ASK JEEVES FOR KIDS

ORIGIN US	A search engine aimed at children, it's simple, safe
SPEED ✓✓✓	and is excellent for homework enquiries and games.
INFO ✓✓✓✓✓	
EASE ✓✓✓✓	

www.all4kidsuk.com

IF YOU'RE LOOKING FOR SOMETHING TO DO

ORIGIN UK	This aims to be a comprehensive directory covering
SPEED ✓✓✓	all your parental needs from activities to schools. It's
INFO ✓✓✓✓✓	got an easy-to-use search engine, where you can
EASE ✓✓✓✓	search by county if you need to.

If you're still stuck try **www.kidsnet.co.uk** which is similar and covers different areas of the country.

www.beritsbest.com
SITES FOR CHILDREN

ORIGIN US	Over 1,000 sites in this directory split into six major
SPEED ✓✓✓	categories, fun, things to do, nature, serious stuff (home-
INFO ✓✓✓✓✓	work), chat and surfing. Each site is rated for speed and
EASE ✓✓✓✓	content and you can suggest new sites as well.

Competitions

www.loquax.co.uk
THE UK'S COMPETITION PORTAL

ORIGIN UK	This site doesn't give away prizes but lists the web
SPEED ✓✓✓✓	sites that do. There are hundreds of competitions
INFO ✓✓✓✓✓	featured, and if you own a web site they'll even run
EASE ✓✓✓✓	a competition for you. There are daily updates and

special features such as 'Pick of the Prizes' which
features the best the web has to offer, with links to
the relevant sites. See also www.webcomp.co.uk and
www.competitions-online.co.uk

Computers

*Its no surprise that the number one place to buy a computer is
the Internet. With these sites you won't go far wrong, and it's
also worth checking out the price checker sites on page 293
before going shopping and checking the software sites on page
333. Mac users should also check out the section on Apple Macs
page 24.*

www.itreviews.co.uk
START HERE TO FIND THE BEST

ORIGIN UK	IT Reviews gives unbiased reports, not only on
SPEED ✓✓✓✓	computer products, but also on software, games and
INFO ✓✓✓✓✓	books too. The site has a good search facility and a
EASE ✓✓✓✓	quick visit may save you loads of hassle when you

come to buy. For other excellent information sites try www.zdnet.co.uk or www.cnet.com both have links to good online stores.

www.pcworld.co.uk
THE COMPUTER SUPERSTORE

ORIGIN UK	A very strong offering from one of the leading
SPEED ✓✓✓	computer stores with lots of offers and star buys.
INFO ✓✓✓✓	They sell a wide range of electronics from cameras
VALUE ✓✓✓✓	to the expected PCs and peripherals.
EASE ✓✓✓✓	

www.simply.co.uk
SIMPLY DOES IT

ORIGIN UK	An award-winning site and company that offers a
SPEED ✓✓✓✓	wide range of PCs and related products. Their
INFO ✓✓✓✓	strengths are speed, quality of service and competi-
VALUE ✓✓✓✓	tive prices. They also sell mobile phones. W?WT
EASE ✓✓✓✓	

www.tiny.com
LATEST TECHNOLOGY AT UNBEATABLE PRICES

ORIGIN UK	A businesslike site that includes all the details you'd
SPEED ✓✓✓✓	need on their range of computers and peripherals for
INFO ✓✓✓✓	home and office use. Tiny are the UK's largest
VALUE ✓✓✓	computer manufacturer and have a history of relia-
EASE ✓✓✓✓	bility and good deals. Shipping costs vary according

to what you buy and where you live.

Other PC manufacturers' site addresses:
Apple – www.apple.com
Dan – www.dan.co.uk
Dell – www.dell.co.uk
Elonex – www.elonex.co.uk
Evesham – www.evesham.com
Gateway – www.gateway.com/uk
Hewlett Packard – www.hp.com/uk
Time – www.timecomputers.com
Viglen – www.viglen.co.uk

Cycles and Cycling

See page 430 for cycling holidays and tours and page 348 for information on cycling as a sport.

www.cycleweb.co.uk
THE INTERNET CYCLING CLUB

ORIGIN UK	A much-improved attempt to bring together all
SPEED ✓✓✓✓	things cycling. Aimed at a general audience rather
INFO ✓✓✓✓✓	than cycling as a sport, it has sections and links on
VALUE ✓✓✓	everything from the latest news to clubs, shops and
EASE ✓✓✓	holidays.

www.bikemagic.com
BIKE MAGIC!

ORIGIN UK	You have to join to get the best out of the site, but
SPEED ✓✓✓	there's plenty here when you do, it has forums on
INFO ✓✓✓	hot bike topics, reviews of equipment, buying
VALUE ✓✓✓	advice, classifieds and an events calendar.
EASE ✓✓✓	

www.bicyclenet.co.uk
UK's NUMBER 1 ONLINE BICYCLE SHOP

ORIGIN UK	Great selection of bikes and accessories to buy with
SPEED ✓✓✓	free delivery to anywhere in the UK. There's also
INFO ✓✓✓	good advice on how to buy the right bike and
VALUE ✓✓✓	they're flexible about method of payment. W?WT
EASE ✓✓✓	

www.cyclesource.co.uk/link.cfm
CYCLE INDUSTRY TRADE ASSOCIATION

ORIGIN UK	How to buy the right bike, find a dealer or browse
SPEED ✓✓✓✓✓	the many links covering the subject – a good-looking
INFO ✓✓✓✓	site that's fast and easy-to-use.
EASE ✓✓✓✓✓	

www.cycling.uk.com
THE CYCLING INFORMATION STATION

ORIGIN UK	A fairly basic site with links to several hundred
SPEED ✓✓✓✓	cycling web sites collected under headings such as
INFO ✓✓✓✓	holidays, legal, tracks, museums, books and events.
EASE ✓✓✓✓	

www.tandem-club.org.uk
CAN YOU RIDE TANDEM?

ORIGIN UK	A pretty basic site devoted to the world of the
SPEED ✓✓✓	tandem with discussion groups, classifieds, buying
INFO ✓✓✓	advice, events and a newsletter.
EASE ✓✓✓	

www.a-nelson,dircon.co.uk/cyclingprelycra
BEFORE THE AGE OF LYCRA

ORIGIN UK	A look at cycling as it used to be before the Lycra
SPEED ✓✓✓✓	clad hordes took to the roads, nicely done and with
INFO ✓✓✓✓	a great nostalgic feel.
EASE ✓✓✓	

Dating

The Net is fast becoming an accepted means to meet people, but be careful about meeting up; many people aren't exactly honest about their details. if in doubt, err on the side of caution.

www.wildxangel.com
THE LOW DOWN

ORIGIN US	An American site that tells it like it is and gives
SPEED ✓✓✓✓	advice about using chat and dating sites, it also gives
INFO ✓✓✓✓	awards for the best ones and there are links too.
EASE ✓✓✓	

www.uksingles.co.uk
FOR ALL UK SINGLES

ORIGIN UK	Not just about dating, this site is devoted to helping
SPEED ✓✓✓✓	you get the most out of life. There are several
INFO ✓✓✓✓✓	sections: accommodation, sport and activities, holi-
EASE ✓✓✓	days, help for single parents, and listings for match-

making and dating services. All the companies that advertise in the directories are vetted too.

Here are some additional sites, there's not much to choose between them, it's all a matter of taste. All are secure and allow you to browse and join in, in relative safety.

www.dateline.co.uk – 30 years experience at the dating game gives Dateline lots of credibility and it's a good site too, easy-to-use and reassuring.

www.datingdirect.com – claims to be the UK's largest agency with over 135,000 members, the site is not as sophisticated as some, though they seem to have lots of success stories.

www.dinnerdates.com – one of the longest estab- lished and most respected dining and social events clubs for unattached single people in the UK, find out how you can get involved here.

www.match.com – leading site in the US, get your
profile matched to someone or join in the chat,
there's an excellent magazine too.

www.singles121.com – newish dating club, good site
but lots of annoying adverts.

www.singlesearchuk.com – introduction service –
discrete and you only get introduced if your
profile matches to 60%, whatever that means.

www.tiggle.com – seven-days free registration and a
nice site, but you have to register to gain access.

www.udate.com – US site for over 25s only, good-
looking site with a good search facility.

Do-It-Yourself

*The web doesn't seem a natural home for do-it-yourself, but
there are some really useful sites, some great offers on tools and
equipment and plenty of sensible advice. The good news is that
in the past year there has been a great improvement in the quality
of sites in this area.*

www.homepagesonline.com

START HERE

ORIGIN UK
SPEED ✓✓✓
INFO ✓✓✓✓✓
EASE ✓✓✓✓

This excellent site has a massive amount of information to help you solve a DIY problem or get help
with a project. There are six major areas:

1. Books – where to buy and what's available.
2. Articles – articles from trade magazines on a wide
   variety of subjects.
3. Events.
4. Hints and tips – all sorts of useful stuff sorted by
   category.
5. Project guides – help with all sorts of DIY jobs.
6. Directory – where to find it all.

Superstores

www.diy.com
THE DIY SUPERSTORE

ORIGIN	UK
SPEED	✓✓✓
INFO	✓✓✓✓
VALUE	✓✓✓✓
EASE	✓✓✓✓

B&Q has a bright and busy site with lots of advice, inspiration, tips and information on projects for the home and garden. It also has an excellent searchable product database. There are also plenty of offers and the store has a good selection of products covering all the major DIY areas. Delivery costs vary according to how much you buy and how fast you want it. Returns can be made to the stores.

www.homebase.co.uk
CREATE YOUR IDEAL HOME, FROM HOME

ORIGIN	UK
SPEED	✓✓✓✓
INFO	✓✓✓✓
VALUE	✓✓✓✓
EASE	✓✓✓✓

Massively improved site, with a fairly large selection of products to buy, you can also get help with projects, plenty of inspirational ideas for each room of the house, as well as offers and competitions. Delivery charges vary, although the minimum is £5. Helpfully, you can return unwanted or faulty goods to your nearest store. W?WT

www.wickes.co.uk
DIY SPECIALISTS

ORIGIN	US
SPEED	✓✓✓
INFO	✓✓✓✓✓
VALUE	✓✓✓
EASE	✓✓✓

Good ideas, inspiration and help are the key themes for this site, it's easy-to-use and genuinely helpful with well laid out project details. You can visit their showrooms for product information and even take a 3-D tour of a conservatory. There's a handy calculator section where you can work out how many tiles or rolls of wallpaper you may need. The site does suffer from lots of graphic errors though.

www.focusdoitall.co.uk
Focus Do-it-All

ORIGIN	UK
SPEED	✓✓✓
INFO	✓✓✓✓✓
VALUE	✓✓✓✓
EASE	✓✓✓

A functional site, which attempts to put over lots of ideas and inspiration, it also carries a wide range of products at good prices. Delivery is £4.99 minimum and you can return unwanted goods to your nearest store.

Other DIY stores worth checking out are:

www.jewson.co.uk – Jewson's site is more corporate than anything but it does have a great set of DIY links.

www.globalpower.co.uk – rather oddly designed but has some good offers nonetheless. **W?WT**

www.decoratingdirect.co.uk – functional and easy-to-use site that concentrates on home décor products at excellent prices.

Buying tools and equipment

www.screwfix.com
Products for all DIY needs

ORIGIN	UK
SPEED	✓✓✓✓
INFO	✓✓✓✓✓
VALUE	✓✓✓✓✓
EASE	✓✓✓✓

Rightly considered to be one of the best online stores, Screwfix offer excellent value for money with free delivery and wholesale prices on a massive range of DIY products. If only all online shops were like this.

www.cooksons.com
Tools a-plenty

ORIGIN	US
SPEED	✓✓✓
INFO	✓✓✓✓
VALUE	✓✓✓✓
EASE	✓✓✓

Over 50,000 tools are available here, with free delivery on orders over £45. There are plenty of special offers and a loyalty scheme for regulars. **W?WT**

www.diytools.co.uk
MORE TOOLS

ORIGIN	UK
SPEED	✓✓✓✓
INFO	✓✓✓✓
VALUE	✓✓✓✓
EASE	✓✓✓✓

Another well-designed and extensive tool store, with over 23,000 products, there's also free delivery for orders over £30. www.toolfast.co.uk is also worth checking out. (W?WT)

DIY help and advice

www.fmb.org.uk/consumers
THE FEDERATION OF MASTER BUILDERS

ORIGIN	UK
SPEED	✓✓✓
INFO	✓✓✓✓✓
EASE	✓✓✓

Get help to avoid cowboys and advice on getting the best out of a builder. There's information and articles on most aspects of home maintenance, plus hints on finding reputable help.

www.homepro.com
THE HOME IMPROVEMENT SPECIALISTS

ORIGIN	UK
SPEED	✓✓✓✓
INFO	✓✓✓✓✓
EASE	✓✓✓✓✓

An excellent and very helpful site split into four major sections, a 24-hour emergency call out service for your area, a 'find a professional' service for any household job, a help and advice section and lastly a superb inspirational section where you can go for ideas for your home. You can access via WAP or call the helplines too.

www.improveline.com
FIND A CONTRACTOR AND IDEAS

ORIGIN	UK
SPEED	✓✓✓✓
INFO	✓✓✓✓✓
EASE	✓✓✓✓

Well-designed site offering information and inspiration for home improvements, there's also a service that puts you in touch with someone to do small jobs on the house within the hour. Inspiration comes in the form of thousands of categorised pictures, which are easily pulled up via a good search facility. You can also ask an expert and get advice on financing your project.

www.hometips.com
EXPERT ADVICE FOR YOUR HOME

ORIGIN US	American the advice may be, but there is plenty here
SPEED ✓✓✓	for every homeowner. Split into six sections: there is
INFO ✓✓✓✓	a buying guide; advice on home care; DIY help; a tip
EASE ✓✓✓	sheet with reviews of other sites and books; a guide

to how your house works; and lastly, dang good ideas. For a similar but less entertaining site try **www.naturalhandyman.com** or alternatively, there is the well-designed **http://homedoctor.net/main.html** or the extensive **www.doityourself.com** which is very detailed.

www.diyfixit.co.uk
ONLINE DIY ENCYCLOPAEDIA

ORIGIN UK	Get help with most DIY jobs using the search engine
SPEED ✓✓✓	or browse by room or job type. The information is
INFO ✓✓✓✓	good but some guidance and more illustrations
EASE ✓✓✓	would help. It's also worth checking out

www.diymate.com

www.architect-net.co.uk
ARCHITECTS AND BUILDING CONTRACTORS DIRECTORY

ORIGIN UK	Find an architect to design your next home using the
SPEED ✓✓✓	regional directory. Not a great site, but useful for
INFO ✓✓✓	good links to related sites.
EASE ✓✓✓	

www.ebuild.co.uk
BUILD YOUR OWN HOUSE

ORIGIN UK	All the information and contacts you need if you're
SPEED ✓✓✓	thinking of buying that plot of land and getting
INFO ✓✓✓✓✓	stuck in. There's also a continually updated list of
EASE ✓✓✓	what plots of land are available and where.

Specialists

www.bathroomexpress.co.uk
BETTER BATHROOMS

ORIGIN UK	A wide range of bathrooms and accessories
SPEED ✓✓✓	are available at decent prices, with some
INFO ✓✓✓✓	interesting luxury items such as aprés-shower
VALUE ✓✓✓✓	driers and some unique toilet seats.
EASE ✓✓✓✓	Delivery is based on how much you spend. W?WT

www.plumbworld.co.uk
AN ONLINE PLUMBING SHOP

ORIGIN UK	Good selection of plumbing tools at competitive
SPEED ✓✓✓	prices. Not exactly the most informative site as you
INFO ✓✓✓	have to assume much and there's very little informa-
EASE ✓✓✓	tion about shipping for example, which is free when

you spend £50 or more. If you need to find a
plumber try the directory of plumbers at
www.plumbers.uk.com or for information on how
to do work yourself try **www.plumbnet.com** or
www.guidetoplumbing.com

www.handlesdirect.co.uk
HANDLES GALORE

ORIGIN	UK
SPEED	✓✓✓✓
INFO	✓✓✓✓
VALUE	✓✓✓
EASE	✓✓✓

A natty-looking site where you can buy, well, handles. It's also got a selection of locks, switches and sockets that match certain handles. The emphasis is on contemporary style, and there's a good advice section, which shows you how to fit them.

www.doorsdirect.co.uk
DOORS AND HANDLES

ORIGIN	UK
SPEED	✓✓✓✓
INFO	✓✓✓✓
VALUE	✓✓✓
EASE	✓✓✓✓

Features replacement doors for kitchens and bathrooms, you can order made-to-measure or standard and there's a selection of fittings as well.

www.salvo.co.uk
SALVAGE AND RECLAMATION

ORIGIN	UK
SPEED	✓✓✓
INFO	✓✓✓✓✓
VALUE	✓✓✓
EASE	✓✓✓✓

Salvo provides information on where to get salvaged and reclaimed architectural and garden antiques. The site is comprehensive and easy-to-use with interesting information such as what buildings are due to be demolished and when, so you can be ready and waiting.

Paint and wallpaper

www.dulux.co.uk
DULUX

ORIGIN	UK
SPEED	✓✓✓
INFO	✓✓✓✓✓
EASE	✓✓✓✓

Great for information and tips on how to use colour in your home, there's an interactive colour schemer, a kids' zone if you really want to get mucky and lots of advice on combining colour. You can't buy from the site although there is a list of stockists. Crown has a similar site that can be found at **www.crownpaint.co.uk**

www.farrow-ball.co.uk
Traditional paint and paper

ORIGIN UK	Excellently designed web site featuring details on
SPEED ✓✓✓	how their paint and paper is manufactured, a thing
INFO ✓✓✓✓	they obviously take pride in. You can also order
VALUE ✓✓✓	from the site or request samples. For that traditional
EASE ✓✓✓✓	Mediterranean look try **www.casa.co.uk** who have a

good selection and a nice site to buy from.

www.sanderson-online.co.uk
William Morris amongst other wallpaper

ORIGIN UK	Find out about the company, its heritage and what
SPEED ✓✓✓	designs they have – new and old. You can also order
INFO ✓✓✓✓	a brochure and visit the Morris & Co pages where
VALUE ✓✓✓	they have all the favourite designs. For more
EASE ✓✓✓	information on William Morris try visiting

www.morrissociety.org.

www.thedesignstudio.co.uk
Get the right design

ORIGIN UK	This is an excellent database of wallpaper and fabric
SPEED ✓✓	samples, which is easy-to-use and good fun. Once
INFO ✓✓✓✓	you've selected your swatch you can then find the
EASE ✓✓✓	nearest supplier. You need some patience, as it can

be quite slow.

Inspiration, design and interiors

www.bhglive.com
Better Homes and Gardens

ORIGIN US	There's more to this than DIY, but superb graphics
SPEED ✓✓	and videos give this site the edge. It's American, so
INFO ✓✓✓✓✓	some information isn't applicable to the UK. The
EASE ✓✓✓	Home Encyclopaedia is excellent.

www.bluedeco.com
DESIGN ONLINE

ORIGIN UK/ LUXEMBOURG
SPEED ✓✓✓
INFO ✓✓✓✓
VALUE ✓✓✓
EASE ✓✓✓

This site offers a superb selection of designer products for the home, from furniture to ceramics, with free delivery to the UK. Unfortunately, returns have to go to Luxembourg.

www.brightbeige.co.uk
STYLE QUESTIONS ANSWERED

ORIGIN UK
SPEED ✓✓✓
INFO ✓✓✓✓✓
EASE ✓✓✓✓

Great looking site with answers to all those basic decorating questions like 'how do I make this room brighter?' It's easy-to-use and there's a quiz to discover your style as well as inspirational photos to help you along the way. There's also an excellent shop directory.

www.chiasmus.co.uk
FRESH AND FUNKY PRODUCTS FOR THE HOME

ORIGIN UK
SPEED ✓✓✓
INFO ✓✓✓✓
VALUE ✓✓✓
EASE ✓✓✓

Cute looking site with plenty of trend-setting products, especially good if you're looking for something a bit different. Free delivery on orders over £30. **W?WT**

www.design4living.co.uk
ULTIMATE IN HOME DESIGN

ORIGIN UK
SPEED ✓✓
INFO ✓✓✓
VALUE ✓✓✓
EASE ✓✓✓

A magazine, a directory and a shop all rolled into one in a nice looking site, although some links don't work and graphics occasionally overlap. There are about 100 products to choose from and the shop needs patience to use.

www.design-gap.co.uk
DESIGNER DIRECTORY

ORIGIN	UK
SPEED	✓✓✓
INFO	✓✓✓✓✓
EASE	✓✓✓

A directory of UK-based designers and manufacturers with some 300 pages to browse through. They are arranged alphabetically by first name or company name as well as by category. The illustrations are excellent.

www.design-online.co.uk
NEED A DESIGNER?

ORIGIN	UK
SPEED	✓✓✓
INFO	✓✓✓✓
EASE	✓✓✓

Design Online's mission is to put buyers and suppliers in touch with each other and to use the Internet to promote the use of well-designed products and services. You just search for the service you want and a list of suitable suppliers with contact details quickly appears. Could do with some illustrations and examples of the work that they are trying to promote.

www.geomancy.net
FENG SHUI

ORIGIN	UK
SPEED	✓✓✓
INFO	✓✓✓✓
EASE	✓✓

What a mess of a site! Considering that it's supposed to promote the principles of light and harmony, it isn't very well designed. However, there's an excellent set of links and you can learn all you need to know about Feng Shui.

www.habitat.co.uk
HABITAT STORES

ORIGIN	UK
SPEED	✓✓✓✓
INFO	✓✓✓✓
EASE	✓✓✓✓

An information only site with lots of details about their product range all wrapped up in a funky design.

www.hi-revolution.com
HOME IMPROVEMENT WITHOUT HASSLE

ORIGIN UK
SPEED ✓✓✓
INFO ✓✓✓✓✓
EASE ✓✓✓✓

A nice idea, this is a service that matches your job requirement to the right trade professional, it also assesses your chosen company on how well you think they performed the job. There's also an advice section and an area you can just browse for inspiration, and there's the 'Home-pro emergency call-out', which sounds a bit dodgy but it's a service that can get a quality tradesman to you really quickly.

www.homesbydesign.co.uk
WHATEVER YOUR NEEDS

ORIGIN UK
SPEED ✓✓✓
INFO ✓✓✓✓✓
EASE ✓✓✓✓

Excellent magazine-style site with great advice on most DIY and home projects, they have regional listings of specialist suppliers and stores as well as features such as celebrity spots and ask a designer. You have to register to get the best out of it.

www.ikea.com
IKEA STYLE

ORIGIN SWEDEN
SPEED ✓✓✓
INFO ✓✓✓✓
EASE ✓✓✓✓

You can't buy from the site but you can check whether a store has the item you want to buy in stock before you go, it would be great if more stores did this. Otherwise the site is more the usual store fare with plenty of ideas, articles and product lists.

www.maelstrom.co.uk
CONTEMPORARY SELECTION

ORIGIN UK
SPEED ✓✓
INFO ✓✓✓✓
VALUE ✓✓✓
EASE ✓✓✓

A wide selection of contemporary gifts, accessories, gadgets and furniture in a good-looking site. Delivery is generally 10% of the value of order, but there are several options. **W?WT**

www.next.co.uk
NEXT HOME WARE

ORIGIN UK
SPEED ✓✓✓
INFO ✓✓✓✓
VALUE ✓✓✓
EASE ✓✓✓

A good selection of Next homeware with an excellent next day delivery service that costs £2.50 whatever you buy.

Education

Using the Internet for homework or study has become one of its primary uses; these sites will help enormously, especially alongside the reference and encyclopaedia sites listed on page 301. There is also a section aimed at students on page 371.

www.a-levels.co.uk
'A' LEVELS – A DODDLE?

ORIGIN UK
SPEED ✓✓✓✓
INFO ✓✓✓
EASE ✓✓✓

Great links providing masses of information on key topics. It's still being developed so not all A level subjects completed – worth checking out though.

www.accessart.org.uk
MAKING ART ACCESSIBLE

ORIGIN UK
SPEED ✓✓✓✓
INFO ✓✓✓✓✓
EASE ✓✓✓✓

A really good, colourful site dedicated to helping you get to grips with the art world and the meaning behind art. There are online workshops to provide advice for teachers and pupils alike.

www.bbc.co.uk/education
GET EQUIPPED FOR LIFE

ORIGIN UK
SPEED ✓✓✓✓
INFO ✓✓✓✓
EASE ✓✓✓

Great for homework with information on all the BBC education-related programs and activities; each section tends to be tied to a particular programme rather than subject. There are also sections on French, Italian, German and Spanish.

www.bigchalk.com
HOMEWORK CENTRAL

ORIGIN US
SPEED ✓✓✓✓
INFO ✓✓✓✓
EASE ✓✓✓

Click on the student's area and you get put through to Homework Central, which has well categorised links to lots of excellent information, web sites and subjects. There's help and information for parents and a teacher's section full of good resources in spite of the US bias.

www.cln.org/int_expert.html
ASK AN EXPERT

ORIGIN CANADA
SPEED ✓✓✓✓
INFO ✓✓✓
EASE ✓✓✓

This site lists almost a hundred sites by subject, where you can ask an expert your homework question – what a doddle! North American bias though.

www.educate.org.uk
EDUCATE YOURSELF

ORIGIN UK
SPEED ✓✓✓✓
INFO ✓✓
EASE ✓✓✓

For parents there is loads of advice on how to get the best out of the system to help your children achieve, and with over 2,500 primary lesson plans, the site is great for teachers. The web search is comprehensive for homework help (Key Stage 1 through GCSE), there's educational news, a schools guide and listings for child-friendly days out. However, it can be a bit slow and, with the exception of web search, is aimed at primary.

www.eduweb.co.uk
THE INTERNET SERVICE FOR TEACHERS AND PUPILS

ORIGIN UK
SPEED ✓✓✓✓
INFO ✓✓✓
VALUE ✓✓
EASE ✓✓✓

EduWeb provides access to a massive amount of curriculum-based data for use on homework. There's also tons of education news and information aimed at teachers and parents from advice on projects to info on good schools. Many features are free but you have to subscribe to get some services.

DiscoverySchool.com
ANSWERS TO HOMEWORK, FREE

ORIGIN US
SPEED ✓✓✓✓
INFO ✓✓✓✓
EASE ✓✓✓

This huge database is one of the biggest online homework sites, with some 600 links to a variety of reference sites. In theory, homework was never so easy, however, to British eyes, it can seem a bit odd.

www.en.eun.org
THE EUROPEAN SCHOOL NET

ORIGIN BELGIUM
SPEED ✓✓✓✓
INFO ✓✓✓
EASE ✓✓✓

Click on the tiny word 'pupils' and you get through to a section with links to other useful web sites with a strong European cross-cultural bias, also pen pals and the latest news – great for Euro-homework.

www.gcse.com
GCSE ANSWERS

ORIGIN UK
SPEED ✓✓✓✓
INFO ✓✓✓✓
EASE ✓✓✓

This site has tests and past papers for English, maths, physics and French GCSE exams, but it's building. Includes tips on how to get good results and information on the various examination boards.

www.homeworkelephant.co.uk
LET THE ELEPHANT HELP

ORIGIN UK
SPEED ✓✓✓✓
INFO ✓✓✓✓✓
EASE ✓✓✓✓

An excellent site with some 5,000 resources aimed at helping children achieve great results, there's help with specific subjects, hints and tips, help for parents and teachers. The agony elephant is great if you get really stuck. It's constantly being updated, so worth checking regularly.

www.homeworkhigh.co.uk
LEARN WITH CHANNEL 4

ORIGIN UK
SPEED ✓✓✓✓
INFO ✓✓✓✓✓
EASE ✓✓✓✓

Split into eight sections: history, geography, science, maths, English, French, news and a chat room, this is one of the better-looking homework sites. Teachers are online for live sessions to help you out. You ask questions, find out lots of information and you can chat with fellow homework sufferers. Excellent.

www.learn.com
SMARTEST PLACE ON THE WEB

ORIGIN US
SPEED ✓✓✓✓
INFO ✓✓✓✓✓
EASE ✓✓✓

Once you've registered (very easy) you're entitled to free access to some online courses, which range from how to bake spicy fries to how to convert centigrade into Fahrenheit. It's not easy to find specific facts, but if you have a project to do there's bound to be something here to help you out. Be warned that many of the courses they offer do cost.

www.pupilline.net
FOR US BY US

ORIGIN UK
SPEED ✓✓✓✓
INFO ✓✓✓✓✓
EASE ✓✓✓✓

A massive, comprehensive site by pupils for pupils, it doesn't stop at education either, it covers social issues as well, in fact everything any pupil would want to know. As it's put together by them it speaks in their language – er a wicked site then.

www.samlearning.com
EXAM REVISION

ORIGIN UK
SPEED ✓✓✓✓
INFO ✓✓✓✓✓
EASE ✓✓✓

SAM stands for self-assessment and marking, on this brilliant site you can do just that, it has mock exams covering every major subject and key stage plus GCSE and A level. There are top tips on taking exams and the chance to win some great prizes when you register. There is a 14-day free trial then you need to pay £4.99 per month as a home user.

www.schoolzone.co.uk
UK's TOP EDUCATIONAL SEARCH ENGINE

ORIGIN UK
SPEED ✓✓✓✓
INFO ✓✓✓✓✓
EASE ✓✓✓

With over 30,000 sites and bits of resource, all checked by teachers, Schoolzone has masses of information. All the sites and information are rated according to how useful they are. There is free software to download, plus homework help, career advice, teacher support (they do need it apparently) and much more. Don't be put off by the confusing layout; it's worth sticking with.

www.startribune.com/homework
HOMEWORK ON THE BRAIN

ORIGIN US
SPEED ✓✓✓
INFO ✓✓✓✓
EASE ✓✓✓

Just click on the right bit of the cartoon brain and you get put through to the subject you're after. There are lots of links to other learning web sites as well as bags of tips and information; you can even e-mail a question. They try to reply within 24 hours.

Pre-school and infant education

www.enchantedlearning.com
FROM APES TO WHALES

ORIGIN US
SPEED ✓✓✓✓
INFO ✓✓✓
EASE ✓✓

It's messy, uncool and largely aimed at young children, but there's loads of good information and activities hidden away, especially on nature. Use the search engine to find what you need.

www.underfives.co.uk
WEB RESOURCE FOR PRE-SCHOOL

ORIGIN UK
SPEED ✓✓✓
INFO ✓✓✓✓✓
EASE ✓✓✓✓

Loads of things to do and see here, from games and activities to download to help and advice for parents. Like the best educational sites it's educational bias is not obvious or overwhelming, the tone is just right, it's also easy-to-use and fast.

National Curriculum

www.dfee.gov.uk/nc
NATIONAL CURRICULUM REVEALED

ORIGIN UK
SPEED ✓✓✓✓
INFO ✓✓✓✓
EASE ✓✓✓✓

Very detailed explanation of the National Curriculum and prescribed standards. For more information on the national curriculum see www.qca.org.uk For information on the Scottish education system see www.sqa.org.uk

Post 16 and adult education

www.ngfl.gov.uk
THE NATIONAL GRID FOR LEARNING

ORIGIN UK
SPEED ✓✓✓✓
INFO ✓✓✓
EASE ✓✓✓

The official government education site with sections on every aspect of learning. There's something for everyone, whatever your needs. It is particularly good for info on further and adult education. There are also details on key museums, galleries and libraries plus a section on international education.

www.learndirect.co.uk
ADULT LEARNING

ORIGIN UK	A government backed site which aims to bring
SPEED ✓✓✓	education to everyone whatever their needs. The site
INFO ✓✓✓✓	explains the background to the initiative plus details
EASE ✓✓✓✓	of courses and how you can find one that meets

your requirements. There's also help for businesses and a jobs advice section.

Electrical Goods, Gadgets and Appliances

In this section we cover stores that sell the usual electrical goods, but also offer a bit more in terms of range, offers or service. There's also the odd spy camera and gadget shop.

www.comet.co.uk
ALWAYS LOW PRICES, GUARANTEED

ORIGIN UK	Lots of products, split into: kitchen and home, for
SPEED ✓✓✓	washing machines, microwaves and cookers; house-
INFO ✓✓✓✓✓	hold with vacuums, irons, ionisers and air purifiers;
VALUE ✓✓✓✓	entertainment featuring TV, music, games and
EASE ✓✓✓✓	keyboards; computing and communication offering

PCs and mobiles, phones and faxes. Finance deals and offers abound and there's information on the products. Delivery costs vary.

www.dixons.co.uk
OFFERS GALORE

ORIGIN UK	The Dixons site has plenty of offers and reflects
SPEED ✓✓✓	what you'd find in their stores very well. It has a
INFO ✓✓✓	similar but slightly wider product range to Comet,
VALUE ✓✓✓✓	with an additional photographic section. Delivery is
EASE ✓✓✓✓	£3.25 per item.

www.maplin.co.uk
ELECTRONICS CATALOGUE

ORIGIN	UK
SPEED	✓✓
INFO	✓✓✓✓
VALUE	✓✓✓
EASE	✓✓

Maplin is well-established and it's a bit of an event when the new catalogue is published. Now you can always have access to the latest innovations and basic equipment at this well put together site. It features the expected massive range with online ordering, unfortunately, the process is laborious and quite slow.

www.priceright.co.uk
ONE STOP SHOP FOR ELECTRICAL APPLIANCES

ORIGIN	UK
SPEED	✓✓✓✓
INFO	✓✓✓✓
VALUE	✓✓✓✓✓
EASE	✓✓✓✓

Priceright have a good reputation for value and you can sense it straight away as the site unfolds. Free delivery on all products is the first thing you see, followed by automatic 5% discount when you join. Their range is excellent, covering most of the major brands and product categories.

www.hed.co.uk
HOME ELECTRICAL DIRECT

ORIGIN	UK
SPEED	✓✓✓✓
INFO	✓✓✓
VALUE	✓✓✓✓✓
EASE	✓✓✓✓

Their motto is 'the lowest prices guaranteed all year round, and that's a promise'. They have a very large range of goods covering all the key product categories minus cameras. Delivery is free. W?WT

Other electrical retailers worth checking out are:
www.electricalappliancesdirect.co.uk
www.applianceonline.co.uk W?WT
www.bestbuyappliances.co.uk W?WT

www.value-direct.co.uk

IF CHOICE IS WHAT YOU'RE LOOKING FOR

ORIGIN	UK	A much wider range than average, from
SPEED	✓✓✓	kitchen equipment to music.
INFO	✓✓✓✓	Good prices and an attractive site make
VALUE	✓✓✓✓	Value Direct stand out from the crowd. W?WT
EASE	✓✓✓✓	

www.richersounds.com

PROMISES TO BEAT EVERY OTHER WEB SITE BY £50

ORIGIN	UK	Bargain hunters will want to include this site on
SPEED	✓✓✓	their list, similar to the other electrical goods retail-
INFO	✓✓	ers but with a leaning towards music and TVs, with
VALUE	✓✓✓✓	plenty of offers and advice. There is now a search
EASE	✓✓✓✓	facility, but delivery isn't free. W?WT

www.appliancespares.co.uk

FIX IT YOURSELF

ORIGIN	UK	Ezee-Fix has thousands of spare parts for a massive
SPEED	✓✓✓✓	range of products, nearly all illustrated, including
INFO	✓✓✓	fridges, cookers, microwaves, vacuum cleaners, etc.
VALUE	✓✓✓	All it needs is online fitting instructions, and more
EASE	✓✓✓	details on the products and it would be perfect.

www.flyingtoolbox.com

IF YOU CAN'T FIX IT YOURSELF

ORIGIN	UK	With Flying Toolbox you can find someone to repair
SPEED	✓✓✓✓	your faulty item. Type in your location and details
INFO	✓✓✓✓	of the repair and they will provide a list of repairers
VALUE	✓✓✓	in your area with information on charges and a
EASE	✓✓✓✓	rating from previous customers. Good though it is,
		could it be just a way of selling insurance policies?

www.bull-electrical.com

FOR THE SPECIALIST

ORIGIN	UK
SPEED	✓✓✓✓
INFO	✓✓✓✓
VALUE	✓✓✓✓✓
EASE	✓✓✓

Fascinating to visit, this site offers every sort of electronic device, from divining rods, to radio kits to spy cameras. There are four basic sections:

1. Surplus electronic – scientific and optical goods – even steam engines.
2. Links to specialist shops – such as spy equipment and hydroponics.
3. Free services.
4. Web services – shopping cart technology for example.

www.innovations.co.uk

NEW TECHNOLOGY

ORIGIN	UK
SPEED	✓✓✓
INFO	✓✓✓✓
VALUE	✓✓✓
EASE	✓✓✓

Some 600 innovative, unusual or just plain daft items for sale, all on a neat web site, the best bit is probably the gift selector, which helps you find the perfect gift when you're stuck for something to buy. Other places for technology geeks to get their kicks are **www.thegagetshop.co.uk** who have free delivery and a free returns policy, **www.firebox.com** for a really wide range of gadgets amongst other boys toys and lastly, the macho **www.big-boys-toys.net**

Fashion, Accessories and Beauty Products

The big brands have never been cheaper. Selling fashion and designer gear is another Net success, as customers flock to the great discounts that are on offer. Many people still prefer to try clothes on before buying but the good sites all offer a convenient returns policy. Beauty product retailers have now cottoned on to the Internet so we've featured a few of the best ones here.

Fashion

www.fuk.co.uk
FASHION UK

ORIGIN	UK
SPEED	✓✓✓✓
INFO	✓✓✓✓✓
EASE	✓✓✓

All you ever need to know about the latest in UK and world fashion, updated daily. There's also a section on beauty, a good links library, competitions, chat and, of course, shopping. It's all packaged into a really attractive site, which initially looks cluttered but is OK once you get used to it.

www.fashionlive.com
A FASHION E-ZINE

ORIGIN	UK
SPEED	✓✓✓✓
INFO	✓✓✓✓
EASE	✓✓✓✓

Check out the latest styles and get the inside view on what's really happening and which styles are 'truly ready to wear'. You can search by designer or just browse; there are plenty of interviews, profiles, plus beauty and fashion tips to keep you amused.

See also **www.firstview.com** which provides access to the top designers' most recent collections and a glimpse at what could be available in the shops the following season.

www.vogue.co.uk
THE LATEST NEWS FROM BRITISH VOGUE

ORIGIN UK	An absolute must for the serious follower of fashion.
SPEED ✓✓✓✓	There's the latest catwalk news and views, and a
INFO ✓✓✓✓	handy who's who of fashion. There's also a section
EASE ✓✓✓✓	on jobs, and you can order a subscription too.

For a similar experience try **www.elle.com** or
the slightly less fashion-oriented but more fun
www.cosmomag.com

www.intofashion.com
GET INTO FASHION

ORIGIN UK	With sections on jewellery, hair accessories, scarves,
SPEED ✓✓✓✓	bags and, of course, clothes, Intofashion offers a
INFO ✓✓✓✓	complete service, backed by excellent and stylish
VALUE ✓✓✓✓	design and great picture quality. You can search the
EASE ✓✓✓✓	site by designer or by product or browse the best

buys. Delivery is free in the UK. For an alternative try
www.theclothesstore.com who also have a good selection of clothes and accessories, but the site isn't easy
to navigate and they charge for delivery to the UK.

www.fashionmall.com
FASHION STORE DIRECTORY

ORIGIN US	A huge number of stores listed by category, packed
SPEED ✓✓✓✓	with offers and the latest new designs. Most stores
INFO ✓✓✓✓	are American and their ability to deliver outside the
VALUE ✓✓✓✓	US and delivery charges vary considerably. The site
EASE ✓✓✓✓	is well-designed and easy to browse.

www.littleblackdress.co.uk
FASHION FAST

ORIGIN UK
SPEED ✓✓✓✓
INFO ✓✓✓✓
VALUE ✓✓✓
EASE ✓✓✓✓

If you need a designer dress in a hurry then The Little Black Dress Company can supply one in two days with no delivery charges. This site is well designed and easy-to-use, you can browse by item, range or by the mood you want to create.

www.yoox.com
TOP DESIGNERS

ORIGIN UK
SPEED ✓✓✓✓
INFO ✓✓✓✓
VALUE ✓✓✓✓
EASE ✓✓✓✓

Great looking site with top offers from the top designers, it's well laid out and easy to navigate with a good returns policy. You can search by designer or category and the quality of the photos is good. Offers range from a few pounds to massive discounts.

www.zercon.com
CUT-PRICE DESIGNER CLOTHES FOR MEN AND WOMEN

ORIGIN UK
SPEED ✓✓✓✓
INFO ✓✓✓✓
VALUE ✓✓✓✓
EASE ✓✓✓✓

Not a big range of clothes but excellent prices. Clear, no-nonsense design, makes the site easy-to-use. W?WT

www.apc.fr
FRENCH CHIC FROM A.P.C.

ORIGIN FRANCE
SPEED ✓✓✓
INFO ✓✓✓
VALUE ✓✓
EASE ✓✓✓✓

Unusual in style and for something a little different A.P.C.'s site is worth a visit. Delivery is expensive in line with the clothes, which are beautifully designed and well presented. For more of the French look go to **www.redoute.co.uk**

www.gap.com
FOR US RESIDENTS ONLY

ORIGIN US	A clear, uncluttered design makes shopping here
SPEED ✓✓✓	easy if you live in the United States! For UK resi-
INFO ✓✓✓✓	dents it's window-shopping only.
VALUE ✓✓✓	
EASE ✓✓✓✓	

www.next.co.uk
THE NEXT DIRECTORY

ORIGIN UK	The online version of the Next catalogue is available
SPEED ✓✓✓	including clothes for men, women and children as
INFO ✓✓✓✓	well as products for the home. Prices are the same as
VALUE ✓✓✓	the directory, next day delivery is £2.50 and return
EASE ✓✓✓✓	of unwanted goods is free. You can order the full
	catalogue for £3.

www.designerheaven.co.uk
UK AND IRISH DESIGNERS FOR MEN

ORIGIN UK	All the top British and Irish names such as
SPEED ✓✓✓	Mulberry and Aquascutum are featured in
INFO ✓✓✓✓	this attractive and easy-to-use site, which
VALUE ✓✓✓	offers free delivery in the UK. W?WT
EASE ✓✓✓✓	

www.arcadia.co.uk
THE ARCADIA GROUP– THE UK'S LEADING FASHION RETAILER

ORIGIN UK	The Arcadia Group has over 1,200 stores in the UK,
SPEED ✓✓✓	and the web sites are accessible, easy-to-use and
INFO ✓✓✓✓	offer good value for money. Each has its own
VALUE ✓✓✓✓	personality that reflects the high street store.
EASE ✓✓✓✓	Delivery charges vary.

www.su214.co.uk – men's fashion
www.racinggreen.co.uk – fashion
www.dorothyperkins.co.uk – women's clothes

www.tops.co.uk – Topshop
www.topman.co.uk – men's clothes
www.burtonmenswear.co.uk – men's clothes
www.hawkshead.com – outdoor clothes
www.principles.co.uk – for both men and women
www.zoom.co.uk – fashion
www.evans.co.uk – for mature women

www.fashionbot.com
THE FASHION SEARCH ENGINE

ORIGIN	UK	Quickly searches the major online stores (mainly those from the Arcadia Group) and compares prices. Just click on the item you want to check. If you can't find what you want here try **www.fashion.net** an American site that also offers news, jobs and a good set of links to other fashion sites.
SPEED	✓✓✓✓	
INFO	✓✓✓✓	
VALUE	✓✓✓✓	
EASE	✓✓✓✓	

Where the top designers hang out:

www.armaniexchange.com – Armani
www.tedbaker.co.uk – Ted Baker
www.jpgaultier.fr – Jean Paul Gaultier
www.christian-lacroix.fr – Christian Lacroix
www.alexandermcqueen.net – Alexander McQueen
www.bensherman.co.uk – Ben Sherman

General clothes stores

www.kaysnet.com
KAYS CATALOGUE

ORIGIN	UK	Massive range combined with value for money is the formula for success with Kays. While they lead with clothes there are plenty of other sections outside of that: jewellery, home entertainment, toys, etc. Delivery charge depends on how much you spend.
SPEED	✓✓✓✓	
INFO	✓✓✓✓	
VALUE	✓✓✓✓	
EASE	✓✓✓✓	

www.freemans.co.uk
FREE DELIVERY IN THE UK AND GOOD PRICES

ORIGIN UK
SPEED ✓✓✓
INFO ✓✓✓✓
VALUE ✓✓✓✓
EASE ✓✓✓✓

A new look site, not the full catalogue but there's a wide range to choose from including top brands. Split into four major sections; women, men, children and sports, they offer free delivery for UK customers. There are also prizes to be won, a special feature on the latest trends and fashions and information on how to get the full catalogue.

See also the excellent **www.shoppersuniverse.com** for the Great Universal Stores' catalogue, and **www.grattan.co.uk** for Grattan's catalogue.

www.thebestofbritish.com
GREAT FOR THE TRADITIONAL AND THE NEW

ORIGIN UK
SPEED ✓✓✓
INFO ✓✓✓✓
VALUE ✓✓✓✓
EASE ✓✓✓✓

Owned by the *Daily Telegraph*, all the brands are here, covering a wide variety of goods, but mainly clothes and accessories. Search the site by designer, brand or product type. Delivery is charged although check as occasionally it's free. **W?WT**

Specialist clothes stores

www.asseenonscreen.com
BUY WHAT YOU SEE ON FILM OR TV

ORIGIN UK
SPEED ✓✓✓✓
INFO ✓✓✓✓
VALUE ✓✓✓
EASE ✓✓✓✓

Now you can buy that bit of jewellery or cool gear that you've seen your favourite TV or film star wearing, 'As seen on screen' specialises in supplying just that. You can search by star or programme, it isn't cheap but you'll get noticed. You can also request products too if you've seen something and they'll try and get it for you.

www.noveltytogs.com

FOR CHARACTER MERCHANDISE

ORIGIN	UK
SPEED	✓✓✓
INFO	✓✓✓✓
VALUE	✓✓✓
EASE	✓✓✓✓

Merchandise for *Pokemon*, *The Simpsons*, *South Park*, *Garfield* and *Peanuts*, there are the usual T-shirts plus boxer shorts, socks and nightshirts. Delivery is free for the UK and there are links to other character web sites. W?WT

www.bloomingmarvellous.co.uk

MATERNITY WEAR

ORIGIN	UK
SPEED	✓✓✓✓
INFO	✓✓✓✓
VALUE	✓✓✓✓
EASE	✓✓✓✓

The UK's leading store in maternity and babywear has an attractive site that features a good selection of clothes and nursery products. There are no discounts on the clothes, but they do have regular sales with some good bargains. Delivery in the UK is £3.95 per order.

www.tienet.co.uk

THE INTERNET TIE STORE

ORIGIN	UK
SPEED	✓✓✓✓
INFO	✓✓✓✓
VALUE	✓✓✓✓
EASE	✓✓✓✓

Hundreds of ties in seemingly every colour and design, there are sections on fashion ties, bow-ties, tartan and character ties. Selection and payment is simple, but some of the pictures are quite blurred and the patterns are sometimes difficult to see. Delivery charge depends on size of order. W?WT

www.shoe-shop.com

EUROPE'S BIGGEST SHOE SHOP

ORIGIN	UK
SPEED	✓✓✓✓
INFO	✓✓✓✓
VALUE	✓✓✓✓
EASE	✓✓✓✓

A massive selection of shoes and brands to chose from, the site is nicely designed with good pictures of the shoes, some of which can be seen in 3D, a facility they are expanding. Delivery is included in the price and there's a good returns policy.
For an alternative try the straightforward **www.shoesdirect.co.uk** who have a similar offer.

Underwear and lingerie

www.smartbras.com
BRAS, BASQUES AND BRIEFS

ORIGIN	UK
SPEED	✓✓✓✓
INFO	✓✓✓✓
VALUE	✓✓✓
EASE	✓✓✓✓

The easy, embarrassment-free way to buy underwear. Choose from a selection of around 200 lingerie products including brand names at high street prices. Delivery is £2.50 for the UK.

For up-market lingerie try **www.rigbyandpeller.com**, for value for money go to the excellent **www.easyshop.co.uk**, for style go for **www.victoriassecret.com**. For specialists in men's underwear try **www.kiniki.com** for underwear with pulling power.

Accessories and jewellery

www.jewellers.net
THE BIGGEST RANGE ON THE NET

ORIGIN	UK
SPEED	✓✓✓✓
INFO	✓✓✓✓
VALUE	✓✓✓
EASE	✓✓✓✓

Excellent range of products, fashion jewellery, gifts, gold and silver, the watch section is particularly strong. There is also information on the history of gems, the manufacturers and brands available. Delivery to the UK is free for orders over £50, and there is a 30-day no quibble returns policy. **W?WT**

Also check out **www.abooga.com** who offer a wide range and also **www.jewellerycatalogue.co.uk** who guarantee low prices.

www.topbrands.net
WATCH HEAVEN

ORIGIN	UK
SPEED	✓✓✓✓
INFO	✓✓✓✓
VALUE	✓✓✓
EASE	✓✓✓✓

A large range of watches including Swatch, Casio, G Shock, Baby G and Seiko are available here. The site is fast and easy-to-use, but a better search facility would save time. Delivery is free for the UK, but prices appear to be similar to the high street. **W?WT**

www.conran.com
TERENCE CONRAN STYLE

ORIGIN	UK
SPEED	✓✓✓
INFO	✓✓✓
VALUE	✓✓✓
EASE	✓✓✓✓

As well as information on all his restaurants this site has an online shopping facility, which allows you to buy Conran-designed accessories as well as stuff for the home.

Cosmetics

ADVICE AND HELP

www.beautyconsumer.com
COMPLETE GUIDE TO SKIN CARE

ORIGIN	UK
SPEED	✓✓✓
INFO	✓✓✓✓✓
EASE	✓✓✓✓✓

An excellent web site with help and information on all forms of skin care as well as beauty tips and product information, there's even a section especially for men. Two people experienced in the field put it together and the information is very easy to access. Two American sites also worth checking out are **www.cosmetics.com** and **www.skinstore.com**

www.lookfantastic.com
LOOK FANTASTIC

ORIGIN UK	A good-looking and well-designed retailer offering
SPEED ✓✓✓	some really good discounts, shipping costs are
INFO ✓✓✓✓	reasonable too. It also offers advice guides on how
VALUE ✓✓✓✓✓	to use make-up, shampoo and conditioners, in fact
EASE ✓✓✓✓	virtually everything a girl needs – it's war out there after all.

www.aliennails.com
DR NAILS

ORIGIN US	A strange-looking site that has a great deal of infor-
SPEED ✓✓✓	mation on caring for your nails as well as a gallery
INFO ✓✓✓✓	of nail art if you're feeling short of ideas on what
EASE ✓✓	colour to paint them.

SHOPPING

www.bodyshop.co.uk
ISSUES, SELF-ESTEEM AND COSMETICS

ORIGIN UK	Balancing the rights of the under-privileged with the
SPEED ✓✓✓	demands of a commercial cosmetics company. There
INFO ✓✓✓✓✓	is good product information but you can't buy
EASE ✓✓✓✓	online. However, download and play with the virtual makeover.

www.fragrancenet.com
WORLD'S LARGEST DISCOUNT FRAGRANCE STORE

ORIGIN US	A massive range of perfumes for men and women,
SPEED ✓✓✓✓	every brand is represented and there are some excel-
INFO ✓✓✓✓	lent offers. However, the site is American with ship-
VALUE ✓✓✓	ping costs of up to $24 dollars for five items or
EASE ✓✓✓✓	more.

www.directcosmetics.com
WIDE RANGE AND THE BEST PRICES

ORIGIN UK
SPEED ✓✓✓✓
INFO ✓✓✓✓
VALUE ✓✓✓✓
EASE ✓✓✓✓

They claim to offer a wide range of perfumes with up to 90% off UK recommended retail prices plus the latest news from the big brand names.
The site is quick and easy-to-use and the offers are genuine; however, delivery costs £3.95. See also **www.perfumeshopping.com** who offer 1,000 perfumes and fragrances, and Smellsearch, a facility which matches a perfume to the smells you stipulate. W?WT

www.beauty4you.co.uk
SHOPPING AND ADVICE

ORIGIN UK
SPEED ✓✓✓✓
INFO ✓✓✓
VALUE ✓✓✓
EASE ✓✓✓✓

A good-looking store with an extensive range of cosmetics and beauty products including aromatherapy and a gift service. There's also a good set of links to other related sites and advice on how to apply make-up. Delivery for the UK is £3.50 on everything.

It's also worth visiting these online chemists: **www.allbeautyproducts.com www.boots.co.uk** and **www.superdrug.co.uk**

www.lush.co.uk
SOAP WITHOUT THE SCENT

ORIGIN UK
SPEED ✓✓✓✓
INFO ✓✓✓✓
VALUE ✓✓✓✓
EASE ✓✓✓✓

Lush offer a wide range of soaps and associated products from their site, it's easy to shop and if you like their soap but find the smell of the high street shops over powering then it's perfect. Postage & packing is £2.95.

Finance, Banking and Shares

The Internet is proving to be a real winner when it comes to personal finance, product comparison and home share dealing, with these sites you will get the latest advice and may even make some money.

General finance information sites, directories and mortgages

www.fsa.gov.uk
FINANCIAL SERVICES AUTHORITY

ORIGIN UK	The regulating body that you can go to if you need
SPEED ✓✓✓	help with your rights or if you want to find out
INFO ✓✓✓✓	about financial products; it will also help you to
EASE ✓✓✓✓	verify that the financial institution you're dealing
	with is legitimate.

www.find.co.uk
INTERNET DIRECTORY FOR FINANCIAL SERVICES

ORIGIN UK	Access to over 6,000 financial sites; split into eight
SPEED ✓✓✓✓	sections: investment, insurance, information, advice
INFO ✓✓✓✓✓	and share dealing, banking and saving, mortgages
EASE ✓✓✓✓	and loans, business services and a centre for
	Independent Financial Advisers. Superb.

www.ft.com
www.ftyourmoney.com
FINANCIAL TIMES

ORIGIN UK	FT.com offers up to date news and information. Your
SPEED ✓✓✓	Money section is biased towards personal finance, it
INFO ✓✓✓✓	is easy-to-use although it looks daunting and provides
EASE ✓✓✓✓	sound, independent advice for everyone.

www.moneyextra.com
THE UK'S PERSONAL FINANCE GUIDE

ORIGIN UK
SPEED ✓✓✓
INFO ✓✓✓✓✓
EASE ✓✓✓✓

Three old sites combined to form a very comprehensive personal finance guide; there are comparison tables for mortgages, loans and other financial services, advice for investors, an excellent financial glossary as well as tax and mortgage calculators. There's also an online mortgage broker with support from several leading lenders.

www.fool.co.uk
THE MOTLEY FOOL

ORIGIN US
SPEED ✓✓✓
INFO ✓✓✓✓
EASE ✓✓✓✓

Finance with a sense of fun, The Fool is exciting and a real education in shrewdness. It not only takes the mystery out of share dealing but gives great advice on investment and personal finance. You need to register to get the best out of it.

www.thisismoney.com
MONEY NEWS AND ADVICE

ORIGIN UK
SPEED ✓✓✓✓
INFO ✓✓✓✓✓
EASE ✓✓✓✓

Easy-to-use, reliable, 24-hour financial advice from the *Daily Mail* group. It has loads of information on all aspects of personal finance and is particularly good for comparison tools, especially mortgages.

www.iii.co.uk
INTERACTIVE INVESTOR INTERNATIONAL

ORIGIN UK
SPEED ✓✓✓✓
INFO ✓✓✓✓✓
VALUE ✓✓✓✓
EASE ✓✓✓✓

In a short space of time iii has built a strong reputation and offer a well-designed, jargon-free site. There are several key sections, which cover share dealing, investments, personal finances, advice and you can even go shopping as a reward.

www.blays.co.uk
BLAYS GUIDES

ORIGIN UK
SPEED ✓✓✓✓
INFO ✓✓✓✓✓
EASE ✓✓✓✓

Excellent design and impartial advice make the Blays guide a must visit site for personal finance. It has all the usual suspects: mortgages, savings etc, plus very good sections for students. Look at the 'which is best value' section for phone service and utilities.

www.moneynet.co.uk
IMPARTIAL AND COMPREHENSIVE

ORIGIN UK
SPEED ✓✓✓
INFO ✓✓✓✓
EASE ✓✓✓✓

Rated as one of the best independent personal finance sites, it covers over 100 mortgage lenders, has a user-friendly search facility plus help with conveyancing and financial calculators.

For other similar sites go to:

www.marketplace.co.uk – 'independent' advisers from Bradford and Bingley help you make the right financial choices from mortgages to investments and pensions.

www.moneybrain.co.uk – a slick site offering a wide range of financial products and independent advice.

www.moneyfacts.co.uk – a no-nonsense information site which shows the cheapest and best value financial products with lots of authority, it's also a comparatively fast site and less tricky than some.

www.moneysupermarket.com – a very good all-rounder with help in most of the important areas of personal finance, good site layout and lots of practical advice add to the package.

www.virtuallyanywhere.co.uk – your local store of financial advisers, particularly good for tax advice and offers a good value accounting service, also personal financial help. Nice design too.

www.thedeal.net
The Deal MAGAZINE

ORIGIN UK
SPEED ✓✓✓
INFO ✓✓✓✓
EASE ✓✓✓✓

A 'financial lifestyle' magazine, with some good deals on mortgages especially if you're patient. There's also an interesting plus in the form of the magazine bit which offers news, gossip, competitions as well as features on the home, travel and entertainment.

www.unbiased.co.uk
FIND AN INDEPENDENT FINANCIAL ADVISER

ORIGIN UK
SPEED ✓✓✓✓
INFO ✓✓✓✓
EASE ✓✓✓✓

A good independent financial adviser is hard to come by, if you need one, then here's a good place to start. Just type in your postcode and the services you need and up pops a list of specialists in your area.

Mortgage specialists

www.charcoalonline.co.uk
INDEPENDENT ADVICE

ORIGIN UK
SPEED ✓✓✓
INFO ✓✓✓✓
EASE ✓✓✓✓

This established independent adviser offers over 500 mortgages from over 45 lenders. There are also sections on pensions, investments and insurance. For other independent advice try **www.mortgages-online.co.uk** alternatively, *Your Mortgage* magazine at **www.yourmortgage.co.uk** presents the latest news and deals from their well-designed and easy-to-use site.

It's worth shopping around so check out these sites too:
www.mortgagepoint.co.uk – geared towards first time buyers and those with a less than perfect credit history.

www.mortgageman.u-net.com – aimed at the self-employed or those having difficulty getting a mortgage from the usual lenders, or with CCJs.

www.moneygator.co.uk – they have wide range of financial products on offer, but are especially good for mortgage comparisons.

www.fredfindsmortgages.com – a great site and a fun way to find a mortgage but it hasn't the sophistication of the likes of some sites and you have to hunt for some details.

Insurance

www.insurancewide.com
HOME OF INSURANCE ON THE WEB

ORIGIN UK	Claiming to be the fastest way to get insurance
SPEED ✓✓✓	cover, they offer a wide range of insurance
INFO ✓✓✓✓✓	policies covering life, travel, transport, home and
EASE ✓✓✓✓	business.

www.easycover.com
UK'S BIGGEST INDEPENDENT INSURANCE WEB SITE

ORIGIN UK	This is a fast-developing site where you can get a
SPEED ✓✓✓	wide range of quotes just by filling in one form.
INFO ✓✓✓✓✓	The emphasis is on convenience and speed.
EASE ✓✓✓✓✓	

Other sites worth checking out:

www.theaa.co.uk – AA Insurance covers travel, cars and home.

www.screentrade.co.uk – the right deal on your motor, home and travel insurance.

Investing and share dealing

www.schwab-worldwide.com
CHARLES SCHWAB EUROPE

ORIGIN	US
SPEED	✓✓✓
INFO	✓✓✓✓✓
EASE	✓✓✓✓

Although you'll need to register and put up a deposit, this is the biggest and probably the most reliable Internet share dealer for the UK. You can trade online from various different accounts depending on how much you trade and your level of expertise.

Any of the following are worth checking out, they are all good sites, each with a slightly different focus, so find the one that suits you.

www.barclays-stockbrokers.co.uk – good value for smaller share deals, 1% commission and a minimum of £11.99, possibly the best for beginners. Can be slow.

www.tdwaterhouse.co.uk – slightly more expensive than Barclays, but still quite good value, well designed but could do with a glossary.

www.sharepeople.com – now owned by American Express, it has a nice design, easy-to-use with lots of explanation on what goes on. Works on a 'the price you see is the price you get' basis, with fees varying according to the type of trading you do.

www.sharexpress.co.uk – the Halifax share dealing service that is a good beginner's site and charges competitively.

www.ukinvest.com – part of the Freeserve network, its strengths are in news and company information. Shares are traded via **www.stockacademy.com**

www.itsonline.co.uk – a well-designed site that concentrates on explaining and campaigning for investment trusts.

www.freequotes.co.uk – an all singing and dancing site with the latest share information, tips and links to related and important sites.

http://uk.csfbdirect.com – allows you to open an account to trade on the London stock exchange or to trade on the U.S. market. It's straightforward and offers a reliable service with good customer backup.

Pensions

www.pensionsorter.com
FIND A PENSION

ORIGIN UK	Excellent site if you need help around the pensions
SPEED ✓✓✓✓	minefield, with lots of jargon-free and independent
INFO ✓✓✓✓✓	information. It tells you how to buy one, how much
EASE ✓✓✓✓✓	you should be paying and advice on what you

should be saving if you want a golden retirement. See also **www.pensionpartnership.co.uk**

www.pensionguide.gov.uk
KNOW YOUR OPTIONS

ORIGIN UK	An impartial guide to pensions from the govern-
SPEED ✓✓✓✓	ment, which aims to help you choose the right
INFO ✓✓✓✓✓	option, there's also information for employers and
EASE ✓✓✓✓✓	current pension holders.

Banks

www.bankfacts.org.uk
BRITISH BANKERS ASSOCIATION

ORIGIN UK	Answers to the most common questions about bank-
SPEED ✓✓✓	ing, advice about Internet banks, the banking code
INFO ✓✓✓✓✓	and general information. There's also a facility that
EASE ✓✓✓✓	helps you resurrect dormant accounts.

*Here are the high street and Internet banks, building
societies and the online facilities they currently offer:*

www.abbeynational.co.uk – full service up and
running including a very competitive Internet-only
savings account. Following the trend for high
street banks to set up Internet-only banks with
wacky names, Abbey National have set up
Cahoot at **www.cahoot.com** and they also offer a
competitive service wrapped up in a neat web site.

www.alliance-leicester.co.uk – a comprehensive
service offering mortgages, insurance and banking. The site is slow due to the large amount of
graphics involved.

www.bankofscotland.co.uk – Home and Office Banking
(HOBS) is an established system, which allows for an
efficient and wide ranging personal banking service.
Re-designed and soon to be re-launched as Internet
banking with extended facilities.

www.barclays.co.uk – one of the original innovators
in Internet banking, they offer an exhaustive
service covering all aspects of personal and small
business banking. Also an ISP but is slow.

www.bradford-bingley.co.uk – basic site showing
information on the B&B and their services,
Internet banking is on the way.

www.citibank.co.uk – very impressive site with a
complete Internet personal banking service with
competitive rates. Citibank have few branches
and this is their attempt at a bigger foothold in
the UK.

www.co-operativebank.co.uk – acknowledged as the
most comprehensive of the banking sites and it's
easy-to-use. Excellent, but they have also
launched the trendier and more competitive Smile
banking site **www.smile.co.uk** which is aimed at a
younger audience.

www.egg.co.uk – low rates combined with an attempt at individuality make Egg a bank with a difference. Caters for the young by offering WAP banking plus all the usual facilities. You can also go shopping at 100 retailers via the site and get up to 3% cash back if you use your Egg card.

www.first-e.com – owned by a French bank – Banque d'Escompte, First-e call themselves the Internet bank, and they offer a full service including insurance and WAP access.

www.halifax.co.uk – comprehensive range of services via an easy-to-use and well-designed site and you'll find a great deal of advice and information all clearly explained. Their Internet-only banking offshoot is called Intelligent Finance, which is excellent and can be found at the easy to remember **www.if.com**

www.banking.hsbc.co.uk – straightforward and easy-to-use site offering online banking alongside the usual services from HSBC, like most other big banks they've also launched a trendier Internet bank called **www.firstdirect.co.uk** which offers all the expected features plus WAP banking from an impressive site.

www.lloydstsb.co.uk – combined with Scottish Widows, The Post Office and Cheltenham and Gloucester, Lloyds offer a more rounded and comprehensive financial service than most. The online banking is well established and efficient, and there is help for small businesses too.

www.nationwide.co.uk – don't be put off by the dated appearance of the Nationwide site which looks rather like a tabloid newspaper, they offer a complete online banking service as well as loans and mortgages.

www.natwest.com – NatWest offer both online and WAP banking and share dealing, with good sections for students and small businesses. It's got a nice design, it's easy-to-use and there is a non-animated version as well.

www.newcastlenet.co.uk – a nice-looking and easy-to-use site from one of the smaller banking/building societies, offering all the usual services including online mortgage applications.

www.woolwich.co.uk – online banking, car buying (**www.motorbase.co.uk**) and a WAP mobile phone banking service plus all the other usual personal financial services make the Woolwich site a little different.

www.virgin-direct.co.uk – access to Virgin's comprehensive financial services site featuring a share dealing service, pension advice, banking, mortgages and general financial advice.

www.ybs.co.uk – no online service but you can get details of the Yorkshire Building Societies very competitive rates on mortgages and savings.

Tax

www.inlandrevenue.gov.uk

TALK TO THE TAXMAN

ORIGIN	UK
SPEED	✓✓✓✓
INFO	✓✓✓✓✓
EASE	✓✓✓

The Inland Revenue has a very informative site where you can get help on all aspects of tax. You can even submit your tax return over the Internet and get a £10 discount if you pay electronically too. There's a good set of links to other government departments.

www.tax.org.uk/
CHARTERED INSTITUTE OF TAXATION

ORIGIN UK
SPEED ✓✓✓
INFO ✓✓✓✓✓
EASE ✓✓✓

A great resource, they don't provide information on individual questions but they can put you in touch with a qualified adviser. It's a good place to start if you have a problem with your tax. For the latest tax news go to http://e-tax.org.uk, which is comprehensive and has an excellent set of links. For a list of sites all relating to tax go to www.taxsites.com

http://listen.to/taxman
UK PAYE TAX CALCULATOR

ORIGIN UK
SPEED ✓✓✓
INFO ✓✓✓✓
EASE ✓✓✓✓✓

Amazingly fast, just input your gross earnings and your tax and actual earnings are calculated.

www.e-taxreturns.co.uk
ONLINE TAX HELP

ORIGIN UK
SPEED ✓✓✓✓
INFO ✓✓✓✓
VALUE ✓✓
EASE ✓✓✓✓

Accountants Ashley & Co has set up a site where you can fill in all your details on line and they'll do the rest for you. You can get a free quote but the service costs from £75.

Business

www.economist.com
The Economist MAGAZINE

ORIGIN UK
SPEED ✓✓✓✓✓
INFO ✓✓✓✓✓
EASE ✓✓✓✓

The airports' best-selling magazine goes online with a wide-ranging site that covers business and politics world-wide. You can get access to the archive and also their excellent country surveys. If you're in business you need this in your favourites box.

www.asiannet.com
BUSINESS INFORMATION ON ASIA

ORIGIN US
SPEED ✓✓✓
INFO ✓✓✓✓
EASE ✓✓✓

Market information, news, services and links all geared to the main Asian markets of which each has a feature site. There are company profiles as well as an online shop where you can contact companies to get product samples.

www.islamiq.com
ISLAMIC FINANCE AND BUSINESS

ORIGIN UK
SPEED ✓✓✓✓
INFO ✓✓✓✓✓
EASE ✓✓✓✓

Excellent British site aimed at being in their words 'a finance and investment portal synchronised with Islamic principles'. There is a great deal of information about personal finance, share dealing and investing as well as news and shopping. Can be slow.

www.uk.sage.com
BUSINESS SOFTWARE

ORIGIN UK
SPEED ✓✓✓
INFO ✓✓✓✓
VALUE ✓✓✓
EASE ✓✓✓✓

If you need accounting software to solve virtually any sort of problem or provide a new service, you should find it here. Sage has a good reputation for helping small businesses.

Miscellaneous

www.young-money.co.uk
ONLINE MONEY GAME SHOW

ORIGIN UK
SPEED ✓✓✓
INFO ✓✓✓✓
EASE ✓✓✓✓

Combines general knowledge and financial games aimed at turning the little ones into financial whizkids of the future. There's a lot that most adults can learn from the site as well as it's a fun way of learning about the world of finance. You need Shockwave for it to work.

Finding Someone

Where to find a phone number, contacts for business and the home.

www.yell.co.uk

THE YELLOW PAGES ONLINE – JUST YELL!

ORIGIN UK
SPEED ✓✓✓
INFO ✓✓✓✓✓
EASE ✓✓✓✓✓

Split into five key services:

1. The search engine – this enables you to search for the business or service you want by region, type or name. It is very quick, and you get plenty of details on each entry.
2. Travel – which links you up with one of the biggest online travel agents www.expedia.com
3. Property – links to www.homesight.co.uk an advice site for moving house or for looking up the details of a region or town.
4. Shopping – a directory for online stores covering mainstream merchandise.
5. Business – provides sections on international trading, UK business, and a business-to-business direct marketing channel.

There is an equivalent service in the USA with the intriguing title of **www.bigfoot.com** It is very similar to Yell, except there is a feature that enables you to search for personal, as well as business e-mail addresses. If you're still stuck then try **www.bigyellow.com**

www.scoot.co.uk

THE SIMPLE WAY TO FIND SOMEONE

ORIGIN UK
SPEED ✓✓✓
INFO ✓✓✓✓✓
EASE ✓✓✓✓✓

Register, type in the person's name or profession then hit the scoot button and your answer comes back in seconds.

www.thomweb.co.uk

THE ANSWER COMES OUT OF THE BLUE

ORIGIN UK
SPEED ✓✓✓✓
INFO ✓✓✓✓✓
EASE ✓✓✓✓

Thomson's local directories are available online. It's an impressive site and has been much improved since the last review.

It's divided up into five major categories:
1. A business finder – search using a combination of name, type of business or region.
2. People finder – track down phone numbers and home or e-mail addresses.
3. Comprehensive local information – available on the major cities and regions.
4. News.
5. Net search and directory.

www.phonenumbers.net

THE PHONE NUMBER OF VIRTUALLY EVERYONE WHO'S LISTED

ORIGIN EUROPE
SPEED ✓✓✓✓
INFO ✓✓✓✓
EASE ✓✓✓✓

Start by clicking on the country or area you need, then you can easily find the phone, fax or e-mail address of anyone who is in the book. It also has a section with a number of links to other search engines such as Yell.

www.bt.com

BRITISH TELECOM SERVICES

ORIGIN UK
SPEED ✓✓
INFO ✓✓✓✓
EASE ✓✓

BT offers a site that gives a very thorough overview of its services. To get the best out of it you need to register; have your account number handy and you can view your telephone bill. To find what service you need click on the 'Go To' button and type it in. Alternatively, **www.bt.com/phonenetuk/** takes you right to the online phone book.

See also:
www.ukphonebook.com – simple to use, quick with a no-nonsense design, also has mapping, a business finder and lots of adverts.

www.whatsmynumber.co.uk – good attempt to put together a national mobile phone directory, sign up and you may win a prize.

www.192.com
THE UK'S LARGEST DIRECTORY SERVICE

ORIGIN UK	192 has changed, there's now more available for
SPEED ✓✓✓✓	non-fee payers such as people and business finders,
INFO ✓✓✓✓	directories and route planning. For £200 per annum
VALUE ✓✓	you get access to other things like the electoral role,
EASE ✓✓✓✓	company reports and the UK-info CD.

Flowers

www.interflora.co.uk
TURNING THOUGHTS INTO FLOWERS

ORIGIN UK	Interflora can send flowers to over 140 countries
SPEED ✓✓✓✓	many on the same day as the order. They'll have a
INFO ✓✓✓✓	selection to send for virtually every occasion and
VALUE ✓✓✓	they offer a reminder service. The service is excel-
EASE ✓✓✓✓	lent, although they are not very up front on delivery

costs, which can be high.

If you can't get what you need here then try **www.teleflorist.co.uk** who offer a similar service.

www.flyingflowers.com
EUROPE'S LEADING FLOWERS BY POST COMPANY

ORIGIN UK	Freshly picked flowers flown from Jersey to the UK
SPEED ✓✓✓✓	from £8.99. All prices include delivery and you save
INFO ✓✓✓✓	at least £1 on all bouquets against their standard
VALUE ✓✓✓	advertised off-line prices. They'll also arrange next
EASE ✓✓✓✓	day delivery in the UK. The site is simple and there's

a reminder service just to make sure you don't forget anyone.

www.clareflorist.co.uk

STYLISH BOUQUETS AND PRETTY PICTURES

ORIGIN	UK
SPEED	✓✓✓✓
INFO	✓✓✓✓
VALUE	✓✓✓✓
EASE	✓✓✓✓

You know what you're sending as all the bouquets are photographed. Cost reflects the sophistication of the flowers. Easy-to-use with good customer services and free delivery to UK with surcharge for same day delivery.

www.daisys2roses.com

MAKE YOUR OWN BOUQUET

ORIGIN	UK
SPEED	✓✓
INFO	✓✓✓✓
VALUE	✓✓✓
EASE	✓✓✓✓

A simple to use, step-by-step approach to making up a bouquet of your choice. You can select from a large range of flowers and there's help to get you started, you can even search by flower type. Delivery is free in the UK. Unfortunately, the process is a bit laborious, but persistence pays.

Food and drink

Whether you want to order from the comfort of your own home, indulge yourself, find the latest food news or get a recipe, this collection of sites will fulfil your foodie desires. It features supermarkets, online magazines and information sites, specialist food retailers, vegetarian, organic, drinks, kitchen equipment and eating out.

Supermarkets and general food stores

www.icelandfreeshop.com

FROZEN FOOD SPECIALIST DELIVERS

ORIGIN UK
SPEED ✓✓
INFO ✓✓✓✓
VALUE ✓✓✓
EASE ✓✓✓✓

Iceland's online service is considered one of the best with nearly all of the UK covered. Easy-to-navigate, but can be ponderous to use. Your order is saved each time, which then acts as the basis for your next order. Information on the products is good, and there's a wide range available, orders must be £40 or more.

www.waitrose.co.uk

IF YOU ARE REALLY INTO FOOD

ORIGIN UK
SPEED ✓✓✓
INFO ✓✓✓✓✓
VALUE ✓✓✓
EASE ✓✓✓✓

Waitrose is offering a very good comprehensive and well laid out site that oozes quality, and it's simple to do your grocery shopping online. You can buy wine, gifts, organics and some John Lewis products.

In addition it also has all the features you'd expect from an Internet Service Provider, including the excellent *Waitrose Illustrated Food Magazine* (also at www.wfi.co.uk), *Hardens Restaurant Guide*, gardening and travel sections along with news and even a section on food education.

www.tesco.co.uk

THE LIFESTYLE SUPERSTORE

ORIGIN UK
SPEED ✓✓✓
INFO ✓✓✓✓
VALUE ✓✓✓✓
EASE ✓✓✓

This functional site has a comprehensive offering and they've tried to make it more attractive. It has details of areas covered by their home delivery service, which is similar to the Iceland service, but on the whole less straightforward to use. Food aside, there's a wide range of goods on offer though, including electrical goods, clothes and books. There's also a section on personal finance.

www.sainsburys.co.uk
NOT JUST GOOD TASTE

ORIGIN UK
SPEED ✓✓✓✓
INFO ✓✓✓✓✓
VALUE ✓✓✓
EASE ✓✓✓✓

Sainsbury's site is similar, (but jollier) in content to Tesco, but without the financial advice. More fun to use, and faster too, with the emphasis being on good food, cooking, recommendation and taste – although the site has a reputation for crashing as you're placing orders (something Sainsbury's are tackling). There's also links to the Carlton Food Network, restaurant guides, lifestyle magazines, health advice and much more.

www.somerfield.co.uk
MEGADEALS

ORIGIN UK
SPEED ✓✓✓✓
INFO ✓✓✓
VALUE ✓✓✓
EASE ✓✓✓✓

The emphasis is firmly on offers with a rolling feature, which changes every few seconds, but there's also a recipe finder, wine guide and essential food facts. Delivery covers most of the UK and it's free if you spend more than £25, provided you live near enough to the store.

www.asda.co.uk
VALUE MAD

ORIGIN UK
SPEED ✓✓
INFO ✓✓✓✓
VALUE ✓✓✓✓✓
EASE ✓✓✓

A much-improved site, which is still pretty dull, but clearer than the last time we reviewed it. There's lots of information about the company and what it stands for plus links to its online shop and clothing brand George. Delivery is free, but they don't cover the whole of the UK at time of writing.

www.safeway.co.uk
FOR THE FAMILY WITH YOUNG CHILDREN

ORIGIN	UK
SPEED	✓✓✓
INFO	✓✓✓✓
EASE	✓✓✓✓

Well they've brightened it up, but it still doesn't hide the fact that it's not that good compared to the other supermarkets – you can't actually shop from the site yet. However, it does have good advice sections on parties and on the family, with lots of good advice for parents of young children. Also information about the company and loyalty card, a recipe finder and a pointless shopping list facility.

www.heinz-direct.co.uk
DELIVERING MORE THAN 57 VARIETIES OF FOOD

ORIGIN	UK
SPEED	✓✓
INFO	✓✓✓
VALUE	✓✓✓✓
EASE	✓✓✓✓

To get the best value for money it's best to order in bulk, as delivery charges can be high. It can be very slow to use and is split into product feature sections: Weightwatchers, canned grocery, Heinz and Farley's baby food, hampers, and sauces and pickles.

www.homefarmfoods.com
DELICIOUS FROZEN FOOD DELIVERED FREE

ORIGIN	UK
SPEED	✓✓✓
INFO	✓✓✓
VALUE	✓✓✓✓✓
EASE	✓✓✓✓

Good selection of frozen foods and huge range of ready meals with a good use of symbols indicating whether the product is low fat, microwavable, vegetarian etc. Can't make up your mind – then order the Eat for a Week selection! With free delivery, it's especially good value, and there is no minimum order.

See also **www.foodhall.co.uk** who have a good selection of specialist stores to choose from.

www.farmersmarkets.net
NATIONAL ASSOCIATION OF FARMERS MARKETS

ORIGIN	UK
SPEED	✓✓✓✓
INFO	✓✓✓✓
EASE	✓✓✓✓

A farmer's market sells locally produced goods, locate your nearest market or get advice on how to set one up.

Asian and Indian cookery

www.curryhouse.co.uk
EVERYTHING YOU NEED TO KNOW ABOUT CURRY

ORIGIN UK	Curryholics can get their fill of recipes, recommen-
SPEED ✓✓✓	dations, taste tests, interviews with famous chefs
INFO ✓✓✓✓✓	and a restaurant guide. Spices and curry mixes can
VALUE ✓✓✓	be bought from Chilli Willies online shop, all orders
EASE ✓✓✓✓✓	charged £2.99 p&p. W?WT

See also **www.curryworld.com** the home of
National Curry Day apparently. While at
www.currysauce.com you can get all the sauces
delivered and even win a year's supply.

www.chinesefood.org
ULTIMATE CHINESE FOOD SITE

ORIGIN US	An impressive site which gives an overview of
SPEED ✓✓✓	Chinese cooking, recipes and cooking methods. The
INFO ✓✓✓✓✓	site also shows you how to use chopsticks and make
EASE ✓✓✓✓	great Dim Sum. If you want to order Chinese ingre-

dients then try **www.qinglung.co.uk**

www.straitscafe.com
RECIPES FROM SINGAPORE

ORIGIN SINGAPORE	A straightforward site with lots of recipes not only
SPEED ✓✓✓	from Singapore, but also Japan and China, there's
INFO ✓✓✓✓	also a good set of links and a gallery. For Indonesian
EASE ✓✓✓✓	cooking go to the enjoyable Henks Hot Kitchen

which can be found at **www.indochef.com**

www.japanweb.co.uk
JAPANESE CUISINE

ORIGIN	JAPAN
SPEED	✓✓✓✓
INFO	✓✓✓✓
VALUE	✓✓✓
EASE	✓✓✓✓

An interesting and growing site covering the basics of Japanese cooking along with recipes and a UK restaurant guide, it also has a glossary and tips on etiquette. 'Itadakimasu' as they say.

www.thai-food.co.uk
DIRECTORY AND RECIPES

ORIGIN	US
SPEED	✓✓✓✓
INFO	✓✓✓✓
EASE	✓✓✓

An overview of Thai restaurants in the South East, plus some great recipes and advice on how to cook Thai, there's also links to related sites.

See also www.thaicuisine.com

www.spiceguide.com
SPICY

ORIGIN	US
SPEED	✓✓✓✓
INFO	✓✓✓✓
EASE	✓✓✓✓

A very useful online spice encyclopaedia, which also includes recipes and a history of spice.

Barbecues

www.barbecuen.com
BARBECUES

ORIGIN	US
SPEED	✓✓✓
INFO	✓✓✓✓✓
EASE	✓✓✓✓

In the unlikely event that our weather will be good enough to have a barbecue, then here's a site with all you need to know on the subject.

British and Irish cookery

www.hwatson.force9.co.uk
BEST OF BRITISH

ORIGIN	UK
SPEED	✓✓
INFO	✓✓✓✓
EASE	✓✓✓✓

Helen Watson is a champion of British cuisine and here you'll find her online cookbook, there's also a magazine and a guide to regional cooking. The site is slow but the content is very good. Check out **www.greatbritishkitchen.co.uk** too, and also **www.recipes4us.co.uk** who have 1,700 recipes although some are international. About.com has an excellent page on UK food at **http://ukfood.about.com**

www.zedtee.com
ENGLISH COOKERY

ORIGIN	UK
SPEED	✓✓✓✓
INFO	✓✓✓
EASE	✓✓✓✓

Raising the profile of English food on the Internet this fairly oddly designed site has a few classic recipes to relish.

www.btinternet.com/~scottishcookery/
CLASSIC SCOTTISH COOKERY

ORIGIN	UK
SPEED	✓✓
INFO	✓✓✓✓
EASE	✓✓✓✓

You need patience with this site but again the recipes are well worth the wait, and they are well illustrated.

www.tasteofireland.com
A TASTE OF IRELAND

ORIGIN	EIRE
SPEED	✓✓✓
INFO	✓✓✓
EASE	✓✓✓✓

Recipes, a restaurant guide and a shop all in one, it's not that comprehensive but well worth a visit nonetheless.

www.red4.co.uk/recipes.htm
WELSH RECIPES

ORIGIN UK
SPEED ✓✓✓
INFO ✓✓✓
EASE ✓✓✓✓

Here are over 120 traditional recipes including lava bread, wines, cawl and Welshcakes.

www.baxters.co.uk
TRADITIONAL FARE

ORIGIN UK
SPEED ✓✓✓
INFO ✓✓✓✓
VALUE ✓✓✓✓
EASE ✓✓✓✓

An old Scottish firm offering their range of soups, jams, sauces, hampers and gift foods online through a well-designed and easy-to-use site. Shipping charges vary according to destination.

Celebrity chefs

www.delia.co.uk
DELIA SMITH

ORIGIN UK
SPEED ✓✓✓✓
INFO ✓✓✓✓
EASE ✓✓✓✓

The queen of British cookery has a clean, well-designed site with lots of recipes, which can be accessed by the good search facility. If you join you get added features such as daily tips, competitions and the chance to chat to Delia. There's also a section on what Delia is up to and you can ask questions and get advice at the cookery school.

www.jamieoliver.net
NAKED COOKING!

ORIGIN UK
SPEED ✓✓✓✓
INFO ✓✓✓
EASE ✓✓✓✓

A nice-looking site featuring Jamie's Diary where you can see what he's up to, get recipes which change seasonally, there's also a kid's club which is aimed at getting kids to enjoy cooking and also information on Jamie's band.

www.bbc.co.uk/rhodesclassics
GARY RHODES

ORIGIN UK
SPEED ✓✓✓
INFO ✓✓✓✓
EASE ✓✓✓✓

A page from the BBC web site, which has lots of British recipes as well as biographical details on Gary, you can also take a culinary tour of the UK.

www.rickstein.co.uk
PADSTOW, STEIN AND SEAFOOD

ORIGIN UK
SPEED ✓✓✓
INFO ✓✓✓✓
VALUE ✓✓✓
EASE ✓✓✓✓

Information on Rick, his restaurants and cookery school all wrapped up in a tidy web site. You can also book a table or a room as well as order products from the online deli.

www.rosemary-conley.co.uk
CONLEY'S DIET AND FITNESS CLUBS

ORIGIN UK
SPEED ✓✓✓
INFO ✓✓✓✓
EASE ✓✓✓✓

Get information on how to stay fit and keep healthy as well as recipes and details of her books.

www.kenhom.com
KEN HOM

ORIGIN UK
SPEED ✓✓✓✓
INFO ✓✓✓
EASE ✓✓✓✓

A web site that rhymes! Ken's site is nicely designed and has a small selection of recipes and products, which you can buy.

Cheese

www.cheese.com
IT'S ALL ABOUT CHEESE!

ORIGIN US
SPEED ✓✓✓✓
INFO ✓✓✓✓✓
EASE ✓✓✓✓

Not a shop, but a huge resource site about 652 types of cheese. There's advice about the best way to eat cheese, a vegetarian section, a cheese bookshop and links to other cheese-related sites and online stores. You can even find a suitable cheese searching by texture, country or type of milk. For more cheese information try the attractive Cheesenet site at www.wgx.com/cheesenet or the American Dairy associations www.ilovecheese.com which also offers a cheese profiler so that you can find the perfect cheese to suit you.

www.cheesemongers.co.uk
OPULENT SITE FROM UK'S OLDEST CHEESEMONGERS

ORIGIN UK
SPEED ✓✓✓✓
INFO ✓✓✓✓
VALUE ✓✓
EASE ✓✓✓✓

Paxton and Whitfield, the royal cheesemongers, provide a very clear and easy-to-use online shop but charge £7.50 to ship goods. A superb selection of cheese and luxury produce, with hampers, cheese kitchen, accessories and wine. A pleasure to browse and it's tempting to buy; you can also join the Cheese Society.

www.teddingtoncheese.co.uk
BRITISH AND CONTINENTAL CHEESEMONGERS

ORIGIN UK
SPEED ✓✓✓
INFO ✓✓✓✓
VALUE ✓✓✓
EASE ✓✓✓✓

Much-acclaimed site offering over 130 types of cheese at competitive prices. The sections are split by country and there's a good system for showing whether the cheese is suitable for vegetarians, pregnant women, etc. There is also a small selection of wine and other produce, and you can even design your own hamper. When buying you can stipulate how much cheese you want in grams (150 minimum.), standard shipping is £5.95 for the UK.

www.fromages.com
TRADITIONAL FRENCH CHEESE

ORIGIN	FRANCE
SPEED	✓✓✓✓
INFO	✓✓✓✓
VALUE	✓✓
EASE	✓✓✓✓

French cheese available to order and delivered within 24 hours along with wine recommendations and express shipping from France. Delivery is included in the price but if you're worried about cost you probably shouldn't be shopping here.

Confectionery, cake and chocolate

www.chocexpress.com
DEDICATED TO GOOD CHOCOLATE

ORIGIN	UK
SPEED	✓✓✓✓
INFO	✓✓✓✓
VALUE	✓✓✓✓
EASE	✓✓✓✓

They've made over 1 million deliveries and offer free delivery to the UK. They also offer a wide range of chocolate-related gifts and you can even buy in bulk! There's a gift finder and you can specify a particular day for delivery.

www.thorntons.co.uk
WELCOME TO CHOCOLATE HEAVEN

ORIGIN	UK
SPEED	✓✓✓✓
INFO	✓✓✓
VALUE	✓✓✓
EASE	✓✓✓✓

Though not as good value as ChocExpress, Thorntons offer a comprehensive and easy-to-use site, with an emphasis on selling. The range is extensive and they supply world-wide – at a cost. All orders are £3.95 for the UK. There are product sections for continental, premier, gifts and hampers.

www.mailacake.co.uk
FOR ALL SPECIAL OCCASIONS

ORIGIN UK
SPEED ✓✓✓✓
INFO ✓✓
VALUE ✓✓
EASE ✓✓✓✓

You've only got one choice of rich 2lb fruitcake, albeit with two different toppings – cherries and nuts and marzipan and icing, you can have it plain too. Add any message you like and have it delivered in the UK for the all-inclusive price of £16.50. There's also a corporate service.

DIET AND NUTRITION

www.3fatchicks.com
THE SOURCE FOR DIET SUPPORT

ORIGIN US
SPEED ✓✓✓✓
INFO ✓✓✓✓✓
EASE ✓✓✓✓✓

The awesome Three Fat Chicks have produced one of the best food web sites. It's entertaining and informative about dieting or trying to stay healthy. There are food reviews, how to live on fast food, recipes, links to other low fat sites, a section for chocoholics, diet tips and 'tool box' which has calorie tables and calculators; also getting started on losing weight and how to get free samples.

www.fatfreekitchen.com
LOW FAT VEGETARIAN

ORIGIN US
SPEED ✓✓✓✓
INFO ✓✓✓✓
EASE ✓✓✓✓

Recipes and great advice on healthy eating make this site stand out, along with good design and information on healthy living.

www.cookinglight.com
THE BEST FROM *Cooking Light* MAGAZINE

ORIGIN US
SPEED ✓✓
INFO ✓✓✓✓
EASE ✓✓✓✓

One of the world's best-selling food magazines, their slow site offers a huge selection of healthy recipes and step-by-step guides to cooking. There are also articles on healthy living.

http://uk.weightwatchers.com
WELCOME TO WEIGHTWATCHERS UK

ORIGIN	UK
SPEED	✓✓✓✓
INFO	✓✓✓
EASE	✓✓✓✓

A site designed to plug their product rather than to offer genuine online advice, although they've improved the look and content with recipes and advice now available in an archive. There's also advice on keeping fit and how to keep motivated.

www.mynutrition.co.uk
ONLINE GUIDE TO HEALTHY EATING

ORIGIN	UK
SPEED	✓✓✓✓
INFO	✓✓✓✓
VALUE	✓✓
EASE	✓✓✓✓

Find out what you really should be eating from this cool British site, which has been put together by a professional nutritionist. It features:

1. Myconditions – an alphabetical listing of diseases and ailments with a short description of what effect they have on the diet, and advice on dietary needs and supplements.

2. Mynews – a newsletter with all the latest information on nutrition.

3. Mylibrary – with articles and book excerpts by the sites author.

4. Myconsultation – fill in a questionnaire about your health and get the dietary advice on eating and supplements.

5. Mystuff – records how you get on after the consultation so that when you revisit you can check on progress.

6. In Myshopping – buy those vitamins and supplements that have been recommended. Delivery is £1.50 for the UK.

For all its beauty and efficiency, you can't help thinking that this is just a very good vehicle for selling vitamins and supplements.

See also the section on health, page 200.

French food

www.gourmet2000.co.uk
LE GOURMET FRANÇAIS

ORIGIN UK
SPEED ✓✓✓✓
INFO ✓✓✓✓
VALUE ✓✓
EASE ✓✓✓✓

High quality French ingredients and recipes, combined with a nicely-designed site and convenient shopping. Delivery is very pricey at £7.99 for the minimum £20 order, but once you spend £100 it's free.

http://frenchfood.about.com
FRENCH CUISINE

ORIGIN US
SPEED ✓✓✓✓
INFO ✓✓✓✓✓
EASE ✓✓✓✓

About.com have created a superb resource at this site with a huge amount of data, articles and recipes. Every aspect of French cooking seems to be covered from the ingredients to the shops and presentation.

Hygiene and food safety

www.foodsafety.gov/~fsg/fsgadvic.html
FOOD SAFETY

ORIGIN UK
SPEED ✓✓
INFO ✓✓✓✓
EASE ✓✓✓✓

A government site with basic advice on handling foods in all sorts of situations from product-specific advice to helping those with special needs, it's very slow so be patient. There's also good links to related topics.

See also **www.foodstandards.gov.uk/index.htm** home of the Food Standards Association who have lots of information on what is safe to eat.

www.basicfoodhygiene.co.uk
FOOD HYGIENE AWARENESS

ORIGIN	UK
SPEED	✓✓✓
INFO	✓✓✓✓
EASE	✓✓✓✓

Take it all the way and you can get a qualification in food hygiene without leaving your home, but the site is still good for tips and information on how to stay safe if you don't want to take the exam. The site is poorly designed and the spelling is pretty abysmal.

Italian food

www.mangiarebene.net
EAT WELL

ORIGIN	US
SPEED	✓✓✓✓
INFO	✓✓✓✓✓
EASE	✓✓✓✓

An award-winning site that covers everything to do with Italian cookery. Its aim is to give a grand tour of Italian cuisine – and it succeeds, including some 600 recipes in the English language section, but over 1,600 overall. See also http://italy1.com/cuisine which has good regional cooking and food information as well as lots of recipes.

www.ilovepasta.org
US NATIONAL PASTA ASSOCIATION

ORIGIN	US
SPEED	✓✓✓✓
INFO	✓✓✓✓✓
EASE	✓✓✓✓

250 recipes, tips, fast meals and healthy options all wrapped up in a clear and easy-to-use site. There's also information on the different types of pasta and advice on the right sauces to go with them.

www.getoily.com
OLIVE OIL

ORIGIN	UK
SPEED	✓✓✓✓
INFO	✓✓✓✓
VALUE	✓✓✓
EASE	✓✓✓✓

All you need to know about olive oil, cooking with it, health benefits and history, oh and you can buy it too, along with a good selection of other Mediterranean products.

www.dominos.co.uk
PIZZA DELIVERY

ORIGIN UK	Order your pizza online and get it delivered to your
SPEED ✓✓✓	home providing you live near enough to one of their
INFO ✓✓✓	outlets that is. It's a nicely-designed site, which also
VALUE ✓✓✓	has a few games if you get bored waiting.
EASE ✓✓✓✓	

Kitchen equipment

www.lakelandlimited.co.uk
EXCELLENT CUSTOMER SERVICE

ORIGIN UK	Lakeland pride themselves on service and it shows,
SPEED ✓✓✓✓	they aim to get all orders dispatched in 24 hours and
INFO ✓✓✓✓	delivery on orders over £35 is free. The product list-
VALUE ✓✓✓	ing for both kitchen and homeware is comprehen-
EASE ✓✓✓✓	sive, and there's a special section of products

recommended by Delia Smith.

See also www.kitchenware.co.uk who also have a
good range, with postage for the UK being £2.95
per order. Divertimenti are also worth a look at
www.divertimenti.co.uk they go for quality and they
are good for gifts.

www.pots-and-pans.co.uk
QUALITY SECONDS

ORIGIN UK	Scottish company offering kitchen equipment
SPEED ✓✓✓✓	through a good online store; it's good value but
INFO ✓✓✓✓	delivery charges may vary.
VALUE ✓✓✓✓	
EASE ✓✓✓✓	

Luxury food sites, delis and gifts

www.stgeorgessquare.com

A VIRTUAL VILLAGE MARKET SQUARE

ORIGIN UK
SPEED ✓✓✓✓
INFO ✓✓✓
VALUE ✓✓✓
EASE ✓✓✓✓

St Georges Square features an expanding range of gifts, incentives and prizes for delivery in the UK and overseas. You can send, flowers, chocolates, fruit, wine, and a range of themed hampers, Edinburgh crystal, or simply send a gift voucher. It's fast and easy-to-use, with some good offers too. Delivery depends on type of order placed.

www.allpresent.com

GIFTS FOR THE DISCERNING

ORIGIN UK
SPEED ✓✓✓✓
INFO ✓✓✓✓
VALUE ✓✓
EASE ✓✓✓✓

An Amazon-style shop offering gifts in the form of chocolates, drinks and bakery items such as cakes and biscuits all beautifully boxed. They also sell flowers and cards; delivery costs vary according to what you buy.

Other similar shops worth checking out are:
www.giftbox.co.uk – nice design and large selection.
www.hampers.uk.com – hampers large and small.
www.giftwarren.co.uk – good selection,
    free delivery. W?WT

www.fortnumandmason.co.uk

EXQUISITE GIFTS

ORIGIN UK
SPEED ✓✓✓
INFO ✓✓✓✓
VALUE ✓✓
EASE ✓✓✓✓

A wide range of gift chocolates, hampers and more from one of the leading luxury stores, UK residents have a wider choice including condiments, teas and wines. Carriage is £6 for UK residents unless you're a F&M account holder then it's free when you spend £50.

www.bluemango.co.uk
SPREADS THE WORD

ORIGIN	UK
SPEED	✓✓✓✓
INFO	✓✓✓✓✓
VALUE	✓✓✓
EASE	✓✓✓✓

This highly-acclaimed site sells everything that you can spread. There are also offers, recipes and a list of links to other food retailers. Everything is well explained, and the food on offer has ingredients listed. It's quick, easy-to-use and delivery is £4 per order. There's also a recipe section and you can buy gift sets. See also **www.jams.co.uk** who offer a good selection of luxury preserves.

www.realmeatco.sageweb.co.uk/
FLAVOUR WITHOUT EQUAL, WELFARE WITHOUT COMPROMISE.

ORIGIN	UK
SPEED	✓✓✓✓
INFO	✓✓✓✓
VALUE	✓✓✓
EASE	✓✓✓✓

Produces meat in a caring and compassionate way, they are against things like livestock markets for example. You can buy online or visit one of the approved list of butchers. The shop is split into several areas featuring different meat products, its easy-to-use but the minimum order is £35.

www.traditionalbutcher.com
A TRADITIONAL BUTCHER

ORIGIN	UK
SPEED	✓✓✓✓
INFO	✓✓✓✓
VALUE	✓✓✓
EASE	✓✓✓✓

John Miles is based in Herefordshire and knows a thing or two about meat, you can buy meats and deli products online, there's a good range and delivery is charged at cost. They seem to take a great deal of care on quality. See also **www.meatdirect.co.uk**

Miscellaneous food sites

www.leapingsalmon.co.uk
STRESS IS FOR OTHER FISH

ORIGIN	UK
SPEED	✓✓✓✓
INFO	✓✓✓✓✓
VALUE	✓✓✓
EASE	✓✓✓✓

This well publicised site is about providing creative and inspirational products to make gourmet cooking fun and achievable in the home. Each meal kit is created for two people by a top chef with step-by-step instructions, order your meal the day before and it gets delivered overnight so that the food is as fresh as possible. They deliver anywhere in the UK for £4.50. Same day delivery is available in London. It really works.

www.reluctantgourmet.com
GOURMET COOKING FOR BEGINNERS

ORIGIN	US
SPEED	✓✓✓✓
INFO	✓✓✓✓✓
EASE	✓✓✓✓

Basically a beginner's cookery book, it's well-designed and easy to follow with a glossary, guide to techniques, equipment, tips and recipes.

Recipes, general food sites and magazines

www.kitchenlink.com
YOUR GUIDE TO WHAT'S COOKING ON THE NET

ORIGIN	US
SPEED	✓✓✓
INFO	✓✓✓✓✓
EASE	✓✓✓

A bit clunky to use, but it has so many links to other key foodie sites and food-related sections that it has to be the place to start your online food and drink experience. The design can make it irritating to use and it's got a little slow, but persevere and you'll be rewarded with a resource that is difficult to beat.

*Other American sites worth checking out are these,
all have loads of recipes and it's just a matter of
finding one you like.*

www.cyber-kitchen.com – excellent for links and
    specialised subjects.

www.foodstop.com – excellent articles about food.

www.ichef.com – good search facility.

www.meals.com – good for meal planning and
    recipes.

www.pastrywiz.com – great for links and tips.

www.recipezaar.com – the world's smartest cook-
    book.

www.ucook.com – the ultimate cookbook.

www.yumyum.com – good fun.

www.tudocs.com

THE ULTIMATE DIRECTORY OF COOKING SITES

ORIGIN US
SPEED ✓✓✓✓
INFO ✓✓✓✓✓
EASE ✓✓✓✓

The main difference with Tudocs is that it grades
each cookery site on its site listing. The listing is
divided up into 19 sections, such as meat, beverages,
low fat and ethnic. British cookery is in the ethnic
section. See also **www.cookingindex.com**

http://epicurious.com

FOR PEOPLE WHO EAT

ORIGIN US
SPEED ✓✓✓✓
INFO ✓✓✓✓✓
EASE ✓✓✓✓

Owned by Condé Nast, this massive site combines
articles from their magazines with information
generated by the Epicurious team. There are over 33
different sections such as recipe search, tips, a food
dictionary, restaurant reviews, live-chat, forums,
wine and a kitchen equipment shop. It's fast, easy to
navigate and international in feel.

www.foodlines.com
FOR THOSE WITH A PASSION FOR FOOD

ORIGIN CANADA	It's easy to find the right recipe at this comprehen-
SPEED ✓✓✓✓	sive site with a modern touch. There are some good
INFO ✓✓✓✓	recipes, as well as food quizzes and food jokes.
EASE ✓✓✓✓	

www.taste.co.uk
GOOD FOOD

ORIGIN UK	This was simplyfood.com by the Carlton Food
SPEED ✓✓✓✓	Network, now combined with Sainsburys to
INFO ✓✓✓✓	produce this new magazine, which is spoiled slightly
VALUE ✓✓	by the amount of advertising. Updated daily, it
EASE ✓✓✓✓	features thousands of recipes, food news, celebrity

interviews, reviews on the latest products, a restaurant search and review, nutritional information and competitions.

www.allrecipes.com
THE HOME OF GREAT RECIPES

ORIGIN US	This site gets its own review because it's not overly
SPEED ✓✓✓✓	cluttered, it's just got loads of recipes which can be
INFO ✓✓✓✓✓	found easily and each is rated by people who have
EASE ✓✓✓✓	cooked them.

http://soar.berkeley.edu/recipes
SEARCHABLE ONLINE ARCHIVE OF RECIPES

ORIGIN US	If after all the trying you still can't find a recipe you
SPEED ✓✓✓✓	want then come here, there are over 70,000 recipes
INFO ✓✓✓✓✓	catalogued, albeit in a fairly boring site.
EASE ✓✓✓✓	

Vegetarian and organic

www.organicfood.co.uk
A WORLD OF ORGANIC INFORMATION

ORIGIN UK
SPEED ✓✓✓
INFO ✓✓✓✓✓
EASE ✓✓✓✓

A very informative site which gives the latest news on organic food. There are sections on why you should shop organic, recommendations on retailers, lifestyle tips, shopping and chat. There's also links to key related sites.

www.organicsdirect.co.uk
ORGANIC FOOD DELIVERED NATIONWIDE

ORIGIN UK
SPEED ✓✓✓✓
INFO ✓✓✓✓
VALUE ✓✓✓✓
EASE ✓✓✓✓

An award-winning site, this company offers a wide variety of organic food and other related products. The whole thing is well put together with the emphasis on ethical living and it's much better value than supermarkets, delivery (UK) is £5.95 up to 20kg, with a further 25p a kilo after that.

Another good organic supermarket to try out is www.purelyorganic.co.uk which is similar in scope to Organicsdirect. But it does sell meat. Delivery charges are £6 for orders under £70, with orders over £70 free. One shop to watch is www.crueltyfreeshop.com the animal-friendly super-store, who are going through a re-vamp, but will be worth checking out once they're back online.

www.freshfood.co.uk
THE FRESH FOOD COMPANY

ORIGIN UK
SPEED ✓✓✓
INFO ✓✓✓✓
VALUE ✓✓✓✓
EASE ✓✓

Another combined supermarket and information site with over 100 different lines to choose from, this one has a recipe section too. They have a subscription system, which delivers your chosen goods on a regular basis. Delivery charges are £5 for a minimum order of £30 with discounts if you subscribe to a regular order.

www.veg.org
THE INTERNET'S DEFINITIVE GUIDE FOR VEGETARIANS

ORIGIN US
SPEED ✓✓✓✓
INFO ✓✓✓
EASE ✓✓✓✓

A huge resource site that covers everything a vegetarian could want to know, but at time of writing it is being updated and re-vamped, you can still visit the old site though. There is information on animal rights, health, nutrition, news and hundreds of links to related sites.

www.vegsoc.org
THE VEGETARIAN SOCIETY

ORIGIN UK
SPEED ✓✓✓✓
INFO ✓✓✓✓✓
VALUE ✓✓✓
EASE ✓✓✓✓

This is the official site of the UK branch with sections on: news, new veggies, environment, business opportunities, recipes and the Cordon Vert school, youth with virtual schoolroom, health, membership info and online bookstore. Each section is packed with information, written in plain English, and there is a search engine for information on any veggie topic.

www.vegweb.com
VEGGIES UNITE!

ORIGIN US	If you're a vegetarian this is a great place, though
SPEED ✓✓✓	not a great design. There are hundreds of recipes,
INFO ✓✓✓✓✓	plus features, chat and ideas in the VegWeb newslet-
EASE ✓✓	ter. Shopping is a confusing affair but at time of
	writing they don't supply to the UK anyway.

www.vegansociety.com
AVOIDING THE USE OF ANIMAL PRODUCTS

ORIGIN UK	The official site of the Vegan Society, promotes
SPEED ✓✓✓✓	veganism by providing information, links to other
INFO ✓✓✓✓	related sites and books. You can't shop from the site
VALUE ✓✓✓	but it does recommend suitable retailers.
EASE ✓✓✓✓	

Drink: non-alcoholic

www.thebevnet.com
FOR NON-ALCOHOLICS ONLY

ORIGIN US	Short for the Beverage Network, the idea is to test
SPEED ✓✓✓	non-alcoholic soft drinks and to provide a written
INFO ✓✓✓✓	critique of each. There are over 700 listed, sadly you
EASE ✓✓✓✓	can't order them from the UK. The fun of the site is
	spoilt by too much advertising.

www.whittard.com
SPECIALITY TEAS DELIVERED WORLDWIDE

ORIGIN UK	An excellent site, with a strong selection of teas,
SPEED ✓✓✓✓	coffees and related products and gifts, some 450 in
INFO ✓✓✓✓	all. It's easy-to-use and they will ship throughout the
VALUE ✓✓✓✓	world. Delivery is £2.95 for the UK – free if you
EASE ✓✓✓✓	spend £50 or more. You can also ask an expert, and
	get information on tea, coffee and making the
	perfect cuppa.

www.coffeereview.com
COFFEE BUYER'S GUIDE

ORIGIN UK	The coffee review gives points out of 100 to the
SPEED ✓✓✓	world's coffees after sampling them. They have
INFO ✓✓✓	several experts on the subject, the reviews are well
EASE ✓✓✓✓	worth a read and there are also articles on coffee

too. A re-launched site hopes to provide information on over 500 coffees later in the year.

Drink: beer

www.camra.org.uk
THE CAMPAIGN FOR REAL ALE STARTS HERE

ORIGIN UK	A comprehensive site that has all the news and views
SPEED ✓✓✓	on the campaign for real ale. Sadly, it only advertises
INFO ✓✓✓	its *Good Beer Guide* and local versions, with only a
EASE ✓✓✓✓	small section on the best beers. Includes sections on

beer in Europe, cider and festivals.

www.beersite.com
THE BEER SEARCH ENGINE

ORIGIN US	More than 1,400 links to beer and brewing sites, it's
SPEED ✓✓✓✓	straightforward and easy-to-use.
INFO ✓✓✓✓	
EASE ✓✓✓✓✓	

Drink: wine and spirits

There are many web sites selling wine and spirits, these are the best so far.

www.berry-bros.co.uk or www.bbr.co.uk

THE INTERNET WINE SHOP

ORIGIN UK
SPEED ✓✓✓
INFO ✓✓✓✓✓
VALUE ✓✓✓
EASE ✓✓✓✓

This attractive and award-winning site offers over 1,000 different wines and spirits at prices from £4 to over £4,000. There is a great deal of information about each wine and advice on the different varieties. You can also buy related products such as cigars. Delivery for orders over £100 is free; otherwise it's £7.50 for the UK. They will deliver abroad and even store the wine for you.

www.winecellar.co.uk

NOT JUST WINE AND GOOD VALUE

ORIGIN UK
SPEED ✓✓✓✓
INFO ✓✓✓✓
VALUE ✓✓✓✓
EASE ✓✓✓

They also sell spirits as well as wine and, while the choice isn't as good as some online wine retailers, Wine Cellar are good value. Use the search facility to find the whole range which isn't obvious from the home page. Delivery is free for orders of 12 bottles or more; otherwise it's £3.99.

www.chateauonline.co.uk

THE WINE SPECIALIST ON THE INTERNET

ORIGIN UK
SPEED ✓✓✓
INFO ✓✓✓✓✓
VALUE ✓✓✓
EASE ✓✓✓✓✓

This much advertised retailer offers some 800 wines, and if you know a bit about wine, then this is a good site with lots of expert advice and recommendation. They claim to be up to 30% cheaper than other wine retailers, but you really have to order 12 bottles. Delivery is £5.99 for the UK. There is also a section with good links to other wine-related sites.

www.wine-lovers-page.com
ONE OF THE BEST PLACES TO LEARN ABOUT WINE

ORIGIN US
SPEED ✓✓✓✓
INFO ✓✓✓✓✓
VALUE ✓✓✓
EASE ✓✓✓

Highly informative for novices and experts alike, this site has it all. There are categories on learning about wine, reading and buying books and tasting notes for some 50,000 wines. Also within the 28 sections there's a glossary, a label decoder, a list of Internet wine shops, wine writers archive, wine search engine and much more.

www.winespectator.com
THE MOST COMPREHENSIVE WINE WEB SITE

ORIGIN US
SPEED ✓✓✓
INFO ✓✓✓✓✓
EASE ✓✓✓✓

From *Wine Spectator* magazine you get a site packed with information. There are eleven comprehensive sections, including news, features, a wine search facility, forums, weekly features, a library, the best wineries, wine auctions and travel. The dining section has a world restaurant guide, tips on eating out, wine matching and a set of links to gourmet food. You can subscribe to the whole site, which includes access to their archive material for $29.95 a month.

www.wine-pages.com
A GREAT BRITISH NON-COMMERCIAL WINE SITE

ORIGIN UK
SPEED ✓✓✓
INFO ✓✓✓✓✓
EASE ✓✓✓

Most independently written wine sites are poor, however wine expert Tom Cannavan has put together a strong offering, which is updated daily. It's well written, informative and links to other good wine sites and online wine merchants.

www.wineanorak.com

THE WINE ANORAK

ORIGIN UK
SPEED ✓✓✓
INFO ✓✓✓✓✓
EASE ✓✓✓

For another good British independent wine site, try the Wine Anorak, it's just a great wine magazine, with lots of advice, articles, issues of the day and general information on wines and regions.

www.jancisrobinson.com

TV WINE EXPERT

ORIGIN UK
SPEED ✓✓✓
INFO ✓✓✓
EASE ✓✓✓

Jancis Robinson has a bright site with wine news, tips, and features on the latest wines and information on her books and videos.

www.ozclarke.com

OZ ON OZ

ORIGIN UK
SPEED ✓✓✓
INFO ✓✓✓✓
EASE ✓✓✓

Lots about Oz and what he's up to plus information on how to get his books and CD-ROM. There's also his wine magazine to browse, which includes tips on tasting, producer profiles, wine basics and the latest news.

Other wine sites worth checking out are:
www.drinks365.com – wide range, and plenty of offers.
www.cyberbacchus.com – wine portal with hundreds of links.
www.cephas.co.uk – superb images of wines and vineyards around the world.
www.englishwineproducers.co.uk – info on English wine-making.
www.wineontheweb.com – good wine magazine.
www.wineloverspage.com – comprehensive guide and magazine.

www.wineplanet.co.uk – powered by virgin wines
this site offers a comprehensive wine list with
good offers, recommendations and a wine
magazine.

www.wine-searcher.com – a wine search engine,
type in the wine you want and up pops a selection
from various retailers from around the world and
UK, all suppliers are vetted for quality and
service.

www.drinkboy.com
ADVENTURES IN COCKTAILS

ORIGIN US	You can't shop from this site, but it contains virtu-
SPEED ✓✓✓✓	ally everything you need to know about cocktails
INFO ✓✓✓✓	including instructions for around 100. There is also
EASE ✓✓✓✓✓	a section in the making on party games.

www.barmeister.com
THE ONLINE GUIDE TO DRINKING

ORIGIN US	Packed with information on everything to do with
SPEED ✓✓✓	drink, there are over 1,300 drink recipes available
INFO ✓✓✓✓	and over 400 drinking games. If you have another,
EASE ✓✓✓✓	then send it to be featured in the site.

Eating out

www.goodguides.com
HOME OF THE GOOD PUB GUIDE

ORIGIN UK	Once you've registered it has an easy-to-use regional
SPEED ✓✓✓✓	guide to the best pubs, which are rated on food,
INFO ✓✓✓✓	beer, value, good places to stay and good range of
EASE ✓✓✓✓	wine. You can also get a listing by award winner. It
	also houses the *Good Guide to Britain*, which is a
	good resource for what's on where.

www.dine-online.co.uk

UK-BASED WINING, DINING AND TRAVEL REVIEW

ORIGIN UK
SPEED ✓✓✓✓
INFO ✓✓✓✓
EASE ✓✓✓✓

A slightly pretentious, but a sincere attempt at an independent eating out review web site. It has a good and expanding selection of recommended restaurants, covers wine and has some well-written feature articles. It relies heavily on reader recommendation, so there's a good deal of variation in coverage and review quality.

www.restaurants.co.uk

FIND THE RIGHT PLACE TO EAT, ANYWHERE IN THE UK

ORIGIN UK
SPEED ✓✓✓
INFO ✓✓✓✓
EASE ✓✓

A confusing site that lists nearly all the UK's restaurants from pits to palaces. You can add your review or go to another review site, but on the whole it doesn't recommend. There are also sections on catering suppliers, recipes and pub food. There's a drive to get advertising on the site, and always seems a little out of date.

www.theaa.co.uk

NOT JUST MOTORING AND TRAVEL ADVICE

ORIGIN UK
SPEED ✓✓✓
INFO ✓✓✓✓✓
EASE ✓✓✓✓✓

The superb AA site has a little known gem in its hotels section – an excellent regional restaurant guide to the UK. Each hotel and restaurant is graded and there are comments on quality of food, ambience, an idea of the price and, of course, how to get there.

Other restaurant review sites worth looking at before you go out are:
www.restaurantreview.co.uk – good design but London only.
www.ukrestaurantguide.com – great potential, good for links.

     www.cuisinenet.co.uk – book online at selected
       restaurants, nice design.
     www.local-restaurant.com – special offers, slow
       and some links don't work.

Free Stuff

*Free stuff is exactly what the term suggests, and these are sites
whose owners have trawled the Net or been offered free services,
software, trial products and so on. It's amazing what you can
find but as most sites are American some offers won't apply.*

www.allforfree.co.uk
DELIVERED DAILY IN YOUR E-MAIL

ORIGIN UK	All for free will let you know all the latest 'free'
SPEED ✓✓✓	news with their e-mail service. There's a lot here, the
INFO ✓✓✓✓✓	highlights being how to ensure that you are getting
VALUE ✓✓✓✓✓	the most out of government services, free Internet
EASE ✓✓✓✓	access, free magazines and where to go for the best

competitions. Members get even more tips and
information. You could also try
www.thefreezone.co.uk which has less available; it's
more of a collection of link pages.

www.free.com
GET SOMETHING FOR NOTHING

ORIGIN US	One of the best and largest sites of its type, there are
SPEED ✓✓✓	literally hundreds of pages of free goodies waiting to
INFO ✓✓✓✓✓	be snapped up. Very wide-ranging and very much
VALUE ✓✓✓✓✓	geared towards the US, but with over 8,000 links
EASE ✓✓✓✓✓	you should find something.

www.2001freebies.co.uk
ONE STOP SHOP FOR FREE STUFF

ORIGIN	UK
SPEED	✓✓✓✓
INFO	✓✓✓✓
VALUE	✓✓✓✓
EASE	✓✓✓✓

Nothing but UK freebies here, so it's all available from computer accessories, games, masses of samples and software to books and magazines. The site is well-designed and simple to use.

Other sites worth looking into are these listed below, but they are American so some offers may not apply for the UK.
www.1freestuff.com – one of oldest and best categorised.
www.freeandfun.com – they'll e-mail offers tailored to your interests.
www.totallyfreestuff.com – massive selection.
www.thefreesite.com – more of the same.

Furniture

Believe it or not it's becoming quite common to order items of furniture for the home over the Net, or at least to browse online catalogues before venturing out into the stores.

www.mfi.co.uk
MFI HOMEWORKS

ORIGIN	UK
SPEED	✓✓✓
INFO	✓✓✓✓
VALUE	✓✓✓
EASE	✓✓✓✓

MFI offer a nicely designed site with all the best aspects of online shopping and a wide range of surprisingly good furniture for home and office available for order online or via a hotline. Delivery is included in the price.

www.habitat.net
DESIGN OVER CONTENT

ORIGIN UK	A clever if slightly irritating web site giving an
SPEED ✓✓✓	overview of what Habitat are about and what they
INFO ✓✓✓	stock, you can't order online though.
EASE ✓✓✓	

www.mccord.uk.com
McCORDS CATALOGUE

ORIGIN UK	McCords offer a huge range of furniture, gift ideas
SPEED ✓✓✓	and accessories for the home via their online cata-
INFO ✓✓✓✓✓	logue. It's very quick, easy-to-use, good value and
EASE ✓✓✓	delivery is £2.95 per order. Straightforward returns policy.

www.furniture123.co.uk
SMART PLACE TO BUY FURNITURE

ORIGIN UK	This company has a well laid out web site offering a
SPEED ✓✓✓✓	good range of furniture, many offers, tips and free
INFO ✓✓✓✓	delivery and show 3D views of some of the items.
VALUE ✓✓✓✓	There's also a magazine with the latest in trends and
EASE ✓✓✓✓	ideas for the home.

www.heals.co.uk
STYLISH CONTEMPORARY DESIGN

ORIGIN UK	Heals has a beautifully designed web site which
SPEED ✓✓✓✓	gives information about the store and inspiration for
INFO ✓✓✓✓	the home. There's an online store which stocks
VALUE ✓✓✓	primarily gifts and home accessories, but there's a
EASE ✓✓✓✓	special services section where you can get informa-
	tion on furniture and interior design.

www.ancestralcollections.co.uk
REPRODUCTIONS FROM THE BEST HOMES

ORIGIN UK
SPEED ✓✓✓✓
INFO ✓✓✓✓
VALUE ✓✓✓✓
EASE ✓✓✓

If you've ever fancied a Regency stool or any decent piece of antique furniture but couldn't run to the expense then this company will supply you with a reproduction. They have a wide range of products not just furniture and are great for unusual gifts too.

Other furniture retailers that may be worth a virtual visit are:

www.cjfurniture.com – contemporary furniture with high delivery costs.

www.davidlinley.com – posh contemporary classics.

www.mufti.co.uk – more posh beautifully designed furniture.

www.new-heights.co.uk – simple, stylish solid wood.

www.amazingemporium.com – a wide range of high quality beds and furniture on a high quality site with good pictures and descriptions of the products.

Gambling and Betting Sites

Gambling sites abound on the Internet and they often use some of the most sophisticated marketing techniques to keep you hooked, new screens pop up as you click on the close button tempting you with the chance to win millions. All the gaming sites are monitored by gaming commissions but above all be sensible, it's easy to get carried away.

www.national-lottery.co.uk

IT COULD BE YOU

ORIGIN UK
SPEED ✓✓✓
INFO ✓✓✓✓
EASE ✓✓✓✓

Find out about Camelot, good causes, the National Lottery and whether you've won. Also, find out whether your premium bonds are worth anything at **www.nationalsavings.co.uk**, you need your bond-holder number handy.

www.jamba.co.uk

WHERE THE WEB IS FUN

ORIGIN UK
SPEED ✓✓✓
INFO ✓✓✓✓
VALUE ✓✓✓✓
EASE ✓✓✓✓

Owned by Carlton TV, this is probably the most complete set of games and trivia; in the gaming section you can place serious or fun bets and go shopping as well. You have to register to take part in the prize-winning games.

www.prizes.com

FREE INSTANT WIN GAMES

ORIGIN US
SPEED ✓✓✓✓
INFO ✓✓✓
VALUE ✓✓✓✓✓
EASE ✓✓✓✓✓

Basically free online scratch-cards, you can win cash or play for tokens that you can later exchange for cash.

www.24ktgoldcasino.com

THE ONLINE CASINO

ORIGIN US
SPEED ✓✓✓✓
INFO ✓✓✓✓
EASE ✓✓✓✓

Excellent graphics and fast response times make this great fun, but you need a decent PC to download the software. It is regulated just like any other casino and the odds are the same. There are 37 games and you can either play for fun or for money.

For a similar experience try **www.intercasino.com** who say they're the safest bet on the Internet. They've got 34 games to choose from.

www.ukbetting.com
LIVE INTERACTIVE BETTING

ORIGIN UK
SPEED ✓✓✓✓
INFO ✓✓✓✓
EASE ✓✓✓✓

Concentrating on sports betting, this is a clear, easy-to-use site; take a guest tour before applying to join. You need to open an account to take part, using your credit or debit card, bets are £1 minimum.

The heavily advertised, and popular www.bluesq.com also offers a similar service, but with a football bias and special bets on things like soap operas, presidential elections and *Who Wants To Be A Millionaire?* See also www.inter-bet.com which is easy-to-use, with loads of options and is probably better value than most sites, and there's www.sportingbet.co.uk which is similar again.

www.racingpost.co.uk
THE RACING POST

ORIGIN UK
SPEED ✓✓✓✓
INFO ✓✓✓✓
EASE ✓✓✓✓

A combination of news, racing and betting on a clearly laid out and well-designed site. Also features greyhounds and information on bloodstock.

www.ladbrokes.co.uk
UK'S NUMBER 1 BOOKMAKER

ORIGIN UK
SPEED ✓✓✓✓
INFO ✓✓✓✓
EASE ✓✓✓✓

Ladbrokes offer a combination of news, information and betting, which is geared to sport with excellent features on racing, golf and the other major sporting events. There's even a casino and lottery coverage.

www.willhill.com

THE MOST RESPECTED NAME IN BOOKMAKING

ORIGIN UK   The best online betting site in terms of speed, layout
SPEED ✓✓✓✓   and design, it has the best event finder, results
INFO ✓✓✓✓   service and betting calculator. The bet finder service
EASE ✓✓✓✓✓   is also very good and quick. All the major sports are
featured and there is a specials section for those out
of the ordinary flutters. Betting is live as it happens.

www.tote.co.uk

BET ON THE HORSES, LIVE

ORIGIN UK   Devoted to horse racing, the Tote fairly successfully
SPEED ✓✓✓✓   attempts to bring you the excitement and feel of live
INFO ✓✓✓✓   betting online. It explains what the bets mean and has
EASE ✓✓✓✓   a very good set of links relating to horses and racing.

www.thedogs.co.uk

GONE TO THE DOGS

ORIGIN UK   Everything you need to know about greyhounds and
SPEED ✓✓✓   greyhound racing. You can adopt or get advice on
INFO ✓✓✓✓✓   buying a dog, find the nearest track, get the latest
EASE ✓✓✓✓   results and learn how to place bets. You can't
gamble from the site but they provide links.

Games

*There's a massive selection of games on the Internet, here's just
some of the very best ones; from board games to quizzes to your
everyday 'shoot 'em up' type. There are more games for macs
listed on page 26.*

*It's worth remembering that before downloading a game from
a site it's wise to check for viruses. If you've not got virus software on your PC then you can download a good one free from
Innoculate at their site* **http://antivirus.cai.com**

Finding games

http://gamespotter.com
GAMES SEARCH ENGINE

ORIGIN US
SPEED ✓✓✓✓
INFO ✓✓✓✓
EASE ✓✓✓✓

A really handy site where you can get links to virtually every type of game whether it be a puzzle or action. Alternatively, you can use the search facility to find something. Each game on the list is reviewed as well.

www.electricgames.com
LINK AND REVIEWS

ORIGIN US
SPEED ✓✓✓✓
INFO ✓✓✓✓
EASE ✓✓✓✓

A good combination of search engine, links and reviews make Electric Games a good starting place on your quest for the perfect game. Where many other sites overload the information, this is well laid out and easy-to-use, especially if you're new to it all.

Games magazines

www.avault.com
THE ADRENALINE VAULT

ORIGIN US
SPEED ✓✓✓✓
INFO ✓✓✓✓
EASE ✓✓✓✓

A comprehensive games magazine with demos, reviews and features on software and hardware – good looking too. There's also a good cheats and hints section.

www.gamespy.com
GAMINGS HOMEPAGE

ORIGIN US
SPEED ✓✓✓
INFO ✓✓✓✓
EASE ✓✓✓✓

Lots here, apart from the usual reviews and features. There are chat and help sections and links to the arcade section with over 150 free games to play.

www.gameplay.com
THE GATEWAY TO GAMES

ORIGIN US
SPEED ✓✓✓✓
INFO ✓✓✓✓
EASE ✓✓✓✓

A really nice design helps make Gameplay one of the most visited games sites. Its magazine *(Spank!)* is good and up-to-date and you're taken to the Wireplay site to play games online. You can buy games too.

www.gamers.com
A MOMENT ENJOYED IS NOT WASTED

ORIGIN US
SPEED ✓✓✓✓
INFO ✓✓✓✓
EASE ✓✓✓✓

A great-looking site with all the features you'd expect from a games magazine but it has more in the way of downloads and games to play. There is also a chat section and competitions.

www.gamesdomain.co.uk
THE GAMES DOMAIN

ORIGIN US
SPEED ✓✓✓✓
INFO ✓✓✓✓
EASE ✓✓✓✓

A strong combination of freebies, competitions and good links, news and reviews make this site a great place to start online gaming. It's clear, fast and easy-to-use.

www.gameweek.com
GAMES NEWS

ORIGIN US
SPEED ✓✓✓✓
INFO ✓✓✓✓
EASE ✓✓✓✓

A very newsy site with lots on the latest developments and upcoming games. More for the industry than the normal punter, but good if you want to keep up-to-date.

www.happypuppy.com
GAMES REVIEWED

ORIGIN	US
SPEED	✓✓✓✓
INFO	✓✓✓✓✓
EASE	✓✓✓✓

Happy Puppy has been around a while now reviewing games in all the major formats. Each is given a thorough test, then it's rated and given a review. There are also links to related games sites. It's all packaged on a really good web site, which is quick and user-friendly.

www.pcgame.com
ALL ON ONE SITE

ORIGIN	US
SPEED	✓✓✓✓
INFO	✓✓✓✓✓
EASE	✓✓✓✓

The aim is to get as much information about games and gaming as possible all on one site and all in a simple package; and it largely succeeds. The design is great, the information current and the links work. There's more than enough information including reviews, cheats and demos of the latest games.

Games to play

www.barrysworld.com
GAMES ONLINE

ORIGIN	UK
SPEED	✓✓✓✓
INFO	✓✓✓✓✓
EASE	✓✓✓

Barrysworld specialise in providing online servers for players to play their games and you can take part in several from this site. There's also more information and links than you'll ever need, which makes it a little daunting at first, but it's also helpful and very well written.

www.classicgaming.com
OLD CLASSIC GAMES REVIVED

ORIGIN US

SPEED ✓✓✓✓

INFO ✓✓✓

EASE ✓✓✓✓

Probably one for older gamers but there's some good stuff on here so it's at least worth a look and it's amazing how new some of the games are.

www.gamehippo.com
OVER 700 FREE GAMES

ORIGIN US

SPEED ✓✓✓✓

INFO ✓✓✓✓✓

EASE ✓✓✓✓

Enough to keep you occupied for hours with games of every type from board to action to puzzles and sports. There's also a really good set of links to other sites. It's worth checking out www.freeloader.com which has a more modern selection available, but you have to register and jump through a few hoops to get them.

www.gamearchive.com
PINBALL MACHINES

ORIGIN US

SPEED ✓✓✓✓

INFO ✓✓✓

EASE ✓✓✓✓

A site devoted to pinball machines and similar games put together by real fans. There's also a selection of video games and links to similar sites.

www.gamebrew.com
JAVA GAMING

ORIGIN US

SPEED ✓✓✓

INFO ✓✓✓✓

EASE ✓✓✓✓

The Java program gives gaming an extra edge with brilliant graphics in particular. Gamebrew specialise in Java games and there are some brilliant ones to download and play here. Send them to your friends...

http://games.yahoo.com
YAHOO!

ORIGIN	US
SPEED	✓✓✓
INFO	✓✓✓✓
EASE	✓✓✓✓

The world's favourite search engine has its own games section. Here you can play against others or yourself online. The emphasis is on board games, puzzles and quizzes although there are other games available plus links to games sites.

www.ogl.org
ONLINE GAMING LEAGUE

ORIGIN	US
SPEED	✓✓✓
INFO	✓✓✓✓
EASE	✓✓✓✓

Join a community of gamers who play in leagues for fun. You can play all the major online games and compete in the leagues and ladders if you like. To quote them: 'What matters is that people are meeting and interacting with other people on the Internet via our services and their game.'

www.pokemon.co.uk
Pokemon GAMES FANS GO HERE

ORIGIN	UK
SPEED	✓✓✓✓
INFO	✓✓✓✓
VALUE	✓✓
EASE	✓✓✓

If you're into *Pokemon* there are games to play, download and buy, links, news, latest updates cartoons and comics.

www.planetquake.com
THE EPICENTRE OF *Quake*

ORIGIN	US
SPEED	✓✓
INFO	✓✓✓✓
EASE	✓✓✓✓

Quake is the most popular game played on the Internet, and this slightly slow site gives you all the background and details on the game. It's got loads of links and features as well as reviews and chat.

www.shockwave.com
SHOCKWAVE GRAPHICS

ORIGIN US	Shockwave's fantastic site offers much more than
SPEED ✓✓✓✓	games, there are cartoons, greeting cards and music
INFO ✓✓✓✓✓	too. Click on 'games' and you get access to five
EASE ✓✓✓✓	sections: action, adventure, sports, jigsaws and

board games plus two sections of arcade games. The
graphics are superb.

www.surfmonkey.com
GAMES FOR KIDS

ORIGIN US	Although primarily a colourful kid's site, the games
SPEED ✓✓✓	section of Surf Monkey offers over 500 games from
INFO ✓✓✓✓	the very simple to the quite complicated. Great for
EASE ✓✓✓✓	beginners.

www.lysator.liu.se/tolkien-games
LORD OF THE RINGS

ORIGIN SWEDEN	Get immersed in Tolkien's Middle Earth with some
SPEED ✓✓✓✓	100 games. It's got action games, quizzes and
INFO ✓✓✓✓✓	puzzles, strategy games and, of course, role playing
EASE ✓✓✓	games.

www.videogames.org
HOME VIDEO GAME HISTORY

ORIGIN US	An odd site that basically consists of links to other
SPEED ✓✓✓	sites that specialise in video games, although there
INFO ✓✓	are some older games on site. That's it really. Plans
EASE ✓✓✓	are to revamp it and create a much better site with

games for sale.

www.wireplay.com
THE GAMES NETWORK

ORIGIN US	Gameplay's free games site is excellent. The site
SPEED ✓✓✓✓	supports a good selection of online games on their
INFO ✓✓✓✓✓	server all with good graphics. This is combined with
VALUE ✓✓✓✓	news updates, demos and patches (files that update
EASE ✓✓✓✓	current games).

www.zone.com
MICROSOFT GAMES ZONE

ORIGIN US	With over 100 games to choose from you shouldn't
SPEED ✓✓✓	be disappointed. There's also a selection of games to
INFO ✓✓✓✓	buy or you could get involved in their premium
VALUE ✓✓✓	section which are highly inventive multiplayer games
EASE ✓✓✓✓	for which you have to pay a subscription.

Game manufacturers and console games

www.dreamcast.com
DREAMCAST FROM SEGA

ORIGIN US	Get the latest information on what's coming, try it
SPEED ✓✓✓✓	out or play online; you can also get the latest tech-
INFO ✓✓✓✓	nology. See also **www.dreamcastmag.co.uk** which
EASE ✓✓✓✓	has more information, reviews and games.

www.eidosnet.co.uk
EIDOS

ORIGIN UK	Sign up to Eidosnet the server and you get access to
SPEED ✓✓✓	games via **www.mplayer.com**. Eidos themselves are
INFO ✓✓✓✓✓	responsible for games like *Tomb Raider* and
VALUE ✓✓✓	*Championship Manager*. This method gives better
EASE ✓✓✓	than average quality and online access but you are
	tied to their games.

www.gbstation.com
Game Boy NEWS

ORIGIN UK	Here you can get all the latest information on *Game*
SPEED ✓✓✓✓	*Boy*, plus reviews and features such as chat forums
INFO ✓✓✓✓✓	and cheats. You can also buy from the site.
VALUE ✓✓✓	
EASE ✓✓✓✓	

www.hasbrointeractive.com
HASBRO GAMES

ORIGIN US	No games to download, but there are details of all
SPEED ✓✓✓✓	the games they sell and you can get patches on the
INFO ✓✓✓✓	site. The most useful bit is the links to sites that
EASE ✓✓✓✓	either sell games or allow you to play online.

www.nintendo.com
OFFICIAL NINTENDO

ORIGIN US	Get the latest news from Nintendo and its spin-offs
SPEED ✓✓✓✓	– N64, *Game Boy* and *Game Cube*. There's also
INFO ✓✓✓✓✓	information on the hardware and details of the
EASE ✓✓✓✓	games new and old. For further information try the

superbly designed **www.n64europe.com** which is
brilliant for news and information. For a site with
wider Nintendo info go to **www.nintendojo.com**

http://uk.playstation.com
OFFICIAL PLAYSTATION SITE

ORIGIN US	Looks good but doesn't tell you much except where
SPEED ✓✓✓✓	to buy, although there is some background informa-
INFO ✓✓✓✓	tion on the history of Playstation.
EASE ✓✓✓✓	

For a more positive experience check out:
www.psxnews.com
www.psx2unicom.com
www.psxextreme.com
www.absolute-playstation.com

www.planetxbox.com
INFORMATION ON XBOX

ORIGIN US
SPEED ✓✓✓✓
INFO ✓✓✓✓
EASE ✓✓✓✓

Xbox is Microsoft's new toy and this site gives you the latest information on it. It promises much and will be released in the States late 2001.

www.station.sony.com
SONY ONLINE GAMES

ORIGIN US
SPEED ✓✓✓
INFO ✓✓✓✓✓
VALUE ✓✓✓✓
EASE ✓✓✓✓✓

Sony have put together an exceptional site for online gaming, and with over 6 million members, it's one of the most popular. It's well designed and easy-to-use. There are lots of games to choose from, even official ones such as *Trivial Pursuit*. Providing you can put up with the adverts, it's a real treat to use.

www.segaweb.com
SEGA AND DREAMCAST

ORIGIN US
SPEED ✓✓✓✓
INFO ✓✓✓✓
EASE ✓✓✓✓

News, reviews, cheats and much more including chat and a letters section. For the official site with links and information on the products go to www.sega-europe.com

www.dreamleague.com
PLAY FANTASY SPORT

ORIGIN US
SPEED ✓✓✓✓
INFO ✓✓✓✓
EASE ✓✓✓✓

Dream League offer fantasy games in five sports: football, tennis, rugby, golf and cricket. Even with the sports you can play foreign leagues. It's easy to register and join in – and it's free.

www.fantasyleague.com
FANTASY FOOTIE

ORIGIN	UK
SPEED	✓✓✓✓
INFO	✓✓✓✓✓
EASE	✓✓✓

Be a football manager, play for yourself, in a league, or even organise a game for your workplace or school. Get the latest team news on your chosen players and how they're doing against the rest. It's also worth checking out http://uk-fantasyfootball.20m.com

www.primagames.com
PRIMA

ORIGIN	US
SPEED	✓✓✓✓
INFO	✓✓✓✓
EASE	✓✓✓✓

The largest fantasy game publisher offers a site packed with reviews, demos and articles. You can also buy a book on virtually every strategy game. There's also a good section on strategy games at About.com http://compstratgames.about.com with links and background on the games.

Cheats, hints and tips

www.cheatstation.com
THE CHEAT STATION

ORIGIN	US
SPEED	✓✓✓✓
INFO	✓✓✓✓✓
EASE	✓✓✓

Select the console or game type that you want a cheat on, then drill down the menus until you get the specific game or cheat that you want. There are cheats for almost 7,000 games so you should find what you're looking for. If you can't, check out www.xcheater.com who have a smaller selection, but you never know your luck.

Games shops

*If you know which game you want then it's probably better to use a price checker such as Kelkoo (**http://uk.kelkoo.com**) to find the best price on the game. They will put you through to the store offering the best all round deal.*

If you want to browse, then these are considered the best online stores for a wide range of games:

> **www.chipsworld.co.uk** – good for Sega and Nintendo. (UK)
>
> **www.eb.uk.com** – Electronic Boutique is easy-to-use with a good loyalty scheme. (UK)
>
> **www.gamespot.co.uk** – wide range, lots of info as well. (UK)
>
> **www.gamesstreet.co.uk** – part of the Streets Online group one of the top shops on the Internet – good kids' section. Free delivery in the UK. (UK)
>
> **www.game-retail.co.uk** – simple to use, good range and a loyalty scheme. (UK) **W?WT**
>
> **www.telegames.co.uk** – around 5,000 types of game in stock, covering all makes. Also has a bargain section. (UK)
>
> **www.ukgames.com** – excellent range and good prices. (UK)

www.gameswapshop.com
DON'T BUY NEW GAMES, SWAP THEM

ORIGIN UK	You have to go through an annoying registration
SPEED ✓✓✓✓	system and loads of adverts but eventually you get
INFO ✓✓✓✓	to a user-friendly site with a secure swapping
EASE ✓✓✓	system. You can swap games with anyone in the UK who is also registered.

www.wargames.co.uk
WAR GAMES FORUM

ORIGIN	UK
SPEED	✓✓
INFO	✓✓✓✓
EASE	✓✓✓

All you need to know about war-gaming on one site, albeit a slow one. There are links to specialist traders and to every aspect of the game from figurines to books to software.

Miscellaneous

www.etch-a-sketch.com
REMEMBER ETCH-A-SKETCH?

ORIGIN	UK
SPEED	✓✓✓
INFO	✓✓✓
EASE	✓✓✓

For those of you who don't remember back that far, Etch-a-Sketch is a rather annoying drawing game. It's been faithfully recreated here and it's still just as difficult to do curves. There are also a few other simple games and some links to children's games sites.

Board and card games

www.chess.co.uk
ULTIMATE CHESS

ORIGIN	UK
SPEED	✓✓✓✓
INFO	✓✓✓✓
EASE	✓✓✓

Massive chess site that's got information on the game, news and views, reviews and shopping. There are lots of links to other chess sites and downloads. Check out the similar **www.bcf.ndirect.co.uk** for the British Chess Federation. If you want to play chess, try the excellent **www.chessed.com** where you can play others live online.

www.gammon.com
BACKGAMMON

ORIGIN	US
SPEED	✓✓✓✓
INFO	✓✓✓✓
EASE	✓✓✓

If you like backgammon, here's the place to start. There's links to live game playing and masses of related information. Also check out **www.bkgm.com**

www.msoworld.com
BOARD GAMES, PUZZLES AND QUIZZES

ORIGIN	US
SPEED	✓✓✓✓
INFO	✓✓✓✓
VALUE	✓✓✓✓
EASE	✓✓✓✓

The ultimate site of its type, there are over 100 board games and masses of quizzes and tests; on top of that, there are over 1,000 links to games sites.

www.scrabble.com
SCRABBLE

ORIGIN	US
SPEED	✓✓✓✓
INFO	✓✓
EASE	✓✓✓✓

Scrabble addicts start here, unfortunately you can't play the game online, but there are some good word games on the site such as hangman. You can also get loads of tips and word lists, which will help you get to grips with the real game.

www.thehouseofcards.com
LOADS OF CARD GAMES

ORIGIN	US
SPEED	✓✓✓✓
INFO	✓✓✓✓
EASE	✓✓✓✓

Huge number of card games to play and download – there's not much missing here and there's also sections on card tricks, history, links and word games too. See also **www.igames.com** and **www.pagat.com** for alternatives.

www.playsite.com
EASY TO PLAY

ORIGIN US	A collection of straightforward games, specialising
SPEED ✓✓✓	in cards and board games. There's also a good selec-
INFO ✓✓✓✓	tion of fantasy games.
EASE ✓✓✓✓	

www.solitairegames.com
SOLITAIRE

ORIGIN US	Play online or download a game onto your PC,
SPEED ✓✓✓✓	there's plenty to choose from and it's quick. There's
INFO ✓✓✓✓	also a good set of links to other online card games.
EASE ✓✓✓✓	

Crosswords, puzzles and word games

www.cluemaster.com
CROSSWORDS AND WORD PUZZLES

ORIGIN UK	1,000 pages of puzzles, word games and crosswords,
SPEED ✓✓✓✓	all free. It's all on a pretty straightforward site,
INFO ✓✓✓✓	although you have to register to get the best out of
EASE ✓✓✓✓	it. Check out **www.wordcross.net** which is a high
	tech version where you can win prizes as well if
	you're over 18.

www.riddler.com
GREAT GRAPHICS, GREAT GAMES

ORIGIN US	You have to register to play and pretend to be
SPEED ✓✓✓✓	American (just put some nonsense where it says zip
INFO ✓✓✓✓	code) but once in you are treated to one of the best-
VALUE ✓✓✓✓	looking sites around. Most of the games are tradi-
EASE ✓✓✓✓	tional or puzzles and all are entertaining. Once

you've become a member you can send out game challenges to friends. Unfortunately, only Americans can win the prizes.

www.pocketgamer.org
GAMES FOR POCKET PCs

ORIGIN	UK
SPEED	✓✓✓✓
INFO	✓✓✓✓
VALUE	✓✓✓
EASE	✓✓✓✓

OK so you've bought your handheld PC, you've impressed the boss, now, what do you really use it for? Oh yes, play games! There's a lot here for most different types of operating systems, if not, then there are links to related sites. See also www.puzzleexpres.com for word games and puzzles for Windows CE and www.handango.com

Quizzes and general knowledge

www.trivialpursuitonline.com
TEST YOUR KNOWLEDGE

ORIGIN	US
SPEED	✓✓✓
INFO	✓✓✓✓
EASE	✓✓✓✓

This site is a site for *Trivial Pursuit* addicts everywhere. You have to download the program but, once that's done and you've chosen your character, you can play others at the game.

For alternatives check out these sites:

> **www.coolquiz.com** – several different types of quiz from sports to movies and quotes. Nice wacky design. (USA)

> **www.quiz.co.uk** – 1,000 questions in several unusual categories including kids, nature, food and sport. (UK)

> **www.trivia.co.uk** – excellent for fans of soap operas, plus pop, movies and much more, you have to register. (UK)

> www.test.com – mainly serious tests, but you can
> find out your IQ and find out how creative you
> are. Visit the family section to take tests on enter-
> tainment and sports amongst others. You have to
> pay for some of the tests. (USA)

www.thinks.com
FUN AND GAMES FOR PLAYFUL BRAINS

ORIGIN US	Massive collection of games, puzzles and quizzes
SPEED ✓✓✓	with something for everyone, in fact there are over
INFO ✓✓✓✓✓	20 categories. It's easy to navigate and free – unless
EASE ✓✓✓✓	you take into consideration the advertising!

www.mensa.org.uk
THE HIGH IQ SOCIETY

ORIGIN UK	Mensa only admit people who pass their high IQ
SPEED ✓✓✓	test – see if you've got what it takes. The site has a
INFO ✓✓✓✓	few free tests and, if eligible, you can join the club.
EASE ✓✓✓	

Gardening

*There's been several high quality British gardening sites launched
in the past year, but many sites are still based in America, so bear
this in mind for tenderness, soil and climate advice. Sites recommended give good general information and good links to specialist sites. Due to regulations on importing of seeds and plants
these can't be imported from outside the UK.*

www.gardenworld.co.uk
THE UK'S BEST

ORIGIN UK
SPEED ✓✓✓✓
INFO ✓✓✓✓
VALUE ✓✓✓
EASE ✓✓✓✓

Described as the UK's best garden centre and horticultural site. It includes a list of over 1,000 garden centres, with addresses, contact numbers and e-mail addresses. Outstanding list of links to other sites on most aspects of gardening. Truly comprehensive with sections on wildlife, books, holidays, advice, societies and specialists. However, it lacks a good plant finder service.

www.gardening365.co.uk
COMPREHENSIVE GARDENING

ORIGIN UK
SPEED ✓✓✓
INFO ✓✓✓✓✓
EASE ✓✓✓✓

This was Oxalis.co.uk, which was comprehensive, but cumbersome to use; now as part of the 365 network it's much better, in fact there's so much here it takes a while to find your way around. It features sections on gardens to visit, finding a gardener, tips, chat, what's on, weather reports, a plant selector and articles written by celebrities and well known gardeners. It's also got an excellent selection of online shops and links to related sites.

www.expertgardener.com
GARDENING COMMUNITY

ORIGIN UK
SPEED ✓✓✓✓
INFO ✓✓✓✓✓
EASE ✓✓✓✓

Advice and articles from experts such as Alan Titchmarsh and other award-winning gardeners combined with good design makes this site stand out. There are links to a good selection of online shops, a magazine and access to chat rooms and communities on various subjects from urban gardening to plantaholics corner.

www.gardenweb.com
GARDEN QUESTIONS ANSWERED

ORIGIN UK
SPEED ✓✓✓✓
INFO ✓✓✓✓✓
EASE ✓✓✓✓

Probably the best site for lively gardening debate; it's enjoyable, international, comprehensive and has a nice tone. There are several discussion forums on various gardening topics, garden advice, plant dictionary and competitions such as guess the mystery plant. Using the forums is easy and fun, and you're sure to find the answer to almost any gardening question.

www.kew.org.uk
ROYAL BOTANIC GARDENS

ORIGIN UK
SPEED ✓✓✓✓
INFO ✓✓✓✓
VALUE ✓✓✓✓
EASE ✓✓✓✓

Kew's mission is to increase knowledge about plants and conserve them for future generations. This site gives plenty of information about their work, the collections, features and events. There are also details of the facilities at the gardens, conservation, educational material and lots of links to related sites.

Other gardening advice sites well worth trying are:
www.plants-magazine.com – very good garden magazine, broad in scope but particularly strong on new plants.
www.drgreenfingers.com – gardening meets Benny Hill! Still there's some good advice available for beginners and those who don't take their gardening too seriously.
www.garden-uk.org.uk – a gardener's web-ring and chat room which is great for links to other related and specialist sites. It's quite slow though and the site needs a re-design.

> **www.gardenlinks.ndo.co.uk** – links to gardening
> sites in 32 categories, a good place to start search-
> ing for something specific.
> **www.gonegardening.com** – nice design, wide rang-
> ing magazine and shop.
> **www.gardenguides.com** – a useful American
> resource site with loads of information on every
> aspect of gardening. It has lots of tips, handy
> guides, and a free online newsletter.

Gardening stores

www.dig-it.co.uk
GARDENING IN STYLE

ORIGIN	UK
SPEED	✓✓✓✓
INFO	✓✓✓✓
VALUE	✓✓✓
EASE	✓✓✓✓

This is a beautifully designed garden shop and
magazine, although sometimes the graphics overlap.
The magazine section offers features, tips and well-
written articles, while in the consultancy bit you can
get online advice or e-mail a gardening expert.
The shop offers a wide range of plants and
gardening equipment and related products,
delivery to mainland UK is £3.95 or £15 if you
live on the islands. (W?WT)

www.crocus.co.uk
GARDENERS BY NATURE

ORIGIN	UK
SPEED	✓✓✓✓
INFO	✓✓✓✓
VALUE	✓✓✓✓
EASE	✓✓✓✓

A good-looking site full of ideas enhanced by excellent photographs. There are some good articles and
features, but it's basically a gorgeous shop with over
8,000 plants and products to choose from and some
good offers. Delivery costs depend on where you live
and, at time of writing, they don't deliver to most of
Scotland or Ireland, if in doubt give them a call.

www.blooms-online.com
ONE-STOP GARDENER'S RESOURCE

ORIGIN UK
SPEED ✓✓✓
INFO ✓✓✓
VALUE ✓✓
EASE ✓✓

A beautiful site that will supply all your garden needs and desires. In addition to ordering your seeds and buying your garden furniture, there's a great plant search where you can find plants of specific size and colour for that difficult hole in the border. There's DIY projects and a design service too, a gardener's club and advice. Delivery cost depends on your order or you can pick up at their nearest store.

Other gardening shops worth checking out are:
www.greenfingers.com – good for gardening advice and information with a well priced shop.
www.glut.co.uk – the Gluttonous Gardener provides unusual presents for every gardener.
www.chilternseeds.co.uk – a bit slow, this superb site offers a massive selection of seeds (over 5,000 types) and growing information.
www.earth-to-earth.com – supplies natural and environmentally friendly products.

Garden design

www.dreamgardens.co.uk
TURNING DREAMS INTO REALITY

ORIGIN UK
SPEED ✓✓✓
INFO ✓✓✓✓
VALUE ✓✓✓
EASE ✓✓✓

Complete Anne and Suze's questionnaire from which you'll get a suggested ideal garden, it's easy-to-use and full of good ideas, but the real design costs from £25. For more ideas try **www.creativegardener.com** which is devoted to providing inspiration for your garden.

Organic gardening

www.hdra.org.uk
HENRY DOUBLEDAY RESEARCH ASSOCIATION

ORIGIN UK
SPEED ✓✓✓
INFO ✓✓✓✓✓
EASE ✓✓✓

The leading authority on organic gardening, this site offers a superb resource if you're into gardening the natural way. It's particularly good if you're growing vegetables with fact sheets and details on why you should garden organically.

For information, compost lovers should go to **www.oldgrowth.org/compost** and for shopping go to the excellent **www.greengardener.co.uk**

British wildflowers and plants

www.nhm.ac.uk/science/projects/fff
FLORA AND FAUNA

ORIGIN UK
SPEED ✓✓✓
INFO ✓✓✓✓✓
EASE ✓✓✓

Using the postcode search, find out the plants that are native to your area, where to get seeds and then how to look after them once they're in your garden. Sponsored by the Natural History Museum.

www.british-trees.com
FORESTRY AND CONSERVATION

ORIGIN UK
SPEED ✓✓
INFO ✓✓✓✓
EASE ✓✓✓✓

Information on British trees which, while comprehensive, could really do with more illustrations. It has also got a good set of links and a list of books and magazines.

www.wildflowergardening.co.uk
WILDFLOWER LINKS

ORIGIN UK
SPEED ✓✓✓✓
INFO ✓✓✓✓
EASE ✓✓✓✓

The aim of this directory is to make it easy for you to discover relevant UK wildflower-related sites, and it succeeds. There are a dozen categories covering the information you need from specialist nurseries to plant information.

www.wildflowers.co.uk
BRITISH WILDFLOWERS

ORIGIN UK
SPEED ✓✓✓
INFO ✓✓✓
EASE ✓✓✓

An online store specialising in British wildflowers with advice on how to grow them, there's also a search engine where you can find the plants you need using common or Latin names.

Specific plants and specialists

www.herbnet.com
'GROWING, COOKING HERBS, GOOD LINKS

ORIGIN US
SPEED ✓✓✓
INFO ✓✓✓✓
EASE ✓✓✓

An American network specialising in herbs, with links to specialists, trade and information sites. It can be hard work to negotiate, but there's no doubting the quality of the content.
See also the excellent Breckland nursery site at
http://herbs.get-the-web.com

www.flowerbase.com
FLOWERFINDER EXTRAORDINARY

ORIGIN HOLLAND
SPEED ✓✓✓✓
INFO ✓✓✓✓
EASE ✓✓✓✓

Part of a Dutch network of sites called 'Flowerweb'. An excellent resource that allows you to look up any plant and get its picture; it searches on part words.

www.discoveringannuals.com
ANNUALS GALORE

ORIGIN UK
SPEED ✓✓✓
INFO ✓✓✓✓
EASE ✓✓✓✓

Based on the successful book, this site offers information on hardy annuals, half-hardy annuals, biennials and seed-raised bedding plants of all kinds. There's an A-Z listing on the plants and it tells you where you can buy them.

www.windowbox.com
CONTAINER GARDENING

ORIGIN US
SPEED ✓✓✓✓
INFO ✓✓✓✓✓
EASE ✓✓✓✓

A really good American site which is well worth a look if you're into container gardening in any form, it's well laid out and very well written with great ideas for unusual plant combinations. Worth a long browse.

www.rareplants.co.uk
RARE PLANT NURSERY

ORIGIN UK
SPEED ✓✓✓
INFO ✓✓✓✓
EASE ✓✓✓✓

A site developed by a specialist nursery, which is well illustrated, and pretty comprehensive, it offers information on the plants and can supply plants worldwide. Delivery costs vary.

www.rosarian.com
ROSES

ORIGIN UK
SPEED ✓✓✓✓
INFO ✓✓✓✓✓
EASE ✓✓✓✓

As this is a generalist guide we wouldn't normally review such a specialist site, but it's so well-designed in terms of how an online magazine should look for its audience, that we couldn't resist including it. If you love roses or just need information on them, drop in here for a good, long browse.

TV tie-ins

www.bbc.co.uk/gardening
GARDENING AT THE BEEB

ORIGIN UK
SPEED ✓✓✓✓
INFO ✓✓✓✓
EASE ✓✓✓✓

A set of web pages from the BBC site which offer a great gardening magazine, with celebrities mixed with helpful advice and features such as plant profiles, ask the expert and what to expect in the month ahead.

www.barnsdalegardens.co.uk
GEOFF HAMILTON'S GARDEN

ORIGIN UK
SPEED ✓✓✓
INFO ✓✓✓✓
VALUE ✓✓✓
EASE ✓✓✓✓

To many people the real home of *Gardener's World*, this site tells you all about Barnsdale and has features about the garden, Geoff and his work. There's also an online store selling a limited range of products and a good set of gardening site links.

Visiting gardens

www.gardenvisit.com
GARDENS TO VISIT AND ENJOY

ORIGIN UK
SPEED ✓✓✓
INFO ✓✓✓✓
EASE ✓✓✓✓

With over 1,000 gardens listed world-wide, this site offers information on all of them and each is rated for design, planting and scenic interest with Sissinghurst scoring top marks. There's also information on the history of gardening, tours and hotels with good gardens.

See also **www.nationaltrust.org.uk** which offers information on their gardens and places of interest. For the RHS go to **www.rhs.org.uk** who have an excellent site which also offers advice and information about their work. For the grandest garden scheme of them all go to **www.edenproject.com** who also have a top site covering all the progress they're making along with visiting times and details.

www.ngs.org.uk
NATIONAL GARDEN SCHEME

ORIGIN UK
SPEED ✓✓✓✓
INFO ✓✓✓
EASE ✓✓✓✓

This is basically the famous yellow book converted into a web site with details on over 2,000 gardens to visit for charity. It's still under construction at time of writing and will develop into a really useful site.

Gardeners with special needs

www.thrive.org.uk
NATIONAL HORTICULTURAL CHARITY

ORIGIN UK
SPEED ✓✓✓
INFO ✓✓✓✓
EASE ✓✓✓✓

This charity exists to provide expert advice on gardening for people with disabilities and older people who want to continue gardening with restricted mobility. The site give information on how the charity works and links to related sites. See also **www.gardenforever.com** who offer lots in the way of horticultural therapy.

Gay and Lesbian

www.rainbownetwork.com
LESBIAN & GAY LIFESTYLE

ORIGIN UK
SPEED ✓✓✓
INFO ✓✓✓✓✓
EASE ✓✓✓✓

A very well thought out magazine-style web site catering for all aspects of gay and lesbian life. It primarily covers news, fashion, entertainment and health. There are also forums and chat sections, classified ads as well as profiles on well-known personalities.

www.queercompany.com
QUEER LIFE

ORIGIN UK
SPEED ✓✓✓
INFO ✓✓✓✓✓
EASE ✓✓✓✓

A superb example of what can be achieved for a community on the Internet, this portal and magazine site is in tune with its readers and market, it has attitude and an obvious style without being too inclusive and indulging in the usual clichés. The writing is also good and the links are comprehensive.

For other good gay/lesbian sites try:
www.uk.gay.com – British page from the big American magazine site.
www.glinn.com – the gay gateway to the web.
www.gaypride.co.uk – gay Britain network – strong on links and great design.
www.gay365.co.uk – chat and dating.

Genealogy

www.sog.org.uk
THE SOCIETY OF GENEALOGISTS

ORIGIN UK
SPEED ✓✓✓✓
INFO ✓✓✓✓
EASE ✓✓✓✓

This is the first place to go when you're thinking about researching your family tree. It won't win awards for web design, but it contains basic information and there is an excellent set of links you can use to start you off. See also the excellent **www.cyndislist.com** where you'll find almost 100,000 links in 150 categories to help with your family research.

www.pro.gov.uk
PUBLIC RECORD OFFICE

ORIGIN UK
SPEED ✓✓✓
INFO ✓✓✓✓✓
EASE ✓✓✓✓

To quote the introduction 'The Public Record Office is the national archive of England, Wales and the United Kingdom. It brings together and preserves the records of central government and the courts of law, and makes them available to all who wish to consult them. The records span an unbroken period from the 11th century to the present day.' The site is easy-to-use, the information is concisely presented and easy to access. See also www.familyrecords.gov.uk which can help enormously with tracing your family tree, the links selection is excellent.

www.accessgenealogy.com
GENEALOGY WEB PORTAL

ORIGIN US
SPEED ✓✓✓✓
INFO ✓✓✓✓
EASE ✓✓✓✓

A massive number of links and access to different countries' web rings give this site 'must check out' status. It is biased to an American audience but it's very useful none-the-less. See also another portal site www.genealogyportal.com which is less cluttered.

www.everton.com
GENEALOGICAL HELPER

ORIGIN US
SPEED ✓✓✓✓
INFO ✓✓✓
EASE ✓✓✓✓

No we haven't gone mad and put a football team in the wrong section, *Everton* is the name of one of the best magazines devoted to genealogy. It has articles and features on the subject along with tips on how to conduct your search.

www.origins.net
DEFINITIVE DATABASES

ORIGIN UK
SPEED ✓✓✓✓
INFO ✓✓✓✓
EASE ✓✓✓✓

This site has information provided from the Society of Genealogists' records, from Scotland going back to 1553 and from England going back to 1568, and unlike many other sites in this area, it's also well-designed and easy-to-use. There's also search tips and access to discussion groups.

www.brit-a-r.demon.co.uk
THE OFFICIAL BRITISH ANCESTRAL RESEARCH SITE

ORIGIN UK
SPEED ✓✓✓✓
INFO ✓✓✓
VALUE ✓✓
EASE ✓✓✓✓

For £375 they will research one surname or line, for £675 two or a minimum of 6 hours work for £140. They guarantee results to four generations. Not as much fun as doing it yourself though.

www.genuki.org.uk
VIRTUAL LIBRARY OF GENEALOGICAL INFORMATION

ORIGIN UK
SPEED ✓✓✓✓
INFO ✓✓✓
EASE ✓✓✓✓

An excellent British-oriented site with a huge range of links to help you find your ancestors. There is help for those starting out, news, bulletin boards, FAQs on genealogy and a regional search map of the UK and Ireland.

www.ancestry.com
NO 1 SOURCE FOR FAMILY HISTORY

ORIGIN US
SPEED ✓✓✓✓
INFO ✓✓✓
VALUE ✓✓
EASE ✓✓✓✓

Find out about your ancestors for $5 a month. This US-oriented site has 500 million names and access to 2,000 databases. It offers some information for free, but for real detail you have to join. It's especially good if you're searching for someone in the US or Canada. Linked to this is the chat site www.familyhistory.com where you can visit surname discussion groups.

www.surnameweb.org

ORIGINS OF SURNAMES

ORIGIN US
SPEED ✓✓✓✓
INFO ✓✓✓✓✓
EASE ✓✓

A great place to start your search for your family origins. On top of the information about your name, there are thousands of links and they claim 2 billion searchable records.

Government

www.open.gov.co.uk

THE ENTRY POINT FOR GOVERNMENT INFORMATION

ORIGIN UK
SPEED ✓✓✓✓
INFO ✓✓✓✓✓
EASE ✓✓✓✓

A massive web site devoted to the workings of our government, it is a superb resource if you want to know anything official both at a national and a local level. Use the index or the search facility to navigate, as it's easy to get side-tracked. The top features are a list of top 10 web sites, a monarchy section (www.royal.gov.uk) a download section and a feedback service.

There's also a very useful search facility and portal for government and local government at www.ukonline.gov.uk Also check out www.ukstate.com which is a great site devoted to opening up on government information. For information on the goings on at the House of Commons, visit www.parliament.uk/commons/hsecom.htm

For info on the major parties go to:
www.labour.org.uk
www.conservative-party.org.uk
www.libdems.org.uk

If you need to know anything about how the European Parliament works and have a good yawn at the same time go to www.europarl.eu.int For the United Nations go to www.un.org

Greetings Cards

www.intercarte.com
SEND A REAL CARD

ORIGIN UK
SPEED ✓✓✓
INFO ✓✓✓
EASE ✓✓✓

Expensive at £4.99 but they print your message and delivery on orders placed before 5pm will be posted via Royal Mail that day. The site only features the up-market Woodmansterne cards.

www.bluemountain.com
E-CARDS FOR FREE

ORIGIN US
SPEED ✓✓✓
INFO ✓✓✓✓
EASE ✓✓✓✓

Blue Mountain has thousands of cards for every occasion; it's easy-to-use and free. There are all sorts of extras you can build in like music, cartoons and even voice messages. Really annoying music goes with it though! If you can't find what you want here then check out **www.egreetings.com** which is similar but has a different selection, it's slushy and very American. At **www.greeting-cards.com** you'll find even more cards to send.

www.nextcard.co.uk
3D CARDS

ORIGIN UK
SPEED ✓✓✓
INFO ✓✓✓
EASE ✓✓✓

Send three-dimensional cards using this site, there are great pictures of animals, sunsets and mountain scenery to choose from.

www.madopolis.com
GIVE MONEY TO CHARITY AT NO COST TO YOU

ORIGIN UK	At Madopolis for every e-card you send their spon-
SPEED ✓✓✓	sor sends 2p to the charity you choose. There's a
INFO ✓✓✓	good selection with a wide range of good quality
EASE ✓✓✓	pictures and it's easy-to-use but a little slow.

www.charitycards.co.uk
CONTRIBUTIONS TO CHARITY

ORIGIN UK	Buy your cards here and give money to charity, this
SPEED ✓✓✓	is traditionally a Christmas thing but Charitycards
INFO ✓✓✓✓	have turned it into an all year round possibility.
VALUE ✓✓✓✓	There are also discounts available and free postage if
EASE ✓✓✓✓	you buy in quantity and they also sell stamps.

Health Advice

Here are some of the key sites for getting good health advice, featuring online doctors, fitness centres, nutrition and sites that try to combine all three. As with all health sites, there is no substitute for the real thing and if you are ill, your main port of call must be your doctor. Dietary advice sites are listed on page 144, specialist sites aimed at men, on page 231 and for women, on page 451. The advice for parents, page 274 and teens, page 373 may also be useful.

General health

www.nhsdirect.nhs.uk
NHS ADVICE ONLINE

ORIGIN UK
SPEED ✓✓✓✓✓
INFO ✓✓✓✓✓
EASE ✓✓✓✓

NHS Direct is a telephone advice service and this is the Internet spin-off, it comprises an excellent guide to common ailments with the emphasis on treating them at home, a health magazine with monthly features, audio clips on a wide range of health topics and a superb selection of NHS-approved links covering specific illnesses or parts of the body. There's also health information and an A–Z guide to the NHS.

www.bupa.co.uk
BUPA HOMEPAGE

ORIGIN US
SPEED ✓✓✓
INFO ✓✓✓✓✓
EASE ✓✓✓

Health fact-sheets, special offers on health cover, health tips and competitions are all on offer at this well-designed site. You can also find your nearest BUPA hospital and instructions on referral. See also www.ppphealthcare.co.uk who have over 150 fact-sheets available on a wide range of health conditions.

www.healthfinder.com
A GREAT PLACE TO START FOR HEALTH ADVICE

ORIGIN US
SPEED ✓✓✓✓✓
INFO ✓✓✓✓✓
EASE ✓✓✓✓✓

Run by the US Department of Health, this provides a link to more or less every health organisation, medical and fitness site you can think of. In several sections you can learn about hot medical topics, catch the medical news, make smart health choices, discover what's best for you and your lifestyle and use the medical dictionary in the research section. The site is well designed, fast once it's fully downloaded and very easy-to-use.

www.patient.co.uk
FINDING INFORMATION FROM UK SOURCES

ORIGIN UK
SPEED ✓✓✓
INFO ✓✓✓✓✓
EASE ✓✓✓✓✓

This excellent site has been put together by two GPs. It's essentially a collection of links to other health sites, but from here you can find a web site on health-related topics with a UK bias. You can search alphabetically or browse within the site. All the recommended sites are reviewed by a GP for suitability and quality before being placed on the list.

For a second opinion you could visit www.surgerydoor.co.uk which is more magazine-like in style, comprehensive and has an online shop. Also try the well-designed www.netdoctor.co.uk who describe themselves as the 'UK's independent health web site' and offer a similar service.

www.embarrassingproblems.co.uk
FIRST STEP

ORIGIN UK
SPEED ✓✓✓✓
INFO ✓✓✓✓✓
EASE ✓✓✓✓✓

An award-winning and much-recommended site that works well; it's what the Internet should be about really. The site helps you deal with health problems that are difficult to discuss with anyone; it's easy-to-use and comprehensive. Younger people and teenagers should also check out www.coolnurse.com which is an excellent American site with similar attributes.

www.medinex.com
THE SAFE HEALTH SEARCH

ORIGIN UK
SPEED ✓✓✓✓
INFO ✓✓✓✓✓
EASE ✓✓✓✓✓

An award winning site whose goal is to bring you the best and most up-to-date information on health. It's become more commercial in the last year but the excellent lists of sites is still there and with an improved search facility, just click on the Medinex logo.

www.drkoop.com
THE BEST PRESCRIPTION IS KNOWLEDGE

ORIGIN US
SPEED ✓✓✓✓
INFO ✓✓✓✓✓
EASE ✓✓✓✓

Don't let the silly name put you off, Dr C. Everett Koop is a former US Surgeon General and is acknowledged as one of the best online doctors. The goal is to empower you to take care of your own health through better knowledge. You have to register, but the site has been expanded and offers the following services:

1. A search engine that enables you to look up any health topic.
2. Health news.
3. A family health advice section split for men, women, children and seniors.
4. A resource section, including a drug checker, which reassures and gives facts about medications. Links to an online drugstore.
5. The wellness section gives advice about fitness (both physical and mental), nutrition and offers a health check.
6. In community you can chat online with fellow suffers and get support on a number of ailments.
7. Conditions and concerns has up-to-date information on many allergies, ailments and specific health problems.
8. An online medical encyclopaedia in the conditions section, where you can look up any disease or symptom.

www.mayohealth.org
RELIABLE INFORMATION FOR A HEALTHY LIFE

ORIGIN US
SPEED ✓✓✓✓
INFO ✓✓✓✓✓
EASE ✓✓✓✓✓

Mayo has a similar ethic to Dr Koop but is less fussy and very easy-to-use. However, the amount of information can be overwhelming, as they claim the combined knowledge of some 2,000 doctors in the 11 'centres'. Essentially it's a massive collection of articles that combine to give you a large amount of data on specific medical topics. They've recently added guides on how to live a healthy life, first aid and a newsletter.

www.quackwatch.com
HEALTH FRAUD, QUACKERY AND INTELLIGENT DECISIONS

ORIGIN US
SPEED ✓✓✓✓
INFO ✓✓✓✓
EASE ✓✓✓

Exposes fraudulent cures and old wives tales, then provides information on where to get the right treatment. It makes fascinating reading and includes exposés on everything from acupuncture to weight loss. Use the search engine or just browse through it; many of the articles leave you amazed at the fraudulent nature of some medical claims.

www.allcures.com
UK's FIRST ONLINE PHARMACY

ORIGIN UK
SPEED ✓✓✓
INFO ✓✓✓✓
VALUE ✓✓✓
EASE ✓✓✓

After a fairly lengthy but secure registration process you can shop from this site which has all the big brands and a wide range of products. There are also sections on toiletries, beauty, alternative medicine and a photo-shop. You can arrange to have your prescriptions made up and sent to you with no delivery charge. See also **www.academyhealth.com** who deliver free in the UK.

www.medicalanswer.com
THE MEDICAL SEARCH ENGINE

ORIGIN US
SPEED ✓✓✓
INFO ✓✓✓✓
EASE ✓✓✓✓

A search engine that looks rather like yahoo, with some 800 medical and health sites listed and rated.

Fitness and exercise

www.netfit.co.uk
DEFINITIVE GUIDE TO HEALTH AND FITNESS

ORIGIN UK
SPEED ✓✓✓
INFO ✓✓✓✓✓
EASE ✓✓✓✓

Devoted to promoting the benefits of regular exercise with a dedicated team who put a great deal of effort into the site. You can gauge your fitness, there's information on some 200 exercises, tips on eating and dieting, nutrition and links to useful (mainly sport) sites.

www.tummybutton.com
ONLINE HEALTH CLUB

ORIGIN UK
SPEED ✓✓✓
INFO ✓✓✓✓
EASE ✓✓✓✓

This engaging site is a virtual health club aimed at getting you fit and healthy the fun way. Ruby the receptionist will show you round and introduce you to your trainer Todd for exercise routines and your chef Greg for healthy recipes and Fiona for nutrition. You have to register to get the best out of it.

www.hfonline.co.uk
Health & Fitness MAGAZINE

ORIGIN UK
SPEED ✓✓✓
INFO ✓✓✓✓
EASE ✓✓✓

A spin-off site from the magazine, which offers the latest health news and advice, it's attractive and it's quite comprehensive.

www.fitnesslink.com
RESHAPE YOURSELF

ORIGIN US
SPEED ✓✓✓✓
INFO ✓✓✓✓
EASE ✓✓✓

They've successfully re-designed the site to make it more accessible and softer in tone although there are still features on things like 'awesome abs'. The key sections are still there though:

1. The Men's Locker Room provides advice on getting back into shape, muscle tone, how to meet gals at the gym or just look up the pin-up of the week.

2. The Women's Locker Room gives you a pin-up as well as advice on most aspects of exercise. There is a good section on exercises you can do after pregnancy or illness. Alongside this the site offers excellent advice on exercise, especially those specifically aimed at one part of the body, and there are also sections on career management, dieting and a chat room.

www.fitnessonline.com
PROVIDING PERSONAL SUPPORT

ORIGIN US
SPEED ✓✓✓✓
INFO ✓✓✓✓✓
EASE ✓✓✓

This good-looking site is from an American magazine group. It takes a holistic view of health offering advice on exercise, nutrition and health products. In reality what you get is a succession of articles from their magazines, all are very informative but getting the right information can be time-consuming.

www.webphysio.com
ONLINE PHYSIOTHERAPY

ORIGIN US
SPEED ✓✓✓
INFO ✓✓✓✓✓
VALUE ✓✓✓
EASE ✓✓✓✓

Lots of advice and help on how to get the right treatment for everything from neck and back problems to injury recuperation. Excellent design with good graphics and therapist finding service, if you need one.

Alternative medicine and therapies

www.alt-med.co.uk
DIRECTORY OF ALTERNATIVE MEDICINE

ORIGIN UK
SPEED ✓✓✓
INFO ✓✓✓✓
EASE ✓✓✓✓

This directory is aimed at people looking for complementary and alternative health therapies in their area. There are links to other relevant web sites and descriptions and information on the benefits of each of the major therapies. For more information on alternative medicines and therapies also check out **www.therapy-world.co.uk** a magazine site with lots of articles on the subject.

www.medical-acupuncture.co.uk
ACUPUNCTURE

ORIGIN UK
SPEED ✓✓✓✓
INFO ✓✓✓✓
EASE ✓✓✓✓

Information from the British Medical Acupuncture Society on the nature of acupuncture and where to find a practitioner in your area.

www.drlockie.com
HOMEOPATHY MADE EASY

ORIGIN US
SPEED ✓✓✓
INFO ✓✓✓✓
EASE ✓✓✓✓✓

Click on any of the medicine jars to get what you need:
1. Information on homeopathy.
2. Homeopathic news.
3. Treatments for a range of diseases and ailments.
4. Review and add to the list of Most Frequently Asked Questions on homeopathy.
5. Buy Dr Lockie's books via the Amazon book-store.
6. Links to other Homeopathic sites.
7. Search the site.
An interesting, clear and simple site that offers sensible advice at all levels. See also **www.homeopathyhome.com**

www.pilates.co.uk
PURELY PILATES

ORIGIN UK	Keep up with the latest information on pilates; find
SPEED ✓✓✓	out what it can do for you and where to find a
INFO ✓✓✓✓	qualified instructor. There's also a newsletter and an
EASE ✓✓✓	events listing.

www.thinknatural.com
THINK NATURALLY

ORIGIN UK	A nicely designed site with a mass of information on
SPEED ✓✓✓	every aspect of natural health, there's also a very
INFO ✓✓✓✓	comprehensive shop with lots of special offers and a
VALUE ✓✓✓✓	very wide range of products.
EASE ✓✓✓✓	

www.yogauk.com
YOGA

ORIGIN UK	Welcome to the yoga village where you can get
SPEED ✓✓✓	information on yoga in the UK, subscribe to their
INFO ✓✓✓✓	magazine, or browse the links section, which has a
EASE ✓✓✓	comprehensive list of stores. See also
	www.yogaplus.co.uk who offer courses and work-
	shops, and also www.yogatherapy.org

Sites catering for a specific condition or disease

Here is a list of the key sites relating to specific diseases, addictions and ailments, we have not attempted to review them, but if you know of a site we've missed and would like it included in the next edition of this book please e-mail us at goodwebsiteguide@hotmail.com

Alcohol and drug abuse
www.drugnet.co.uk
www.alcoholics-anonymous.org
www.al-anon-alateen.org

Allergies
  www.allergy-info.com
  www.allergy.co.uk
Alzheimers and dementia
  www.alzheimers.org.uk
  www.dementia.ion.ucl.ac.uk
Aids and HIV
  www.tht.org.uk
  www.lovelife.hea.org.uk
  www.avert.org
Arthritis
  www.arc.org.uk
Blindness
  www.rnib.org.uk
  www.sense.org.uk
Brain disease
  www.bbsf.org.uk
Breast Cancer Campaign
  www.bcc-uk.org
Bullying
  www.bullying.co.uk
Cancer
  www.imperialcancer.co.uk
  www.cancerbacup.org
  www.crc.org.uk
  www.bowelcancer.org
Cerebral palsy
  www.scope.org.uk
Chiropody
  www.feetforlife.org
Deafness
  www.britishdeafassociation.org.uk
Dental
  www.gdc-uk.org
  www.priory.co.uk
  www.bda-dentistry.org.uk

Depression
  www.gn.apc.org/da
Dermatology
  www.skinhealth.co.uk
Diabetics
  www.diabetic.org.uk
Disabled
  www.disability.gov.uk
  www.radar.org.uk
Drugs
  www.release.org.uk
  www.yap.org.uk
Epilepsy
  www.epilepsy.org.uk
  www.epilepsynse.org.uk
Eczema
  www.eczema.org
Fertility
  www.ifc.co.uk
Gambling
  www.gamblersanonymous.org.uk
Heart and stroke
  www.bhf.org.uk
  www.stroke.org.uk
  www.familyheart.org
High blood pressure
  www.hbpf.org.uk
Kidney problems
  www.kidney.org.uk
Liver problems
  www.britishlivertrust.org.uk
Meningitis
  www.meningitis-trust.org
Mental health
  www.mentalhealth.com

www.mind.org.uk
www.youngminds.org.uk
www.infoexchange.org.uk
www.uzone.org.uk

Migraine
www.migraine.org.uk

Multiple sclerosis
www.mssociety.org.uk

Smoking
www.ash.org.uk
www.lifesaver.co.uk

Solvent abuse
www.canban.com

Spina bifida
www.asbah.org

Stress
www.stressrelease.com
www.isma.org.uk

History and Biography

The Internet is proving to be a great storehouse, not only for the latest news but also for cataloguing historical events in an entertaining and informative way, here are some of the best sites.

www.thehistorychannel.com

THE BEST SEARCH IN HISTORY

ORIGIN US
SPEED ✓✓✓✓
INFO ✓✓✓✓✓
EASE ✓✓✓

Excellent for history buffs, revision or just a good read, the History Channel provides a site that is packed with information. Search by key word or timeline, by date and by subject, get biographical information or speeches. It's fast and easy to get carried away once you start your search.

www.historytoday.com

World's leading history magazine

ORIGIN UK
SPEED ✓✓✓✓
INFO ✓✓✓✓
EASE ✓✓✓✓

Contains some excellent articles from the magazine, but probably the most useful bit is the related links section, which offers many links to other history sites.

www.newsplayer.com

Relive the last century

ORIGIN UK
SPEED ✓✓✓
INFO ✓✓✓✓✓
VALUE ✓✓
EASE ✓✓✓✓

Relive the events of the past hundred years, witness them at first hand as they happened. A truly superb site with real newsreel footage worth the £25 annual subscription fee.

www.ukans.edu/history/VL

The history virtual library

ORIGIN US
SPEED ✓✓✓✓
INFO ✓✓✓✓✓
EASE ✓✓✓

The folks at the University of Kansas love their history and have put together a huge library, organised by country and historical period. It's got an easy-to-use search engine too.

www.thehistorynet.com

Modern history American-style

ORIGIN US
SPEED ✓✓✓✓
INFO ✓✓✓✓✓
EASE ✓✓✓

Bringing history to life by using the eyewitness accounts of people who were actually there. This site is excellent for the World Wars, technology and American history. There's also a good archive with some pieces on British history too. You could also try www.historyplace.com which is similar and has some great historic photos. There's also www.ibiscom.com who have a large catalogue of historical recollections both ancient and modern.

www.biography.com
FIND OUT ABOUT ANYONE WHO WAS ANYONE

ORIGIN US
SPEED ✓✓✓✓
INFO ✓✓✓✓✓
EASE ✓✓✓

Over 25,000 biographical references and some 2,500 videos make this site a great option if you need to find out about someone in a hurry. There are special features such as a book club and a magazine. There is a shop but at time of going to press they don't ship to the UK.

www.francisfrith.co.uk
HISTORY IN PHOTOGRAPHS

ORIGIN UK
SPEED ✓✓✓✓
INFO ✓✓✓✓
VALUE ✓✓✓✓
EASE ✓✓✓✓

This remarkable archive was started in 1860 and there are over 365,000 photographs featuring some 7,000 cities, towns and villages. The site is very well designed with a good search facility. You can buy from a growing selection of shots, different sizes are available and it's good value too.

www.old-maps.co.uk
FREE OLD MAPS

ORIGIN UK
SPEED ✓✓✓
INFO ✓✓✓✓
EASE ✓✓✓✓

Access to mapping as it was between 1846 and 1899, just type in your town and you get a view of what it looked like in those times. The quality is variable but it's fun to try and spot the changes.

www.museumofcostume.co.uk
COSTUME THROUGH THE AGES

ORIGIN UK
SPEED ✓✓✓
INFO ✓✓✓✓
EASE ✓✓✓

Excellent site showing how the design of costume has changed through the ages. There's a virtual tour and links to other museums based in Bath.

www.blackhistorymap.com
BLACK AND ASIAN HISTORY ACROSS THE BRITISH ISLES

ORIGIN UK
SPEED ✓✓✓
INFO ✓✓✓✓✓
EASE ✓✓✓✓

A beautifully designed and important site which graphically describes how Blacks and Asians have contributed to British history. Search by region, use the timeline or category headings. It's well written and very informative with a wide range of contributions, there's also a selection of videos.

Hobbies

www.yahoo.co.uk/recreation/hobbies
IF YOU CAN'T FIND YOUR HOBBY THEN LOOK HERE

ORIGIN UK
SPEED ✓✓✓✓
INFO ✓✓✓
VALUE ✓✓
EASE ✓✓✓✓

Hundreds of links for almost every conceivable pastime from amateur radio to urban exploration, it's part of the Yahoo service (see page 314); also see **www.about.com** who have a similarly large list but with an American bias.

See also **www.hobbywebguide.com** whose modest list has some good hobby sites and also **www.ehobbies.com** who have plans to ship outside the USA, but are worth a visit anyway for information and links. Try **www.hobbyseek.net/cgi-search/Great_Britain/** which is a German site with good links to modelling sites.

www.cass-arts.co.uk
ONE STOP SHOP FOR ART MATERIALS

ORIGIN UK
SPEED ✓✓✓✓
INFO ✓✓✓
VALUE ✓✓✓
EASE ✓✓✓✓

A huge range of art and craft products available to buy online, also hints and tips and step-by-step guides for the novice. There is an online gallery and a section of art trivia and games. The shop has a decent search engine which copes with over 10,000 items, delivery is charged according to what you spend.

www.sewandso.co.uk
SHOP AT THE SPECIALISTS

ORIGIN	UK
SPEED	✓✓✓
INFO	✓✓✓✓
VALUE	✓✓✓✓
EASE	✓✓✓✓

This site offers a huge range of kits and patterns for cross-stitch, needlepoint and embroidery. In addition, there's an equally large range of needles and threads, some 6,000 products in all. There are some good offers and delivery starts at £1 for the UK, but the cost is calculated by weight.

www.horology.com
THE INDEX

ORIGIN	US
SPEED	✓✓✓✓
INFO	✓✓✓
EASE	✓✓✓

The complete exploration of time, this is essentially a set of links for the committed horologist. It's pretty comprehensive, so if your hobby is tinkering about with clocks and watches, then this is a must.

www.royalmint.com
THE VALUE OF MONEY

ORIGIN	UK
SPEED	✓✓✓✓
INFO	✓✓✓✓✓
VALUE	✓✓✓
EASE	✓✓✓✓

The Royal Mint's web site is informative, providing a history of the Mint, and coins themselves plus details on the coins they've issued. You can buy from the site and delivery is free. For coin news and valuations try www.coin-news.com or www.coin-universe.com all have good lists of links to specialist sites.

www.stangib.com
STAMPS ETC.

ORIGIN	UK
SPEED	✓✓✓✓
INFO	✓✓✓
VALUE	✓✓✓
EASE	✓✓✓✓

The best prices and a user-friendly site for philatelists, you can buy a whole collection or sell them your own. Their catalogue is available online, and you can take part in auctions.

See also www.corbitts.com who auction stamps, coins, notes and medals. www.stamps.co.uk is a good online resource site for stamp collectors,

especially for beginners. For good prices
see also **www.robinhood-stamp.co.uk** and
www.duncannon.co.uk for accessories and albums.

For further information, especially on exhibitions
and events try the Association of British Philatelic
Societies at **www.ukphilately.org.uk/abps**.

www.towerhobbies.com

EXCITING WORLD OF RADIO CONTROLLED MODELLING

ORIGIN US	An excellent, clearly laid out site offering a vast
SPEED ✓✓✓✓	range of radio-controlled models along with thou-
INFO ✓✓✓	sands of accessories and parts. The delivery charge
VALUE ✓✓✓	depends on the size of the order.
EASE ✓✓✓✓	

www.brmodelling.com

BRITISH RAILWAY MODELLING

ORIGIN UK	A high quality magazine site devoted to model rail-
SPEED ✓✓✓✓	ways, it includes a virtual model set for you to play
INFO ✓✓✓✓	with and articles on specific types of trains and rail-
EASE ✓✓✓✓	ways. There's also a forum where you to can chat to

fellow enthusiasts. For model cars go to
www.modelcarsplus.com alternatively try
www.motormodels.co.uk and for model boats check
out **www.modelboats.co.uk**

www.ontracks.co.uk

MODEL AND HOBBY SUPERSTORE

ORIGIN UK	They sell over 35,000 models and hobby items, but
SPEED ✓✓✓	it's tricky to find what you want as the site is a bit
INFO ✓✓✓	messy with lots of annoying graphics. Having said
VALUE ✓✓✓✓	that there's some good special offers and delivery
EASE ✓✓✓	prices are reasonable. **W?WT**

Humour

Jokes, links and directories.

www.amused.com
CENTRE FOR THE EASILY AMUSED

ORIGIN US
SPEED ✓✓✓✓
INFO ✓✓✓✓
EASE ✓✓✓✓

News, jokes, stories, games, trivia, satire and revenge it's all here in what is probably the most comprehensive fun site. There is also a really good set of links to other humour sites.

www.comedy-zone.net
COMPLETE COMEDY GUIDE

ORIGIN UK
SPEED ✓✓✓
INFO ✓✓✓✓✓
EASE ✓✓✓

Excellent and wide-ranging comedy site with lots of links and competitions, alongside quotes, jokes and chat.

www.funny.co.uk
THE COMEDY PORTAL

ORIGIN UK
SPEED ✓✓✓
INFO ✓✓✓✓✓
EASE ✓✓✓✓

Here fun web sites are rated and collated, along with news on who's doing what and where. There are plenty of jokes, and if you register you can post your own and subscribe to their magazine. For a real laugh, join the chat in their forum.

See also **www.funs.co.uk** who aren't as comprehensive but offer more in the way of interactivity.

For loads of jokes go to:
www.jokepost.com – hundreds, all well categorised.
www.jokecenter.com – vote for your favourites.
www.jokes2000.com – e-mail you the latest jokes.

www.funnybone.com – huge database with lots of rude jokes.

www.kidsjokes.co.uk – 10,000 jokes, great for the family.

www.olleysplace.com
VERY NAUGHTY MULTI-MEDIA

ORIGIN US
SPEED ✓✓✓
INFO ✓✓✓✓
EASE ✓✓✓✓

Claiming to have some 5,000 hits per day Olleysplace is justifiably popular for visual and multimedia humour. Its sections include bizarre film clips, voyeur and crazy clips; you should be aware that some of the content is unsuitable for children, and some people may find this site more disturbing than funny. Much of it is geared to selling the accompanying CD-ROM and there's lots of advertising. See also www.jokesnpics.com which has hundreds of animated and visual jokes, plus funny clip-art, all free. Lots of annoying adverts and it's a bit slow.

www.pickthehottie.com
PICK THE HOTTIE!

ORIGIN US
SPEED ✓✓✓
INFO ✓✓✓✓
EASE ✓✓✓✓✓

Probably the best of many sites where people post photos of themselves and their friends (or enemies) the idea being that you vote for the hottest-looking people and the ugliest too.

www.uebersetzung.at/twister/
TONGUE TWISTERS

ORIGIN AUSTRIA
SPEED ✓✓✓✓
INFO ✓✓✓✓
EASE ✓✓✓✓

An international collection of tongue twisters, over 2,000 in 87 languages when we last visited, nearly 400 in English – 'Can you can a can as a canner can can a can?' as they say.

British humour

www.britcoms.com
BRITISH COMEDY LINKS

ORIGIN UK
SPEED ✓✓✓✓
INFO ✓✓✓✓
EASE ✓✓✓✓

If you want to find a link to a British comedy show or comedian, then start here. The sites are selected for quality and there's also a broader selection of links for you to browse. You can also sign up for their newsletter. For traditional humour check out **www.britishcomedy.org.uk**

www.comedybutchers.com
SURREAL BRITISH COMEDY

ORIGIN UK
SPEED ✓✓✓
INFO ✓✓✓✓✓
EASE ✓✓✓

A really good attempt at creating a web site that shows off surreal comedy in the traditional British style, with entertaining news stories, audio sketches and features such as 'Padded Cell' where they highlight the worlds least remembered computer programs.

Stand-up comedy

www.chortle.co.uk
GUIDE TO LIVE COMEDY IN THE UK

ORIGIN UK
SPEED ✓✓✓✓
INFO ✓✓✓✓
EASE ✓✓✓✓

Chortle provides a complete service, listing who's on, where and when – also whether they're any good or not. There's also a comic's A–Z so that you can find your favourites and get reviews on how they're performing, or not, as the case may be.

www.comedyonline.co.uk
STAND UP COMEDY IN YOUR AREA

ORIGIN UK
SPEED ✓✓✓✓
INFO ✓✓✓✓
EASE ✓✓✓✓

News, links, interviews, clubs and listings; its all here at this comprehensive and well put together site, so if you're looking to check out a new comedian or just want to see an old favourite, start here. See also **www.jongleurs.co.uk** whose entertaining site has audio clips and details of what's on and when at their clubs, and also **www.standup.co.uk** which is under construction, but looks promising.

www.thespark.com
TAKE THE SPARK TESTS

ORIGIN UK
SPEED ✓✓✓✓
INFO ✓✓✓✓
EASE ✓✓✓✓

The Spark consists of a humourous news magazine and a few other jokey bits and bobs plus lots of annoying adverts, but its main feature, and the reason why millions visit, is for the tests. From the popular personality test, through bitch and bastard tests to the wealth test, all are good for a laugh and of course very accurate. Dare you take the Death test though?

TV comedy

www.comedycentral.com
THE HOME OF *South Park* AND MORE

ORIGIN US
SPEED ✓✓✓✓
INFO ✓✓✓✓
EASE ✓✓✓✓

Great for *South Park* and selected American TV shows, but also has good stuff on *League of Gentlemen* and *Ab Fab* with clips and background information.

www.thesimpsons.com
HOME OF THE SIMPSONS

ORIGIN US	A much-improved official site with biographies,
SPEED ✓✓✓✓	background, quizzes and more, plus the ever-present
INFO ✓✓✓✓	merchandise store.
VALUE ✓✓	
EASE ✓✓✓✓	If you are a real fan then go to

www.snpp.com the Simpsons archive or
www.fandom.com/simpsons which is a little
more commercial but good nonetheless.

Miscellaneous

www.theonion.com
AMERICA'S FINEST NEWS SOURCE

ORIGIN US	A great send-up of American tabloid newspapers,
SPEED ✓✓✓✓	this is one of the most visited sites on the Internet
INFO ✓✓✓✓✓	and easily one of the funniest. For more satire try
EASE ✓✓✓✓	www.scoopthis.com another very good online

magazine parody, which is now defunct, but the
archives are still available, also check out
www.ourpress.com an entertaining Canadian site.

www.losers.org
THE WEB'S LOSERS

ORIGIN US	A site that catalogues and rates the saddest sites and
SPEED ✓✓✓	sights on the web, note that some of the content is
INFO ✓✓✓✓	strictly adults only. Still, it's one of the most fasci-
EASE ✓✓✓✓	nating giggles available, all web site designers should

see this.

Internet Service Provision

There are so many Internet Service Providers (ISPs) that it would be impossible to review them all and it's moving so fast that any information soon becomes outdated. However, help is at hand and here are some sites that will help you chose the right one for you.

www.net4nowt.com
THE PLACE TO START LOOKING FOR THE BEST ISP

ORIGIN UK	This is a directory of free internet service providers
SPEED ✓✓✓✓✓	offering news and advice on the best ones. There is
INFO ✓✓✓✓✓	an up-to-date critique on each ISP with comments
EASE ✓✓✓✓✓	on costs and reliability. There is also a good

summary table featuring all the ISPs which proves useful for comparisons.

www.ispreview.co.uk
INTERNET NEWS

ORIGIN UK	Find out what's really going on at this impressive
SPEED ✓✓✓✓	site – they are especially good at exposing the worst
INFO ✓✓✓✓✓	performers. There's plenty in the way of news, offers
EASE ✓✓✓✓✓	and a top 10 ISP list. Also check out

www.thelist.com which is international.

Jobs and Careers

There are over 200 sites offering jobs or career advice but it's largely a matter of luck if you come across a job you like. Still, it enables you to cover plenty of ground in a short space of time without trawling the newspapers. These sites offer the most options and best advice.

Career guidance

www.careerguide.net
ONLINE CAREER ADVICE RESOURCE

ORIGIN UK	This is a comprehensive service sadly without career
SPEED ✓✓✓✓	advice. However, there are many sections on job
INFO ✓✓✓✓✓	hunting, vacancies, CVs and professional
EASE ✓✓✓	institutions that can help.

www.careers-gateway.co.uk
THE CAREER GATEWAY

ORIGIN UK	Great advice and lots of information. For example,
SPEED ✓✓✓✓	how to launch a proper career, evaluate your
INFO ✓✓✓✓✓	options and read articles to help you decide what
EASE ✓✓✓✓	you can do with your life.

www.reachforthesky.co.uk
CAREER ADVICE FROM SKY TV

ORIGIN UK	Sky has put together a great web site that doesn't
SPEED ✓✓✓✓	just look good. There are interviews, examples and
INFO ✓✓✓✓✓	information on careers, as well as a section where
EASE ✓✓✓✓	you can just chill out. The questionnaire is a bit of
	fun and may give you a pointer to your personality
	and what type of career could suit you.

www.careersolutions.co.uk
HELP TO GO FORWARD

ORIGIN UK	A good place to start if you're not sure what you
SPEED ✓✓✓	want to do next with your career, or don't know
INFO ✓✓✓✓✓	where to start. Using the site enables you to narrow
EASE ✓✓✓✓	your options and clarify things. The list of links is
	logically laid out and very helpful.

www.careerstorm.com
WHERE DO YOU GO FROM HERE?

ORIGIN HOLLAND
SPEED ✓✓✓
INFO ✓✓✓✓
EASE ✓✓✓✓

A site that will help you make decisions about your next career steps by a series of quizzes and questionnaires designed to find out what you're really good at. It's interesting anyway, and it costs nothing.

Job finders

www.transdata-inter.co.uk/jobs-agencies/
DIRECTORY OF JOB SITES

ORIGIN UK
SPEED ✓✓✓
INFO ✓✓✓✓✓
EASE ✓✓✓✓✓

Don't let the long URL put you off, this is an excellent place to start on your search. The Directory lists all the major online employment agencies and ranks them by the average number of vacancies, the regions they cover, whether they help create and store CVs, and what industries they represent. Clicking on the name takes you right to the site you need.

www.gisajob.co.uk
SEARCH FOR YOUR NEXT JOB HERE

ORIGIN UK
SPEED ✓✓✓✓
INFO ✓✓✓✓
EASE ✓✓✓✓✓

The largest of the UK online job sites with over 60,000 vacancies. You can search by description or sector and browse their top 100 jobs list. It's good for non-senior executive types.

www.workthing.com
IT'S A WORK THING

ORIGIN UK
SPEED ✓✓✓✓
INFO ✓✓✓✓✓
EASE ✓✓✓✓

One of the best-looking job sites with a reputation to match, this site must be one of the first to visit when job hunting across a wide range of industries. They also work with businesses to develop their people skills and recruitment; you can also get advice on training and personal development too.

www.monster.co.uk
GLOBAL JOBS

ORIGIN UK
SPEED ✓✓✓✓
INFO ✓✓✓✓✓
EASE ✓✓✓✓✓

With over 500,000 jobs available worldwide there are plenty to chose from. The site is well-designed and easy-to-use with the usual help features. At time of writing there were 17,000 UK jobs listed in over 20 categories. For another good site try **www.totaljobs.co.uk** who have around 50,000 jobs listed in a wide range of sectors, as has **www.fish4jobs.co.uk**

www.stepstone.co.uk
EUROPEAN INTERNET RECRUITMENT

ORIGIN UK
SPEED ✓✓✓✓
INFO ✓✓✓✓
EASE ✓✓✓✓

Regarded as one of the best, Stepstone has over 75,000 European vacancies and 14,000 in the UK. It's quick, easy-to-use and offers lots of timesaving cross-referencing features. You can also register your CV. For other overseas jobs see **www.overseasjobs.com**

www.i-resign.com/uk/
THE INS AND OUTS OF RESIGNATION

ORIGIN US
SPEED ✓✓✓
INFO ✓✓✓✓✓
EASE ✓✓✓

Pay a visit before you send the letter, it offers a great deal of advice both legal and sensible. The best section contains the funniest selection of resignation letters anywhere. There are also jobs on offer, links to job finder sites and a career guide service.

www.freelancecentre.com
SELF EMPLOYED

ORIGIN UK
SPEED ✓✓✓
INFO ✓✓✓✓
EASE ✓✓✓✓

Great for advice if you're thinking of going it alone, or are looking for help if you're already working for yourself, and a good deal of it is absolutely free.

www.homeworking.com
WORKING FROM HOME

ORIGIN UK
SPEED ✓✓✓✓
INFO ✓✓✓✓✓
EASE ✓✓✓✓

A site full of advice and information for anyone considering or actually working from home. There are links, directories and classified ads, as well as forum pages where you can share experiences with other home workers.

Legal Advice and the Law

We all need help with certain key events in life: marriages, moving house, making a will or getting a divorce. Maybe you need advice on lesser issues like boundary disputes or problems with services or property? Here are several good sites that could really make a difference.

www.lawrights.co.uk
LEGAL INFORMATION AND SERVICES
FOR ENGLAND AND WALES

ORIGIN UK
SPEED ✓✓✓✓
INFO ✓✓✓✓✓
VALUE ✓✓✓✓
EASE ✓✓✓✓

An extremely informative and useful site that covers many aspects of the law in a clear and concise style, there are usable documents – you can download some free, others to buy, case histories, news, tips and plenty of fact-sheets. See also **www.legaladvice-free.co.uk** which provides the answer to many legal questions.

www.lawsolutions.co.uk
FREE LEGAL ADVICE

ORIGIN UK
SPEED ✓✓✓✓
INFO ✓✓✓✓✓
VALUE ✓✓✓✓
EASE ✓✓✓✓

Free written legal advice from a dedicated team of lawyers and barristers on a number of subjects including accidents and injuries, employment, debt and money, landlord and tenant, consumer, road traffic, harassment and bullying and professional negligence problems. They'll also help you with support on other issues such as divorce and motoring offences.

www.uklegal.com
LEGAL RESOURCES AT YOUR FINGERTIPS

ORIGIN UK
SPEED ✓✓✓✓
INFO ✓✓✓✓✓
EASE ✓✓✓✓

This site offers a superb selection of links to everything from private investigators to barristers to legal equipment suppliers.

www.desktoplawyer.net
THE UK'S FIRST ONLINE LAWYER

ORIGIN UK
SPEED ✓✓✓✓
INFO ✓✓✓✓✓
VALUE ✓✓✓
EASE ✓✓✓

This site is quite straightforward if you know what you need and have read through the instructions carefully. First you register, then download the software (Rapidocs) enabling you to compile the document you need. The legal documents you create will cost from £5.99 upwards depending on complexity. You can call for advice or support as well, which costs around £1.75 a minute. The range of documents available is huge and there are more being added. See also www.lawpack.co.uk who offer legal documents such as wills, letting agreements and other contracts from £3.99.

www.legal-aid.gov.uk
FOR HELP WITH LEGAL AID

ORIGIN UK
SPEED ✓✓✓✓
INFO ✓✓✓✓✓
EASE ✓✓

The official line on legal aid with guidance on how to use it, how to get information and news on latest changes to the legal aid scheme. It could be a lot more user-friendly. For Scottish legal aid go to www.slab.org.uk and see also www.legalservices.gov.uk for further help.

www.terry.co.uk
ENGLISH LEGAL ADVICE

ORIGIN UK
SPEED ✓✓✓✓
INFO ✓✓✓✓✓
EASE ✓✓✓✓

The site of an English firm of solicitors that features a very good A–Z of legal terms, with clear, concise explanations in plain language.

www.dumblaws.com
THE DAFTEST, STUPIDEST LAWS

ORIGIN US	Did you realise that in England placing a postage
SPEED ✓✓✓✓	stamp that bears the Queen's head upside down is
INFO ✓✓✓✓	considered treasonable, or that in Kentucky it's ille-
EASE ✓✓✓✓	gal to fish with a bow and arrow? These are just a
	couple of the many dumb laws that you can find on
	this very entertaining site.

Magazines

Where to buy and subscribe to your favourite magazines.

www.britishmagazines.com
BRITISH MAGAZINES DIRECT

ORIGIN UK	Order just about any UK magazine, there are 3,500
SPEED ✓✓✓✓	listed, and get it delivered to your home, free of
INFO ✓✓✓✓	charge. Its fast and easy-to-use, but you have to
VALUE ✓✓✓	register. See also www.whsmith.co.uk who have
EASE ✓✓✓✓	some good offers but you have to pay for delivery.
	www.worldofmagazines.co.uk also have a wide
	range but is less easy-to-use.

www.newsrack.com
JOHN MENZIES

ORIGIN UK	Search for the web site of the magazine or newspa-
SPEED ✓✓✓✓	per you want, then use the links. It covers most of
INFO ✓✓✓✓	the world, but you can't order from this site. For
EASE ✓✓✓✓	another site with masses of links to newspapers and
	magazines sites try www.actualidad.com

Men

Not what you think, these are just a few sites especially for blokes, lads and real men.

Magazines

www.fhm.co.uk
FHM MAGAZINE

ORIGIN UK	A good reflection of the real thing, with sections on
SPEED ✓✓✓	everything from serious news to the lighter side,
INFO ✓✓✓✓	with the usual blokey features such as the jug-o-
EASE ✓✓✓✓	meter, bingatron, joke of the day, in fact you can
	even do the bloke test online.

www.gqmagazine.co.uk
GENTLEMEN'S QUARTERLY

ORIGIN UK	A stylish site, which gives a flavour of the real maga-
SPEED ✓✓✓✓	zine. It contains a few stories, competitions, fashion
INFO ✓✓✓	tips and a random selection of 'cool stuff'.
EASE ✓✓✓✓	

www.sharpman.com
SHARP!

ORIGIN UK	While a little odd, it's good fun and there's some
SPEED ✓✓✓✓	useful advice. Split into six key sections:
INFO ✓✓✓✓	Dating – with tips on conversation and repartee.
EASE ✓✓✓✓	Health – how to keep in tip-top condition.
	Work – getting the best out of the Internet.
	Travel – staying sharp abroad.
	Grooming – looking the part.
	Toys – the best advice on windsurfing.

www.fathersdirect.com
A MAGAZINE FOR FATHERS

ORIGIN UK
SPEED ✓✓✓✓
INFO ✓✓✓✓
VALUE ✓✓✓
EASE ✓✓✓✓

Written by fathers for fathers, this entertaining e-zine has all the advice and support you need if you're a new dad or you're trying to fit in both work and kids. There are competitions, a rant section where you can let off steam and a games room. Rather twee graphics let it down somewhat. See also **www.dadah.co.uk** who support stay-at-home fathers.

www.loaded.co.uk
LOADED MAGAZINE

ORIGIN UK
SPEED ✓✓✓
INFO ✓✓✓
EASE ✓✓✓

All the features, articles and regular naughtiness you'd expect from the magazine.

Health

www.menshealth.co.uk
MEN'S HEALTH MAGAZINE

ORIGIN UK
SPEED ✓✓✓✓
INFO ✓✓✓✓✓
EASE ✓✓✓✓

Lots of advice on keeping fit, healthy and fashion-able too. There's also an excellent section on the number one topic – sex.

www.menshealthforum.org.uk
STOP MOANING!

ORIGIN UK
SPEED ✓✓✓✓
INFO ✓✓✓✓✓
EASE ✓✓✓✓

An excellent all-rounder revealing the truth behind the state of men's health and lots of discussion about specific and general health issues facing men today – good for links too.

Other men's health sites:

www.malehealth.co.uk – comprehensive site where you can check the state of your health and your health knowledge; excellent links and advice make up the picture.

www.orchid-cancer.org.uk – promotes the awareness of testicular and prostate cancer.

www.vasectomy-clinic.co.uk – no scalpel vasectomy – honest!

www.impotence.org.uk – the Impotence Association.

Shopping

www.firebox.com
WHERE MEN BUY STUFF

ORIGIN UK	An online shop aimed totally at boy's toys,
SPEED ✓✓✓✓	with it's own bachelor pad containing all you
INFO ✓✓✓✓	need for the lifestyle. There's masses of games,
VALUE ✓✓✓	videos, toys and, of course, the latest gadgets.
EASE ✓✓✓✓	Delivery costs vary. (W?WT)

See also **www.big-boys-toys.net** and **www.boysstuff.co.uk** both are worth a visit if you can't find what you want at Firebox.

www.condomsdirect.co.uk
CONDOMS UK

ORIGIN UK	Many different types of condoms are available
SPEED ✓✓✓✓	to buy, and you get free delivery if you spend
INFO ✓✓✓✓	more than £10 – there's even a price promise.
VALUE ✓✓✓✓	For more information it's worth checking out
EASE ✓✓✓✓	**www.condomania.com**

Motorcycles

www.bmf.co.uk
BRITISH MOTORCYCLISTS FEDERATION

ORIGIN UK	At this site you can join the BMF, get involved with
SPEED ✓✓✓	their activities or just use the site for information or
INFO ✓✓✓✓	for their magazine *Rider*. You can also get club
EASE ✓✓✓✓	information and e-mail them on any issues. For the
	international governing body go to **www.fim.ch/en**

www.motorcycle.co.uk
THE UK'S MOTORCYCLE DIRECTORY

ORIGIN UK	Essentially a list of links by brand, dealer,
SPEED ✓✓✓	importer, classics, gear, books and auctions.
INFO ✓✓✓	For more information on motorcycle clubs
EASE ✓✓✓✓	go to **www.motorcycle.org.uk**

www.moto-directory.com
THE WORLD MOTORCYCLE DIRECTORY

ORIGIN US	US-oriented, but links to over 800 sites ensure that
SPEED ✓✓✓	you'll know what's going on in motorcycling and
INFO ✓✓✓✓✓	find the information you need.
EASE ✓✓✓	

www.motorworld.com
ALL YOU NEED TO KNOW ABOUT MOTORCYCLES

ORIGIN US	Good coverage of both machines and events with
SPEED ✓✓✓	multimedia features. Although the site is American
INFO ✓✓✓✓	there's a good British section. See also the better
EASE ✓✓✓	designed **www.bikenet.com** which is more UK-
	centric.

www.motorcycle-search.co.uk
FREE CLASSIFIED ADS

ORIGIN UK
SPEED ✓✓✓✓
INFO ✓✓✓✓
EASE ✓✓✓✓

A good, fast site with a good selection of used bikes, luggage, clothing, parts and accessories. See also Bike Exchange at **www.biketrader.co.uk** who also offer other services such as insurance and finance.

Movies

All you need to know about films and film stars including where to go to get the best deals on DVDs and videos. For information on film stars also check out the celebrities section on page 63.

http://uk.imdb.com
INTERNET MOVIE DATABASE

ORIGIN US
SPEED ✓✓✓✓
INFO ✓✓✓✓✓
VALUE ✓✓✓✓
EASE ✓✓✓✓

The best and most organised movie database on the Internet. It's very easy-to-use and every film buff's dream. In 'What's Hot' check out the latest releases, get the latest movie news and reviews, do the quizzes, leave a review or take up a recommendation. There's also a handy 'if you liked, then you'll just love' section, and check out the stars' birthdays. Another good database site is **www.allmovie.com** which has a really good search engine.

www.filmworld.co.uk
THE ONE STOP FILM SHOP

ORIGIN	UK
SPEED	✓✓✓✓
INFO	✓✓✓✓
VALUE	✓✓✓✓
EASE	✓✓✓✓

A brilliant film buff's site. What really makes this site stand out is its very good search facility and the way it combines a great review site with an excellent shop. The shop offers film memorabilia, finds 'out of print' movies, and offers up to 25% off current ones. Delivery is £1.25 for the UK and only £1.80 for Europe – and it's often guaranteed to a specific time. There are also trailers, competitions and lots of information.

www.aintitcoolnews.com
AIN'T IT JUST COOL

ORIGIN	US
SPEED	✓✓✓✓
INFO	✓✓✓✓✓
EASE	✓✓✓

A renowned review site that can make or break a movie in the US, it's very entertaining and likeable, albeit a bit messy. Harry Knowles' movie reviews are by far the best bit of the site, although they can go on a bit. You can search the archive for a particular review or contribute a bit of juicy gossip by e-mailing Harry direct. See also **www.moviecritic.com** where you can also rate movies yourself, but you have to become a member.

www.corona.bc.ca/films
COMING ATTRACTIONS

ORIGIN	US
SPEED	✓✓✓
INFO	✓✓✓✓
EASE	✓✓✓✓

An excellent site that previews upcoming movie releases, giving background information on how films were made (or are progressing), gossip and links. You can join in with your own film ratings or just read the articles, which are generally well written. It's not perfect but it's very entertaining.

www.popcorn.co.uk
EVERYTHING FROM POSTERS TO WHAT'S ON WHERE

ORIGIN UK
SPEED ✓✓✓
INFO ✓✓✓✓✓
EASE ✓✓✓✓

Almost the complete package from Carlton TV, a great site for movie buffs as well as reliable local cinema listings complete with trailers giving you a taster before you put your coat on. Takes a long time to download but it's worth it.

www.insidefilm.com
THE INSIDER'S VIEW

ORIGIN US
SPEED ✓✓✓
INFO ✓✓✓✓
EASE ✓✓✓✓

The latest gossip, news and views from tinsel town, Inside Film is essentially a very good magazine site. Also check out www.hollywood.com which has over 1 million pages of information and trailers, and also www.mrshowbiz.go.com

www.eonline.com
E IS FOR ENTERTAINMENT

ORIGIN US
SPEED ✓✓✓✓
INFO ✓✓✓✓
EASE ✓✓✓✓

This is one of the most visited entertainment news sites and it has a reputation for being first with the latest gossip and movie news. It's well designed and has a tongue in cheek style, which is endearing; sadly some of the reporters prattle on.

www.variety.com
Variety MAGAZINE

ORIGIN US
SPEED ✓✓✓
INFO ✓✓✓✓✓
EASE ✓✓✓✓

A show business stalwart magazine online with an excellent and entertaining site with all the hot topics, news and background information you'd expect plus biographies and international film news.

www.oscars.com
THE ACADEMY AWARDS

ORIGIN US
SPEED ✓✓✓✓
INFO ✓✓✓✓
EASE ✓✓✓✓

Stylish and as glitzy as you'd imagine it should be, this is the official tie-in site for the Oscars. There's an archive and even some games to play. For the Golden Globes go to www.goldenglobes.org

www.bafta.org
BRITISH ACADEMY OF FILM & TELEVISION ARTS

ORIGIN UK
SPEED ✓✓✓✓
INFO ✓✓✓✓
EASE ✓✓✓✓

A site giving all the information you need on the Baftas, their history and how it all works.

www.bfi.org.uk
BRITISH FILM INSTITUTE

ORIGIN UK
SPEED ✓✓✓✓
INFO ✓✓✓✓✓
EASE ✓✓✓✓

A top site from the BFI packed with information on how the film industry works with archive material, links and how to make movies. Refreshing that there's not much mention of Hollywood.

www.britmovie.co.uk
DEDICATED TO BRITISH CINEMA

ORIGIN UK
SPEED ✓✓✓✓
INFO ✓✓✓✓✓
EASE ✓✓✓✓

A site devoted to the history of British cinema and its wider contribution to film-making in general. There's a great deal of information and background and it's all well cross-referenced, although it could do with a search facility. There's also a section which features video clips and trailers of classic British cinema.

Cinemas

www.abccinemas.co.uk
MORE FUN THAN CHOCOLATE

ORIGIN UK
SPEED ✓✓✓✓
INFO ✓✓✓✓
VALUE ✓✓✓✓
EASE ✓✓✓✓

Top marks go to ABC for not producing a boring site simply geared to selling tickets. While that's essentially what it does, it also provides one of the most entertaining movie sites with excellent graphics, links and information on the films and stars.

www.virgin.net/cinema
VIRGIN CINEMA

ORIGIN UK
SPEED ✓✓✓✓
INFO ✓✓✓✓
VALUE ✓✓✓
EASE ✓✓✓✓

Excellent magazine-style film site with links to their shop and what's on guide. There are sections on gossip, news and coming soon, as well as competitions and a chat room.

Other cinema company sites:
www.cineworld.co.uk – straightforward and easy-to-use guide.
www.odeon.co.uk – at time of writing undergoing a re-vamp.
www.showcasecinemas.co.uk – lots here to see and do, but a little slow to download.
www.uci-cinemas.co.uk – good looking site with all the usual information and previews.
www.warnervillage.co.uk – excellent site with online booking.

Movie humour

www.moviesounds.com
LISTEN TO YOUR FAVOURITE MOVIES

ORIGIN US	Download extracts from over 50 movies, it's a little
SPEED ✓✓✓✓	confusing at first but once you've got the technology
INFO ✓✓✓✓	sorted out it's good fun.
EASE ✓✓✓✓	

http://rinkworks.com/movieaminute/
DON'T HAVE TIME TO WATCH IT ALL?

ORIGIN US	Summaries of the top movies for those who either
SPEED ✓✓✓✓	can't be bothered to watch them or just want to
INFO ✓✓✓✓	pretend they did, either way it's really funny.
EASE ✓✓✓✓	

www.moviecliches.com
THE MOVIE CLICHÉ LIST

ORIGIN US	Clichés listed by topic from aeroplanes to wood,
SPEED ✓✓✓✓	there's something for everyone here...
INFO ✓✓✓	
EASE ✓✓✓✓	

www.moviebloopers.com
BLOOPERS GALORE

ORIGIN US	A catalogue of mistakes and continuity errors from
SPEED ✓✓✓✓	many of the world's greatest films – rather than be
INFO ✓✓✓✓	funny though, it just makes you wonder how long
EASE ✓✓✓✓	some people study films to spot such small errors!
	There are also reviews and quizzes.

Film companies

Some of the best web sites are those that promote a particular film. Here is a list of the major film producers and their web sites, all of which are good and have links to the latest releases. Most have clips, downloads, screensavers and lots of advertising.

> www.disney.com
> www.mca.com
> www.miramax.com
> www.paramount.com
> www.spe.sony.com
> www.foxmovies.com
> www.uip.com
> www.universalpictures.com
> www.warnerbros.com

Buying movies

It's probably best to start with visiting a price checker site first such as www.kelkoo.com (see page 293) but these are the best of the movie online stores.

www.blackstar.co.uk
THE UK'S BIGGEST VIDEO STORE

ORIGIN UK	The biggest online video and DVD retailer, it claims
SPEED ✓✓✓✓	to be able to get around 50,000 titles. Blackstar is
INFO ✓✓✓✓	very good value, boasts free delivery, and has a
VALUE ✓✓✓✓	reputation for excellent customer service. If you
EASE ✓✓✓✓	want to shop around try www.blockbuster.com who

have a less packed site and offers on a wide variety of films.

www.dvdstreet.infront.co.uk
FOR DVD ONLY

ORIGIN UK	Part of the Streets Online group, this is a great value
SPEED ✓✓✓✓	and easy-to-use site that only sells DVD. There are lots
INFO ✓✓✓✓	of other movie-related features too, such as the latest
VALUE ✓✓✓✓	news and gossip or reviews. Delivery is free for the
EASE ✓✓✓✓	UK. See also the good-looking **www.musicbox.cd** who

have good offers and delivery is £1 whatever the order.

www.movietrak.com
RENT A DVD MOVIE

ORIGIN UK	The latest films are available to rent for £2.99 for
SPEED ✓✓✓✓	seven days. Pick the title of your choice and it's
INFO ✓✓✓✓	dispatched the same day, you then return it seven
VALUE ✓✓✓	days later in the pre-paid envelope. The range
EASE ✓✓✓✓	offered is excellent covering ten major categories

plus the latest releases, coming soon and a good
search facility too.

www.in-movies.co.uk
IT'S IN THE MOVIES

ORIGIN UK	The latest trailers, short films, competitions and DVD
SPEED ✓✓✓✓	rental are just some of the things you can see and do
INFO ✓✓✓✓	here at this good-looking site. DVD rental is £15 a
VALUE ✓✓✓	month but you can take out as many as you like.
EASE ✓✓✓✓	

www.reel.com
OVER 100,000 MOVIES

ORIGIN US	Here is a mixture of news, gossip, interviews, event
SPEED ✓✓✓✓	listings and US-style outright selling. The content is
INFO ✓✓✓✓	good and you can get carried away browsing. The
VALUE ✓✓✓	search facility is very good but shipping to the UK
EASE ✓✓✓✓	costs a minimum of $6. Watch out for local taxes

and ensure that you can actually play the video in
the UK. Also sells DVD and CDs.

Memorabilia

www.vinmag.com
POSTERS, CARDS AND T-SHIRTS

ORIGIN UK	Vintage magazines stand-up cutouts and magazine
SPEED ✓✓✓✓	covers complete the picture from this established
INFO ✓✓✓✓	dealer. Shipping to the UK starts at around $2, but it
VALUE ✓✓✓	depends on how much you spend.
EASE ✓✓✓✓	

www.asseenonscreen.com
AS SEEN ON SCREEN

ORIGIN UK	At this site you can buy what you see on the screen,
SPEED ✓✓✓✓	your favourite star's shirt or dress can be replicated
INFO ✓✓✓	just for you. You have to register first, and then you
VALUE ✓✓✓	get access to the product list, which is vast. You can
EASE ✓✓✓✓	also search by film and TV show.

www.propstore.co.uk
PROPS FOR SALE

ORIGIN UK	An extensive selection of props and replicas await
SPEED ✓✓✓✓	you here with everything from snow globes to cloth-
INFO ✓✓✓✓	ing. Each piece is unique and has been bought from
VALUE ✓✓	the relevant film company and a provenance is
EASE ✓✓✓✓	provided.

Music

*Before spending your hard earned cash on CDs it's worth investi-
gating MP3. MP3 technology allows the compression of a music
track into a file, which can be stored and played back.*

*An MP3 player can be downloaded free onto your PC from several
sites, the best being the original at* **www.mp3.com** *or the popular*
www.real.com *and its RealPlayer. It takes minutes to download the
player and if you play CDs on your PC it will also record them.*

You'll then be able to listen to samples available on music stores. Once you've joined the MP3 revolution, there's an amazing amount of free music available, start at either web site where there are excellent search facilities. Other good MP3 players can be found at:

www.winamp.com
www.sonique.com
www.liquidaudio.com

Sonique is the best looking, but you can do more with Winamp.

Other sites with lots of MP3 downloads that are worth checking out are listed below.

www.artistdirect.com – great design, with the latest music news and tunes from over 100,000 artists.

www.audiofind.com – brilliant search engine, many free downloads.

www.eclassical.com – many free classical greats and many more to buy.

www.eatsleepmusic.com – free karaoke! You need RealPlayer to play.

www.emusic.com – over 6,700 artists, great but you have to pay.

www.listen.com – good for previewing a wide variety of music.

www.mp3example.com – well categorised, great for links.

www.mp3-mac.com – MP3 for Mac users.

www.mp3meta.com – excellent for links and information on MP3.

www.soundresource.net – great for sound effects – some rude!

Have a look at www.100topmp3sites.com *who list all the good MP3 sites including specialist ones.*

If you're in a band you can apply to have your music available to download on some of the sites, BT's specialist site www.getoutthere.bt.com *is particularly good, but also try the excellent* www.2bdiscovered.com *and* www.iuma.com

www.taxi.com
FOR UNSIGNED BANDS

ORIGIN US	Looking to get a music contract for your band? You
SPEED ✓✓✓✓	should start here, there's loads of information,
INFO ✓✓✓✓	contacts and links that will help you on the rocky
EASE ✓✓✓✓	road to success and stardom – well that's the theory
	anyway! British bands can try **www.burbs.co.uk**

www.joescafe.com/bands
BAND NAMES

ORIGIN US	So you can't think of a name for your band? Here is
SPEED ✓✓✓✓	the 'Band-o-matic' which will offer all sorts of never
INFO ✓✓✓✓	before used band names in seconds. We got Batman
VALUE ✓✓✓✓	the Giant Walking Dildo...
EASE ✓✓✓✓	

Downloading free music

www.napster.com
THE NAPSTER MUSIC COMMUNITY

ORIGIN US	Much has been written about Napster and its effect
SPEED ✓✓✓	on the music industry and its demise has been exag-
INFO ✓✓✓✓	gerated as you can still get lots of free music there.
VALUE ✓✓✓✓✓	Once you've downloaded the Napster program, you
EASE ✓✓✓	can locate and download your favourite music in
	MP3 format from one convenient, easy-to-use web
	site. This means that you can literally share the
	downloaded music of thousands of other MP3 fans

for free. All the court cases and the judgements against it will mean that eventually we'll have to start paying, which, for the artists involved, will be a good thing.

Try also visiting Open Nap at **http://opennap.sourceforge.net** this is a free program where you can select some of the many specialist and general servers which hold music, (see **www.napigator.com** for a server list) then use the program to search them for the music you like.

You could also check out the more complicated world of Gnutella (**www.gnutella.co.uk**), which sounds like something you spread on toast, but is basically a mini search engine and file sharing system in one site. It's really a network of thousands of computer users, all of whom use Gnutella software 'clones' which link them directly to other users to find music, movies and other files. At **www.gnutelliums.com** you'll find more similar programs that do the same thing, but may be easier to use or just more efficient.

Other similar sites:

www.aimster.com – Aimster combines AOL's instant message service with the ability to search for files and trade them with other users of the network, of Gnutella or even of Napster. The new version includes encryption software, so nobody can monitor your files while they're in transit and will even tell you which other AOL messenger buddies use it.

www.imesh.com – iMesh is really a Napster clone; you type in an artist and song, and then a list of available matches from a centralised server appears. Since it's an Israeli site, it's likely to be immune from U.S. copyright lawsuits, so it'll probably be around for a while yet.

www.espra.net – a new version of espra is now available to download, it offers anonymity because it doesn't work from a central point like the other sharing software, so, in theory, you can download to your heart's content.

www.musicnet.com – Musicnet is due to be launched in autumn 2001, it will offer official downloads from some of the biggest music companies and top stars, but you'll have to pay for them.

Buying Music

It's as well to start by checking prices of CDs through price comparison sites such as those listed on page 293. These will take you to the store offering the best combination of price and postage.

All the stores listed below offer good value plus a bit extra.

www.jungle.com
JUNGLE MANIA!

ORIGIN	UK
SPEED	✓✓✓✓
INFO	✓✓✓✓
VALUE	✓✓✓
EASE	✓✓✓✓

Jungle is easy but it's lost some of the fun and value it used to have. You get all the latest in music and a massive back catalogue and there's good information even on obscure albums. They also have offers on DVDs and videos, phones, electrical goods and games for PCs and other formats, plus a wide selection of computers, software, hardware and consumables (discs, ink cartridges etc). There is a loyalty scheme but delivery is no longer free, it starts at just over £1. Jungle also offers e-mail and an order tracking service.

www.hmv.co.uk
HIS MASTERS VOICE ONLINE

ORIGIN UK	Excellent features and offers on the latest CDs and
SPEED ✓✓✓✓	videos. There are sections on most aspects of music
INFO ✓✓✓✓✓	as well as video, DVD and games with a good
VALUE ✓✓✓	search facility. You can listen to selections from
EASE ✓✓✓✓	albums before buying if you have RealPlayer.
	Spoken word or books on tape are available as well.

www.virginmega.com
THE VIRGIN MEGA-STORE

ORIGIN US	Loads of music categories means that you are spoilt
SPEED ✓✓✓	for choice and you get good prices, though delivery
INFO ✓✓✓✓	is expensive. There is the usual search facility and
VALUE ✓✓✓	loads of recommendation to help you. Become a
EASE ✓✓✓✓	Virgin V.I.P. and get special offers just for you. An
	interesting feature is the Virgin free radio. The site is
	a little slow.

www.cdnow.com
NOT JUST CDs

ORIGIN US	One of the original music sites and one of the easiest
SPEED ✓✓✓✓	to use, it has lots of features: downloads which
INFO ✓✓✓✓✓	enable you to sample albums for 30 days; a video
VALUE ✓✓✓	section; and a recommendation service.
EASE ✓✓✓✓	Unfortunately, UK residents can't take advantage of
	the excellent custom CD service.

www.cduniverse.com
FOR THE WIDEST RANGE AND GREAT OFFERS

ORIGIN US	Probably the site with the very best offers. There is a
SPEED ✓✓✓	massive range to choose from and delivery normally
INFO ✓✓✓✓	takes only five days. You can also buy games, DVDs
VALUE ✓✓✓✓	and videos. Excellent, but can be quite slow.
EASE ✓✓✓✓	

For more great offers on CDs try these sites:

www.101cd.com – renowned for offering good
value, 1.6 million titles to choose from.

www.recordstore.co.uk – choose from thousands of
vinyl records, CDs, T-shirts, record bags and
assorted DJ gear.

www.musicbox.cd – CDs, videos and DVD and
postage is only £1 whatever the size of order. Nice
design too.

www.towerrecords.co.uk – wide variety and some
good offers – better service than you get from the
real store.

www.cd-wow.com – chart music at great prices.

www.amazon.co.uk – as good as you'd expect from
Amazon.

www.audiostreet.co.uk – some good prices, free
delivery in UK.

www.secondsounds.com – used and new CDs from £7.

www.htfr.co.uk
HARD TO FIND RECORDS

ORIGIN	UK
SPEED	✓✓✓
INFO	✓✓✓✓
VALUE	✓✓✓
EASE	✓✓✓

Although they specialise in new and deleted house,
garage, techno, electro, disco, funk, soul and hip-
hop vinyl, they will try and find any record previ-
ously released. They also offer a complete service to
all budding and serious DJs.

Bands, groups and stars

www.ubl.com
THE ULTIMATE BAND LIST

ORIGIN US	It is the place for mountains of information on
SPEED ✓✓✓✓	groups or singers. It has a totally brilliant search
INFO ✓✓✓✓✓	facility, and you can buy from the site as well,
VALUE ✓✓✓✓	although the prices are not as good as elsewhere.
EASE ✓✓✓✓	

For a similar, but better organised site try
www.allmusic.com where you can also get excellent
information and videos too.

www.eartothesound.fsnet.co.uk
REVIEWS AND RATINGS

ORIGIN US	They call themselves the ultimate review site and it's
SPEED ✓✓✓✓	really great, except that they concentrate almost
INFO ✓✓✓✓	entirely on rock music, so if that's your poison then
EASE ✓✓✓✓	it's perfect.

Music TV and magazine sites

www.bbc.co.uk/totp/
www.totp.beeb.com
Top of the Pops

ORIGIN UK	The *Top of the Pops* sites are different, the site at
SPEED ✓✓✓✓	bbc.co.uk is more of a magazine, the one at
INFO ✓✓✓✓✓	beeb.com basically a shop and both are aimed at
EASE ✓✓✓	teenagers. That said, there are loads of good features

and articles as well as competitions and trivia and
lots of information in both of them, so maybe it
doesn't matter which you go to.

www.cdukweb.com
UK's NUMBER ONE MUSIC SHOW

ORIGIN UK
SPEED ✓✓✓✓
INFO ✓✓
EASE ✓✓✓✓

Considering their boast, the web site is a bit of a disappointment, with not much in the way of information or interaction. There are some quizzes, competitions and you can download a few things but it has none of the buzz of the show.

www.mtv.co.uk
MUSIC TELEVISION

ORIGIN UK
SPEED ✓✓✓✓
INFO ✓✓✓✓✓
EASE ✓✓✓

MTV offers loads of info on events, shows and the artists as well as background on the presenters and creative bits like movie and music video clips. Great design.

www.music365.com
MUSIC NEWS

ORIGIN UK
SPEED ✓✓✓✓
INFO ✓✓✓✓✓
EASE ✓✓✓

Fantastic for all the latest gossip and news from the pop world, hot stories, charts, competitions, reviews and you can even sample some of the latest releases too.

www.music-mag.com
NEWS AND REVIEWS

ORIGIN UK
SPEED ✓✓✓✓
INFO ✓✓✓✓
EASE ✓✓✓✓

A good, cool-looking all rounder covering all aspects of modern music in a straightforward style, it has a really good section on clubbing and the latest dance news. There's also a good links section.

www.nme.com
NEW MUSICAL EXPRESS

ORIGIN UK
SPEED ✓✓✓
INFO ✓✓✓✓✓
EASE ✓✓✓✓

If you're a rock fan then this is where it's at. There's all the usual information, it's well laid out and easy to access. The archived articles are its greatest asset, featuring 150,000 artists and every article, feature and review they've ever published plus full UK discographies, pictures, e-cards and links to the best web sites.

www.q4music.com
Q MAGAZINE

ORIGIN UK
SPEED ✓✓✓
INFO ✓✓✓✓✓
EASE ✓✓✓✓

A music magazine site that reflects its parent magazine extremely well, with over 18,000 reviews, plus features and articles that cover most aspects of music, it doesn't miss much.

www.popworld.com
WHERE POP COMES FIRST

ORIGIN UK
SPEED ✓✓✓✓
INFO ✓✓✓✓
EASE ✓✓✓

Brilliant new site that concentrates on pop, it's fun and has great graphics. You have to register to join but once you're in you get access to competitions, features on your favourite bands, clips from Popworld TV, fashion tips and much more. You need the latest Flash download from Macromedia to get the best out of it.

www.thebox.co.uk
SMASH HITS YOU CONTROL

ORIGIN UK
SPEED ✓✓✓✓
INFO ✓✓✓✓
EASE ✓✓✓✓

Similar to 365 and Q but with added features such as the ability for you to select a tune to be played on their TV channel and you can influence their overall selection by voting for your favourite songs.

www.musicstation.com/musicnewswire
MUSIC STOP-PRESS

ORIGIN US	All the latest music headlines plus background arti-
SPEED ✓✓✓✓	cles and links to hundreds of music sites.
INFO ✓✓✓✓✓	
EASE ✓✓✓✓	

Sites for specific types of music

www.darkerthanblue.com/
HOME OF BLACK MUSIC

ORIGIN UK	Very well-designed site dedicated to black-influenced
SPEED ✓✓✓✓	music and musicians, it has all the latest news, gig
INFO ✓✓✓✓✓	guides, artist features and downloads as well as
EASE ✓✓✓✓	sections on reggae, garage, soul and hip-hop.

www.bluesworld.com
HOMAGE TO THE BLUES

ORIGIN US	If you're into the blues then this is your kind of site.
SPEED ✓✓✓	There are interviews, memorabilia, 78's auctions,
INFO ✓✓✓✓	bibliographies, discographies and lists of links to
EASE ✓✓✓✓	other blues sites. You can order CDs via 'Roots and
	Rhythm' and if the mood takes you, order a guitar
	too.

www.classicalmusic.co.uk
EVERYTHING YOU NEED TO KNOW ABOUT
CLASSICAL MUSIC

ORIGIN UK	Excellent for lovers of classical music, with articles,
SPEED ✓✓✓✓	guides, reviews and concert listings, you can also
INFO ✓✓✓✓✓	buy CDs from the Global Music Network who
EASE ✓✓✓	aren't the cheapest so it may pay to buy elsewhere.

www.operadata.co.uk
OPERA NOW MAGAZINE

ORIGIN	UK
SPEED	✓✓✓✓
INFO	✓✓✓✓✓
EASE	✓✓✓

This site offers opera listings and provides background to the history of opera. To get the most out of it you have to subscribe to *Opera Now* magazine. For the *Opera* magazine site go to www.opera.co.uk

Other key classical music sites:
www.classical.net – great for information.
www.classicalhub.com – reviews and articles.
www.eclassical.com – download MP3s, many are free.
www.mdcmusic.co.uk – good offers on CDs.
www.orchestranet.co.uk – excellent selection of links.

www.countrymusic.org.uk
UK COUNTRY MUSIC SCENE

ORIGIN	UK
SPEED	✓✓✓✓
INFO	✓✓✓✓
EASE	✓✓✓✓

A pretty naff-looking site with lots of links and information on the country music scene in Britain. See also www.thatscountry.com which is excellent if a little slow.

www.anthems.com
DANCE, HOUSE AND GARAGE

ORIGIN	UK
SPEED	✓✓✓✓
INFO	✓✓✓✓✓
EASE	✓✓✓

Great design combined with brilliant content, there's everything here for dance fans, news, and info on raves, samples of the latest mixes or if you're feeling rich you can buy them too, although you'll probably find cheaper elsewhere.

For an alternative view of the dance scene try www.fly.co.uk who have a real urban look to their site. For links to over 500 dance-related sites and a complete listing of new releases go to www.juno.co.uk

www.burnitblue.com
BURN IT BLUE

ORIGIN UK
SPEED ✓✓✓✓
INFO ✓✓✓✓✓
EASE ✓✓✓✓

Concentrating on dance and club culture this coolly designed site offers up all the information you need to keep up with the scene; it's been critically acclaimed as one of the best sites of its type.

www.folkmusic.net
FOLK ON THE WEB

ORIGIN UK
SPEED ✓✓✓✓
INFO ✓✓✓✓
EASE ✓✓✓✓

A straightforward site from *Living Traditions* magazine, a collection of articles, features, reviews and news.

www.thedsc.com
HIP-HOP AND RAP

ORIGIN UK
SPEED ✓✓✓✓
INFO ✓✓✓✓
EASE ✓✓✓✓

Da saga continues... news, reviews and features on hip-hop, there's a good selection of links to other related sites and if you're a real fan you can voice your opinions by becoming a writer for them. See also **www.britishhiphop.co.uk** for information on the UK scene.

www.playlouder.com
INDIE MUSIC

ORIGIN US
SPEED ✓✓✓
INFO ✓✓✓✓
EASE ✓✓✓✓

Great graphics and excellent design make Playlouder stand out from the crowd, it covers the Indie music scene in depth with all the usual features, but with a bit more style. Another really well-designed web site covering Indie music in great depth is Channel Fly **www.channelfly.com** – take your pick!

www.jazzonln.com
JAZZ ONLINE

ORIGIN US
SPEED ✓✓✓✓
INFO ✓✓✓✓✓
EASE ✓✓✓✓

Whether you need help in working your way through the minefield that is jazz music, or you know what you want, Jazz Online can provide it. Its easy format covers all styles and it has a brill search facility. There is a good chat section and you can ask 'Jazz Messenger' just about anything. You can't buy from the site but there are links to Amazon's music section. Try also www.jazze.com and the beautifully designed www.jazzcorner.com

www.rbpage.com
R&B AND SOUL

ORIGIN US
SPEED ✓✓✓✓
INFO ✓✓✓✓
EASE ✓✓✓✓

The R&B page is the place to go if you've got soul, and you've got it bad. You can sample the latest releases, catch up on the R&B news, read reviews or artist biographies and there's a great set of links too.

www.icrunch.co.uk
ALTERNATIVE MUSIC

ORIGIN UK
SPEED ✓✓✓✓
INFO ✓✓✓✓
VALUE ✓✓✓
EASE ✓✓✓✓

Download music and keep up with the latest bands in the alternative music scene at this really well-designed site. It offers exclusive DJ mixes, live performances and prides itself on its quality.

Music information

www.clickmusic.co.uk
EVERYTHING YOU NEED TO KNOW ABOUT MUSIC

ORIGIN UK
SPEED ✓✓✓✓
INFO ✓✓✓✓✓
EASE ✓✓✓✓

This is great for all music fans. It has quick access to details on any particular band, tickets, and downloads, gigs or gossip. Shopping is straightforward using their Best 10 listings, just click on the store or use the search engine to find something specific. The search engine needs improving though. See also **www.musites.com** where you can find a rather variable but improving music search engine.

www.dotmusic.com
ALL THE MUSIC NEWS

ORIGIN UK
SPEED ✓✓✓✓
INFO ✓✓✓✓✓
VALUE ✓✓
EASE ✓✓✓✓

Get the latest 'insider' views from the music industry, with reviews, charts, chat and a good value online shop. These combined with great design make this an excellent site. You can also access this site from some WAP phones.

www.musicsearch.com
THE INTERNET'S MUSIC SEARCH ENGINE

ORIGIN US
SPEED ✓✓✓✓
INFO ✓✓✓✓
EASE ✓✓

Not that easy-to-use, but keep at it if you need to find that track or artist, or need information on a particular instrument or commercial aspect of music. You can search the online stores for good deals or where to get the best range.

Learning music

www.listensmart.com/learn/music/
LEARN ABOUT MUSIC

ORIGIN US
SPEED ✓✓✓✓
INFO ✓✓✓✓✓
EASE ✓✓✓✓

Excellent overview of most major musical instruments, plus links to related web sites. It also has descriptions for the general structure of music, as well as sound demos, history and much more. Check out **www.learnmusic.iwarp.com/main.html** which is a British site that also has good information. Long-winded though the site URL is, it's worth visiting **www.si.umich.edu/chico/mhn/enclpdia.html** where you can find a music encyclopaedia in which you can sample the sound of many instruments.

www.happynote.com/music/learn.html
LEARN MUSIC WITH A GAME

ORIGIN US
SPEED ✓✓✓✓
INFO ✓✓✓✓
EASE ✓✓✓✓

You download the game, which helps you learn the basics, but the more you learn and the better you get the higher the score. See also **www.talentz.com/MusicEducation/index.mv**

Sites for specific instruments

General
www.harmony-central.com – all sorts of instruments reviewed and rated.

Strings
www.guitar.com – good all rounder, all you need to know.
www.guitarsite.com – masses of information.
www.aic.se/basslob – playing the bass.
www.sitar.co.uk – comprehensive plus good links.

www.violin-world.com – complete resource for all string instruments.

Percussion
www.drummersweb.com – drummers' delight.
www.drumnetwork.com – includes a virtual drum kit and the latest hot licks!
www.thepercussionist.com – masses of information and lessons.

Wind
www.brassworld.co.uk – guide for all types of brass player.
www.wfg.sneezy.org – woodwind.
www.saxophone.org – great for info and links.

Electronic
http://nmc.uoregon.edu/emi – great introduction to electronic music and instruments.

Keyboard
www.artdsm.com/music.html – complete piano course.
www.pianoshop.co.uk – masses of links, pianos for sale and information on learning.

Sheet music

www.sunhawk.com
DOWNLOAD SHEET MUSIC

ORIGIN US	Well-designed site where you can download music
SPEED ✓✓✓	from a wide variety of styles including pop,
INFO ✓✓✓✓	Christian, country, Broadway, jazz and classical, you
VALUE ✓✓✓	have to pay but there are some freebies.
EASE ✓✓✓✓	

Lyrics

www.lyrics.com
THE WORDS TO HUNDREDS OF SONGS

ORIGIN US	There are songs from over 100 bands and artists
SPEED ✓✓✓✓	including Oasis, Madonna, Britney Spears and
INFO ✓✓✓✓	Queen. You can also make requests and see if you
VALUE ✓✓✓✓	know the words to any of the songs in the 'most
EASE ✓✓✓✓	wanted' section. Don't expect to find any old
	favourites or classics though.

Other good lyric sites:
www.execpc.com/~suden – songs from the 50s, 60s and 70s.
www.songfile.com – 2 million songs!
www.sing365.com – listed by artist, good search engine.

www.kissthisguy.com
MISHEARD LYRICS

ORIGIN US	Mr Misheard lists all those lyrics that you thought
SPEED ✓✓✓✓	were being sung but in reality you were just not
INFO ✓✓✓✓	quite listening properly. We liked 'I am the fire
EASE ✓✓✓✓	starter' misheard as 'I am a big fat hamster' but
	there are hundreds more.

Concerts and tickets

www.liveconcerts.com
WELCOME TO THE CYBERCAST

ORIGIN US	Watch live concerts online! A great idea but let
SPEED ✓✓✓	down by 'net congestion'. You need RealPlayer to
INFO ✓✓✓✓	see the concerts and listen to the interviews and
VALUE ✓✓✓	recordings. It's very good for sampling different
EASE ✓✓✓✓	types of music and you can buy CDs as well. See
	also **www.primeticket.com**

www.bigmouth.co.uk
UK's MOST COMPREHENSIVE GIG GUIDE

ORIGIN	UK
SPEED	✓✓✓✓
INFO	✓✓✓✓
EASE	✓✓✓✓

UK based, with lots of links to band sites, news, events listing and information on what's up and coming. Great search facilities and the ability to buy tickets make this a really useful site for gig lovers everywhere. It's geared to rock and pop though. For tour dates in the USA try www.tourdates.com

www.ticketmaster.co.uk
TICKETS FOR EVERYTHING

ORIGIN	UK
SPEED	✓✓✓✓
INFO	✓✓✓✓✓
VALUE	✓✓✓✓
EASE	✓✓✓

Book tickets for just about anything and you can run searches by venue, city or date. The site is split into four key sections:

Theatre – theatre, classical, dance, comedy and events.

Concerts – gigs, jazz, clubs, rock and pop.

Family – shows, anything from Disney on Ice to air shows.

Sports – tickets for virtually every sporting occasion.

www.concertphoto.co.uk
PHOTOS OF YOUR FAVOURITE BANDS

ORIGIN	UK
SPEED	✓✓✓✓
INFO	✓✓✓✓
VALUE	✓✓✓
EASE	✓✓✓✓

OK so you've been to the gig and you didn't take a camera, well the chances are that Pete Still has a photo available for you to buy from this great web site. There are hundreds of bands to choose from both old and new and he's covered the major festivals too. Costs vary according to size and quantity.

Nature and the environment

The Internet offers charities and organisations a chance to high-light their work in a way that is much more creative than ever before, it also offers the chance for us to get in-depth information on those species and issues that interest us.

www.panda.org
THE WORLD WIDE FUND FOR NATURE

ORIGIN UK
SPEED ✓✓✓
INFO ✓✓✓✓✓
EASE ✓✓✓✓

Called the WWF Global Network, this is the official site for the WWF. Information on projects designed to save the world's endangered species by protecting their environment. You can: find out about the charity and how to contribute; visit the photo, video and art galleries; or use the kids' section to teach children about wildlife. If you want to get involved you can 'take action today' over issues such as the location of dams or more rainforest going under the saw.

An American organisation called the National Wildlife Fund has a similar excellent site at **www.nwf.org**

www.nhm.ac.uk
THE NATURAL HISTORY MUSEUM

ORIGIN UK
SPEED ✓✓✓
INFO ✓✓✓✓✓
EASE ✓✓✓✓

A superb user-friendly web site that covers every-thing from ants to eclipses. You can get the latest news, check out exhibitions, take a tour, browse the Dinosaur database or explore the wildlife garden. There are details on the collections and contacts for answers to specific questions. See also the Smithsonian National Museum of Natural History who also has a great site at **www.mnh.si.edu**

www.bbc.co.uk/nature.

WILDLIFE EXPOSED

ORIGIN UK
SPEED ✓✓✓
INFO ✓✓✓✓
VALUE ✓✓
EASE ✓✓✓✓

A brilliant nature offering from the BBC with sections on key wildlife programmes and animal groups. The information is good and enhanced by view clips. Also visit www.bbcwild.com the commercial side of the BBC wildlife unit with over 100,000 wildlife images available to buy. It's aimed at commercial organisations but plans to offer pictures for personal use at £15 each. It is a great place to browse for the remarkable images in the premium selection.

www.naturenet.net

COUNTRYSIDE, NATURE AND CONSERVATION

ORIGIN UK
SPEED ✓✓✓
INFO ✓✓✓✓✓
EASE ✓✓✓✓

Ignore the rather twee graphics and you'll find a great deal of information about nature in the UK. Their interests include: countryside law, upkeep of nature reserves, voluntary work, education and environmental news. You can also search the site for specifics and there is a good set of links to related sites. See also www.wildlifetrust.org.uk who care for over 2,000 of Britain's nature reserves. For details on all our nature reserves go to www.englishnature.org.uk who supply maps, photos and information on why reserves are so important – all on an excellent site.

www.foe.co.uk

FRIENDS OF THE EARTH

ORIGIN UK
SPEED ✓✓✓✓
INFO ✓✓✓✓
EASE ✓✓✓✓

Not as worthy as you might imagine, this site offers a stack of information on food, pollution, green power, protecting wildlife in your area and the latest campaign news.

www.envirolink.org
THE ONLINE ENVIRONMENTAL COMMUNITY

ORIGIN US
SPEED ✓✓✓✓
INFO ✓✓✓✓✓
EASE ✓✓✓

A huge site focused on personal involvement in environment issues. There are seven key sections: organisations, educational resources, jobs, governmental resources, actions you can take to help, environment links and information on the contributors. There is also a good search facility on environment-related topics.

For real campaigners go to the Greenpeace site **www.greenpeace.org** where you can find out about their latest activities and how to get involved. For more campaign work check out the International Fund for Animal Welfare who do a great deal of work protecting animals and their environment. Find out how you can help by going to **www.ifaw.org**

www.planetdiary.com
WHAT'S REALLY HAPPENING ON THE PLANET

ORIGIN US
SPEED ✓✓✓
INFO ✓✓✓✓✓
EASE ✓✓✓✓

Every week Planetdiary monitors and records world events in geological, astronomical, meteorological, biological and environmental terms and relays them back via this web site. It's done by showing an icon on a map of the world, which you then click on to find out more. Although very informative, a visit can leave you a little depressed.

http://library.thinkquest.org/C003603
FORCES OF NATURE

ORIGIN US
SPEED ✓✓✓✓
INFO ✓✓✓✓✓
EASE ✓✓✓✓

An amazing site which covers all the known natural disasters, giving background information, simulations and multimedia explanations with experiments for you to try at home. See also **www.naturalhazards.org**

www.coralcay.org
HOW YOU CAN JOIN IN

ORIGIN UK
SPEED ✓✓
INFO ✓✓✓✓
EASE ✓✓✓✓

In Coral Cay's words its aim is 'providing resources to help sustain livelihoods and alleviate poverty through the protection, restoration and management of coral reefs and tropical forests'. Sign up for an expedition or a science project in Honduras or the Philippines. See also www.ecovolunteer.com if you want to give your services to a specific animal benefit project.

Animals

www.arkive.org.uk
RAISING AWARENESS OF ENDANGERED SPECIES

ORIGIN UK
SPEED ✓✓✓
INFO ✓✓✓✓✓
EASE ✓✓✓✓

Sponsored by the Wildscreen Trust this site will eventually catalogue and picture all the world's endangered species. Each animal and plant has a page devoted to it giving details on how and where it lives, including pictures and movie clips. You can help by donating pictures and film.

www.wdcs.org
WHALE AND DOLPHIN SOCIETY

ORIGIN UK
SPEED ✓✓✓✓
INFO ✓✓✓✓
EASE ✓✓✓✓

All the latest news and developments in the fight to save whales and dolphins. There's also information on them, how and where they live, a sightings and strandings section and details of how to book a whale-watching holiday. See also the excellent www.cetacea.org where you can get background info on every species of dolphin, whale and porpoise. For fish, try www.flmnh.ufl.edu/fish where you can find a good overview plus links and a good selection of photographs.

Take a visit to the excellent Sea Watch site **www.seawatchfoundation.org.uk** you can learn more about cetaceans, and their sightings around the UK.

www.africam.com
ALWAYS LIVE, ALWAYS WILD

ORIGIN	S.AFRICA
SPEED	✓✓✓
INFO	✓✓✓✓✓
EASE	✓✓✓✓

Web cameras have come a long way and this is one of the best uses of them. There are strategically placed cameras at water holes and parks around Africa and other of the world's wildlife areas, and you can tap in for a look at any time. You have to register to get the best out of it, but even a quick visit is rewarding. See also the excellent elephant only site at **http://elephant.elehost.com** and for large carnivores check out **www.lioncrusher.com** who have a good picture archive.

www.bugbios.com
BUGS AND INSECTS

ORIGIN	US
SPEED	✓✓✓✓
INFO	✓✓✓✓✓
EASE	✓✓✓✓

A beautifully designed site exposing insects as miracles of nature, with amazing macro-photography, information and links. For 'The Bug Club' go to **www.insect-world.com/insects** which is more comprehensive, but less entertaining than Bugbios.

www.birds.com
ALL ABOUT BIRDS

ORIGIN	US
SPEED	✓✓✓
INFO	✓✓✓✓✓
EASE	✓✓✓

An online directory and guide to birds covering both wild and pets, biased to America but excellent except that it's a bit too commercial. For the RSPB go to **www.rspb.org.uk** who have a nice site detailing what they do, and how you can help. Also try **www.ornithology.com** which is dedicated to wild birds.

For a run down on British birds go to
www.birdsofbritain.co.uk which is a monthly web
magazine for bird watchers.

www.prehistoricplanet.com
PREHISTORIC PLANET

ORIGIN US	A great site put together by some dinosaur enthusi-
SPEED ✓✓✓✓	asts. It's got information on what the planet looked
INFO ✓✓✓✓✓	like in prehistoric times, you can ask a palaeontolo-
EASE ✓✓✓✓	gist a question or just browse the many articles. For

other dinosaur sites try **www.dinosaur.org** which is
a bit messy, but packed with facts or the excellent
BBC site **www.bbc.co.uk/dinosaurs**.

Zoos and safari parks

www.safaripark.co.uk
SAFARI ONLINE

ORIGIN UK	A detailed site on the UK's safari parks including
SPEED ✓✓✓	opening times, animal information and facts on
INFO ✓✓✓✓	endangered species. At **www.zoo-keeper.co.uk** you
EASE ✓✓✓	get information on the most common zoo animals

and some background about what it's like to work
with them.

www.sandiegozoo.org
SAN DIEGO ZOO

ORIGIN US	Probably the best zoo site. You can get conservation
SPEED ✓✓✓✓	information, check out the latest arrivals and
INFO ✓✓✓✓	browse their excellent photo gallery. The highlight is
EASE ✓✓✓✓	definitely the Panda Cam.

Other good zoo sites:

www.bristolzoo.co.uk – good looking and fun for kids.

www.dublinzoo.ie – slow but good content.

www.marwell.org.uk – masses to see and do.

www.londonzoo.co.uk – excellent and comprehensive zoo site, also covers Whipsnade Wildlife Park.

www.bornfree.co.uk
Zoo check

ORIGIN	UK
SPEED	✓✓✓
INFO	✓✓✓✓
EASE	✓✓✓✓

Zoo Check is a charity whose mission is to promote Born Free's core belief that wildlife belongs in the wild. They expose the suffering of captive wild animals and investigate neglect and cruelty. They want tighter legislation and the phasing out of all traditional zoos. If you want to know more then this is where to go.

News and the media

The standard of web sites in this sector is usually very high making it difficult to pick out one or two winners, just find one which appeals to you and you won't go far wrong.

www.sky.co.uk/news
The ultimate news site

ORIGIN	UK
SPEED	✓✓✓
INFO	✓✓✓✓✓
EASE	✓✓✓✓

Sky News has fast developed a reputation for excellence and that is reflected in their web site. It has a well rounded news service with good coverage across the world as well as the UK. You can view news clips, listen to news items or just browse the site. There are special sections on sport, business, technology and even a few games.

www.bbc.co.uk/news
FROM THE BBC

ORIGIN UK	As you'd expect the BBC site is excellent – similar to
SPEED ✓✓✓	Sky but without the adverts. You can also get the
INFO ✓✓✓✓✓	news in several languages and tune into the World
EASE ✓✓✓✓	Service or any of their radio stations.

www.itn.co.uk
INDEPENDENT TELEVISION NEWS

ORIGIN UK	A good site in that it doesn't bombard you with
SPEED ✓✓✓✓	everything at once, you get the main headline and a
INFO ✓✓✓✓	sections listing for further information. See also
EASE ✓✓✓✓✓	www.teletext.co.uk who offer a similar very clearly
	laid out site.

www.cnn.com
THE AMERICAN VIEW

ORIGIN US	CNN is superb on detail and breaking news with
SPEED ✓✓✓	masses of background information on each story.
INFO ✓✓✓✓✓	Has plenty of feature pieces too. However, it is
EASE ✓✓✓✓	biased towards the American audience, for a similar
	service try www.abcnews.com

www.telegraph.co.uk
NEWSPAPERS ONLINE

ORIGIN UK	The *Telegraph* has the best site for news and layout
SPEED ✓✓✓	with all its sections mirrored very effectively on the
INFO ✓✓✓✓	site. The other major newspapers with sites worth a
EASE ✓✓✓✓	visit can be found here:

www.dailymail.co.uk – not so much the paper as a
   portal for Associated Newspapers, which is disappointing.

www.guardian.co.uk – clean site with lots of added
   features and guides.

www.thesun.co.uk – very good representation of the
paper with all you'd expect.

www.fish4news.co.uk
LOCAL NEWS MADE EASY

ORIGIN UK	An outstanding web site, just type in your postcode
SPEED ✓✓✓✓	and back will come a collated local 'newspaper'
INFO ✓✓✓✓✓	with regional news headlines, sport and links to the
EASE ✓✓✓✓	source papers sites and small ads.

www.whatthepaperssay.co.uk
WHEN YOU'VE NOT GOT TIME

ORIGIN UK	Can't be bothered to sift through the papers? At this
SPEED ✓✓✓	site you can quickly take in the key stories and be
INFO ✓✓✓✓✓	linked through to the relevant newspaper site too.
EASE ✓✓✓✓	You can also sign up to its daily e-mail bulletin so
	you need never buy a paper again.

www.ecola.com
NEWS DIRECTORY

ORIGIN US	A listing service that concentrates on news, it has
SPEED ✓✓✓	links to every major US news site, newspaper, maga-
INFO ✓✓✓✓	zine and resources such as a travel planner. Also has
VALUE ✓✓	excellent features on Europe.
EASE ✓✓✓✓	

www.newsnow.co.uk
NEWS NOW!

ORIGIN UK	A superb news gathering and information service
SPEED ✓✓✓	that you can tailor to your needs and interests. The
INFO ✓✓✓✓✓	layout is confusing at first but it allows you to flick
EASE ✓✓✓	between latest headlines from 3,000 leading news
	sources without visiting each site separately, you can
	then read their choice of stories in full on the

publishers' web sites. See also Moreover, at
www.moreover.com who also offer a free news
service, but with further services such as monitoring
the Net for mentions of your company for example.
They are one to watch for the future.

www.drudgereport.com
Now for the real news

ORIGIN US	One of the most visited sites on the web. It's a pain
SPEED ✓✓✓	to use, but the gossip and tips about upcoming
INFO ✓✓✓✓✓	features in the papers make it worthwhile. One of its
EASE ✓✓	best features is its superb set of links to other news
	sources.

www.foreignreport.com
Predict the future

ORIGIN UK	The Foreign Report team attempt to pick out trends
SPEED ✓✓	and happenings that might lead to bigger interna-
INFO ✓✓✓✓	tional news events. Browsing through their track
EASE ✓✓✓	record shows they're pretty good at it too.

www.wwevents.com
World events

ORIGIN UK	Details of events that are happening in the world
SPEED ✓✓✓✓	today, tomorrow and this weekend all available at
INFO ✓✓✓✓	the touch of a button, it really is that simple. You
EASE ✓✓✓✓	can search by country or even region and county.

Organiser and Diary

www.organizer.com
ORGANISE YOURSELF

ORIGIN US
SPEED ✓✓
INFO ✓✓✓✓
EASE ✓✓✓✓

An American site that is just what it says it is, an organiser that allows you to list all your commitments and it will send e-mail reminders in good time.

www.opendiary.com
THE ONLINE DIARY FOR THE WORLD

ORIGIN US
SPEED ✓✓✓
INFO ✓✓✓✓
EASE ✓✓✓

Your own personal organiser and diary, easy-to-use, genuinely helpful and totally anonymous. Simply register and away you go but follow the rules faithfully or you get deleted. Use it as you would any diary, go public or just browse other entries.

Over 50s

If you're over 50 then you're part of the fastest growing group of Internet users, and some sites have cottoned on to the fact with specific content just for you.

www.idf50.co.uk
I DON'T FEEL FIFTY

ORIGIN UK
SPEED ✓✓✓✓
INFO ✓✓✓✓✓
EASE ✓✓✓

Graham Andrews is retired and this is his irreverent and opinionated magazine site. It's very positive about the power of being over 50 and it has a great deal of motivational advice on how to get the best out of life combined with a superb set of links to useful sites. See also **www.60-plus.co.uk** which is also good fun, and of course, *The Oldie* magazine which can be found at **www.theoldie.co.uk**

www.vavo.com

ONLINE COMMUNITY

ORIGIN UK
SPEED ✓✓✓✓
INFO ✓✓✓✓
VALUE ✓✓✓✓
EASE ✓✓✓

This well laid out site is aimed at over 45s, but it offers a great deal if you register, in terms of special deals on travel, health info, financial advice, consumer tips, education and features on history and politics. There's an online shop with some very good offers and also a great section on making retirement work for you. You can also reminisce and take part in the chat rooms and forums. See also www.age-net.co.uk who take a magazine-style approach and www.maturetymes which is more of online newspaper in style.

http://ourworld.compuserve.com/homepages/SMilne6/silv.htm

SILVER LINKS

ORIGIN UK
SPEED ✓✓✓
INFO ✓✓✓✓✓
EASE ✓✓✓

A long-winded URL, but you are rewarded with an excellent set of links to sites for senior citizens.

www.ageconcern.co.uk

WORKING FOR ALL OLDER PEOPLE

ORIGIN UK
SPEED ✓✓✓✓
INFO ✓✓✓✓✓
EASE ✓✓✓✓

Learn how to get involved with helping older people, get information and practical advice on all aspects of getting old. You can also make a donation. There are also over 50 links to related and special interest sites.

www.passport5oplus.org.uk
LEGAL ADVICE

ORIGIN UK
SPEED ✓✓✓✓
INFO ✓✓✓✓
EASE ✓✓✓✓

A very straightforward site from an organisation that specialises in giving legal advice and information to the over 50s.

www.arp.org.uk
ASSOCIATION OF RETIRED PERSONS

ORIGIN UK
SPEED ✓✓✓✓
INFO ✓✓✓✓✓
EASE ✓✓✓✓

ARP's mission is to change the attitude of society and individuals towards age in order to enhance the quality of life for people over 50 – and this site goes a long way to achieving that. It has great design and plenty of features aimed at helping you get the most out of life. It's excellent for a place to chat if nothing else.

www.hairnet.org
TECHNOLOGY EXPLAINED

ORIGIN UK
SPEED ✓✓✓✓
INFO ✓✓✓✓
EASE ✓✓✓✓

So you've bought the PC and now you need to know how to work it properly? Hairnet explains all through a series of forums and specific courses designed to help you get the most from technology. See also **www.seniornet.org**

www.age-exchange.org.uk
MAKE YOUR MEMORIES MATTER

ORIGIN UK
SPEED ✓✓✓✓
INFO ✓✓✓✓
EASE ✓✓✓✓

Share your experiences and pass them on, Age Exchange aims to 'improve the quality of life for older people by emphasizing the value of their memories to old and young, through pioneering artistic, educational, and welfare activities', they are also active in improving care for older people. This site gives details of how you can join in.

www.sagaholidays.com
HOLIDAYS FOR THE OVER 50S

ORIGIN	UK
SPEED	✓✓✓✓
INFO	✓✓✓✓
VALUE	✓✓✓
EASE	✓✓✓✓

A superbly illustrated and rich site from Saga who've been specialising in holidays for older people for many years. Here you'll find everything from top quality cruises to weekend breaks.

Parenting

As a source of advice the Internet has proved its worth and especially so for parents. As well as information, there are great shops and useful sites that filter out the worst of the web and give advice on specific problems. Some of the education web sites also have useful resources for parents as do the health sites. In addition, there is loads of useful stuff for parents about taking children on holiday and what to do with the children in the UK in the travel section, page 429.

Advice and information

www.babyworld.co.uk
BE PART OF IT

ORIGIN	UK
SPEED	✓✓✓
INFO	✓✓✓✓✓
EASE	✓✓✓✓

Babyworld is an online magazine that covers all aspects of parenthood, there's excellent advice on how to choose the right products for your baby and for the pregnancy itself. Its shopping service was under review at time of writing and some of the graphics were awry.

www.babycentre.co.uk
A HANDS-ON GUIDE

ORIGIN UK
SPEED ✓✓✓
INFO ✓✓✓✓✓
EASE ✓✓✓✓

A superb site with a massive amount of information and links to all aspects of pregnancy, childbirth and early parenthood. The content is provided by experts and you can tailor-make your profile so that you get the right information for you. There's also a series of buying guides to help you make the right decision on baby shopping.

www.breastfeeeding.co.uk
ADVICE ON BREASTFEEDING

ORIGIN UK
SPEED ✓✓✓
INFO ✓✓✓✓✓
EASE ✓✓✓✓

A nice-looking and informative site on breastfeeding; it's got a good sense of fun and it's easy-to-use.

www.babyzone.com
PARENTAL ADVICE

ORIGIN US
SPEED ✓✓✓✓
INFO ✓✓✓✓✓
EASE ✓✓✓

This massive, comprehensive, American site on parenting gives a week-by-week account of pregnancy, information on birth and early childhood. The shop is not open to UK residents, but they have a good set of links to stores that are. See also the similarly well-put-together **www.parentsoup.com** and the basic but informative website **www.amipregnant.com**

www.ukparents.co.uk
YOUR PARENTING LIFELINE

ORIGIN UK
SPEED ✓✓✓✓
INFO ✓✓✓
VALUE ✓✓✓
EASE ✓✓✓✓

Chat, experiences, stories and straightforward advice make this site worth a visit – there's even a forum where you can buy and sell baby goods.

www.miriamstoppard.com
MIRIAM STOPPARD LIFETIME

ORIGIN UK
SPEED ✓✓✓✓
INFO ✓✓✓✓
EASE ✓✓✓✓

An excellent web site from the best selling author with lots of advice on being a parent, how to cope with pregnancy and keeping you and your family healthy. The site is continually being added to, so it's very up-to-date and will become a great resource for parents.

www.babydirectory.com
A–Z OF BEING A PARENT

ORIGIN UK
SPEED ✓✓✓
INFO ✓✓✓
EASE ✓✓✓✓

The Baby Directory catalogue is relevant to most parts of the UK. It lists local facilities plus amenities that care for and occupy your child. The quality of information varies by area though.

www.babyweb.co.uk
BABY PICTURES

ORIGIN UK
SPEED ✓✓✓
INFO ✓✓✓
VALUE ✓✓✓
EASE ✓✓✓

If you want to have a picture of your new arrival and a personalised web page with all the birth details highlighted for all to coo over, here's where to go!

www.gingerbread.org.uk
SUPPORT FOR LONE PARENT FAMILIES

ORIGIN UK
SPEED ✓✓✓
INFO ✓✓✓
EASE ✓✓✓

Gingerbread is an established charity run by lone parents with the aim of providing support to lone parents. The site is fun to use and well designed, the best aspect being that it's available in several languages.

See also **www.oneparentfamilies.org.uk** and Families Need Fathers at **www.fnf.org.uk**

Childcare

www.bestbear.co.uk
MARY POPPINS ONLINE

ORIGIN	UK
SPEED	✓✓✓✓
INFO	✓✓✓✓
EASE	✓✓✓✓

Select your postcode and they will provide you with a list of reputable childcare agencies or nurseries in your area. There are also homepages for parents, childcarers and agencies all with information and ideas. There is also a parents' forum. See also www.sitters.co.uk

www.daycaretrust.org.uk
CHILDCARE ADVICE

ORIGIN	UK
SPEED	✓✓✓
INFO	✓✓✓
EASE	✓✓✓

Daycare Trust is a national childcare charity which works to promote high quality, affordable childcare for all. This site is designed to give you all the information you need on arranging care for your child, there are sections on finance, news and you can become a member.

Shopping

www.bloomingmarvellous.co.uk
MATERNITY, NURSERY AND BABY WEAR

ORIGIN	UK
SPEED	✓✓✓✓
INFO	✓✓✓✓
VALUE	✓✓✓✓
EASE	✓✓✓✓

Excellent online store with a selection of maternity, baby and nurseryware available to buy, or you can order their catalogue. Delivery in the UK is £3.95.

www.mothercare.com
MOTHERCARE

ORIGIN	UK
SPEED	✓✓✓✓
INFO	✓✓✓✓
VALUE	✓✓✓✓
EASE	✓✓✓✓

A nice-looking site with a good selection of baby and toddler products, also clothing, entertainment and equipment. It's good value and there are some excellent offers, delivery is free if you spend over £60, £3 below that. It's not all about shopping though, there are advice sections on baby care, finance, tips on how to keep kids occupied and chat rooms where you can share your experiences.

www.go-help.co.uk
SHOP AND GIVE

ORIGIN	UK
SPEED	✓✓✓
INFO	✓✓✓✓
VALUE	✓✓✓✓
EASE	✓✓✓✓

Go-help is about allowing you to make money for a good cause, whether it is a school, charity or club, of your choice from your Internet shopping. It's basically a store list set in the usual shopping categories, with each store pledging a certain percentage of the amount you spend with them to your chosen beneficiary.

Dealing with areas of concern

BULLYING

www.bullying.co.uk
HOW TO COPE WITH BULLYING

ORIGIN	UK
SPEED	✓✓✓✓
INFO	✓✓✓✓
EASE	✓✓✓✓

Advice for everyone on how to deal with a bully; there are sections on tips for dealing with them, school projects, problem pages and links to related sites.

COMPUTERS AND THE INTERNET

www.cyberpatrol.com
INTERNET FILTERING SOFTWARE

ORIGIN US
SPEED ✓✓✓
INFO ✓✓✓✓
VALUE ✓✓✓
EASE ✓✓✓✓

The best for filtering out unwanted web sites, images and words. As with all similar programs, it quickly becomes outdated but will continue to weed out the worst. You can download a free trial from the site. See also **www.netnanny.com** whose site offers more advice and seems to be updated more regularly.

www.pin-parents.com
PARENTS INFORMATION NETWORK

ORIGIN US
SPEED ✓✓✓✓
INFO ✓✓✓✓✓
VALUE ✓✓✓
EASE ✓✓✓✓

Provides good advice for parents worried about children using computers. It has links to support sites, guidance on how to surf the Net, evaluations of software and buyers guides to PCs.

DRUGS

www.nodrugs.org.uk
YOU DON'T NEED DRUGS TO FEEL GOOD

ORIGIN UK
SPEED ✓✓✓
INFO ✓✓✓✓
EASE ✓✓✓✓

This site gives information on the effects of taking drugs, what they do and how to get help. There are facts and figures on everything from alcohol to ecstasy to tobacco as well as good advice to go with them.

DYSLEXIA

www.bda-dyslexia.org.uk
BRITISH DYSLEXIA ASSOCIATION

ORIGIN UK
SPEED ✓✓✓✓
INFO ✓✓✓✓
EASE ✓✓✓✓

A good starting point for anyone who thinks that their child might be dyslexic. There is masses of information on dyslexia, choosing a school, a list of local Dyslexia Associations where you can get assessment and teaching, articles on the latest research and educational materials for sale. There is also information on adult dyslexia. For similar material visit **www.dyslexia-inst.org.uk** who also offer testing and teaching through their centres.

EATING DISORDERS

www.edauk.com
EATING DISORDERS ASSOCIATION

ORIGIN UK
SPEED ✓✓✓
INFO ✓✓✓✓
EASE ✓✓✓✓

If you think you have a problem with eating then at this site you can get advice and information. It does-n't replace going to the doctor but it's a place to start. There's a youth helpline – 01603 765 050.

HEALTH

www.iemily.com
GIRL'S HEALTH

ORIGIN US
SPEED ✓✓✓
INFO ✓✓✓✓
EASE ✓✓✓✓

A massive A–Z listing of all the issues and problems you might face, it's easy-to-use and the information is straight to the point and often accompanied by articles relating to the subject. If you can't find what you need here try **www.prematuree.com** which is especially useful for older teenage girls. See also section on Health Advice page 200.

MISSING CHILDREN

www.missingkids.co.uk
UK'S MISSING CHILDREN

ORIGIN	UK
SPEED	✓✓✓
INFO	✓✓✓✓✓
EASE	✓✓✓✓

This site is dedicated to reuniting children with their families, the details of those missing are based on police and home office data. You can search by town or date and there's also a section on those who've got back together.

Also try:
www.salvatioarmy.org.uk for their family tracing service, www.missingpersons.org the missing persons helpline or www.icmec.co.uk for the International Centre for Missing Children.

RACISM

www.britkid.org
DEALING WITH RACISM

ORIGIN	UK
SPEED	✓✓✓
INFO	✓✓✓✓✓
EASE	✓✓✓✓

A game that shows how different ethnic groups live in the Britain of today, full of interesting facts and information. There's a serious side, which has background information on dealing with racism, information on different races and their religious beliefs.

SAFETY

www.childalert.co.uk
CHILD SAFETY

ORIGIN	UK
SPEED	✓✓✓
INFO	✓✓✓✓✓
VALUE	✓✓✓
EASE	✓✓✓✓✓

This is about bringing up children in a safe environment; there are tips, product reviews and a shop, stories, links and masses of advice and information. Except for the shop, the site is well-designed and it's easy to find things.

SEX

www.lovelife.uk.com
HERE TO ANSWER YOUR QUESTIONS

ORIGIN UK	Great site that has lots of information on sex as well
SPEED ✓✓✓✓	as games and links to related sites. The emphasis is
INFO ✓✓✓✓✓	on safe sex and AIDS prevention. See also the
EASE ✓✓✓✓	Terence Higgins Trust at **www.tht.org.uk** this is the
	leading AIDS charity. See also section on Health
	page 200.

www.fpa.org.uk
FAMILY PLANNING ASSOCIATION

ORIGIN UK	Straightforward and informative, you can find out
SPEED ✓✓✓	where to get help and there's a good list of web links
INFO ✓✓✓✓	too. See also the British Pregnancy Advisory service
EASE ✓✓✓✓	at **www.bpas.org**

SPEECH

www.speechcontacts.co.uk
SPEECH THERAPY

ORIGIN UK	Information, help and advice on what to do if your
SPEED ✓✓✓	child has speech problems and communication
INFO ✓✓✓	difficulties, with a free regular newsletter.
VALUE ✓✓✓	
EASE ✓✓✓✓	

STRESS AND MENTAL HEALTH

www.at-ease.nsf.org.uk
YOUR MENTAL HEALTH

ORIGIN UK	At-ease offers loads of good advice on how to deal
SPEED ✓✓✓	with stress and is aimed specifically at young people.
INFO ✓✓✓✓	Go to the A–Z section which covers a large range of
EASE ✓✓✓✓	subjects from dealing with aggression to exam stress
	to how to become a volunteer to help others.

www.isma.org.uk/exams.htm
EXAM STRESS

ORIGIN UK	Top tips on coping with exams from the
SPEED ✓✓✓	International Stress Management Association.
INFO ✓✓✓✓	
EASE ✓✓✓✓	

Pets

Pet web sites and online pet shops were one of the biggest growth areas in 1999, but this has tailed off and there have been some closures in the past few months. Some of the sites are very well designed and other retailers should take note.

www.pets-pyjamas.co.uk
THE COMPLETE PETS WEB SITE

ORIGIN UK	An excellent site now split into four sections:
SPEED ✓✓✓	1. Entertainment – quizzes and chat.
INFO ✓✓✓✓	2. Services – vet finder, insurance and a funeral
VALUE ✓✓✓	service.
EASE ✓✓✓✓	3. News and information – topics such as health.
	4. Shopping – via their own shop plus
	www.animail.co.uk a more general value-led
	pet shop and a specialist bookstore.

There are also subsections on dogs, cats and small animals.

For other good online pet information and stores visit:

www.mypetstop.com – superb for information and health advice.

www.petplanet.co.uk – good for the shop and up-to-the-minute news.

www.petpark.co.uk – great for a bargain, catering for a broad range of pets.

www.ukpets.co.uk – a directory of pet shops and suppliers, plus advice.

www.pethealthcare.co.uk

PET INSURANCE

ORIGIN UK	This is a good place to start looking for insurance to
SPEED ✓✓✓	cover your vet's bill.
INFO ✓✓✓✓	
VALUE ✓✓✓	
EASE ✓✓✓✓	

www.pets-on-holiday.com

UK HOLIDAYS WITH PETS

ORIGIN UK	This site is devoted to finding holiday accommoda-
SPEED ✓✓✓	tion where your pets are always welcome simply
INFO ✓✓✓✓	arranged by region, easy. There's also a bookshop
EASE ✓✓✓✓	and a good set of links. See also the useful

www.petswelcome.co.uk and **www.preferredplaces.co.uk** who offer a similar service. For information on quarantine laws go to **www.maff.gov.uk/animalh/quarantine//**

Animal charities

www.rspca.org
THE RSPCA

ORIGIN UK	News (some of which can be quite disturbing) and
SPEED ✓✓✓	information on the work of the charity plus animal
INFO ✓✓✓✓	facts and details on how you can help. There's also a
EASE ✓✓✓	good kids' section. It's a good site but a bit tightly
	packed.

Other charity sites:

www.aht.org.uk – applying clinical and research
   techniques to help animals.
www.animalrescuers.co.uk – a directory of centres
   and people who will help distressed animals.
www.animalrescue.org.uk – fight animal pain and
   suffering.
www.bluecross.org.uk – excellent site with information, help and advice.
www.pdsa.org.uk – Peoples Dispensary for Sick
   Animals has a good-looking site with details on
   how to look after pets and how you can help.
www.petrescue.com – home of the pet action league.
www.nwnet.co.uk/terryreader// – index of charities
   and animal rescue centres.

www.giveusahome.co.uk
RE-HOMING A PET

ORIGIN UK	A nice idea, a web site devoted to helping you
SPEED ✓✓✓	save animals that need to be re-homed, it's
INFO ✓✓✓✓	got a large amount of information by region
EASE ✓✓✓	on shelters, vets and the animals themselves
	as well as an entertaining cartoon for kids.
	See also **www.giveapetahome.co.uk**

TV-related

www.channel4.com/petrescue
PET RESCUE

ORIGIN UK
SPEED ✓✓✓✓
INFO ✓✓✓✓
EASE ✓✓✓✓

Details of the program plus information and links on animal charities and sites, there are also stories, games and chat. See also the excellent BBC web pages on pets which can be found at **www.bbc.co.uk/nature/animals/pets**

Sites for different species

BIRDS

www.avianweb.com
FOR BIRD ENTHUSIASTS

ORIGIN US
SPEED ✓✓✓✓
INFO ✓✓✓✓✓
EASE ✓✓✓✓

A massive site devoted to birds, it's especially good for information on parrots. There are sections on species, health and equipment as well as advice on looking after birds. See also **www.rspb.org.uk**

www.bird-shop.co.uk
BIRDS AND EXOTIC PETS

ORIGIN UK
SPEED ✓✓✓✓
INFO ✓✓✓
VALUE ✓✓✓
EASE ✓✓✓✓

Online pet shop devoted mainly to birds but also covers more exotic animals too, there's advice on food and a breeder's directory. It could do with more information and unless you really like bird-calls, turn the sound off. **www.birdcare.co.uk** is another commercial site with useful information.

CATS

www.cats.org.uk
HOME OF CAT PROTECTION

ORIGIN	UK
SPEED	✓✓✓✓
INFO	✓✓✓✓
VALUE	✓✓✓
EASE	✓✓✓✓

A well-designed and informative site, with information on caring, re-homing, news and general advice, there's even a section for children called 'Kitten Club' and an archive of cat photos. The online shop offers free delivery in the UK. For more information on cats go to **www.moggies.co.uk** home of the Online Cat Guide, not an easy site to use, but has exceptional links to pet sites. See also **www.fabcats.org** – a charity devoted to cat care.

DOGS

www.dogsonline.co.uk
DOGS, DOGS AND MORE DOGS

ORIGIN	UK
SPEED	✓✓✓
INFO	✓✓✓✓✓
VALUE	✓✓
EASE	✓✓✓✓

All you'd ever want from a web site about dogs. There's information on breeding, where to get dogs, events, directories, how to find hotels that accept dogs, classified ads and insurance.

For more information on dogs try **www.canismajor.com/dog** an American magazine site, the comprehensive **www.canineworld.com** or **www.the-kennel-club.org.uk** for the official line on dogs and breeding with information on Crufts and links to related web sites.

www.ncdl.org.uk
NATIONAL CANINE DEFENCE LEAGUE

ORIGIN UK
SPEED ✓✓✓✓
INFO ✓✓✓✓✓
VALUE ✓✓✓
EASE ✓✓✓✓

Excellent web site featuring the charitable works of the NCDL the largest charity of its type. Get advice on how to adopt a dog, tips on looking after one and download a doggie screensaver. For Battersea Dogs Home go to **www.dogshome.org** who have a well-designed site.

FISH

www.ornamentalfish.org
ORNAMENTAL AQUATIC TRADE ASSOCIATION

ORIGIN UK
SPEED ✓✓✓
INFO ✓✓✓✓
EASE ✓✓✓✓

An excellent site beautifully designed and well executed. Although much of it is aimed at the trade and commercial side, there is a great deal of information for the hobbyist about looking after and buying fish.

HORSES

www.equiworld.net
GLOBAL EQUINE INFORMATION

ORIGIN UK
SPEED ✓✓✓
INFO ✓✓✓✓✓
EASE ✓✓✓✓

A directory, magazine and advice centre in one with incredible detail plus some fun stuff too. The shop consists of links to specialist traders. For health advice go to **www.horseadvice.com** which supplies a huge amount of information. See also the very comprehensive **www.equine-world.co.uk**

RABBITS

http://www.rabbit.org
HOUSE RABBIT SOCIETY

ORIGIN UK
SPEED ✓✓✓✓
INFO ✓✓✓✓✓
EASE ✓✓✓✓

It's all here, from feeding, breeding, behaviour, health advice and even info on house-training your rabbit. Has a nice kids' section and plenty of cute pictures. For a personal tribute to rabbits see **www.rabbitworld.com** which also has information on caring for your fluffy friend.

Photography

www.rps.org
THE ROYAL PHOTOGRAPHIC SOCIETY

ORIGIN UK
SPEED ✓✓✓
INFO ✓✓
EASE ✓✓✓

A worthy, dull site dedicated to the works of the RPS; you can get details of the latest exhibitions and the collection, become a member, get the latest news about the world of photography. Good for links to other related sites. Sadly there aren't many pictures, which is an opportunity missed.

www.nmpft.org.uk
NATIONAL MUSEUM OF PHOTOGRAPHY, FILM AND TELEVISION

ORIGIN UK
SPEED ✓✓✓
INFO ✓✓✓✓
EASE ✓✓✓✓

Details of this Bradford museum via a high tech web site, opening times and directions, what's on, education resources and a very good museum guide. Kids can also have fun and educational games at the 'Magic Factory'.

www.eastman.org
THE INTERNATIONAL MUSEUM OF PHOTOGRAPHY

ORIGIN US
SPEED ✓✓✓
INFO ✓✓✓✓
EASE ✓✓✓✓

George Eastman founded Kodak and this New York-based museum too. This site is comprehensive and amongst other things you can learn about the history of photography, visit the photographic and film galleries, or obtain technical information. Become a member and you're entitled to benefits such as free admission and copies of their *Image* magazine.

www.nationalgeographic.com/photography
HOME OF THE NATIONAL GEOGRAPHIC MAGAZINE

ORIGIN US
SPEED ✓✓✓✓
INFO ✓✓✓✓✓
EASE ✓✓✓✓

Synonymous with great photography, this excellent site offers much more. There are sections on travel, exhibitions, maps, news, education, and for kids. In the photography section pick up tips and techniques, follow their photographers' various locations, read superb articles and accompanying shots in the 'Visions Galleries'. Good links to other photographic sites.

www.masters-of-photography.com
ONLINE GALLERIES

ORIGIN US
SPEED ✓✓✓
INFO ✓✓✓✓✓
EASE ✓✓✓✓✓

A simple site with a superb array of galleries devoted to the real masters of the art of photography – you can spend hours browsing here.

www.pathfinder.com/Life/
LIFE MAGAZINE

ORIGIN US
SPEED ✓✓✓
INFO ✓✓✓✓
VALUE ✓✓
EASE ✓✓✓

Life Magazine, it's wonderfully nostalgic and still going strong. There are several sections, features with great photos, excellent articles, and an option to subscribe; however they could do much more and it's a little frustrating to use.

www.corbis.com
THE PLACE FOR PICTURES ON THE INTERNET

ORIGIN	US
SPEED	✓✓✓
INFO	✓✓✓✓✓
VALUE	✓✓✓
EASE	✓✓✓✓

Another Microsoft product, this is probably the world's largest online picture library. Use the pictures to enhance presentations, web sites, screen-savers, or to make e-cards for friends. You can also buy pictures framed or unframed which are good value, but shipping to the UK can be expensive. You can also now buy high quality digital images at $3 a go. See also **www.freefoto.com** who offer the largest free image database.

www.bjphoto.co.uk
THE BRITISH JOURNAL OF PHOTOGRAPHY

ORIGIN	UK
SPEED	✓✓✓
INFO	✓✓✓✓
EASE	✓✓✓✓

An online magazine with loads of material on photography. Access their archive of articles or visit picture galleries that contain work from contemporary photographers; find out about careers in photography and where to buy the best photographic gear.

www.betterphoto.com
TAKE BETTER PICTURES

ORIGIN	UK
SPEED	✓✓✓✓
INFO	✓✓✓✓✓
EASE	✓✓✓✓

A very well laid out and comprehensive advice site for new and experienced photographers with a buyer's guide and introductions to and overviews of traditional and digital photography.

www.jessops.com
TAKE ADVICE TAKE GREAT PICTURES

ORIGIN UK
SPEED ✓✓✓
INFO ✓✓✓✓
VALUE ✓✓✓
EASE ✓✓✓✓

Jessops are the largest photographic retailer in the UK and they offer advice on most aspects of photography plus courses and free software for their digital printing service. They do give you an opportunity to go shopping for your camera and accessories, of course.

www.whichcamera.co.uk
FIND THE RIGHT CAMERA

ORIGIN UK
SPEED ✓✓✓✓
INFO ✓✓✓✓✓
EASE ✓✓✓

Get advice on the best camera for you then use links to find your local dealer or to the manufacturer direct. The information is very good, there's a good search engine and camera finder service too. The graphics could be better though. See also **www.camerareview.com**

www.ditigal-photography.org
GO DIGITAL

ORIGIN UK
SPEED ✓✓✓✓
INFO ✓✓✓✓✓
EASE ✓✓✓

A messy site that has masses of information about the world of digital photography with lots of reviews and links to related sites. See also **www.photobuzz.com** for the latest digital news. At the Digital Photo review **http://photo.askey.net** you can get reviews and join in forums on various digital topics.

www.fotango.com
ONLINE DEVELOPERS

ORIGIN UK
SPEED ✓✓✓✓
INFO ✓✓✓✓
VALUE ✓✓✓
EASE ✓✓✓✓

Fotango will take your film and digitise it, then place your pictures on a secure site for you to view and select for printing the ones you like. The service is quick and easy-to-use; costs don't seem much

different from the high street although single
prints can be expensive. See also Boots'
version at www.bootsphoto.com and also
www.photoscrapbook.com

Price Checkers

*Here's a good place to start any online shopping trip – a price
comparison site. There are many price checker sites, however, the
sites listed here allow you to check the prices for online stores
across a much wider range of merchandise than the usual books,
music and film.*

www.kelkoo.com
COMPARE PRICES BEFORE YOU BUY

ORIGIN	EUROPE
SPEED	✓✓✓
INFO	✓✓✓✓✓
VALUE	✓✓✓✓✓
EASE	✓✓✓✓

Kelkoo is probably the best price-checking site with
20 categories in their shop directory. The price
comparison section has 14 sections including books,
wine, white goods, even cars. There are plenty of
bargains to be had in that section, in fact they keep
popping up on every page. In the features section
you'll find reviews and news of the latest goods and
consumer advice.

www.shopsmart.co.uk
SHOP SMART

ORIGIN	UK
SPEED	✓✓✓✓
INFO	✓✓✓✓✓
VALUE	✓✓✓✓✓
EASE	✓✓✓✓

A wide ranging shop review site which is fully
reviewed in the shopping section, but it deserves a
place here for its excellent price checking facility
which covers books, DVD & video, games,
computer hardware and electronics.

www.checkaprice.com
CONSTANTLY CHECKING PRICES

ORIGIN UK
SPEED ✓✓✓
INFO ✓✓✓✓
VALUE ✓✓✓✓✓
EASE ✓✓✓✓

Compare prices across nearly 60 different product types, from the usual books to cars, holidays, mortgages and electrical goods. If it can't do it for you, it patches you through to a site that can.

Other good sites:

www.buy.co.uk – excellent for the utilities – gas, water and electrical as well as credit cards and mobile phones.

www.dealtime.co.uk – easy-to-use directory and price checker covering a wide range of goods.

www.pricechecker.co.uk – straightforward site, also covers flights and telephone tariffs.

www.pricescan.com – all the usual, plus watches, sports goods and office equipment – good store finder.

www.price-search.net – mainly computers and gadgets.

www.pricewatch.co.uk – good for computers and personal finance.

www.priceoffers.co.uk – not really a checker, but has access to the best bargains, also a regular newsletter covering the latest offers.

Property

Every estate agent worth their salt has got a web site, and in theory finding the house of your dreams has never been easier. These sites have been designed to help you through the real life minefield.

www.upmystreet.com

FIND OUT ABOUT WHERE YOU WANT TO GO

ORIGIN UK	Type in the postcode and up pops almost every
SPEED ✓✓✓	statistic you need to know about the area in ques-
INFO ✓✓✓✓✓	tion. Spooky, but fascinating, it's a good guide
EASE ✓✓✓	featuring not only house prices, but also schools, the

local MP, local authority information, crime and
links to services. It also has a classified section and
puts you in touch with the nearest items to your
area.

www.conveyancing-cms.co.uk

CONVEYANCING MARKETING SERVICE

ORIGIN UK	Conveyancing is a bit of a minefield if you're new to
SPEED ✓✓✓	it, this site aims to help with advice and competitive
INFO ✓✓✓✓	quotes. See also **www.easier2move.com** which is
VALUE ✓✓✓✓	nicely designed.
EASE ✓✓✓	

www.reallymoving.com

MAKING MOVING EASIER

ORIGIN UK	A directory of sites and help for home buyers includ-
SPEED ✓✓✓	ing mortgages, removal firms, surveyors, solicitors,
INFO ✓✓✓✓✓	van hire and home improvements. You can get
EASE ✓✓✓	online quotes on some services and there's good

regional information. The property search is fast
and has plenty to choose from.

www.hagglepages.com

LET SOMEONE HAGGLE FOR YOU

ORIGIN UK	If you're not comfortable with haggling for a home
SPEED ✓✓✓✓	then try this service, they'll also find the best deals
INFO ✓✓✓✓	on mortgages, insurance and surveyors. The site is
VALUE ✓✓✓✓	expanding and deserves to succeed.
EASE ✓✓✓	

www.propwise.com
PROPERTY WISE

ORIGIN UK
SPEED ✓✓✓
INFO ✓✓✓✓
EASE ✓✓✓

This site makes it easier for you to search for the most appropriate property-related sites, all the leading sites dealing with buying, selling, rental, mortgages or area guides have been listed, evaluated and rated. The information is very good and its easy-to-use, if a little slow at times.

www.freehomeindex.com
ADVERTISE YOUR PROPERTY FOR FREE

ORIGIN UK
SPEED ✓✓✓
INFO ✓✓✓✓
EASE ✓✓✓

As well as free advertising, get mortgage and insurance advice, area information and browse the houses for sale. The site has improved and there's more information available, though it's still slow and the search facility still could be much better. See also **www.homefreehome.co.uk**

For more properties try these sites:
www.08004homes.com – good, magazine-style site with 100,000 homes listed.
www.assertahome.com – excellent site with lots of advice, information, houses and associated services.
www.easier.co.uk – the Internet Property Index will sell your house around the world.
www.bambooavenue.com – moving help, advice and service quotes, good layout and simple to use.
www.beach-huts.co.uk – great site, providing you want to buy or rent a beach hut.
www.findaproperty.com – over 20,000 properties, good for the South East.
www.heritage.co.uk – covers listed buildings for sale only plus information on their upkeep.

www.hol365.com – really good site design and a massive range of services and properties from 6,000 estate agents.

www.homelet.co.uk – claim to take the risk out of renting by offering sound advice and insurances for both tenants and landlords – good design.

www.houseweb.co.uk – comprehensive advice and 150,000 properties for sale!

www.itlhomesearch.com – independent home search that also covers Spain and Ireland – rent or buy.

www.knightfrank.com – world-wide service, easy-to-use site.

www.propertyfinder.co.uk – Britain's biggest house database.

www.propertylive.co.uk – advice and properties from the National Association of Estate Agents.

www.property-sight.co.uk – easy-to-use and comprehensive.

www.rightmove.com – very clear information site with a good property search engine.

www.smartnewhomes.com – dedicated to new homes.

www.ukpropertyshop.com – claims to be the most comprehensive covering 3,000 towns in the UK.

www.ukpg.co.uk – the ultimate guide to moving home, apparently.

Property abroad

www.french-property.com
NO. 1 FOR FRANCE

ORIGIN FRANCE
SPEED ✓✓✓✓
INFO ✓✓✓✓
EASE ✓✓✓

If you are fed up with the UK and want to move to France this is the site to start with, they offer properties for rent or for sale in all regions and can link you with other estate agents.

www.spanish-property-online.com
MOVING TO SPAIN

ORIGIN UK
SPEED ✓✓✓✓
INFO ✓✓✓✓
EASE ✓✓✓

Avoid all the pitfalls by stopping off for a browse at this informative site that covers all you need to know about buying property in Spain. Sections on France, Portugal, Cyprus, Portugal, Italy and Florida are due soon.

Radio

You need a decent downloadable player such as RealPlayer (see Introduction) or Windows Media Player before you start listening. RealPlayer in particular gives you access to loads of stations and allows you to add more. The downside is that quality is sometimes affected by 'Net congestion'.

www.mediauk.com/directory
DIRECTORY OF RADIO STATIONS

ORIGIN UK
SPEED ✓✓✓✓
INFO ✓✓✓✓✓
EASE ✓✓✓✓

Excellent site. You can search by station, presenter or by type, there's also background on the history of radio and articles on topics such as digital radio. The site also offers similar information on television and magazines. See also the superb **http://windows-media.com** home to Microsoft's media listings, which is also comprehensive. If you still can't find what you want then try **www.webradionow.com** who list some 1,000 stations. Go to Yahoo's **www.broadcast.com/radio** for another massive list of stations.

www.radioacademy.org
UK's GATEWAY TO RADIO

ORIGIN UK
SPEED ✓✓✓
INFO ✓✓✓✓✓
EASE ✓✓✓✓

Radio Academy is a charity that covers all things to do with radio including news, events and its advancement in education and information. It has a list of all UK stations including those that offer web casts.

www.bbc.co.uk/radio
THE BEST OF THE BBC

ORIGIN UK
SPEED ✓✓✓
INFO ✓✓✓✓✓
EASE ✓✓✓✓

Listen to the news and the latest hits while you work, just select the station you want. There's also information on each major station, as well as a comprehensive listing service. Some features such as football commentary on certain matches will be missing due to rights issues. Most of the stations have some level of interactivity, with Radio 1 being the best and most lively, you can also tap into their local stations and of course the World Service.

www.virginradio.co.uk
VIRGIN ON AIR

ORIGIN UK
SPEED ✓✓✓
INFO ✓✓✓✓✓
EASE ✓✓✓✓

Excellent, if slightly messy site, with plenty of stuff about the station, its schedule and stars. There's a good magazine with the latest music news. The site has an annoying amount of advertising though. You can listen if you have Quicktime, Windows Media Player or RealPlayer.

Other independent radio stations online are:
www.classicfm.com – classical music and background information.
www.jazzfm.com – live broadcasts.
www.galaxyfm.co.uk – good range of music.
www.capitalfm.com – Capital Radio.

www.coolfm.co.uk – Northern Ireland's number
  one.
www.heart1062.co.uk – London's heart.
www.lbc.co.uk – the voice of London.
www.wwfm.co.uk – international, pop all-rounder.
www.comfm.fr – a French site with access to over
  4,500 stations.
www.webradio.com – a wide ranging US site.

www.netradio.net
RADIO TAILORED JUST FOR YOU

ORIGIN UK
SPEED ✓✓✓
INFO ✓✓✓✓✓
EASE ✓✓✓✓

Pick any one of its specialist 100 or so channels;
tune in using RealPlayer or Windows Media Player,
and if you like the track you can also buy the album.
A specialist has programmed each channel to play a
type of music and the selection is consistently good.
This site has a real 'wow' factor. See also the excellent www.sonicbox.com and www.radio.mp3.com
where you can also customise your radio experience.

Railways

*These are sites aimed at the railway enthusiast. For information
on trains and timetables see page 435.*

www.nrm.org.uk
NATIONAL RAILWAY MUSEUM

ORIGIN UK
SPEED ✓✓✓✓
INFO ✓✓✓✓
EASE ✓✓✓✓

An excellent museum site packed with information
and details on their collection, you can even take a
virtual tour. See also Great Western's new museum
site at www.steam-museum.org.uk it's not hi-tech
but it's very informative.

http://ukhrail.uel.ac.uk
HERITAGE RAILWAY ASSOCIATION

ORIGIN UK
SPEED ✓✓✓✓
INFO ✓✓✓✓✓
EASE ✓✓✓✓

This site offers an online guide to the entire heritage railway scene in the UK, including details of special events and operating days for all heritage railways with lots of links world-wide.

www.narrowgauge.f2s.com
NARROW GAUGE HEAVEN

ORIGIN UK
SPEED ✓✓✓✓
INFO ✓✓✓✓
EASE ✓✓✓✓

If you're into narrow gauge railways, then this is the place to come. It's got regional information on all the UK's railways plus details of where to stay, news, a photo gallery and a links page.

www.gbrail.org.uk
A LIGHTER LOOK

ORIGIN UK
SPEED ✓✓✓✓
INFO ✓✓✓✓
EASE ✓✓✓

A real enthusiast's site and the nearest thing we could find to a quality magazine, it's comprehensive and well written with a good sense of humour. The links section is excellent. There's a guide to track numbering and a free game of battleships!

Reference and Encyclopaedia Sites

If you are stuck with your homework or want an answer to any question, then this is where the Internet really comes into its own. With these sites you are bound to find what you are looking for.

www.refdesk.com
THE BEST SINGLE SOURCE FOR FACTS

ORIGIN US
SPEED ✓✓✓
INFO ✓✓✓✓✓
EASE ✓✓✓✓

Singled out for its sheer size and scope, this site offers information and links to just about anything. Its mission is 'only about indexing quality Internet sites and assisting visitors in navigating these sites'. It's won numerous awards and it never fails to impress.

www.xrefer.co.uk
FREE REFERENCE

ORIGIN UK
SPEED ✓✓✓✓
INFO ✓✓✓✓✓
EASE ✓✓✓✓✓

The UK's answer to RefDesk with access to some 50 books and reference works, and it's pretty comprehensive. Its real strength is in the speed of its search engine and its clean user-friendly design.

www.knowuk.co.uk
ALL ABOUT BRITAIN

ORIGIN UK
SPEED ✓✓✓
INFO ✓✓✓✓✓
EASE ✓✓✓✓

A subscription service which offers a massive amount of data about the UK from the arts to the civil service, education, the *Hutchinson Encyclopaedia*, government, law, travel and sport. Although most of the information can be accessed through separate sites, the advantage here is that you only need the one. Prices aren't listed on the site but you can contact them for a free trial.

www.about.com
IT'S ABOUT INFORMATION

ORIGIN US
SPEED ✓✓✓
INFO ✓✓✓✓✓
EASE ✓✓✓✓✓

A superb resource, easy-to-use and great for beginners learning to search for information, experts help you to find what you need every step of the way. It offers information on a wide range of topics from the arts and sciences to shopping. Also worth a visit is **www.libraryspot.com** which is similar in scope but has a more literary emphasis. It has an entertaining 'lists' section for those obsessed by top tens and useless facts.

www.ipl.org
THE INTERNET PUBLIC LIBRARY

ORIGIN US	Another excellent resource, there are articles on a
SPEED ✓✓✓	vast range of subjects concentrating on literary criti-
INFO ✓✓✓✓✓	cism. Almost every country and its literature is
EASE ✓✓✓	covered. If there isn't anything at the library, there is

invariably a link to take you to an alternative web site. It also has sections for young people.

www.allexperts.com
ASK AN EXPERT

ORIGIN US	Staffed by expert volunteers, you can ask any ques-
SPEED ✓✓✓✓	tion in some thirty-six categories from arts to TV, in
INFO ✓✓✓✓✓	fact there's an expert covering most subject or topic
EASE ✓✓✓✓	no matter how inane.

www.homeworkelephant.co.uk
LET THE ELEPHANT HELP WITH HOMEWORK

ORIGIN UK	A resource with some 700 links aimed at helping
SPEED ✓✓✓✓	students achieve great results. There's help with
INFO ✓✓✓✓✓	specific subjects, hints and tips, help for parents and
EASE ✓✓✓✓	teachers. It's constantly being updated, so worth

checking regularly. See also **www.homeworkhigh.co.uk** Channel 4's homework help site. For still more homework links see **www.kidsclick.org** and the wide-ranging **www.studyweb.com** with over 160,000 URL's listed.

www.maths-help.co.uk
E-MAIL YOUR MATHS PROBLEMS

ORIGIN UK
SPEED ✓✓✓
INFO ✓✓✓✓✓
EASE ✓✓✓✓✓

Send your queries to maths-help and they'll e-mail you back the answers in a couple of days. You can also visit the knowledge bank to see past queries and answers. See also **www.mathacademy.com** for a more fun view of maths.

www.eserver.org
THE ENGLISH SERVER

ORIGIN US
SPEED ✓✓✓
INFO ✓✓✓✓✓
EASE ✓✓✓

A much-improved humanities site, which provides a vast amount of resource data about almost every cultural topic, there are some 20,000 texts, articles and essays available on subjects from the arts, fiction through to web design.

http://classics.mit.edu
THE INTERNET CLASSICS ARCHIVE

ORIGIN US
SPEED ✓✓✓✓
INFO ✓✓✓✓✓
EASE ✓✓✓✓

An excellent site for researching into the classics, it's easy-to-use and fast, with more than enough information for homework whatever the level. See also **www.bibliomania.com** for a wider range of resource materials.

www.omsakthi.org/religions.html
RELIGION WORLD-WIDE

ORIGIN US
SPEED ✓✓✓
INFO ✓✓✓✓✓
EASE ✓✓✓

This site provides a clear description of each world religion including values and basic beliefs with links to books on each one.

www.ntu.edu.sg/library/stat/statdata.htm
STATISTICS AND MORE STATISTICS

ORIGIN US
SPEED ✓✓✓
INFO ✓✓✓✓✓
EASE ✓✓✓

Free information and statistics about every world economy, not that easy-to-use at first, but it's all there. See also **www.population.com** which has a huge amount of data and information. For the UK go to the source of the statistics at **www.statitistics.gov.uk**

www.atlapedia.com
THE WORLD IN BOTH PICTURES AND NUMBERS

ORIGIN US
SPEED ✓✓
INFO ✓✓✓✓✓
EASE ✓✓✓✓

Contains full colour political and physical maps of the world with statistics and very detailed information on each country. It can be very slow, so you need patience, but the end results are worth it.

Encyclopaedias

http://encarta.msn.com
THE ENCARTA ENCYCLOPAEDIA

ORIGIN US
SPEED ✓✓✓✓
INFO ✓✓✓✓✓
EASE ✓✓✓✓

Even though the complete thing is only available to buy, there is access to thousands of articles, maps and reference notes via the concise version. It's fast and easy-to-use.

www.whsmith.co.uk/education
THE HUTCHINSON ENCYCLOPAEDIA

ORIGIN UK
SPEED ✓✓✓✓
INFO ✓✓✓✓✓
EASE ✓✓✓✓

Smiths have a good, concise education site with access to some 18,000 entries from the established Hutchinson Encyclopaedia, with a quick search facility, useful links and homework help.

Other useful encyclopaedias:

http://i-cias.com/e.o/index.htm – Encyclopaedia of the Orient – for North Africa and the Middle East.

www.si.edu/resource – encyclopaedia and links to the massive resources of the Smithsonian.

http://encyclozine.com – wide range of topics covered plus good use of games, quizzes and trivia.

www.babloo.com – encyclopaedia aimed at kids.

www.dk.com – Dorling Kindersley's site is not what it once was but still an excellent place to go for homework help.

www.eb.com – Encyclopaedia Britannica for $5 per month.

www.ehow.com – instructions on how to do just about anything.

www.encyberpedia.com – some 500 links to reference sites.

www.encyclopedia.com – the most comprehensive free encyclopedia on the net.

www.infoplease.com – the biggest collection of almanacs, plus an encyclopedia and an atlas.

www.utm.edu/research/iep – the Internet Encyclopaedia of Philosophy.

www.digitalcentury.com/encyclo – Jones Digital Century with a wide range of resources and the usual encyclopaedia.

www.quibs.co.uk – a massive database of lists.

www.spartacus.schoolnet.co.uk – Spartacus Encyclopaedia is excellent for history homework.

http://plato.stanford.edu – Stanford Encyclopaedia of philosophy.

www.wsu.edu/DrUniverse/ – ask Dr Universe a question – any question...

Dictionaries and thesauruses

www.cup.cam.ac.uk/elt/dictionary
CAMBRIDGE UNIVERSITY

ORIGIN UK	This site has five dictionaries including English,
SPEED ✓✓✓✓	American English, Idioms, Phrasal Verbs and a
INFO ✓✓✓✓	Learner's dictionary – all free. See also
EASE ✓✓✓✓✓	www.oed.com where you can find the Oxford

English Dictionary, which you have to subscribe to.

www.thesaurus.com
IF YOU CAN'T FIND THE WORD

ORIGIN US	Based on Roget's Thesaurus, this site will enable you
SPEED ✓✓✓	to find alternative words, useful but not worth turn-
INFO ✓✓✓✓✓	ing your PC on for in place of the book. For the
EASE ✓✓✓✓	equivalent dictionary site, go to the useful

www.dictionary.com where you can play word
games as an added feature.

For a dictionary that specialises in jargon and
Internet terms only go to www.jargon.net or
www.netdictionary.com for enlightenment.

www.onelook.com
DICTIONARY HEAVEN

ORIGIN US	Onelook claim to offer access to almost 700 dictio-
SPEED ✓✓✓	naries and nearly 3 million words, at a fast, user-
INFO ✓✓✓✓✓	friendly site, it also offers a price checking service
EASE ✓✓✓✓	for online shopping.

www.plumbdesign.com/thesaurus/
THE VISUAL THESAURUS

ORIGIN US	If you get bored looking up words or looking for
SPEED ✓✓✓	alternative meanings for words in the usual way,
INFO ✓✓✓✓	then check out the Visual Thesaurus at Plumb
EASE ✓✓	Design. It's fun to use if a bit weird.

http://dictionaries.travlang.com
FOREIGN LANGUAGE DICTIONARIES

ORIGIN US	There are 16 language dictionaries on this site, just
SPEED ✓✓✓✓	select the dictionary you want, and then type in the
INFO ✓✓✓✓✓	word or sentence to be translated – it couldn't be
EASE ✓✓✓✓✓	simpler. Originally aimed at the traveller, but it's
	very useful in this context.

www.peevish.u-net.com/slang
DICTIONARY OF SLANG

ORIGIN UK	A comprehensive dictionary of English slang as used
SPEED ✓✓✓✓	in the UK, with good articles and search facility.
INFO ✓✓✓✓	
EASE ✓✓✓	

www.acronymfinder.com
WHAT DO THOSE INITIALS STAND FOR?

ORIGIN US	If you don't know your MP from your MP3 here's
SPEED ✓✓✓✓	where to go, with over 150,000 acronyms you
INFO ✓✓✓✓	should find what you're looking for.
EASE ✓✓✓✓✓	

www.symbols.com
WHAT DOES THAT SYMBOL MEAN?

ORIGIN US	Here you can find the meaning of over 2,500
SPEED ✓✓✓✓	symbols, with articles on their history.
INFO ✓✓✓✓	
EASE ✓✓✓✓	

Science

The Internet was originally created by a group of scientists who wanted faster, more efficient communication and today, scientists around the world use the Net to compare data and collaborate. In addition, the layman has access to the wonders of science in a way that's never been possible before, and as for homework – well now it's a doddle.

www.sciseek.com
ONLINE RESOURCE FOR SCIENCE AND NATURE

ORIGIN US
SPEED ✓✓✓
INFO ✓✓✓✓
EASE ✓✓✓

A good place to start, Sciseek lists over 1,000 sites on everything from agriculture to chemistry to health to physics, each site is reviewed and you have the opportunity to leave comments too.

www.royalsoc.ac.uk
THE ROYAL SOCIETY

ORIGIN UK
SPEED ✓✓✓
INFO ✓✓✓
EASE ✓✓✓✓

An attractive site where you can learn all about the workings of the society, how to get grants, and what events they are running. You can't help thinking that the site should have more on it, especially to encourage young scientists.

www.sciencemag.org
SCIENCE MAGAZINE

ORIGIN US
SPEED ✓✓✓
INFO ✓✓✓✓✓
EASE ✓✓✓

A serious overview of the current science scene with articles covering everything from global warming to how owls find their prey. The tone isn't so heavy that a layman can't follow it and there are plenty of links too. You need to register to get the best out of it.

www.sciencemuseum.org.uk
THE SCIENCE MUSEUM

ORIGIN UK
SPEED ✓✓✓
INFO ✓✓✓✓
EASE ✓✓✓✓

An excellent site detailing the major attractions at the museum with 3D graphics and features on exhibitions and forthcoming attractions, you can also shop and browse the galleries. See also **www.exploratorium.edu** a similar site by an American museum.

www.madsci.org
THE LAB THAT NEVER SLEEPS

ORIGIN US
SPEED ✓✓✓
INFO ✓✓✓✓
EASE ✓✓✓

A site that successfully combines science with fun, you can ask a question of a mad scientist, browse the links list or check out the archives in the library.

www.howstuffworks.com
HOW STUFF REALLY WORKS

ORIGIN US
SPEED ✓✓✓✓
INFO ✓✓✓✓✓
EASE ✓✓✓✓✓

A popular site, for nerds and kids young and old; it's easy-to-use and fascinating, there are 27 sections ranging from the obvious like engines and technology, through to food and the weather. The current top ten section features the latest answers to the questions of the day. It's written in a very concise, clear style with lots of cross-referencing.

http://freeweb.pdq.net/headstrong
BIZARRE STUFF YOU CAN MAKE IN YOUR KITCHEN

ORIGIN US
SPEED ✓✓✓✓
INFO ✓✓✓✓
EASE ✓✓✓

The entertaining Bizarre Stuff is devoted to daft experiments that most boys (and some girls) have attempted at some time in their lives; from goo to solar ovens to crystal gardens it's all here and described in loving detail. See also the more worthy but still interesting **www.doscience.com** who have lots of straightforward experiments and check out Fun Science at **www.funsci.com**

www.voltnet.com
DON'T TRY THIS AT HOME!

ORIGIN	US
SPEED	✓✓✓✓
INFO	✓✓✓✓
EASE	✓✓✓✓

This is literally a high voltage site devoted to electricity and how it works. While there is a serious side, by far the best bit is where they 'stress test' all sorts of objects by sending 20,000 volts through them – a Furby was getting the treatment when this review was written.

www.innovations.co.uk
GADGETS GALORE

ORIGIN	UK
SPEED	✓✓✓
INFO	✓✓✓✓
VALUE	✓✓✓
EASE	✓✓✓

Impress your friends with your knowledge of the newest gadgets, innovations or what's likely to be the next big thing. Innovations is well established and has one of the best online stores and a wide range, there's a reward scheme but they're a bit vague about delivery costs. See also **www.streettech.com** who specialise in the latest hardware and also **www.firebox.com** where apparently 'men buy stuff', whatever, they've got lots to choose from.

www.21stcentury.co.uk
YOUR PORTAL TO THE FUTURE

ORIGIN	UK
SPEED	✓✓✓✓
INFO	✓✓✓✓
EASE	✓✓✓✓

A stylish site that gives an overview of the latest technology put over in an entertaining way. Whether you're using it for homework or just for a browse, it's useful and interesting, they have 12 categories from cars through to humour, people and technology, they even cover fashion.

www.nesta.org.uk
THE CREATIVE INVENTOR'S HANDBOOK

ORIGIN UK
SPEED ✓✓✓✓
INFO ✓✓✓✓
EASE ✓✓✓✓

The National Endowment for Science Technology not only helps inventors get their ideas off the ground with support and guidance, but also encourages creativity and innovation. They'll also inspire you, as a visit to this well designed site will show.

www.newscientist.com
NEW SCIENTIST MAGAZINE

ORIGIN US
SPEED ✓✓✓
INFO ✓✓✓✓✓
EASE ✓✓✓✓

Much better than the usual online magazines because of its creative use of archive material which is simultaneously fun and serious. It's easy to search the site or browse through back features – the 'Even More Bizarre' bit is particularly entertaining. For a more traditional science magazine site go to *Popular Science* at **www.popsci.com** great for information on the latest gadgets.

www.discovery.com
THE DISCOVERY CHANNEL

ORIGIN UK
SPEED ✓✓✓
INFO ✓✓✓✓✓
EASE ✓✓✓✓

A superb site for science and nature lovers, it's inspiring as well as educational. Order the weekly newsletter, get information on the latest discoveries as well as features on pets, space, travel, lifestyle and school. The 'Discovery Kids' section is very good with lots going on.

www.webelements.com
THE PERIODIC TABLE

ORIGIN US
SPEED ✓✓✓✓
INFO ✓✓✓✓✓
EASE ✓✓✓✓

So you don't know your halides from your fluorides, with this interactive depiction you can find out. Just click on the element and you get basic details plus an audio description.

www.science-frontiers.com
SCIENTIFIC ANOMALIES

ORIGIN US
SPEED ✓✓✓✓
INFO ✓✓✓
EASE ✓✓✓

Science Frontiers is a bimonthly newsletter providing digests of reports that describe scientific anomalies; that's, 'those observations and facts that challenge prevailing scientific paradigms'. There's a massive archive of the weird and wonderful, it takes patience but there are some real gems.

www.mentalmuscles.com
BRAIN WAVES

ORIGIN US
SPEED ✓✓✓✓
INFO ✓✓✓✓
EASE ✓✓✓✓

The Brainwaves Centre 'provides the general public with practical applications of current research in the neurosciences to improve and maintain mental skills' which shouldn't put you off as it's very entertaining and well written with lots of facts and information. You can test your brain and memory skills and find out what you can do to improve them.

Search engines

The best way to find what you want from the Internet is to use a search engine. Even the best only cover at most 60% of the available web sites; so if you can't find what you want from one, try another. These are the best and most user friendly. For children's search engines see page 80.

www.searchenginewatch.com
A GUIDE TO SEARCHING

ORIGIN US
SPEED ✓✓✓✓
INFO ✓✓✓✓✓
EASE ✓✓✓✓

This site rates and assesses all the search engines and it's a useful starting point if you're looking for a good or specific search facility. There's a newsletter and statistical analysis plus strategies on how to

make the perfect search. See also **www.searchengi-
neshowdown.com** who do much the same thing but
it's less comprehensive.

http://uk.yahoo.com
FOR THE UK AND IRELAND

ORIGIN US
SPEED ✓✓✓✓
INFO ✓✓✓✓✓
EASE ✓✓✓

The UK arm of Yahoo! is the biggest and one of the
most established search engines. It's now much more
than just a search facility as it offers a huge array of
other services: from news to finance to shopping to
sport to travel to games. You can restrict your
search to just UK or Irish sites. It's the place to start,
but it can be a little overwhelming at first.

www.mirago.co.uk
THE UK SEARCH ENGINE

ORIGIN UK
SPEED ✓✓✓✓
INFO ✓✓✓✓✓
EASE ✓✓✓✓✓

Mirago searches the whole web but prioritises the
search for UK families and businesses. It's very
quick, easy-to-use and offers many of the services
you get from Yahoo! You can tailor your search very
easily to exclude stuff you won't need. For another
UK-oriented site try **www.ukplus.co.uk**

www.ask.co.uk
ASK JEEVES

ORIGIN US
SPEED ✓✓✓✓
INFO ✓✓✓✓
EASE ✓✓✓✓✓

Just type in your question and the famous old butler
will come back with the answer. It may be a bit
gimmicky but works very well, it's great for beginners and reliable for old hands too.

www.mamma.com
THE MOTHER OF ALL SEARCH ENGINES

ORIGIN US
SPEED ✓✓✓✓
INFO ✓✓✓✓
EASE ✓✓✓✓

Mamma claim to have technology enabling them to search the major search engines thoroughly and get the most pertinent results to your query – it's fast too, your query comes back with the answer and the search engine it came from. You might also try **www.metacrawler.com** which uses similar technology and **www.37.com** which is a bit of a mess but can search 37 other search engines in one go. For a UK-oriented search engine searching site try **www.godado.co.uk**.

www.google.co.uk
BRINGING ORDER TO THE WEB

ORIGIN US
SPEED ✓✓✓✓✓
INFO ✓✓✓✓
EASE ✓✓✓✓✓

Google is all about speed and accuracy. Using a complicated set of rules they claim to be able to give the most relevant results in the quickest time, in fact they even tell you how fast they are. It's easier to use than most and a mass of information doesn't overload you. At this URL you can limit your search to the UK.

www.lii.org
THE LIBRARIANS INDEX TO THE INTERNET

ORIGIN US
SPEED ✓✓✓✓✓
INFO ✓✓✓✓
EASE ✓✓✓✓✓

This is a search engine with a difference in that all the source material has been selected and evaluated by librarians specifically for their use in public libraries. This doesn't stop you using it though, and it is very good for obscure searches and research – like putting together a web site guide for example.

www.dmoz.org
THE OPEN DIRECTORY PROJECT

ORIGIN WORLD
WIDE
SPEED ✓✓✓✓✓
INFO ✓✓✓✓
EASE ✓✓✓✓

The goal is to produce the most comprehensive directory of the web, by relying on an army (some 36,000) of volunteer editors, and if you want to get involved it's easy to sign yourself up. If it can't help with your query it puts you through to one of the mainstream search engines.

Finding the search engine that suits you is a matter of personal requirements and taste, here are some other very good, tried and trusted ones:

www.alltheweb.com – no frills, similar to Google.

http://uk.altavista.com – limited but very efficient.

www.dogpile.com – straightforward and no mess.

www.excite.co.uk – one of the best and most comprehensive.

www.hotbot.com – good for shopping and entertainment.

www.infoplease.com – good for homework.

www.kidtastic.com – safe search for kids.

www.lycos.co.uk – easy-to-use and popular.

www.msn.co.uk – searching is just one of the many things you can do here.

www.northernlight.com – specialist news and information search engine that has broadened out into the mainstream.

www.scotland.org – small Scotland-oriented site.

www.searchopolis.com – excellent for homework.

Ships and Boats

Boats

www.boatlinks.co.uk
BOATING DIRECTORY

ORIGIN UK ✓✓✓✓
SPEED ✓✓✓✓
INFO ✓✓✓✓✓
EASE ✓✓✓✓

A superb directory and the place to start if you're looking for any information on shipping or boating, there are 16 categories in all and several hundred links.

http://boatbuilding.com
THE BOAT BUILDING COMMUNITY

ORIGIN UK
SPEED ✓✓✓
INFO ✓✓✓✓✓
EASE ✓✓✓✓

If you want to repair or build a boat then here's where to go, with features and discussion forums to help you on your way. There's also a very good directory of links to suppliers and resource sites.

www.buyaboat.co.uk
BUY A BOAT MAGAZINE

ORIGIN UK
SPEED ✓✓✓
INFO ✓✓✓✓
EASE ✓✓✓✓

Primarily a vehicle to get you to subscribe to the magazine, the site offers information on brokers and the details of some 7,000 boats for sale.

Ships and Navy

www.royal-navy.mod.uk
THE ROYAL NAVY

ORIGIN UK
SPEED ✓✓✓
INFO ✓✓✓✓
EASE ✓✓✓✓

An excellent site from the Royal Navy giving details of the ships, submarines and aircraft and what it's like to be a part of it all. There's a video gallery featuring a crew's shore visits and a Harrier Jump Jet. Apart from all the information, you can have a go on the interactive frigate. See also **www.ships.co.uk** for more historical information.

www.red-duster.co.uk
RED DUSTER MAGAZINE

ORIGIN UK
SPEED ✓✓✓✓
INFO ✓✓✓✓
EASE ✓✓✓✓

Red Duster is a merchant navy enthusiasts' site offering lots in the way of history covering sail, stream and shipping lines. There's also a section on the history of customs. To find out what the current merchant navy are up to go to **www.merchantnavyofficers.com** where you find information and links.

www.maritimematters.com
OCEAN LINERS AND CRUISE SHIPS

ORIGIN UK
SPEED ✓✓✓
INFO ✓✓✓✓
EASE ✓✓✓✓

An informative site with data on over 100 ships from the earliest liners to the most modern, each has its own page with quality pictures and some virtual tours. It is also good for news and links to related sites.

Other Watercraft

www.hovercraft.org.uk
HOVERCRAFT

ORIGIN UK	If you're into hovercrafts or are just interested,
SPEED ✓✓✓	here's the place to look with 3 sections – Britain,
INFO ✓✓✓	Europe and the world which just about covers it all.
EASE ✓✓✓✓	

www.jetski.ndirect.co.uk
JETSKI

ORIGIN UK	A comprehensive links site with sections on where to
SPEED ✓✓✓	Jetski, how to buy one and look after it, dealers, tips
INFO ✓✓✓	and tricks – all to the sound of Hawaii 5-0's theme
EASE ✓✓✓✓	tune.

Shopping

To many people shopping is what the Internet is all about, and it does offer an opportunity to get some tremendous bargains. Watch out for hidden costs such as delivery charges or finance deals that seem attractive until you compare them with what's available elsewhere.

For help on finding comparative prices, see the price comparison sites on page 293, in fact starting your shopping trip at a site like www.kelkoo.com may prove to be a wise move.

Another good place to start is at the Which? *Magazine web site, www.which.net who run a scheme to protect online shoppers. They sign up retailers to a code of practice that covers the way they trade.*

To quote Which?:
'The *Which?* Web Trader Scheme is designed to make sure
consumers get a fair deal and to provide them with protection if things go wrong. *Which?* Web Traders agree to meet
and abide by our Code of Practice. If we receive complaints
from consumers about the service from a web trader
displaying the *Which?* Web Trader logo, we will investigate
and may withdraw our permission for a trader to display
the logo.'
*In this book we indicate which of the sites listed are part of the
scheme and follow the code of practice with this symbol –* W?WT.
You can get a complete list from the Which? *web site.*

www.tradingstandards.gov.uk
TRADING STANDARDS CENTRAL

ORIGIN UK
SPEED ✓✓✓
INFO ✓✓✓✓
EASE ✓✓✓✓

Find out where you stand and what to do if you
think you're being ripped off or someone is not trading fairly – you can even take a quiz about it. There
are advice guides to print off or download and there
is help and advice to businesses and schools as well
as consumers.

www.dooyoo.co.uk
MAKE YOUR OPINION COUNT

ORIGIN GERMANY
SPEED ✓✓✓
INFO ✓✓✓✓
EASE ✓✓✓✓

Media darling Doo Yoo is a site where you the
consumer can give your opinion or a review on any
product that's available to buy, this way you get
unbiased opinions about them – in theory. The
'products' range in some 18 categories from books
to TV shows and it's easy to contribute, earning
Doo Yoo miles, like Air Miles. See also
www.ciao.com where you can actually get paid a
small amount of money for your opinion

The virtual high street

www.marks-and-spencer.co.uk
CLOTHES AND GIFTS

ORIGIN	UK
SPEED	✓✓
INFO	✓✓✓✓
VALUE	✓✓✓
EASE	✓✓✓✓

This attractive site offers a number of options and there are several hundred lines available to buy:

1. Home – with lots of ideas. Register for the catalogue or wedding service.
2. Gifts – register your wedding gift list, get ideas.
3. Flowers – from orchids to baskets, even outdoor plants.
4. Kids – fashion and schoolwear.
5. Men – the latest fashions, including shoes.
6. Women – their latest collections.
7. Offers – from gifts to clothes.

The delivery charge is variable, but starts at £2.95. There are good features such as the running total and you can buy gift vouchers, but overall you can't help thinking that the process of shopping is too slow to make it worthwhile.

www.wellbeing.com
BOOTS

ORIGIN	UK
SPEED	✓✓✓✓
INFO	✓✓✓✓✓
VALUE	✓✓✓
EASE	✓✓✓✓

A new look and approach from Boots, with a clinical site that offers health advice as well as shopping. There's a comprehensive guide covering health, beauty and baby topics, a good hospital guide, a confidential ask the pharmacist section and a list of specialist stores in your area. The shopping bit is quite understated and is basically split into eight sections; men, fitness, mother and baby, beauty, health, nutrition, gifts and personal care. There's also a good search facility, free delivery on some items and you can also use your Advantage card as in the store. You can't return unwanted goods to a Boots shop though; you have to send it back to Wellbeing.

www.whsmith.co.uk
W.H.SMITH

ORIGIN	UK
SPEED	✓✓✓
INFO	✓✓✓✓✓
VALUE	✓✓✓
EASE	✓✓✓✓

Smiths have re-vamped their site to a much cleaner and easier to navigate format, with content making way for shopping. There is a great deal here though including:

1. Books – with the latest offers and author features.
2. Music – lots of chart offers.
3. DVD and video – more offers as well as the latest film previews.
4. Games – good range and good prices.
5. Magazines – discounts off top sellers.
6. Stationery – great multi-buys and exclusive ranges.

Other sections include a store finder, an excellent education zone and the Hutchinson Encyclopaedia, a photo service and their Amazing Adventures range. Delivery charges start at £2.95, and unwanted goods can be returned to your local store.

www.woolworths.co.uk
WELL WORTH IT

ORIGIN	UK
SPEED	✓✓✓✓
INFO	✓✓✓✓
VALUE	✓✓✓✓
EASE	✓✓✓

A bright and breezy site from Woolworths with all you'd expect in terms of range and prices. They are particularly good on kid's stuff with strong prices on movies, chart music, clothes and mobile phones. There's also gardening, picnicking, pets and sweets. It's not that easy to navigate but there is a good search facility. All in all a much improved offering on last year's effort.

www.argos.co.uk
ARGOS CATALOGUE

ORIGIN UK
SPEED ✓✓✓✓
INFO ✓✓✓✓
VALUE ✓✓✓✓
EASE ✓✓✓✓

Argos offers an excellent range of products (some 8,000) across fourteen different categories as per their catalogue. There are some good bargains to be had. You can now reserve an item at your local store, once you've checked that they have it in stock. They've improved the search facility and you can find a product via its catalogue number if you've a catalogue handy that is. Delivery is £3.95 unless you spend more than £100 in which case it's free. Returns can be made to your local store.

www.debenhams.co.uk
AWARD WINNING FAMILY SERVICE

ORIGIN UK
SPEED ✓✓✓
INFO ✓✓✓✓
VALUE ✓✓✓✓
EASE ✓✓✓✓

Not a common sight on the high street but Debenhams have a very good site aimed at their retailing strengths: gifts, weddings and fashion. Delivery costs vary.

General retailers, directories and online department stores

www.which.net
Which? MAGAZINE

ORIGIN UK
SPEED ✓✓✓✓
INFO ✓✓✓✓✓
VALUE ✓✓✓✓✓
EASE ✓✓✓✓

By joining up you can get access to their product reviews and benefit from special arrangements with selected retailers to get good prices on their best buys. If you're a member there's an excellent selection of reports and articles on consumer subjects. Check out the alphabetical listing of several hundred stores that have met their trading criteria and show the *Which?* Web trader badge; unfortunately they are not listed by shopping category.

www.2020shops.com
THE SHOPPER'S FRIEND

ORIGIN	UK
SPEED	✓✓✓✓✓
INFO	✓✓✓✓✓
VALUE	✓✓✓✓✓
EASE	✓✓✓✓✓

A really likeable site with a great ethic – they don't do cosy deals with other retailers for exposure so the shops they select and rate are there on merit. They are one of the few that give extra information on the shops such as delivery costs, plus some shopping advice. It's fast too. The only site in this book to get full marks.

www.goldfishguide.co.uk
GOLDFISH GUIDES

ORIGIN	UK
SPEED	✓✓✓✓
INFO	✓✓✓✓✓
VALUE	✓✓✓✓
EASE	✓✓✓✓

Another good place for consumer advice and an easy approach to selecting the right store to buy from. The Goldfish guides cover a wide range of shopping categories all written by independent journalists. Essentially the idea is that you read up on it, compare prices on it then buy it – simple really. The site is well designed and easy-to-use.

www.shopsmart.com
ONLINE SHOPPING MADE SIMPLE

ORIGIN	UK
SPEED	✓✓✓
INFO	✓✓✓✓
VALUE	✓✓✓✓✓
EASE	✓✓✓✓

This is probably the best of the sites that offer a directory of links to specialist online retailers. Search within the eighteen categories or the whole site for a particular item or store. Each of the 1000 or so retail sites featured are reviewed and rated using a star system. The reviews are quite kind, and the worst sites are excluded anyway. There's a price comparison service on all the major shopping categories as well.

www.mytaxi.co.uk

SHOP AND SEARCH FOR THE BEST PRICES

ORIGIN UK	Personalise your online shopping experience using
SPEED ✓✓✓	My Taxi to search retailers' web sites for the best
INFO ✓✓✓✓	prices on the goods you are interested in.
VALUE ✓✓✓✓	Particularly strong on music and video, less so on
EASE ✓✓✓	other items. The recommended online stores are

selected according to safety and service, there is no
star rating system; however, they are well
categorised.

www.safestreet.co.uk

SHOP SAFELY

ORIGIN UK	Safe Street provide the technology behind many
SPEED ✓✓✓✓	online stores and they've provided this directory
INFO ✓✓✓✓	which covers some 20 shopping categories from arts
VALUE ✓✓✓✓	and crafts to sports gear, including charities and
EASE ✓✓	travel. The shops aren't rated at all, it's simply a

fairly ad hoc directory, but there are some good
bargains to be had if you're patient.

www.edirectory.co.uk

IF IT'S OUT THERE, BUY IT HERE

ORIGIN UK	A nice looking directory with a wide variety of
SPEED ✓✓✓✓	shops and goods to choose from, it has a good
INFO ✓✓✓✓	reputation for service as well.
VALUE ✓✓✓✓	
EASE ✓✓	

www.shopspy.co.uk

THE GUIDE THAT SHOPS BEFORE IT RATES

ORIGIN UK	A great idea, the shop spy team actually use the
SPEED ✓✓✓✓	shops on their listing and then report back on things
INFO ✓✓✓✓✓	like value, quality of the goods and service then
VALUE ✓✓✓✓	rates them accordingly. The list of more than 400
EASE ✓✓✓	

stores is fairly eclectic and you can easily see the best
rated ones. The site could be much better organised
though.

www.zoom.co.uk
MORE THAN JUST A SHOP

ORIGIN	UK
SPEED	✓✓✓✓✓
INFO	✓✓✓
VALUE	✓✓✓
EASE	✓✓✓✓

This is an excellent magazine-style site, with lots of
features other than shopping, such as free Internet
access, e-mail and a dating service. Shopping
consists of links to specialist retailers. You can earn
loyalty points, enter prize draws and there are a
number of exclusive offers as well. Not always the
cheapest, but an entertaining shopping site.

www.virgin.net/shopping
LIFESTYLE AND SHOPPING GUIDE

ORIGIN	UK
SPEED	✓✓✓
INFO	✓✓✓✓✓
EASE	✓✓✓✓

Virgin's shopping guide is comprehensive covering
all major categories while allowing retailers to
feature some of their best offers. It also attempts to
be a complete service for entertainment and leisure
needs with excellent sections on music, travel and
cinema in particular.

www.shoppingunlimited.co.uk
INDEPENDENT RECOMMENDATION

ORIGIN	UK
SPEED	✓✓✓✓
INFO	✓✓✓✓
VALUE	✓✓✓✓
EASE	✓✓✓✓✓

Owned by the *Guardian* newspaper, this site offers
hundreds of links to stores that they've reviewed. It
also offers help to inexperienced shoppers and guidance on using credit cards online. There are also
links to other *Guardian* sites such as news and
sport.

www.shoppersuniverse.co.uk
GREAT UNIVERSAL STORES

ORIGIN UK
SPEED ✓✓✓✓
INFO ✓✓✓✓
VALUE ✓✓✓✓
EASE ✓✓✓✓✓

Avoid having to shop around by using this clear and simple site that offers a wide variety of products at excellent prices. It also hosts and recommends other stores too.

www.indigosquare.co.uk
NOT JUST FOR BARCLAYCARD OWNERS

ORIGIN UK
SPEED ✓✓✓✓
INFO ✓✓✓
VALUE ✓✓✓
EASE ✓✓✓✓

Barclays' new and hyped site provides a shopping search facility. Once you've found what you're looking for, you'll be directed to the web site of the shop that's selling the product where you can complete your purchase. The shop will then confirm your order and ensure that your goods are delivered to you. All the shops have been vetted as safe sites with good service. The selection of shops you can visit is quite limited compared to other similar sites, however, there are some good bargains and enough to cover most shopper's needs. W?WT

www.thevirtualmall.co.uk
THE VIRTUAL SHOPPING CENTRE

ORIGIN UK
SPEED ✓✓✓
INFO ✓✓✓✓
EASE ✓✓✓✓✓

Literally browse by floor then click on the shop you want to go into. There's no real advantage in using it other than having all the best stores represented graphically in one place, even then some links don't work.

www.screenshop.co.uk
SHOP ON TV, WEB OR CATALOGUE

ORIGIN UK
SPEED ✓✓✓✓
INFO ✓✓✓✓
VALUE ✓✓✓✓
EASE ✓✓✓✓

As a shopping channel on Sky, Screenshop was already successful, this well-put-together site shows off the breadth of their range and, at time of writing, you can earn 5% discount by shopping from the web site.

www.hard2buy4.co.uk
GIFT IDEAS

ORIGIN	UK
SPEED	✓✓✓
INFO	✓✓✓✓✓
VALUE	✓✓✓✓
EASE	✓✓✓✓

Excellent gift shop with a wide range of unusual products including celebrity items, activities and gifts for men, women and children in separate sections, some good offers too. For more unusual gifts and stuff you don't need but would really like, try www.iwantoneofthose.com

www.streetsonline.co.uk
STREETS AHEAD

ORIGIN	UK
SPEED	✓✓✓✓
INFO	✓✓✓✓
VALUE	✓✓✓✓
EASE	✓✓✓✓

One of Britain's most successful online retailers, Streets Online not only offers excellent books, music and movie shops but an entertainment magazine and an exchange service where you can swap your unwanted goods. You can also download trailers, audio clips and e-books.

www.crueltyfreeshop.com
CRUELTY FREE SHOP

ORIGIN	UK
SPEED	✓✓✓✓
INFO	✓✓✓✓
VALUE	✓✓✓
EASE	✓✓✓

A wide range of products on sale all of which are guaranteed not to have had any animal cruelty or exploitation in their production. The range is wide and the prices aren't bad either. It can only improve, a good idea that deserves some success.

www.shoppingmaster.co.uk
SUPPORT YOUR LOCAL SCHOOL

ORIGIN	UK
SPEED	✓✓✓✓
INFO	✓✓✓
VALUE	✓✓✓✓
EASE	✓✓✓✓

Select a school then go shopping using the 'school master directory', then when you purchase something money is paid into a charitable foundation. Each school will be allocated an account into which commission nominated for that school will be paid. The money from the account will be paid to the nominated school at quarterly intervals when the sum exceeds £50.

www.ybag.com
LET SOMEONE ELSE DO THE SHOPPING

ORIGIN	UK
SPEED	✓✓✓✓
INFO	✓✓✓
VALUE	✓✓✓✓
EASE	✓✓✓✓

Tell the Ybag team what you want and what you want to pay, and then they put a seller in touch with you. As long as you don't put in requests at silly prices you won't be disappointed, but be prepared for a wait.

Value for money

www.bigsave.com
SAVE, SAVE, SAVE...

ORIGIN	UK
SPEED	✓✓✓
INFO	✓✓✓
VALUE	✓✓✓✓✓
EASE	✓✓✓✓

Bigsave has six sections: travel, electronics, mobile phones, clothing, jewellery and best buys. The emphasis is on value and the choice has improved massively with some 120,000 items available. Registration is required, but you can track your purchase from order to delivery. Delivery costs vary according to product. **W?WT**

www.onlinediscount.com
THE VERY BEST DISCOUNTS

ORIGIN	UK
SPEED	✓✓✓✓
INFO	✓✓✓
VALUE	✓✓✓✓
EASE	✓✓✓✓

Online Discount specialise in monitoring Internet stores and highlighting those giving the best discounts in any one of sixteen major categories. You are quickly put through to a list of the key shops, unfortunately in a category like 'Books' you get a list of all the major retailers as, of course, they're all discounting in one form or another.

www.priceoffers.co.uk
SUPERMARKETS SORTED

ORIGIN	UK
SPEED	✓✓✓
INFO	✓✓✓✓
VALUE	✓✓✓✓✓
EASE	✓✓✓✓

The online guide to high street bargains, check out the site then choose which supermarket to visit for the best offers. There are several sections: the newsletter offering customised updates; an editor's choice of the best bargains; buy one get one free deals; store deals; and lastly a selection found by shoppers willing to share their bargain finds.

British shopping

www.buckinghamgate.co.uk
THE BEST OF BRITISH QUALITY AND DESIGN

ORIGIN	UK
SPEED	✓✓✓✓
INFO	✓✓✓✓
VALUE	✓✓
EASE	✓✓✓✓✓

Basically a selection of links to posh shops, or that's what it's supposed to look like, as a few are not quite that up-market. However, you can buy Bentley merchandise, book a flight on British Airways and treat yourself to a weekend at a health farm. What ho! **W?WT**

For more quintessentially British shops check out these sites:
www.harrods.co.uk – a small selection of their products available to buy.
www.british-shopping.com – UK shopping links and directory.
www.classicengland.co.uk – the best British products.
www.distinctlybritish.com – a British shop directory with a wide range of food, clothing, gift and children's retailers on offer.

www.scotsmart.com
SCOTSMART

ORIGIN	UK
SPEED	✓✓✓✓
INFO	✓✓✓✓✓
VALUE	✓✓✓
EASE	✓✓✓✓

A Scottish directory of sites, not just for shopping but covering most areas, you can search by theme or category and the shopping section is split into books, clothing, food, gifts and highland wear. See also **www.scotch-corner.co.uk** which is Scottish through and through and the broader reaching **www.scotstore.com**

The rest

There are hundreds, possibly thousands of online stores and shopping malls, it would be impossible to include them all, but here is a list of some of this year's best reviewed sites and what they do.

THE BEST

www.bobsshopwindow.com – Bob's Shop Window is a comprehensive directory of shops, well-categorised but not rated in any way.

www.eshopone.co.uk – posh products and cheap prices. **W?WT**

www.eshops.co.uk – great design, over 7,200 shops listed in the directory with some excellent offers.

www.gotogifts.co.uk – gift ideas in profusion, highlights are the blokes' and girls' guide to gifts. There's also a reminder service.

www.I-stores.com – a very good store search engine.

www.malltraders.com – a well-designed shopping directory aiming to give small businesses a big Net presence.

www.shopeeze.com – nice design and good prices too.

http://theukhighstreet.com – a good UK directory, with the shops rated by you the customer.

www.ukshopsearch.com – above average search engine and quality design make this stand out from the crowd, you can also vent your frustrations out on the shopping experience in the shoppers forum.

COULD BE USEFUL

http://orders.mkn.co.uk – Market Net simply lists retailers and gives delivery times, good for the unusual though.

www.1shop.org – mall supporting small or medium sized UK businesses.

www.catxpress.com – very good for outdoor enthusiasts.

www.eplaza.co.uk – virtual shopping centre, nice design, not many shops though.

www.oneshopforall.co.uk – odd looking shop, good for unusual gifts though. W?WT

www.shopq.co.uk – massive set of shopping links, well categorised.

www.shop-shop-shop.co.uk – search the databases of over 200 shops, good links.

www.shoptour.co.uk – links to 900 secure shops in 14 categories.

www.shoppersempire.com – nice, wide-ranging store with some good offers. W?WT

www.shoppingtrolley.net – lots of shops and categories, boring design.

www.sortal.co.uk – very useful directory of UK shops sorted into 40 categories.

www.theukmall.co.uk – minimalist design, odd ratings and shop selection.

www.ukonlineshopping.com – comprehensive shop listing.

www.ukshops.co.uk – 500 shops this one, it's a bit of a mess design-wise.

LOYALTY SCHEMES AND UNUSUAL SHOPPING

www.beenz.co.uk
A NEW KIND OF MONEY

ORIGIN US	You earn beenz by visiting or spending money at
SPEED ✓✓✓✓	participating retailers, then you can use the beenz
INFO ✓✓✓✓	that you've built up to spend online at those shops.
VALUE ✓✓✓✓	See also Ipoints at **www.ipoints.co.uk**
EASE ✓✓✓✓	

www.smartcreds.co.uk
NO CREDIT CARD NEEDED

ORIGIN UK	You buy Smartcreds, top up you virtual wallet, then
SPEED ✓✓✓✓	you can shop in the UKSmart shop where there are
INFO ✓✓✓✓	over a hundred stores including high street names
VALUE ✓✓✓✓	who will accept Smartcreds as payment. Brilliant for
EASE ✓✓✓✓	children and teenagers. W?WT

Software

If you need to upgrade your software then these are the sites to go to. Shareware is where you get a program to use for a short period of time before you have to buy it, freeware is exactly what you'd think – free.

www.softwareparadise.co.uk
THE SMART WAY TO SHOP FOR SOFTWARE

ORIGIN UK	With over 250,000 titles and excellent offers make
SPEED ✓✓✓✓	this site the first stop. It's easy-to-use, there's a good
INFO ✓✓✓✓	search facility and plenty of products for Mac users.
VALUE ✓✓✓✓	There are links to sister sites offering low cost soft-
EASE ✓✓✓	ware for charities and students. **W?WT**

www.download.com
CNET

ORIGIN US	A superb site covering all types of software and
SPEED ✓✓✓✓	available downloads. There are masses of reviews as
INFO ✓✓✓✓✓	well as buying tips and price comparison tools; it
VALUE ✓✓✓✓	also covers handheld PCs, Linux and Macs.
EASE ✓✓✓	

www.softseek.com
ZDNET

ORIGIN US	Another excellent site with a huge amount of
SPEED ✓✓✓✓	resources to download, it's all a little overwhelming
INFO ✓✓✓✓✓	at first but the download directory is easy-to-use and
VALUE ✓✓✓✓	there's lots of free software available.
EASE ✓✓✓✓	

www.tucows.com
TUCOWS

ORIGIN US	Probably less irritating to use than ZDNet and
SPEED ✓✓✓✓✓	CNet, the software reviews are also entertaining in
INFO ✓✓✓✓✓	their own right, the best thing about it though is
VALUE ✓✓✓✓	that it's quick.
EASE ✓✓✓✓	

If you feel like shopping around a bit more see also:
http://home.netscape.com/plugins – if you're a
  Netscape fan then you can improve its performance with 'plug-ins' from this site.

> **www.completelyfreesoftware.com** – hundreds of free
> programs for you to download, from games to
> useful desktop accessories if it's available free,
> then its here.
> **www.davecentral.com** – lots of shareware, also good
> for Linux fans.
> **www.winplanet.com** – specialises in improving and
> discussing Windows applications.

www.bugnet.com

FIX THAT BUG

ORIGIN US	Subscribe to the Bug Net and they alert you to soft-
SPEED ✓✓✓	ware bugs, keep you up to date with reviews, analy-
INFO ✓✓✓	sis and the tests they carry out. You can then be sure
VALUE ✓✓✓✓	to buy the right fixes.
EASE ✓✓✓	

www.winzip.com

MANAGE FILES

ORIGIN US	Winzip allows you to save space on your PC by
SPEED ✓✓✓	compressing data, making it easier to e-mail files
INFO ✓✓✓✓	and unlock zipped files that have been sent to you. It
EASE ✓✓✓	takes a few minutes to download. For Macs go to
	www.aladdinsys.com

Space

www.space.com
MAKING SPACE POPULAR

ORIGIN US	An education-oriented site dedicated to space;
SPEED ✓✓✓	there's news, mission reports, technology, history,
INFO ✓✓✓✓✓	personalities, a kids' section and plenty of pictures.
VALUE ✓✓	The science section explores the planets and earth.
EASE ✓✓✓	You can buy goods at the space shop with delivery

cost dependent on purchase. See also Thinks Space at **http://library.thinkquest.org/26220** which is great for photos and links.

www.nasa.gov
THE OFFICIAL NASA SITE

ORIGIN US	This huge site provides comprehensive information
SPEED ✓✓✓	on the US National Aeronautical and Space
INFO ✓✓✓✓✓	Administration. There are details on each NASA
EASE ✓✓✓	site, launch timings, sections for news, kids, project

updates, and links to their specialist sites such the Hubble Space Telescope, Mars and Earth observation. For Britain's place in space go to **www.bnsc.gov.uk** or **www.ukspace.com** which is great for links.

www.spacedaily.com
YOUR PORTAL TO SPACE

ORIGIN US	A comprehensive newspaper-style site with a huge
SPEED ✓✓✓	amount of information and news about space and
INFO ✓✓✓✓✓	related subjects. It also has links to similar sister
EASE ✓✓✓	sites covering subjects like Mars, space war and

space travel.

www.astronomynow.com

THE UK'S BEST SELLING ASTRONOMY MAG

ORIGIN UK
SPEED ✓✓
INFO ✓✓✓✓
VALUE ✓✓
EASE ✓✓✓

Get the news and views from a British angle, plus reviews on the latest books. The store basically offers back issues of the magazine and posters.

www.StarTrails.com

STAR TRAILS SOCIETY

ORIGIN US
SPEED ✓✓✓
INFO ✓✓✓✓
EASE ✓✓✓✓

An entertaining magazine site that covers all aspects of popular astronomy. Features include the daily solar weather, classes on breaking science news and the latest astral headlines.

www.seds.org/billa/tnp/

THE NINE PLANETS

ORIGIN UK
SPEED ✓✓✓✓
INFO ✓✓✓✓✓
EASE ✓✓✓✓

A multimedia tour of the nine planets, stunning photography, interesting facts combined with good text. See also Bill Arnett's other interesting site on Nebulae at **http://seds.lpl.arizona.edu/billa/twn** where there are some beautiful pictures.

www.redcolony.com

MARS

ORIGIN US
SPEED ✓✓✓✓
INFO ✓✓✓✓✓
EASE ✓✓✓✓

A superb site all about the red planet. There is a synopsis of its history, plus details on past and future space missions with a focus on the colonisation of Mars. There's a great deal of information on things like terra forming and biogenesis, it's all taken very seriously too.

www.nauts.com
THE ASTRONAUT CONNECTION

ORIGIN US
SPEED ✓✓✓
INFO ✓✓✓✓✓
EASE ✓✓✓

In their words 'The Astronaut Connection has worked to create an educational and entertaining resource for space enthusiasts, young and old, to learn about astronauts and space exploration' and that just about sums up this excellent and informative site.

www.telescope.org
BRADFORD ROBOTIC TELESCOPE PROJECT

ORIGIN UK
SPEED ✓✓
INFO ✓✓✓✓
EASE ✓✓✓

Here you can view the stars and, once you've registered, ask for the telescope to be pointed at anything in the northern sky. There are plenty of images on the site and there's basic information on how the stars and our galaxy were formed.

http://www.heavens-above.com
IT'S ABOVE YOUR HEAD

ORIGIN US
SPEED ✓✓✓✓
INFO ✓✓✓✓✓
EASE ✓✓✓✓

Type in your location and they'll give you the exact time and precise location of the next visible pass of the International Space Station or space shuttle. They also help you to observe satellites and flares from Iridium satellites.

www.setiathome.ssl.berkeley.edu/
GET IN TOUCH WITH AN ALIEN

ORIGIN US
SPEED ✓✓✓
INFO ✓✓✓✓
EASE ✓✓✓

To borrow the official site description 'SETI@home is a scientific experiment that uses Internet-connected computers in the Search for Extraterrestrial Intelligence (SETI).' You can participate by running a free program that downloads and analyses radio telescope data. You could be the first!

Sport

One of the best uses of the Internet is to keep up to date with how your team is performing, or if you're a member of a team or association, keep each other updated.

General sports sites

www.sporting-life.com
THE SPORTING LIFE

ORIGIN UK
SPEED ✓✓✓✓
INFO ✓✓✓✓
EASE ✓✓✓✓

A very comprehensive sport site, with plenty of advice, tips, news and latest scores. It's considered to be one of the best, good for stories, in-depth analysis and overall coverage of the major sports.

www.sports.com
SPORTS NEWS AND SHOPPING

ORIGIN UK
SPEED ✓✓✓
INFO ✓✓✓✓
VALUE ✓✓✓
EASE ✓✓✓✓✓

With a strong international feel, this site offers much in the way of information on all key sports, particularly football, in tandem with a shopping service mainly covering cricket, football and golf.

www.bbc.co.uk/sport
BBC SPORT COVERAGE

ORIGIN UK
SPEED ✓✓✓
INFO ✓✓✓✓✓
EASE ✓✓✓✓✓

They may have lost the right to broadcast many sporting events but their coverage at this level is excellent – much broader than most and it's always up-to-date.

www.skysports.com
THE BEST OF SKY SPORT

ORIGIN UK
SPEED ✓✓✓✓
INFO ✓✓✓✓
EASE ✓✓✓✓

Excellent for the Premiership and football in general, but also covers other sports very well particularly cricket and both forms of rugby. Includes a section featuring video and audio clips, and there are interviews with stars. You can vote in their polls, e-mail programmes or try sports trivia quizzes. Lots of adverts spoil it.

www.rivals.net
THE RIVALS NETWORK

ORIGIN UK
SPEED ✓✓✓✓
INFO ✓✓✓✓✓
EASE ✓✓✓✓

Independent of any news organisations Rivals is basically a network of specialist sites covering the whole gamut of major and minor sports, each site has its own editor who is passionate about the sport they cover. In general it's excellent with good quality content and pictures.

www.talksport.net
HOME OF TALK SPORT RADIO

ORIGIN UK
SPEED ✓✓✓
INFO ✓✓✓✓
VALUE ✓✓
EASE ✓✓✓✓

A pretty down-market site where you can listen to sports news and debate while you work. The information comes from *Sporting Life* but it's up-to-date. There's also an audio archive and scheduling information, view the fantastic sports babe and visit the bookstore. There's also a sister site where you can place bets.

Other good all-rounders, and sites with good links:
www.allstarsites.com – directory of some 2,000 sports sites, you rate the ones you like.
www.EL.com/elinks/sports – list of American-oriented sports links.

www.oldsport.com – very good directory of over
  7,500 sports sites.
www.sportal.co.uk – good, football-oriented magazine site.
www.sportquest.com – excellent search engine and
  directory.
www.sportsonline.co.uk – odd-looking site with
  lots of links and an OK search engine.
www.sportszine.co.uk – excellent search engine and
  directory, all sites are well reviewed.

Sites on specific sports

AMERICAN FOOTBALL

www.nfl.com
NATIONAL FOOTBALL LEAGUE

ORIGIN US
SPEED ✓✓✓
INFO ✓✓✓✓
EASE ✓✓✓✓

American football's online bible, it's a huge
official site with details and statistics bursting
from every page. It's got information on all the
teams, players and likely draft picks; there's
also information on NFL Europe and links to
other key sites. All it really lacks is gossip! See also
the authoritative http://football.espn.go.com/nfl
and also www.nflplayers.com for the latest news
and background on all the key people in the game.

ARCHERY

www.archery.org
INTERNATIONAL ARCHERY FEDERATION

ORIGIN UK
SPEED ✓✓✓
INFO ✓✓✓✓
EASE ✓✓✓✓

Get the official news, events listings, rankings and records information from this fairly mundane site; and you can learn more about field archery at **www.fieldarcher.com** which has a great enthusiastic amateur feel. For a more entertaining and chatty site try **www.theglade.co.uk** which is basically an online magazine, devoted to all forms of archery. Lastly, check out **www.archery.net** for equipment and advice.

ATHLETICS AND RUNNING

www.athletix.net
WORLD ATHLETICS NEWS

ORIGIN GREECE
SPEED ✓✓✓✓
INFO ✓✓✓✓✓
EASE ✓✓✓✓

This is an excellent, comprehensive site that is easy-to-use and covers all aspects of the sport. There are reports on each Grand Prix and other events, with statistics and links to other specialist sites.

To see what Linford Christie is up to these days go to **www.nuff-respect.co.uk**

www.ukathletics.org
THE GOVERNING BODY

ORIGIN UK
SPEED ✓✓✓✓
INFO ✓✓✓✓✓
EASE ✓✓✓

Many official 'governing body' sites are pretty boring affairs, not so UK Athletics which contains lots of features, is newsy and written with an obvious sense of enthusiasm. There are details on forthcoming events, reports on aspects of the sport, records, biographies of key athletes and advice on

keeping fit. See also **www.british-athletics.co.uk**
which is a typical boring site but has a directory of
clubs and regional events.

www.runnersworld.com
RUNNER'S WORLD MAGAZINE

ORIGIN	US
SPEED	✓✓✓
INFO	✓✓✓✓
EASE	✓✓✓✓

A rather dry site with tips from getting started
through to advanced running. There's lots of information, news and records plus reviews on shoes and
gear. See also the less visually exciting but comprehensive **www.runnersweb.com**

www.realrunner.com
A RUNNING COMMUNITY

ORIGIN	UK
SPEED	✓✓✓✓
INFO	✓✓✓✓
EASE	✓✓✓✓

A very well put together site with lots of resources
to help runners in terms of both equipment and
advice. There's an online health check, details of
events, marathons and profiles of the athletes. Good
design ensures that the site is a pleasure to use. For
details on all the tracks in the UK go to
www.runtrackdir.com, while for equipment advice
try Runnersworld **www.runnersworld.ltd.uk**

AUSTRALIAN RULES FOOTBALL

www.afl.com.au
AUSTRALIAN FOOTBALL LEAGUE

ORIGIN	AUSTRALIA
SPEED	✓✓✓
INFO	✓✓✓✓✓
EASE	✓✓✓✓

A top quality site covering all aspects of the game
including team news, player profiles and statistics as
well as the latest gossip and speculation.

BASEBALL

www.mlb.com
MAJOR LEAGUE BASEBALL

ORIGIN US	All you need to know about the top teams and the
SPEED ✓✓✓✓	World Series, it's not the best-designed site but
INFO ✓✓✓✓	there's good information and statistics on the game
EASE ✓✓✓✓	and the key players as well as related articles and

features. If you want to find out more, a good place to try is **www.baseball-links.com** which is easy-to-use; for the British game try **www.gbbaseball.co.uk**

BASKETBALL

www.nba.com
NATIONAL BASKETBALL ASSOCIATION

ORIGIN US	A comprehensive official site with features on the
SPEED ✓✓✓	teams, players and games; there's also an excellent
INFO ✓✓✓✓✓	photo gallery and you can watch some of the most
EASE ✓✓✓✓	important points if you have the right software. For

the official line on British basketball go to **www.bbl.org.uk** or **www.britball.com** which is unofficial but more fun and also covers Ireland.

BOWLS

www.bowlsengland.com
ENGLISH BOWLING ASSOCIATION

ORIGIN UK	Poor design lets the site down, but if you persevere
SPEED ✓✓	you'll find all you need to know about lawn bowls
INFO ✓✓✓✓	in England, including a good set of links to associ-
EASE ✓✓✓	ated sites and even tips on green maintenance.

www.bowlsclubs.co.uk

INFORMATION ON BOWLING CLUBS

ORIGIN UK
SPEED ✓✓✓
INFO ✓✓✓✓
EASE ✓✓✓

A much-improved site in terms of information, you can get the latest news on the game, links, events diary, rules and player profiles.

www.eiba.co.uk

ENGLAND INDOOR BOWLING ASSOCIATION

ORIGIN UK
SPEED ✓✓✓
INFO ✓✓✓✓
EASE ✓✓✓

A very basic site giving an overview of the game, links and background information on competitions and rules.

BOXING

www.houseofboxing.com

HOME FOR BOXING ON THE NET

ORIGIN US
SPEED ✓✓✓
INFO ✓✓✓✓
EASE ✓✓✓✓

A beautifully designed site that gives comprehensive coverage on the world of boxing, including video interviews, reviews and features. See also **www.boxinginsider.com** which is good for chat and stats. There's also **www.heavyweights.co.uk** who cover the hype around heavyweight boxing.

www.world-boxing.com

FRANK WARREN

ORIGIN UK
SPEED ✓✓✓✓
INFO ✓✓✓✓
EASE ✓✓✓✓

A nicely designed site with some big name columnists, interviews and lots of information and statistics plus details of the key fighters.

For the different boxing authorities:
www.wbaonline.com – WBA.
www.ajapa.qc.ca/wbc/index/html – WBC.
www.worldboxingfed.com – WBF.
www.btInternet.com/wbuboxing/ – WBU.

www.femboxer.com – women's boxing.
www.amateurboxing.freeserve.co.uk – Amateur
  Boxing Association of England.

CLAY SHOOTING

www.clayshooting.co.uk
CLAY SHOOTING MAGAZINE

ORIGIN UK	A good introduction to the sport with a beginner's
SPEED ✓✓✓	guide to start you off and a good set of links to key
INFO ✓✓✓✓	suppliers and associated sites. There's also an online
VALUE ✓✓✓	shop where you can buy the odd essential item such
EASE ✓✓✓	as global positioning systems and dog food.

Serious shooters can go to the comprehensive
www.hotbarrels.com

CRICKET

www.uk.cricket.org or www.cricinfo.com
THE HOME OF CRICKET ON THE NET

ORIGIN UK	Simply the best cricket site on the Internet bar none.
SPEED ✓✓✓✓	In depth analysis, match reports, player profiles,
INFO ✓✓✓✓✓	statistics, links to other more specialised sites and
VALUE ✓✓✓	live written commentary. There's also a shop with
EASE ✓✓✓✓	lots of cricket goodies, delivery is included in the

price.

www.khel.com
WORLD CRICKET

ORIGIN INDIA
SPEED ✓✓✓✓
INFO ✓✓✓✓✓
EASE ✓✓✓✓

Another site for the real fan, it's particularly good for checking statistics whether it is on players or matches. It has a comprehensive set of links to other cricket sites too. A real labour of love.

www.wisden.com
WISDEN CRICKET MONTHLY

ORIGIN UK
SPEED ✓✓✓✓
INFO ✓✓✓✓
EASE ✓✓✓✓

The best features from the magazine, created in association with the *Guardian* and its excellent cricket site www.cricketunlimited.co.uk. Some of the best cricket journalism you can get. See also www.cricket.org and www.cricnet.co.uk

www.lords.org
THE OFFICIAL LINE ON CRICKET

ORIGIN UK
SPEED ✓✓✓
INFO ✓✓✓✓✓
EASE ✓✓✓✓

Here you'll find news with plenty of information about the game and players, even a quiz and an excellent section on women's cricket. Good links to governing bodies, associations, the MCC and ECB. If you have RealPlayer, there's access to live games on audio via the BBC.

www.webbsoc.demon.co.uk
WOMEN'S CRICKET ON THE WEB

ORIGIN UK
SPEED ✓✓✓✓
INFO ✓✓✓✓
EASE ✓✓✓

There are not many sites about women's cricket, this is probably the best, with features, news, fixture lists, match reports and player profiles. Nothing fancy, but it works.

CYCLING

These are sites aimed at the more serious sportsman, for more leisurely cycling see page 83 and for holidays turn to page 430.

www.bcf.uk.com/
BRITISH CYCLING FEDERATION

ORIGIN UK	The governing body for cycling, the site doesn't
SPEED ✓✓✓	contain a huge amount of data but you can still
INFO ✓✓✓	get information on events, rules, clubs and
EASE ✓✓✓✓	rankings, as well as contact names for coaching
	and development.

www.bikemagic.com
IT'S BIKETASTIC!

ORIGIN UK	Whether you're a beginner or an old hand, the
SPEED ✓✓✓	enthusiastic and engaging tone of this site will
INFO ✓✓✓✓	convert you or enhance your cycling experience.
VALUE ✓✓✓	There's plenty of news and features, as well as
EASE ✓✓✓✓	reviews on bike parts and gadgets. There's also a
	classified ads section and a selection of links to other

biking web sites, all of which are rated. It's also worth checking out **www.bikinguk.net** who are big on mountain biking.

www.letour.fr
TOUR DE FRANCE

ORIGIN FRANCE	Written in several languages this site covers the Tour
SPEED ✓✓✓✓	in some depth with details on the teams, riders and
INFO ✓✓✓✓	general background information.
EASE ✓✓✓	

DARTS

www.embassydarts.com
EMBASSY WORLD DARTS

ORIGIN UK	Whether you think darts qualifies as a sport or not,
SPEED ✓✓✓✓	this well-designed site gives a great deal of informa-
INFO ✓✓✓✓✓	tion about the game, its players and the tournament.
EASE ✓✓✓✓	See also **www.cyberdarts.com** for more information

and good links to other darts sites. For some
outstanding advice on how to play the game visit
the labour of love that is **www.dartbase.com**

EQUESTRIAN

www.equestrianonline.com
EQUESTRIANS ONLINE

ORIGIN UK	Get all the news and results on the sport with a
SPEED ✓✓✓	bookstore, articles by those involved, profiles of the
INFO ✓✓✓✓✓	riders, owners and trainers, training tips and forums
EASE ✓✓✓✓	on each event. A very well-designed site.

www.bhs.org.uk
BRITISH HORSE SOCIETY

ORIGIN UK	A charity that looks after the welfare of horses, here
SPEED ✓✓✓✓	you can get information on insurance, links, events
INFO ✓✓✓✓	and trials.
EASE ✓✓✓✓	

www.horseonline.co.uk
A DEFINITIVE RESOURCE

ORIGIN UK	Another excellent horse site with lots of news,
SPEED ✓✓✓✓	features and chat, there's also plenty of advice on
INFO ✓✓✓✓	buying and looking after your horse.
EASE ✓✓✓✓	

EXTREME SPORTS

www.bxtreme.net

BE EXTREME

ORIGIN UK	All the major 'extreme' sports are well covered at
SPEED ✓✓✓✓	this excellent web site; from BMX to skydiving to
INFO ✓✓✓✓	wakeboarding. Each section gives an overview of
EASE ✓✓✓✓	the sport, links and photos, plus a chat room.

See also the graphically brilliant but slow
www.adrenalin-hit.com Actually it's worth
a visit just for the design alone.

FISHING

www.fishing.co.uk

HOME OF UK FISHING ON THE NET

ORIGIN UK	A huge site that offers information on where to fish,
SPEED ✓✓✓✓	how to fish, where's the best place to stay near fish,
INFO ✓✓✓✓✓	even fishing holidays. There's also advice on equip-
VALUE ✓✓	ment, a records section and links to shops and shop
EASE ✓✓✓✓	locations. Shop on-site for fishing books and maga-

zines. See also **www.anglersnet.co.uk** for good writing and yet more information and the excellent
www.nimpopo.com for all your tackle needs.

FOOTBALL

www.footballnews.co.uk

MORE COVERAGE THAN THE MILLENNIUM DOME

ORIGIN UK	For depth of coverage this is hard to beat – and
SPEED ✓✓✓✓	they've got Des Lynam. It's less cluttered and easier
INFO ✓✓✓✓✓	to use than most other football sites, it's also
EASE ✓✓✓✓	up-to-date and doesn't miss much.

It's worth just having a look at these other sites listed below; just pick the one you like best.

www.football365.co.uk – outspoken and fun, comprehensive too.

www.guardian.co.uk/football – great writing and irreverent articles.

www.on-the-ball.com – spin off from the magazine, not as good as others.

www.planetfootball.com – news, information and OPTA statistics and the world game.

www.soccerage.com – excellent for world soccer, in 11 languages.

www.soccernet.com – well put together, comprehensive but a bit boring.

www.zoofootball.com – good fun, excellent kids' section.

www.ukfootballpages.com
IT'S WHERE YOU FIND FOOTBALL

ORIGIN	UK	This site offers a huge directory of football-related
SPEED	✓✓✓	links and boasts some 1,200 enquiries a day; also
INFO	✓✓✓✓✓	offers match reports and statistics, and a fantasy
EASE	✓✓✓✓	football game.

www.teamtalk.com
CHECK OUT THE TEAMS!

ORIGIN	UK	The place to go if you want all the latest gossip and
SPEED	✓✓✓	transfer information, it's opinionated but not often
INFO	✓✓✓✓✓	wrong. They have around 90 journalists on their
EASE	✓✓✓✓	books and they also cover rugby and racing too.

www.icons.com
THE WORLD'S LEADING FOOTBALLERS

ORIGIN UK
SPEED ✓✓✓
INFO ✓✓✓✓✓
EASE ✓✓✓✓

Keep up-to-date with transfer news, gossip and hear the word from the players themselves. Each has a page or site devoted to them with a biography and other important details like what they think of their teammates, an interview, achievements to date and the all important gallery.

www.soccerbase.com
SOCCER STATISTICS

ORIGIN UK
SPEED ✓✓✓
INFO ✓✓✓✓✓
EASE ✓✓✓✓

The site to end all pub rows, it's described as the most comprehensive and up-to-date source of British football data on the Internet.

www.fifa.com
FIFA

ORIGIN SWITZERLAND
SPEED ✓✓✓✓
INFO ✓✓✓✓✓
EASE ✓✓✓✓

This is FIFA's magazine where you can get information on what they do, the World Cup and other FIFA competitions. For the UEFA go to **www.uefa.com** where you can see how the British are faring in the Champions League and UEFA cup.

www.englishpremiershipfootball.com
THE PREMIER LEAGUE

ORIGIN UK
SPEED ✓✓✓✓
INFO ✓✓✓✓
EASE ✓✓✓✓

All the news and gossip plus the latest scores and fixture lists. There's also loads of links to team and betting sites. To find out the views of the managers go to **www.leaguemanagers.com** home of the League Managers Association.

GOLF

www.golfix.co.uk
GOLF FIX

ORIGIN	UK
SPEED	✓✓✓✓
INFO	✓✓✓✓✓
EASE	✓✓✓✓

A straightforward and informative site with masses of tips and advice on how to improve your game. Alongside this there's all the information you'd expect from a quality sports site with sections on games, fitness and all the latest news. See also **www.mygolfzone.com** which is similar but less easy-to-use.

www.golftoday.co.uk
THE PREMIER ONLINE GOLF MAGAZINE

ORIGIN	UK
SPEED	✓✓✓
INFO	✓✓✓✓✓
EASE	✓✓✓✓

An excellent site for golf news and tournaments with features, statistics and rankings and also a course directory. It's the best all-round site covering Europe. There are also links to sister sites about the amateur game, shops and where to stay. Golf Today also hosts a comprehensive site on the amateur game; you can find it at **www.amateur-golf.com**

www.golfweb.com
PGA TOUR

ORIGIN	US
SPEED	✓✓✓
INFO	✓✓✓✓✓
EASE	✓✓✓✓

The best site for statistics on the game, and keeping up with tournament scores, it also has audio and visual features with RealPlayer. For the official word on the tour go to **www.pga.com**

www.golf.com
THE AMERICAN VIEW

ORIGIN	US
SPEED	✓✓✓
INFO	✓✓✓✓✓
EASE	✓✓✓

Part of NBC's suite of web sites, this offers a massive amount of information and statistics on the game, the major tours and players, both men and women.

www.uk-golf.com
GOLF TOURISM

ORIGIN UK	A useful directory of courses and hotels with
SPEED ✓✓✓	courses, with links to travel agents for the UK and
INFO ✓✓✓✓	abroad, you can also get information on golf equip-
EASE ✓✓✓	ment suppliers and insurance.

HOCKEY

www.hockeyonline.co.uk
THE ENGLISH HOCKEY ASSOCIATION

ORIGIN UK	A slick site covering the English game with informa-
SPEED ✓✓✓	tion and chat on the players, leagues and teams for
INFO ✓✓✓✓	both the men's and the women's games. For the
EASE ✓✓✓	Welsh game go to **www.welsh-hockey.co.uk** and for

the Scottish **www.scottish-hockey.org.uk** neither are
great on design but give all the relevant information.
For more links to teams and chat sites check out
www.hockeyweb.co.uk

HORSE RACING

www.racingpost.co.uk
THE RACING POST

ORIGIN UK	Superb, informative site from the authority on the
SPEED ✓✓✓	sport, every event covered in-depth with tips and
INFO ✓✓✓✓✓	advice. To get the best out of it you have to register,
EASE ✓✓✓✓	then you access to the database and more. For more

information on the sport go to the British Horse
Racing Board's excellent site at **www.bhb.co.uk**

www.racenews.co.uk
RACING, COURSES AND BETTING

ORIGIN	UK
SPEED	✓✓✓
INFO	✓✓✓✓
EASE	✓✓✓

A slightly different spin from Racenews, they have three main sections: their news service, a course guide and a tipsters column, there's also an excellent links section covering racing world-wide.

www.flatstats.co.uk
FLAT RACING STATISTICS

ORIGIN	UK
SPEED	✓✓✓
INFO	✓✓✓✓
VALUE	✓✓✓
EASE	✓✓✓✓

This site contains masses of unique statistics – horse, trainer, jockey, sire and race statistics, favourites analysis, systems analysis and much more are examined in detail. The site contains two sections, one for turf, and the other for all-weather racing. You have to be a member to get the best out of it.

ICE HOCKEY

www.iceweb.co.uk
THE ICE HOCKEY SUPER-LEAGUE

ORIGIN	UK
SPEED	✓✓✓✓
INFO	✓✓✓✓✓
EASE	✓✓✓

Keep up-to-date with the scores, the games and the players, even their injuries. Good for statistics as well as news. See also **www.puck-off.com** which isn't as fun as it's name may suggest, but for more news and information see also **www.azhockey.com** home of the Encyclopaedia of Ice Hockey.

www.nhl.com
NATIONAL HOCKEY LEAGUE

ORIGIN	US
SPEED	✓✓✓✓
INFO	✓✓✓✓
EASE	✓✓✓

Catch up on the latest from the NHL including a chance to listen to and watch key moments from past and recent games.

MARTIAL ARTS

www.martial-arts-network.com

PROMOTING MARTIAL ARTS

ORIGIN	US
SPEED	✓✓
INFO	✓✓✓✓
EASE	✓✓✓

Possibly qualifies as the loudest introduction sequence, but once you've cut the volume or skipped the intro, the site offers a great deal in terms of resources and information about the martial arts scene, including 'Black Belts' magazine. Its layout is a little confusing and the site is quite slow.

Beginners should go to **www.martialresource.com** a good-looking site which explains the background to each type of martial art and gives hints and tips to those just starting out. Martial Info **www.martialinfo.com** is another slow but comprehensive site with an online magazine.

www.britishjudo.org.uk

JUDO

ORIGIN	UK
SPEED	✓✓✓✓
INFO	✓✓✓✓
EASE	✓✓✓✓

Judo has a proud tradition in the UK, and if you want to follow that you can get all the information you need at the British Judo Association site. It gives a brief history of judo, a magazine and event information.

www.btkf.homestead.com

BRITISH KARATE FEDERATION

ORIGIN	UK
SPEED	✓✓✓✓
INFO	✓✓✓✓
EASE	✓✓✓✓

Information on all forms of the discipline as well as events listings, fun pages and an online martial arts club, which is hosted by Yahoo.

MOTOR SPORT

www.ukmotorsport.com
INFORMATION OVERLOAD

ORIGIN	UK	This site, a great advert for function over design,
SPEED	✓✓✓✓	covers every form of motor racing; it's easy-to-use
INFO	✓✓✓✓✓	and thorough, with lots of links to appropriate sites.
EASE	✓✓✓	

www.linksheaven.com
THE MOST COMPREHENSIVE LINKS DIRECTORY

ORIGIN	US	Whatever, whoever, there's an appropriate link. It
SPEED	✓✓✓	concentrates on Formula 1, CART and Nascar
INFO	✓✓✓✓✓	though.
EASE	✓✓✓	

www.autosport.com
AUTOSPORT MAGAZINE

ORIGIN	UK	Excellent for news and features on motor sport plus
SPEED	✓✓✓	links and a slightly confusing online shopping expe-
INFO	✓✓✓✓✓	rience for related products such as team gear, books
VALUE	✓✓✓	or models.
EASE	✓✓✓	

www.fosa.org
FORMULA ONE SUPPORTERS ASSOCIATION

ORIGIN	UK	An F1 enthusiasts' site, set up by fans to provide
SPEED	✓✓✓	feedback to the people who run the sport. It's infor-
INFO	✓✓✓✓	mative and there are plenty of links, quizzes, statis-
VALUE	✓✓	tics, articles and games.
EASE	✓✓✓✓	

www.itv-f1.com
F1 ON ITV

ORIGIN	UK
SPEED	✓✓✓✓
INFO	✓✓✓✓✓
EASE	✓✓✓✓✓

The TV show may be disappointing, but the web site is excellent. It doesn't miss much and there is plenty of action. There's all the background information you'd expect plus circuit profiles, schedules and a photo gallery. For more news and links to everywhere in F1 go to www.f1-world.co.uk

www.fota.co.uk
FORMULA 3

ORIGIN	UK
SPEED	✓✓✓✓
INFO	✓✓✓✓✓
EASE	✓✓✓✓✓

Formula 3 explained plus info on the teams, drivers and circuits, it's the breeding ground for F1 drivers of the future which adds to the excitement reflected in the energy of this site.

www.rallysport.com
COVERING THE WORLD RALLY CHAMPIONSHIP

ORIGIN	UK
SPEED	✓✓✓✓
INFO	✓✓✓✓
VALUE	✓✓✓
EASE	✓✓✓✓

Good for results and news on rallying in the UK and across the world. See also www.rallyzone.co.uk which is slow but a good magazine nonetheless. You can follow a race stage by stage at www.rally-live.com/gb as well as get all the latest news.

www.btccpages.com
BRITISH TOURING CAR CHAMPIONSHIP

ORIGIN	UK
SPEED	✓✓✓
INFO	✓✓✓✓✓
EASE	✓✓✓✓

This site offers a great deal of information and statistics on the championship, driver and team profiles, photos and links to other related sites. There are also a number of forums you can get involved with if you feel like chatting to fellow enthusiasts.

MOTORCYCLING

www.motorcyclenews.com
NEWS AND VIEWS

ORIGIN UK
SPEED ✓✓✓
INFO ✓✓✓✓✓
EASE ✓✓✓✓

A very good magazine-style site giving all the latest news, gossip and event information, there are also sections on buying a bike, where to get parts and the latest gear, off-road biking and a links directory. There's also a chat room and the obligatory subscription page.

www.acu.org.uk
AUTO-CYCLE UNION

ORIGIN UK
SPEED ✓✓✓✓
INFO ✓✓✓
EASE ✓✓✓✓

The ACU is the governing body for motorcycle sports in the UK and this site gives information on its work and the benefits of being a member. There are also links and details of their magazine. To be honest it's a bit lightweight on information and some graphics annoyingly overlap.

www.motograndprix.com
TRACK AND OFF-ROAD

ORIGIN UK
SPEED ✓✓✓✓
INFO ✓✓✓✓
EASE ✓✓✓✓✓

A well laid out magazine site, which covers track grand prix and dirt biking in equal measure, even some of the more obscure areas of the sport, such as snowcross, are covered.

www.british-speedway.co.uk
SPEEDWAY

ORIGIN UK
SPEED ✓✓✓✓
INFO ✓✓✓
EASE ✓✓✓✓

A pretty basic site giving information on the leagues as well as the latest news, there's also an events calendar and links to related sites.

MOUNTAINEERING AND OUTDOOR SPORTS

www.mountainzone.com

FOR THE UPWARDLY MOBILE

ORIGIN US	Thoroughly covers all aspects of climbing, hiking,
SPEED ✓✓✓	mountain biking, skiing and snowboarding with a
INFO ✓✓✓✓✓	very good photography section featuring galleries
EASE ✓✓✓	from major mountains and climbers.

www.rockandrun.co.uk

ALL THE RIGHT EQUIPMENT

ORIGIN UK	Excellent equipment shop covering climbing and
SPEED ✓✓✓	walking gear, which is also pretty comprehensive on
INFO ✓✓✓✓✓	the information front too; this site is linked with
EASE ✓✓✓	www.ukclimbing.com **W?WT**

Other good climbing sites:

www.cruxed.com – advice on techniques and training, good links.

www.climbing.co.uk – climb UK is wide-ranging
from information on climbing and climbs to chat
and gear suppliers.

www.thebmc.co.uk – good all-round climbing and
hill-walking magazine-style site with good links
pages.

OLYMPICS

www.the5rings.com
INTERACTIVE INTERNET SPORT

ORIGIN	UK
SPEED	✓✓✓✓
INFO	✓✓✓✓✓
EASE	✓✓✓✓

Lots of statistics on the Olympics, plus a review of the Sydney games and details on all the events going back to the beginning of the last century. It's got excellent links to associated sites and information on future games too.

www.olympics.org
BRITISH OLYMPIC ASSOCIATION

ORIGIN	UK
SPEED	✓✓✓✓
INFO	✓✓✓
EASE	✓✓✓✓

A new look site with sections on the forthcoming winter and summer games, information for collectors and also the doping policy, for a history of the games there's the Olympic museum link and links to sports federations and committees.

ROWING

www.total-rowing.org.uk
TOTAL ROWING WEEKLY

ORIGIN	UK
SPEED	✓✓✓✓
INFO	✓✓✓
EASE	✓✓

An odd-looking site that gives an overview of the sport from beginners to Olympic stars mainly through the use of links but there are some good articles if you can be bothered to find them.

www.ara-rowing.org
AMATEUR ROWING ASSOCIATION

ORIGIN	UK
SPEED	✓✓✓
INFO	✓✓✓✓
EASE	✓✓✓✓

This site offers information on the history of the sport, plus the latest news, coaching tips and links, for a better set of international links go to **http://users.ox.ac.uk/~quarell** who also give the latest rowing news.

RUGBY

www.scrum.com
RUGBY UNION

ORIGIN UK
SPEED ✓✓✓
INFO ✓✓✓✓✓
EASE ✓✓✓✓

An excellent site about rugby union with impressively up-to-the-minute coverage, for a similar but lighter and more fun site go to **www.planet-rugby.com** which has a comprehensive round-up of world rugby with instant reports, lots of detail and information on both union and league.

www.rfu.com
RUGBY FOOTBALL UNION

ORIGIN UK
SPEED ✓✓✓✓
INFO ✓✓✓✓
VALUE ✓✓✓
EASE ✓✓✓✓

Masses of features, articles and news from the official RFU site, it's got team news and information, links and a shop where you can buy gear – delivery is £2 for the UK.

www.irb.org
INTERNATIONAL RUGBY BOARD

ORIGIN UK
SPEED ✓✓✓
INFO ✓✓✓✓
EASE ✓✓✓✓

For the official line on rugby union, you will find all the rules and regulations explained, information on world tournaments, history of the game, fixtures and results.

www.rleague.com
WORLD OF RUGBY LEAGUE

ORIGIN UK
SPEED ✓✓✓
INFO ✓✓✓✓✓
EASE ✓✓✓✓

Another very comprehensive site, featuring sections on Australia, New Zealand and the UK, with plenty of chat, articles, player profiles and enough statistics to keep the most ardent fan happy. See also the excellent Australian site **www.smh.com.au/league** which is quite parochial. If it's more the European game you're after then try **www.rugbyleaguer.co.uk**

SAILING

www.madforsailing.com
MAD FOR SAILING

ORIGIN UK	An informative and well laid out site covering all
SPEED ✓✓✓	aspects of sailing both as a sport and as a hobby.
INFO ✓✓✓✓	There are some really good and well written articles
EASE ✓✓✓✓	and features plus weather information.

www.yacht.co.uk
SAILING LINKS

ORIGIN UK	Links categorised into six sections including
SPEED ✓✓✓✓✓	marinas, clubs, official bodies, charts and weather.
INFO ✓✓✓✓	
EASE ✓✓✓	

www.ukdinghyracing.com
UK DINGHY RACING

ORIGIN UK	Devoted mainly to this one aspect of sailing, it
SPEED ✓✓✓	covers the sport comprehensively and gives advice
INFO ✓✓✓✓	on buying and hosts links to auctions and specialist
EASE ✓✓✓✓	shops.

SKIING AND SNOWBOARDING

www.fis-ski.com
INTERNATIONAL SKI FEDERATION

ORIGIN US	Catch up on the news, the fastest times, the rankings
SPEED ✓✓✓	in all forms of skiing at this site. Very good back-
INFO ✓✓✓✓	ground information and an excellent picture gallery
EASE ✓✓✓✓	sets the whole thing off.

www.ski.co.uk
THE PLACE TO START – A SKI DIRECTORY

ORIGIN UK
SPEED ✓✓✓
INFO ✓✓✓✓
EASE ✓✓✓✓

Straightforward site, the information in the directory is useful and the recommended sites are rated. The sections are holidays, travel, weather, resorts, snowboarding, gear, fanatics and specialist services. You can also e-mail them for advice on any aspect of skiing.

www.1ski.com
COMPLETE ONLINE SKIING SERVICE

ORIGIN UK
SPEED ✓✓✓
INFO ✓✓✓✓✓
VALUE ✓✓✓
EASE ✓✓✓✓

With over 250,000 holidays, live snow reports, tips on technique and equipment and the ultimate guide featuring over 750 resorts, it's difficult to go wrong. The site is well laid out and easy-to-use. There's a good events calendar too.

See also the similar www.iglu.com who have a very good search facility.
   Other good ski sites:
www.ifyouski.com – comprehensive skiing site that
   has a very good holiday booking service with lots
   of deals.
www.skimaps.com – much like any other general ski
   site except for its eponymous maps section, which
   has several hundred to download.
www.mountainzone.com – great for features and
   articles.
www.skiclub.co.uk – Ski Club of Great Britain has
   an attractive site with lots of information and
   links.
www.natives.co.uk – aimed at ski workers, there's
   info on conditions, ski resorts, a good job section,
   where to stay and links to other cool sites all
   wrapped up in a very nicely designed site.

www.snowboardinguk.co.uk
UK SNOWBOARDING NEWS

ORIGIN UK
SPEED ✓✓✓
INFO ✓✓✓✓✓
EASE ✓✓✓✓

A surprisingly unpretentious site for what is the coolest of sports, aimed at anyone whether beginner or expert, it offers news, an events diary, resort information, travel information and a links page. You can 'feel the powder' at **www.feelthepow.com** which is really only good for its tips section. For the best board shopping try **www.legendsboardriders.com** which has a nice flash intro sequence.

SNOOKER

www.snookernet.com
ALL ABOUT SNOOKER

ORIGIN UK
SPEED ✓✓✓
INFO ✓✓✓✓
VALUE ✓✓✓
EASE ✓✓✓✓✓

A clearly laid out, easy-to-use site that has comprehensive information on the game, plus a master class from a top player, over 1,000 links, a shop selling snooker merchandise, a club finder and subscription to *SnookerScene* magazine.

From the sponsor, visit **www.embassysnooker.com** have a similar but less comprehensive site.

TENNIS AND RACQUET SPORTS

www.lta.org.uk
LAWN TENNIS ASSOCIATION

ORIGIN UK
SPEED ✓✓✓
INFO ✓✓✓✓
VALUE ✓✓✓
EASE ✓✓✓✓

An excellent and attractively designed all-year tennis information site run by the Lawn Tennis Association, it has information on the players, rankings and tournament news, as well as details on clubs and coaching courses. There's also an online tennis shop where you can buy merchandise and equipment.

See also **www.atptour.com** which gives a less UK biased view of the game, with excellent sections on the players, tournaments and rankings.

www.wimbledon.org
THE OFFICIAL WIMBLEDON SITE

ORIGIN UK
SPEED ✓✓
INFO ✓✓✓✓
VALUE ✓✓
EASE ✓✓✓✓

Very impressive, there's a great deal here and not just in June, but you need to be patient. Apart from the information you'd expect, you can download screensavers, visit the online museum and eventually see videos of past matches. The shop is expensive.

Other tennis sites worth a look:

www.cliffrichardtennis.org – excellent site aimed at encouraging children to take up the game.

www.tennis.net – solid magazine site, with good articles and features.

www.tennis.com – good magazine, with gear guides, tips and hot news.

www.tennisnews.com – the latest news updated daily and e-mailed to you.

www.tmatch.com – another magazine, nice design and good writing.

Badminton

www.badmintonuk.ndo.co.uk
BRITISH BADMINTON

ORIGIN UK
SPEED ✓✓✓✓
INFO ✓✓✓✓
EASE ✓✓✓✓

A clear, easy-to-use site packed with information about badminton, how ladders work, directory of coaches, club directory, rules, but not much news on the game. For that go to **www.baofe.co.uk** the site of the Badminton Association of England, also try **www.intbadfed.org** home of the International Badminton Federation.

Squash

www.squashplayer.co.uk
WORLD OF SQUASH AT YOUR FINGERTIPS

ORIGIN US
SPEED ✓✓✓✓
INFO ✓✓✓✓✓
EASE ✓✓✓✓✓

A really comprehensive round-up of the game, with links galore and a great news section, there's also a section for the UK, which has club details and the latest news. See also **www.worldsquash.org** for a good site on what's going on world-wide.

Table tennis

www.ettu.org
EUROPEAN TABLE TENNIS UNION

ORIGIN UK
SPEED ✓✓✓
INFO ✓✓✓✓
EASE ✓✓✓✓

Find out about the ETTU, its rankings, competition details and results plus a section devoted to world table tennis links. See also **www.ittf.com** which gives a world view.

WATER SPORTS AND SWIMMING

www.swimnews.com
SWIMMING NEWS

ORIGIN UK
SPEED ✓✓✓✓
INFO ✓✓✓✓
EASE ✓✓✓✓

It's up-to-date and offers a wide coverage of news, with other features such as rankings, events calendar, shopping and competition analysis.

Other good swimming sites:
www.swimxtreme.com – for entertaining chat, advice and articles.
www.pullbuoy.co.uk – good site that covers the UK scene, you can find unusual features such as a job finder and time converter.
www.swimnet.fsnet.co.uk – good for results on the major events, but not that up-to-date otherwise.

www.coldswell.co.uk
ULTIMATE GUIDE FOR SURFING THE UK COAST

ORIGIN UK
SPEED ✓✓✓
INFO ✓✓✓
EASE ✓✓✓✓

Includes forecasts for weather and surf, satellite images, live surf web cams from around the world and a complete directory of surfing web sites. For a more traditional and regional approach try **www.surfcall.co.uk** while for links and surf speak go to the expanding **www.surfstation.co.uk**

www.waterski.com
WORLD OF WATER SKIING

ORIGIN US
SPEED ✓✓✓
INFO ✓✓✓✓
EASE ✓✓✓✓

An American site which features information about the sport, how to compete, news, tips, equipment and where to ski. See also the ever-changing **www.waterski-az.co.uk** for the UK view. For forums and chat go to **www.waterski-uk.co.uk**

www.scubauk.co.uk

SCUBA UK

ORIGIN	UK
SPEED	✓✓✓✓
INFO	✓✓✓✓
EASE	✓✓✓✓

A large directory site with lots of links to all the sites you'd associate with scuba diving, there are sections on travel, cave diving, product reviews and you can submit your best photos for the gallery. Good design too.

Sports clothes and merchandise

www.sweatband.com

SHOP BY SPORT

ORIGIN	UK
SPEED	✓✓✓✓
INFO	✓✓✓✓
VALUE	✓✓✓✓
EASE	✓✓✓✓

A wide-ranging shop that supplies equipment for many sports, but it's especially good for tennis, rugby and cricket. Delivery costs depend on the weight of your parcel but they start at only 50p.

www.kitbag.com

SPORTS FASHION

ORIGIN	UK
SPEED	✓✓✓
INFO	✓✓✓✓
VALUE	✓✓✓✓
EASE	✓✓✓✓

Football kits and gear galore from new to retro; covers cricket and rugby too. Free delivery. Also offers shopping by brand and a news service.

www.discountsports.co.uk

UK's LOWEST PRICED SPORTSWEAR

ORIGIN	UK
SPEED	✓✓✓
INFO	✓✓✓✓
VALUE	✓✓✓✓✓
EASE	✓✓✓

Cheap and cheerful approach, with all the major brands represented and much of what they offer has free delivery in the UK, and they have a good product finding facility. **W?WT**

www.sportspages.co.uk
TAKING SPORT SERIOUSLY

ORIGIN	UK
SPEED	✓✓✓✓
INFO	✓✓✓✓
VALUE	✓✓
EASE	✓✓✓✓

Book and video specialists, concentrating on sport, they offer a wide range at OK prices. Great for that one thing you've been unable to find.

Stationery

www.stationerystore.co.uk
STATIONERY STORE

ORIGIN	UK
SPEED	✓✓✓
INFO	✓✓✓✓
VALUE	✓✓✓✓
EASE	✓✓✓✓

A well designed and easy-to-use stationery store supplying everything from paperclips to office machinery. There are also sections on electronics and lots of offers. Delivery is free for orders over £40, £4 if below that.

For other stationery stores try:

www.staples.co.uk – lots of promise, they'll have a full online store up and running in 2002 offering free delivery and a store pick up service.

www.office-world.co.uk – Office World promise a service 'soon'. You can print off an order form and fax them though; delivery is next day and free if you spend over £30.

www.stationery.co.uk – another good W.H.Smith site with some offers and multi-buys but a limited range.

www.greenstat.co.uk
GREEN STATIONERY

ORIGIN	UK
SPEED	✓✓✓
INFO	✓✓✓
VALUE	✓✓✓
EASE	✓✓

Green as in environmentally friendly, they supply a wide range of recycled paper products and desk accessories. It's unsophisticated with delivery costs being well hidden and you have to go through an annoying process of making a note of product code numbers for your order form. It's got good links to other environmentally friendly businesses.

Student Sites

There is masses of information for students on the Net. Here are some sites worth checking out. The links are generally very good, so if the topic isn't covered here, it should be easy to track down.

Universities and colleges

www.ucas.co.uk
THE UNIVERSITY STARTING BLOCK

ORIGIN	UK
SPEED	✓✓✓
INFO	✓✓✓✓✓
EASE	✓✓✓✓

A comprehensive site listing all the courses at British universities with entry profiles. You can view the directory online and order your UCAS handbook and application form. If you've already applied, you can view your application online. There are links to all the universities plus really good links to related sites. There is good advice too. If you want to study abroad you can try finding a course through **www.edunet.com**

www.nusonline.co.uk
STUDENTS UNITE

ORIGIN UK
SPEED ✓✓✓✓
INFO ✓✓✓✓
EASE ✓✓✓

Lots of relevant news and views for students. You need to register to get assess to their discounts directory and special offers. Once in, you can send e-cards and use their mail and storage facilities too.

Working abroad

www.gapyear.com
EVERYTHING YOU NEED TO KNOW

ORIGIN UK
SPEED ✓✓✓✓
INFO ✓✓✓✓✓
EASE ✓✓✓✓

Whether you fancy helping out in the forests of Brazil or teaching in Europe you'll find information and opportunities here. There is loads of advice, past experiences to get you tempted, chat, bulletin boards, competitions and you can subscribe to their magazine (an old-fashioned paper one).

www.payaway.co.uk
FIND A JOB ABROAD OR WORKING HOLIDAY

ORIGIN UK
SPEED ✓✓✓✓
INFO ✓✓✓✓✓
EASE ✓✓✓✓

A great starting place for anyone who wants to work abroad. There is a magazine, reports from travellers and you can register with their online jobs service. They've missed nothing out in their links section from embassies to travel health to Durex.

Discount cards

www.istc.org.uk
INTERNATIONAL STUDENT TRAVEL CONFEDERATION

ORIGIN UK
SPEED ✓✓✓
INFO ✓✓✓✓✓
EASE ✓✓✓

Get your student and youth discount card as well as info on working and studying abroad. Also help with such things as railpasses, phonecards, ISTC registered travel agents world-wide, plus e-mail, voice mail and fax messaging. For a European youth card for discounts within the EU go to **www.euro26.org**.

Magazines

www.studentuk.com
BEER IS LIFE

ORIGIN UK
SPEED ✓✓✓
INFO ✓✓✓✓✓
EASE ✓✓✓

A useful and generally well-written students' magazine featuring news, music and film reviews, going out, chat, even articles on science and politics. Some excellent advice on subjects such as gap years, accommodation and finance.

It's worth checking out **www.ragmag.co.uk** who continue the tradition of rag week all the time, and is a source for all things good. **www.anythingstudent.com** is also worth a look although it could be more fun.

Teenagers

Here's a small selection of the best sites that are aimed at teenagers. If you want more we have created a separate book just for you, called the Cool Web Site Guide *(ISBN: 0752841696 – £2.99), it's got over 750 sites listed and reviewed. Many of the most hyped sites are just heavily disguised marketing and sales operations, treat these with scepticism and enjoy the best which are done for the love of it. We've also indicated the sort of age that the magazines are aimed at.*

Teenage magazines

www.4degreez.com
INTERACTIVE COMMUNITY

ORIGIN US
SPEED ✓✓✓✓
INFO ✓✓✓✓
EASE ✓✓✓✓

A friendly and entertaining site with reviews, poetry, jokes, polls and links to other related sites. You have to become a member to get the best out of it though.
15 plus

www.alloy.com
ALLOY MAGAZINE

ORIGIN US
SPEED ✓✓✓
INFO ✓✓✓✓
EASE ✓✓✓

On the face of it this is great, it's got loads of sections on everything from personal advice to shopping. But it's spoiled by too many adverts and every time you click on a new section another load of boxes pop up with more adverts. It all seems to be geared to getting your name for marketing purposes.
13 plus

www.bbc.co.uk/so
So

ORIGIN UK
SPEED ✓✓✓
INFO ✓✓✓✓✓
EASE ✓✓✓✓

The BBC have done a great job with the colourful *So* mag, it's got really excellent stuff such as quizzes, music, problems, interviews, fashion, weird, links and a chat section. There are also some brilliant competitions, prizes and fun articles too.
10 plus

www.cheekfreak.com
FOR THE FREAK IN ALL OF US

ORIGIN US
SPEED ✓✓✓✓
INFO ✓✓✓✓
EASE ✓✓✓✓

Best for stories, online diaries and free downloads. It's got chat sections, message boards and a search engine. They deserve a medal for the pranks section, which is brilliant.
13 plus

www.cyberteens.com
CONNECT TO CYBERTEENS

ORIGIN	US
SPEED	✓✓✓✓
INFO	✓✓✓✓✓
VALUE	✓✓
EASE	✓✓✓✓

One of the most hyped sites aimed at teenagers, it contains a very good selection of games, news, links and a creativity section where you can send your art and poems. Don't bother with the shop, which was being re-designed at time of writing, but on previous visits it was expensive, as is the credit card they offer.

13 plus

www.globalgang.org.uk
WORLD NEWS, GAMES, GOSSIP AND FUN

ORIGIN	UK
SPEED	✓✓✓
INFO	✓✓✓✓
EASE	✓✓✓

See what the rest of the world gets up to at Global Gang. You can find out what kids in other countries like to eat, what toys they play with, chat to them or play games. Lastly you get to find out how you can help those kids less fortunate than yourself.

10 plus

www.kidsonline.co.uk
BLUE JAM

ORIGIN	UK
SPEED	✓✓✓
INFO	✓✓✓✓✓
EASE	✓✓✓✓

Blue Jam is excellent; it has everything from WAP pets to the latest news, as well as games, reviews, event listings, links and competitions. There's also a good advice section. There's also a version for younger kids too.

10 plus

www.thesite.org.uk
THE SITE

ORIGIN	UK
SPEED	✓✓✓✓
INFO	✓✓✓✓
EASE	✓✓✓✓

This site offers advice on a range of subjects; careers, relationships, drugs, sex, money, legal issues and so on. Aimed largely at 15 to 24 year olds, it's well laid out and very informative.
15 plus

www.teentoday.co.uk
FOR TEENAGERS BY TEENAGERS

ORIGIN	UK
SPEED	✓✓✓✓
INFO	✓✓✓✓✓
EASE	✓✓✓✓

Get your free e-zine mailed to you daily or just visit the site which has much more; games, chat, news, entertainment, free downloads and message boards. It's well designed and genuinely good with not too much advertising.
12 plus

www.dubit.co.uk
GAMES, ARTICLES – THE LOT

ORIGIN	UK
SPEED	✓✓✓
INFO	✓✓✓✓
EASE	✓✓✓

Dubit combines 3D graphics with chat, games, video, music and animations in a fun and interactive way. It's a completely different approach to the normal teen magazine. It takes a while to get your head round but it's worth it in the end.
15 plus

http://goosehead.com
COUNTER CULTURE PROGRAMMING

ORIGIN	UK
SPEED	✓✓✓
INFO	✓✓✓✓✓
EASE	✓✓✓✓

A great teen magazine site with brilliant graphics and lots to do from homework help, chat, horoscopes and all the important things in life like games and web soap – whatever.
13 plus

www.urban75.co.uk
WITH ATTITUDE

ORIGIN UK
SPEED ✓✓✓
INFO ✓✓✓✓✓
EASE ✓✓✓

Probably not one most parents would approve of but it's advert free and punchy. This 'zine has got information on how to be an eco-warrior, sports, news, photography and some really useless games. It tells you how to put on your own rave party and where the best ones are, and best of all, you get to 'punch' your least favourite celebrity. There is some strong language here, but there's no denying its quality.
16 plus

www.mirabilis.com
ICQ – I SEEK YOU

ORIGIN US
SPEED ✓✓✓
INFO ✓✓✓✓
EASE ✓✓

Not so easy for the very young but there's lots here and it's quick. A good site to use combined with a mobile phone with lots of features such as chat, games, money advice, music and lurve.
13 plus

www.terrifichick.com
A FORUM FOR TEENAGE GIRLS

ORIGIN US
SPEED ✓✓✓
INFO ✓✓✓✓✓
EASE ✓✓✓✓

Recommended by Sherry, one of our readers, this excellent site has loads of advice, articles and most importantly some 13 monitored message boards on topics from health to homework.
13 plus

Directories

www.beritsbest.com
SITES FOR CHILDREN

ORIGIN US
SPEED ✓✓✓
INFO ✓✓✓✓✓
EASE ✓✓✓✓

Over 1,000 sites in this directory split into six major categories, fun, things to do, nature, serious stuff (homework), chat and surfing. Each site is rated for speed and content and you can suggest new sites as well. Another similar site to Berits is **www.kids-space.org**, which has some really cute graphics and a better search facility.

www.teen.com
THE ULTIMATE PLACE FOR TEENS

ORIGIN US
SPEED ✓✓✓
INFO ✓✓✓✓✓
EASE ✓✓✓✓

Annoying adverts aside, this is a great site for teenagers, it's more of a magazine than anything but it's here because of the search engine which is excellent. It can be a little slow though.

www.teensites.org
WEB DIRECTORY FOR TEENS

ORIGIN US
SPEED ✓✓✓
INFO ✓✓✓✓✓
EASE ✓✓✓✓

A huge directory of sites covering loads of subjects of interest to teenagers. It's biased to the USA, but if you don't mind that, then it should have everything you need.

Telecommunications

In this section there's information on where to go to buy mobiles, get the best out of them and even have a little fun with them. For phone numbers see the section entitled 'finding someone' on page 130.

www.carphonewarehouse.com
CHOOSING THE RIGHT MOBILE

ORIGIN UK
SPEED ✓✓✓
INFO ✓✓✓✓
VALUE ✓✓✓✓
EASE ✓✓✓✓

You need to take your time to find the best tariff using their calculator, then take advantage of the numerous offers. Excellent pictures and details of all phones and the information is unbiased. There's an online encyclopaedia devoted to mobile phone terminology, a shop that also sells handheld PCs and delivery is free too. You can download a wide range of new phone ring tones, from classical to the latest pop tunes.

Another good site is **www.miahtelecom.co.uk** who, apart from good offers, have an easy-to-use tariff calculator. See also **www.mediaring.com** who offer excellent Internet voice communications products; it's good value too.

www.mobileedge.co.uk
MOBILE INFORMATION

ORIGIN UK
SPEED ✓✓✓✓
INFO ✓✓✓✓
VALUE ✓✓✓
EASE ✓✓✓✓

A really well-designed site with help on buying the right mobile, it also offers information on health and mobiles, links and contact numbers, pre-pay deals, global networks, ring tones, shop and much more.

www.yourmobile.com
NEW RING TUNES FOR YOUR PHONE

ORIGIN UK
SPEED ✓✓✓
INFO ✓✓✓✓
VALUE ✓✓✓✓
EASE ✓✓✓✓

There are several hundred tunes that you can down-load on to your mobile using text messaging. At the time of writing it only works on Nokia, Ericsson and Siemens phones, but it's expanding fast and you'll soon be able to get icons and logos.

Here's where to find the major phone operators:
www.orange.co.uk
www.vodafone.co.uk (**www.vizzavi.co.uk** for their WAP service)
www.one2one.co.uk
www.cellnet.co.uk
www.bt.co.uk
www.virginmobile.com

www.genie.co.uk
WAP PHONES MADE USEFUL

ORIGIN UK
SPEED ✓✓✓✓
INFO ✓✓✓✓✓
VALUE ✓✓✓✓
EASE ✓✓✓✓

A huge site with loads of information on what you can do if you've got a WAP phone, including how to get gossip, results and news. The site is well laid out, there are competitions and you can download ring tones and icons.

Other WAP sites and what they do:
http://wap.fast.no/html – 'the world's largest WAP index' or very good search engine to you and me.
www.2thumbswap.com – large site with lots of WAP information and an especially good down-loads section and good explanations too.
www.anywhereyougo.com – excellent for the latest news and developments, good links and informa-tion too.

www.wapaw.com – another directory site, with over 2,000 sites listed.

www.wapsight.com – excellent WAP news site.

www.wirelessgames.com – the best place to find games to play on your WAP phone.

www.bluetooth.com
AFTER WAP COMES BLUETOOTH

ORIGIN	US
SPEED	✓✓✓✓
INFO	✓✓✓✓
EASE	✓✓✓✓

A superb official Microsoft site devoted to Bluetooth technology which is supposed to come into its own soon. Whether it does or not is still open to question but here's where you can find out about it.

www.chatlist.com/faces.html
TEXT MESSAGING

ORIGIN	UK
SPEED	✓✓✓✓
INFO	✓✓✓✓
EASE	✓✓✓

Confused about your emoticons? %-) Here's a list of several thousand for you to choose from.

www.iobox.com
SMS MESSAGING FROM A PC

ORIGIN	UK
SPEED	✓✓✓
INFO	✓✓✓✓
VALUE	✓✓✓✓
EASE	✓✓✓✓

Get tired of typing messages on your mobile, now you can do it from a PC. You get some free credits when you join up, from then on you can purchase them. Prices start at 1 credit for 6p, but it depends on what service you use, sending an icon costs 20 credits, for example. You can also play games, send e-cards, shop and much more, especially if you have a WAP phone.

Theatre

There's been a great improvement in the sites devoted to the theatre, here's the best of them.

www.whatsonstage.com
HOME OF BRITISH THEATRE

ORIGIN UK	A really strong site with masses of news and reviews
SPEED ✓✓✓✓	to browse through plus a very good search facility
INFO ✓✓✓✓✓	and booking service (through a third party). A real
VALUE ✓✓✓	theatre buff's delight.
EASE ✓✓✓✓	

www.aloud.com
THEATRE SEARCH

ORIGIN UK	You can search by venue, location or by artist, it's
SPEED ✓✓✓✓	fast and pretty comprehensive and there's a hot
INFO ✓✓✓	events section – it also covers music and festivals.
VALUE ✓✓✓	The review section is good and you can buy tickets.
EASE ✓✓✓✓	

www.theatrenet.com
THE ENTERTAINMENT CENTRE

ORIGIN UK	Get the latest news, catch the new shows and, if you
SPEED ✓✓✓	join the club, there are discounts on tickets for
INFO ✓✓✓✓✓	theatre, concerts, sporting events and holidays. You
VALUE ✓✓✓	can also search their archives for information on
EASE ✓✓✓	past productions.

www.uktw.co.uk
UK THEATRE WEB

ORIGIN UK	A cheerful site offering all the usual information on
SPEED ✓✓✓✓	theatre plus amateur dramatics, jobs, chat, competi-
INFO ✓✓✓✓	tions and just gossip.
VALUE ✓✓✓	
EASE ✓✓✓✓	

www.rsc.org.uk
THE ROYAL SHAKESPEARE COMPANY

ORIGIN UK	Get all the news as well as information on perfor-
SPEED ✓✓✓	mances and tours. You can book tickets online
INFO ✓✓✓✓	although it's via a third party site.
EASE ✓✓✓	

www.reallyuseful.com
ANDREW LLOYD WEBBER

ORIGIN UK	At this attractive, hi-tech site you can watch video
SPEED ✓✓✓	and listen to top audio clips, download screen savers
INFO ✓✓✓✓✓	and wallpaper, take part in competitions and chat.
EASE ✓✓✓✓	There's also a good kids' section plus details on the
	shows.

www.nt-online.org
THE NATIONAL

ORIGIN UK	Excellent for details of their shows and forthcoming
SPEED ✓✓✓✓	plays with tour information added. You can't buy
INFO ✓✓✓✓	tickets online, but you can e-mail or fax for them.
EASE ✓✓✓✓	

www.officiallondontheatre.co.uk
SOCIETY OF LONDON THEATRE

ORIGIN UK	The latest news, a show finder service and hot tick-
SPEED ✓✓✓✓	ets are just a few of the services available at this
INFO ✓✓✓✓✓	great site. You can also get a theatreland map, half
VALUE ✓✓✓	price tickets and they'll even fax you a seating plan.
EASE ✓✓✓✓	See also www.thisislondon.co.uk

To book online try the following sites:
www.ticketmaster.co.uk
www.londontheatretickets.com
www.uktickets.co.uk
www.lastminute.com
www.firstcall.co.uk

TV

TV channels, listings and your favourite soap operas are all here – some have great sites, others are pretty naff, especially when you consider they're in the entertainment business.

www.itc.org.uk
INDEPENDENT TELEVISION COMMISSION

ORIGIN UK	The ITC issues the licences that allow commercial
SPEED ✓✓✓✓	TV stations to broadcast and ensures fair play on
INFO ✓✓✓✓	advertising so if you have a complaint about
EASE ✓✓✓✓	commercial TV then go here first.

Channels

www.bbc.co.uk
THE UK'S MOST POPULAR WEB SITE

ORIGIN UK	The BBC site deserves a special feature, it is huge
SPEED ✓✓✓	with over 300 sections and it can be quite daunting.
INFO ✓✓✓✓✓	This review only scrapes the surface. These are the
VALUE ✓✓✓	main sections:
EASE ✓✓✓✓✓	

- News – keep up-to-date with the tickertape facility.
- Weather – 1, 3 or 5 day forecasts and more.
- Sport – catch up on all the scores, news and gossip.
- Arts – literature, classical and art.
- Education – a brilliant section for homework with features from many programmes.
- Entertainment – catch up with popular BBC shows.
- Food – recipes from the stars, tips and what's healthy.

- Gardening – advice and info on plants.
- Health – the latest advice and news.
- History – features from many history programs.
- Homes – antiques, DIY and inspiration.
- Kids – the best of *Blue Peter*, *Newsround* and *Live & Kicking*; also info on the stars, have your say and games.
- Live Chat – talk to the stars of BBC TV and radio.
- Nature – from dinosaurs to frog spawn.
- Radio – find out what's on and visit the listening booth.
- Science – the latest inventions and discoveries.
- Teens – *So* magazine and other cool stuff.
- What's on – listings.
- World Service – sections on world regions, with a live web cast and news bulletins.

There are also regional sections, a web guide as well as tips on how to use the Internet and you can subscribe to a newsletter.

There's also a sister site called **www.beeb.com** where you can go shopping. Using consumer programs to head each major section, the BBC attempt to offer the best shopping, advice and offers available on the web, using links to other online retailers. They only partially succeed, there's better shopping to be had elsewhere.

- Good Homes – advice on buying, selling and improving your home.
- Gardener's World – tips, projects and more advice from the experts.
- Top of the Pops – latest chart news.
- Music Magazine – for classical buffs.
- Top Gear – where to buy and how to run your car.
- Holidays – advice, ski guide and links.

The best BBC products are also available, delivery is charged according to what you spend.

You can also obtain full radio and TV listings by signing up to their ISP **www.freebeeb.com**

www.itv.co.uk
ITV NETWORK

ORIGIN UK
SPEED ✓✓✓
INFO ✓✓✓
EASE ✓✓✓✓

ITV has a pretty straightforward site with links to all the major programs, their related web sites and a 'what's on' guide, plus a few extras such as quizzes.

www.citv.co.uk
CHILDREN'S ITV

ORIGIN UK
SPEED ✓✓
INFO ✓✓✓✓
EASE ✓✓✓

A bright and breezy site that features competitions, chat, safe surfing, features on the programs including all the favourite characters and much more. You need to join to get the best out of it though, and because there's so much on the site, it can be a little slow.

www.channel4.co.uk
CHANNEL 4

ORIGIN UK
SPEED ✓✓✓✓
INFO ✓✓✓✓
EASE ✓✓✓

A cool design with details of programmes and links to specific web pages on the best-known ones. There are also links to other initiatives such as Filmfour and the 4learning programme.

www.channel5.co.uk
CHANNEL 5

ORIGIN UK
SPEED ✓✓✓
INFO ✓✓✓✓
EASE ✓✓✓✓

Similar to Channel 4 except it's brighter and has more in the way of games and competitions. It's also a bit clearer and easier to find your way around.

www.sky.com
SKY TV

ORIGIN UK
SPEED ✓✓✓
INFO ✓✓✓✓✓
EASE ✓✓✓✓

You'd be forgiven for thinking this was a news site, but a closer look reveals that there are links to all the best Sky programmes as well as great features such as games, shopping and links to other sister sites.

www.nicktv.co.uk
NICKELODEON

ORIGIN UK
SPEED ✓✓✓
INFO ✓✓✓✓
EASE ✓✓✓✓

Bright doesn't do this site justice, you need sunglasses! It's got info on all the top programmes: *Sabrina*, *Rugrats* and so on, plus games and quizzes.

TV review and listings sites

www.digiguide.co.uk
THE DOWNLOADABLE GUIDE

ORIGIN UK
SPEED ✓✓✓
INFO ✓✓✓✓✓
VALUE ✓✓✓✓✓
EASE ✓✓✓✓✓

If you have Sky digital you'll be familiar with this guide, it follows a similar format, although you can customise it. Simply download the program and you get 14 days forward programming for up to 200 channels, masses of links and background information. You then need to access the site for updates. The best thing is that it's all free.

www.radiotimes.beeb.com
THE RADIO TIMES

ORIGIN	UK
SPEED	✓✓✓
INFO	✓✓✓✓✓
EASE	✓✓✓✓

Excellent listings e-zine with a good search facility for looking up programme details, plus competitions, links and a cinema guide. There are also sections on the best-loved TV genres – children's, sci-fi, soaps and so on.

See also **www.teletext.co.uk/tvplus** which is a far cry from the listings you get via your television.

www.unmissabletv.com
WHAT'S ON THAT'S UNMISSABLE

ORIGIN	UK
SPEED	✓✓✓✓
INFO	✓✓✓✓✓
EASE	✓✓✓✓

A site that's dedicated to all that's best on UK TV, with links and features on all the programmes including soaps. There are also special features on all the 'in' programmes.

Soaps

www.brookie.com
THE OFFICIAL BROOKSIDE WEB SITE

ORIGIN	UK
SPEED	✓✓
INFO	✓✓✓✓
VALUE	✓✓✓
EASE	✓✓✓✓

You'll get the latest information, gossip or storyline with loads of background info on the cast. There are competitions and you can shop for Brookie merchandise. With the new animated version you can download clips and take a virtual tour, but be patient and the sound effects are really annoying. There are also links to related programs.

www.corrie.net
CORONATION STREET BY ITS FANS

ORIGIN UK
SPEED ✓✓✓✓
INFO ✓✓✓✓✓
EASE ✓✓✓✓

Corrie was formed in 1999 from several fan's sites and has no connection with Granada, the site is written by volunteer fans who have contributed articles, updates and biographies. There are five key sections. One for Corrie newbies (are there any?) with a history of the Street; a catch up with the story section; what's up and coming; profiles on the key characters; a chat section where you can gossip about the goings on. For another fan's eye view try out www.csvu.net

www.coronationstreet.co.uk
THE OFFICIAL CORONATION STREET

ORIGIN UK
SPEED ✓✓✓
INFO ✓✓✓✓
VALUE ✓✓
EASE ✓✓✓✓

This is the official site and it's split into several sections including 'breaking news', chat, storylines, a shop plus topical links. There's also a good archives section and games and quizzes to play.

www.dawsons-creek.com
DAWSONS CREEK

ORIGIN UK
SPEED ✓✓✓
INFO ✓✓✓✓✓
EASE ✓✓✓✓

Everything is here, storylines, interviews, chat and feedback as well as the ability for you to send Dawsons Creek e-cards, have a gossip at the Creek, learn about Cape Cod and download the music. Plus it's all packaged on a nice web site.

www.emmerdale.co.uk
THE OFFICIAL EMMERDALE SITE

ORIGIN UK
SPEED ✓✓✓✓
INFO ✓✓✓✓
EASE ✓✓✓✓

Very similar to the official Coronation Street site, you can: keep up-to-date with the show; play games at the Woolpack; visit the archives; leave messages for other fans; and visit Dingleworld.

Both Emmerdale and Coronation Street are hosted by **www.G-Wizz.com** who also host sites for Granada, Yorkshire TV, LWT and Tyne Tees television.

www.emmerdale.clara.net
THE UNOFFICIAL EMMERDALE SITE

ORIGIN UK
SPEED ✓✓✓✓
INFO ✓✓✓✓
EASE ✓✓✓✓

A much improved, less eccentric site run by a true fan with a less fussy approach than the official site, it is divided up into sections in which you can see things such as future plotlines – spoilers. There are links to other Emmerdale fan sites, a weekly poll, a message board and you can send an e-card.

www.bbc.co.uk/eastenders
THE OFFICIAL EASTENDERS PAGE

ORIGIN UK
SPEED ✓✓✓
INFO ✓✓✓✓✓
EASE ✓✓✓✓✓

A page from the massive BBC site, it's split into several sections: catch up on the latest stories and hints on future storylines; play games and competitions; get pictures of the stars; vote in their latest poll; reminisce and visit the 'where are they now?' section; take a virtual tour and view Albert Square with the Walford Cam.

www.familyaffairs.co.uk
FAMILY AFFAIRS UNOFFICIAL

ORIGIN UK
SPEED ✓✓✓
INFO ✓✓✓✓✓
EASE ✓✓✓✓

A massive site dedicated to the goings on in Charnham, you can download whole episodes if you like, otherwise there's the usual collection of interviews, stories and pictures.

www.summerbay.co.uk
STREWTH, IT'S A HOME AND AWAY SITE

ORIGIN UK
SPEED ✓✓✓
INFO ✓✓✓✓✓
EASE ✓✓✓

As you'd expect, a bright and breezy site, in which you can learn all the facts about the characters that inhabit Summer Bay. There is also loads in the way of things to do – see also **www.homeandaway.org**

www.hollyoaks.com
THE OFFICIAL HOLLYOAKS WEB SITE

ORIGIN UK
SPEED ✓✓✓
INFO ✓✓✓✓✓
EASE ✓✓✓✓✓

A very cool site with lots on it, you can subscribe to the fortnightly newsletter; peek behind the scenes; catch up on the latest news; chat with fellow fans. There's also the expected photos and downloads to be had.

www.baxendale.u-net.com/ramsayst/
NEIGHBOURS WORLD-WIDE FANPAGES

ORIGIN UK
SPEED ✓✓✓
INFO ✓✓✓✓✓
EASE ✓✓✓✓

You can also get them at **www.ramsay-street.co.uk** This is a labour of love by the fans of Neighbours, it has everything you need: storylines past, present and future; info on all the characters; clips from some episodes; complete discographies of the singing stars; and access to all the related web sites through the links page. Unfortunately, you can't buy Neighbours merchandise from the site.

www.soapweb.co.uk
THE LATEST SOAP NEWS

ORIGIN UK
SPEED ✓✓✓✓
INFO ✓✓✓✓✓
EASE ✓✓✓✓

Can't be bothered with visiting each site separately? Then try Soap Web. Here you can keep up-to-date on all the soaps, even the Australian and American ones.

Travel and Holidays

Travel is the biggest growth area on the Internet, from holidays to insurance to local guides. If you're buying, then it definitely pays to shop around and try several sites, but be careful, it's amazing how fast the best deals are being snapped up. You may find that you still spend time on the phone, but the sites are constantly improving.

Starting out

www.abtanet.com
ABTA

ORIGIN	UK
SPEED	✓✓✓✓
INFO	✓✓✓✓
EASE	✓✓✓✓

Make sure that the travel agent you choose is a member of the Association of British Travel Agents as then you're covered if they go bust halfway through your holiday. All members are listed and there's a great search facility with links for you to start the ball rolling. See also the Air Travellers Licensing home page at **www.atol.org.uk** they also cover travel agents.

www.brochurebank.co.uk
BROCHURES DELIVERED TO YOUR HOME

ORIGIN	UK
SPEED	✓✓✓✓✓
INFO	✓✓✓✓
EASE	✓✓✓✓✓

Holiday brochures from over 150 companies can be selected then delivered to your home, free of charge. The selection process is easy and the site is fast. Delivery is through 2nd class postage.

Travel information and tips

www.fco.gov.uk/travel
ADVICE FROM THE FOREIGN OFFICE

ORIGIN UK
SPEED ✓✓✓✓
INFO ✓✓✓✓✓
EASE ✓✓✓

Before you go get general advice, safety or visa information. Just select a country and you get a run-down of all the issues that are likely to affect you when you go there, from terrorism to health.

www.medicineplanet.com
MOBILE HEALTH

ORIGIN UK
SPEED ✓✓✓✓
INFO ✓✓✓✓✓
EASE ✓✓✓

Get advice put through to your mobile phone, gen up on the facts before you go and find out which vaccines and medicines to take. Excellent design makes this site stand out.

For more travel safety information go to:

www.cdc.gov/travel – official American site giving sensible health information world-wide.

www.travelsafetytips.com – starts off by scaring you to death, then gives you straightforward advice on how to keep safe, covers mainly how to avoid crime.

www.tripprep.com – country-by-country risk assessment covering health, safety and politics; it can be a little out of date so check with the foreign office as well.

www.etravel.org – masses of tips to browse through from book reviews to flying advice and weather updates.

www.tips4trips.com – all the tips come from well-meaning travellers and are categorised under sections such as pre-planning, what and how to pack, travelling for the disabled, for women, for men or with children.

www.1000traveltips.org – tips from the very well travelled Koen De Boeck and friends.

www.travel-news.org

TRAVEL NEWS ORGANISATION

ORIGIN UK
SPEED ✓✓✓
INFO ✓✓✓✓
EASE ✓✓✓

A good, but oddly-designed travel magazine packed with the latest news and information, as well as destination reports and event listings. There are also links to airlines, special offers and specialist holidays.

www.guardian.co.uk/travel

FROM THE *Guardian* NEWSPAPER

ORIGIN UK
SPEED ✓✓✓✓
INFO ✓✓✓✓✓
EASE ✓✓✓✓

A good reflection of the *Guardian*'s weekly travel section, which is excellent with guides, information and inspiration throughout. There's also the latest news and links to sites with offers.

www.vtourist.com

THE VIRTUAL TOURIST

ORIGIN US
SPEED ✓✓✓
INFO ✓✓✓✓
EASE ✓✓✓

Explore destinations in a unique and fun way. Travellers describe their experiences, share photos, make recommendations and give tips so others benefit from their experience. See also **www.travel-library.com** which is less entertaining but combines recommendation with hard facts very well.

www.budgettravel.com

BUDGET TRAVEL

ORIGIN US
SPEED ✓✓✓✓
INFO ✓✓✓✓
EASE ✓✓✓

Masses of links and information for the budget traveller plus advice on how to travel on the cheap. It can be difficult to navigate but the information is very good.

Travel services and information

www.xe.net/currency/
ONLINE CURRENCY CONVERTER

ORIGIN US
SPEED ✓✓✓✓✓
INFO ✓✓✓✓✓
EASE ✓✓✓✓✓

The Universal Currency Converter could not be easier to use, just select the currency you have, then the one you want to convert it to, press the button and you have your answer in seconds.

www.taxfree.se
GLOBAL REFUND

ORIGIN
SPEED ✓✓
INFO ✓✓✓✓✓
EASE ✓✓✓

Find out how to make the most out of tax-free shopping at this very useful web site.

www.webofculture.com/worldsmart/gestures.html
GESTURES OF THE WORLD

ORIGIN US
SPEED ✓✓✓
INFO ✓✓✓✓
EASE ✓✓✓✓

Country-by-country, what their gestures mean, what not to do and what's best to do, all in a concise format.

www.whatsonwhen.com
WORLD-WIDE EVENTS GUIDE

ORIGIN UK
SPEED ✓✓
INFO ✓✓✓✓
EASE ✓✓✓✓

An easy-to-use site with information on every type of event you can think of from major festivals to village fêtes.

www.ukpa.gov.uk

UK PASSPORTS

ORIGIN UK	Apply for your passport online and get tips on how
SPEED ✓✓✓	to get the best passport photo.
INFO ✓✓✓✓	
EASE ✓✓✓✓	

Travel Insurance

www.travelinsuranceclub.co.uk

AWARD WINNING TRAVEL INSURANCE CLUB

ORIGIN UK	Unfortunately there isn't one site for collating travel
SPEED ✓✓✓✓	insurance yet, it's a question of shopping around.
INFO ✓✓✓✓	These sites make a good starting point offering a
VALUE ✓✓✓✓	range of policies for backpackers, family and busi-
EASE ✓✓✓	ness travel.

All these companies offer flexibility and good value:
www.columbusdirect.co.uk – good information,
  nice, but fiddly web site and competitive prices.
www.costout.co.uk – did well in a recent *Which?*
  survey.
www.jameshampden.co.uk – wide range of policies,
  straightforward and hassle free.
www.journeywise.co.uk – nice straightforward site,
  also did well in the *Which?* survey.
www.underthesun.co.uk – good for annual and six
  monthly policies.
www.worldwideinsure.com – good selection
  of policies. **W?WT**

Travel shops

www.expedia.co.uk
THE COMPLETE SERVICE

ORIGIN US/UK
SPEED ✓✓✓✓
INFO ✓✓✓✓✓
VALUE ✓✓✓
EASE ✓✓✓

This is the UK arm of Microsoft's very successful online travel agency. It offers a huge array of holidays, flights and associated services, for personal or business use, nearly all bookable online. It's easy and quicker than most, and there are some excellent offers too. Not the trendiest but it's a good first stop. As with all the big operators, you have to register. They've also added sections on business travel, mapping and insurance.

www.lastminute.com
DO SOMETHING LAST MINUTE

ORIGIN UK
SPEED ✓✓
INFO ✓✓✓✓
VALUE ✓✓✓✓
EASE ✓✓✓✓

Last Minute has an excellent reputation not just as a travel agent, but as a good shopping site too. For travellers there are comprehensive sections on hotels, holidays and flights, all with really good prices. There is also a superb London restaurant guide and a general entertainment section. Mostly, you can book online, but a hotline is available.

www.thomascook.com
THE WIDEST RANGE OF PACKAGE HOLIDAYS

ORIGIN UK
SPEED ✓✓✓✓
INFO ✓✓✓✓
VALUE ✓✓✓✓
EASE ✓✓✓✓

This site is easy-to-use and well laid out and, with over 2 million package holidays to chose from, you should be able to find something to your liking. You can also browse the online guide for ideas or search for cheap flights or holiday deals. Again you have to call the hotline to book – 0870 0100 437.

www.its.net
INTERNET TRAVEL SERVICE

ORIGIN	UK
SPEED	✓✓✓✓
INFO	✓✓✓✓✓
EASE	✓✓✓✓✓

An excellent place to start your search for travel information or holidays, with links to over 1,500 travel agents and service providers classified into over 40 specialist sections. See also **www.theinterjet.com**

www.travel.world.co.uk
FOR ALL YOUR TRAVEL REQUIREMENTS

ORIGIN	UK
SPEED	✓✓✓
INFO	✓✓✓✓✓
EASE	✓✓✓

A massive, comprehensive site, it basically includes most available travel brochures with links to the relevant travel agent. It concentrates on Europe, so there are very few American sites, but provides links to hotels, specialist holidays, cruises, self-catering and airlines. For a more global view go to **www.globalpassage.com** who offer 15,000 web sites to browse.

www.holidayauctions.net
BID FOR YOUR HOLIDAY

ORIGIN	UK
SPEED	✓✓✓
INFO	✓✓✓✓
EASE	✓✓✓✓

Some amazing bargains are available from these auction sites – you bid in the same way a normal online auction works. It's fully bonded and if you hit a problem call their hotline 08003 899 553. They also sell conventional holidays. See also the nicely designed **www.lateescapes.com** who were offering holidays from 50p.

www.priceline.co.uk
LET SOMEONE ELSE DO THE WORK

ORIGIN UK
SPEED ✓✓✓
INFO ✓✓✓✓
VALUE ✓✓✓✓
EASE ✓✓✓✓

You could leave it to someone else to do the travel searching for you, here you provide details of the trip you want and how much you're willing to pay, then they try to find a deal that will match your requirements. If you're flexible about timing then there are some great offers. They cover flights, hotels and car hire. For a wider holiday-oriented service see **www.ybag.co.uk** (full review page 329) whose travel service is excellent, and also **www.myown-price.com** both this site and Priceline want your credit card details before you agree to any transaction so you may feel more comfortable using a more traditional route.

Here's a selection of well-proven and independent online travel agents – the choice is yours.

www.a2btravel.co.uk – superb travel resource, great for the UK too.

www.balesworldwide.com – for something special, tailor-made holidays to the exotic parts of the world; hi-tech site is excellent but no online booking.

www.bargainholidays.com – probably the best for quick breaks, excellent for late availability offers. 029 2033 0052.

www.beachtowel.co.uk – good all-round site from an independent travel agent who is ABTA and ATOL covered. 0800 013 1300.

www.e-bookers.com – a little tedious to use, but good for Europe and flight deals, online booking available and a good flight alert service.

www.escaperoutes.com – sister site to Bargain Holidays, good for conventional and destination information.

www.firstchoice.co.uk – bargains from First Choice holidays see also the sister site found at **www.travelchoice.co.uk** – discounts for online booking.

www.firstresort.com – a good all-rounder with some good deals and a price promise, owned by Thomsons – 0870 055 6300.

www.gvillage.co.uk – specialising in independent travellers and students with some great deals and adventure holidays to the world's most interesting places – 020 7692 7770.

www.holiday.co.uk – good deals on package holidays – 01633 627550.

www.lunn-poly.co.uk – lots of holidays and offers on a bright and breezy site – 0800 0278234.

www.packageholidays.co.uk – late bargain holidays and flights from over 130 tour operators including Thomson, Sunworld, Airtours and specialist agents.

www.teletext.co.uk/holidays – much better than browsing the TV, you can now get all those offers on one easy-to-use site. There are also lots of useful travel information to help you on your way.

www.travelagents.co.uk – another all-rounder, nothing special but competent – 0870 010 6233.

www.travelcareonline.com – not a great site but loads of deals and honest information from the UK's largest independent – 0870 902 0033.

www.travelfinder.co.uk – lots of options and great bargains at this simple-to-use site.

www.travelocity.com – one of the oldest online travel agents; it's similar to Expedia and there's a rewards scheme too.

www.trrravel.com – good for something different as

well as the usual bargains, you can even charter a plane and there good links to other travel sites – 0870 013 3152.

www.unmissable.com – dedicated to the sale of extraordinary, exclusive, exceptional and exhila- rating experiences, and it succeeds – just visit for inspiration. It covers events as well.

www.utravel.co.uk – good comprehensive site but you have to register before using it.

www.webweekends.co.uk – specialists in weekend breaks both in the UK and abroad – 0870 848 2222.

Airlines and flights only sites

www.cheapflights.co.uk
NOTHING BUT CHEAP FLIGHTS

ORIGIN	UK
SPEED	✓✓✓✓
INFO	✓✓✓✓✓
VALUE	✓✓✓✓✓
EASE	✓✓✓

You don't need to register here to explore the great offers available from this site; you still need to phone most of the travel agents or airlines listed to get your deal though and some of the prices quoted seem magically to disappear once you've clicked on the link. Having said that, there are obviously some great deals to be had.

www.netflights.com
THE AIRLINE NETWORK

ORIGIN	UK
SPEED	✓✓✓
INFO	✓✓✓✓
VALUE	✓✓✓✓
EASE	✓✓✓

Discount deals on over 100 airlines world-wide make The Airline Network is worth checking out for their flight offers page alone. It's good for flights from regional airports. They also do all the tradi- tional travel agent things and there are some good holiday bargains too.

www.deckchair.com
Relax with Deckchair

ORIGIN UK
SPEED ✓✓✓
INFO ✓✓✓✓✓
VALUE ✓✓✓✓✓
EASE ✓✓✓

Concentrates on getting value for money on flights, it can be a little slow but the results are usually worth it, although they annoyingly show sold out fares and they don't bother showing you the full priced fares. Still, there are some good offers to be had, especially for European flights.

For more cheap flight deals try these sites:
www.bargainflights.com – good search facility and plenty of offers, but you need to be patient.
www.easyjet.co.uk – great for a limited number of destinations, particularly good for UK flights. **W?WT**
www.go-fly.com – limited to selected airports but some excellent offers for Western Europe. Nicely designed site.
www.ryanair.com – very good for Ireland, northern Europe, Italy and France. Clear and easy-to-use web site.
www.travelselect.com – good flight selection and lots of different options available at this very flexible site.

Airport and airline information

www.worldairportguide.com
What are the world's airports really like?

ORIGIN GERMANY
SPEED ✓✓
INFO ✓✓✓✓
EASE ✓✓✓✓

It seems that no matter how out of the way, this guide has details on every airport – how to get there, where to park, facilities, key phone numbers and a map. There are also guides on cities, resorts and even world weather.

www.baa.co.uk
BRITISH AIRPORT AUTHORITY

ORIGIN UK	Details on all the major UK airports that are run by
SPEED ✓✓	the BAA, you get all the essential information plus
INFO ✓✓✓	flight data, weather and shopping information.
VALUE ✓✓✓	
EASE ✓✓✓	

www.airlinequality.com
RANKING THE AIRLINES

ORIGIN UK	An independent ranking of all the world's airlines
SPEED ✓✓✓	and their services, see who's the best and the worst
INFO ✓✓✓	and why. Each airline is rated a number of stars (up
EASE ✓✓✓	to 5) on criteria such as seat quality, catering and
	staff.

Hotels and places to stay

www.hotelguide.com
COMPREHENSIVE

ORIGIN US	With services available in eight languages and
SPEED ✓✓✓	specialist sections such as golfing breaks, this site
INFO ✓✓✓✓	ranks among the best for finding the right hotel. It
VALUE ✓✓✓	lists around 60,000 at time of writing. You can get
EASE ✓✓✓	good deals and save more money with their loyalty
	scheme.

www.from-a–z.com
A–Z OF HOTELS

ORIGIN UK	A well-designed British site with over 15,000 hotels
SPEED ✓✓✓	to choose from in the UK, Eire and France and a
INFO ✓✓✓	further 40,000 world-wide. It's quick and easy-to-
VALUE ✓✓	use and there's online booking available plus plenty
EASE ✓✓	of special discounts.

Other good hotel directory and booking sites:

www.all-hotels.co.uk – another directory of 60,000 hotels with lots of options, American bias.

www.best-inn.co.uk – 60,000 hotels listed but very good for London and links to specialist accommodation.

www.holidayleaders.com – if you need a villa come here first.

www.jamesvillas.co.uk – over 500 villas in the Med.

www.johansens.com/joh_luxury_hotel_guide.html – the posh hotels' guide with links to online reservations.

www.laterooms.co.uk – easy-to-use directory featuring unsold hotel rooms at great prices.

www.openworld.co.uk – a collection of links to hotel sites, just use the interactive world map.

www.placestostay.com – another with an interactive map, you drill down until you find the place you want to stay, then you get a list of hotels, a description, price and online reservation service.

Travel guides

www.mytravelguide.com
ONLINE TRAVEL GUIDES

ORIGIN US	
SPEED ✓✓✓	
INFO ✓✓✓✓✓	
EASE ✓✓✓	

A general American travel site that offers a good overview of most countries, with points of interest, a currency converter, very good interactive mapping and live web cams too. You need to become a member to get the best out of it though.

www.lonelyplanet.com
LONELY PLANET GUIDES

ORIGIN UK
SPEED ✓✓✓✓✓
INFO ✓✓✓✓✓
VALUE ✓✓✓✓
EASE ✓✓✓✓✓

A superb travel site, aimed at the independent traveller, but with great information for everyone. Get a review on most world destinations or pick a theme and go with that; leave a message on the thorn tree; find out the latest news by country; get health reports; read about the travel experiences of others – what's the real story? Maybe the best service is the eKno system which is a combined phone, e-mail and answer machine which offers a great way to stay in touch when you're in the back of beyond.

http://travel.roughguides.com
ROUGH GUIDES

ORIGIN UK
SPEED ✓✓✓✓
INFO ✓✓✓✓✓
VALUE ✓✓✓
EASE ✓✓✓✓

Lively reviews on a huge number of places – some 14,000; general travel information; share your travel thoughts with other travellers; or buy a guide.

www.fodors.com
FODOR'S GUIDES

ORIGIN US
SPEED ✓✓✓✓
INFO ✓✓✓✓✓
EASE ✓✓✓

These guides give an American perspective, but there is a huge amount of information on each destination. The site is much improved on previous visits and is much faster to use.

http://kasbah.com
WORLD'S LARGEST TRAVEL GUIDE

ORIGIN UK
SPEED ✓✓✓✓
INFO ✓✓✓✓
EASE ✓✓✓✓

A claim that it doesn't quite live up to, e.g. Kenya was not listed when we visited, but the information is clear, the site easy-to-use and there's lots of links. The highlights on each destination are useful.

www.packback.com
PACKBACK TRAVEL GUIDE

ORIGIN UK
SPEED ✓✓✓
INFO ✓✓✓✓
VALUE ✓✓✓
EASE ✓✓✓✓

A good looking and useful site with an independent travel guide, a growing membership and a reputation for quality reviews. Includes a discussion forum, travel tools and flight booking.

www.gorp.com
FOR THE GREAT OUTDOORS

ORIGIN US
SPEED ✓✓✓
INFO ✓✓✓✓✓
EASE ✓✓✓

A great title, Gorp is dedicated to adventure, whether it be hiking, mountaineering, fishing, snow sports or riding the rapids. It has an American bias, but is full of relevant good advice and information.

www.timeout.com
TIME OUT GUIDE

ORIGIN UK
SPEED ✓✓✓✓
INFO ✓✓✓✓
EASE ✓✓✓✓

A slick site with destination guides covering many European cites and some further afield such as New York and Sydney. Not surprisingly, it's outstanding for London and you can also book tickets and buy books via other retailers.

www.bradmans.com
BRADMAN'S FOR BUSINESS TRAVELLERS

ORIGIN US
SPEED ✓✓✓✓
INFO ✓✓✓✓✓
EASE ✓✓✓✓

A really excellent city guide with none of your fancy graphics, just a straightforward listing of countries and sensible information on each one. Includes tips on orienting yourself in the city and restaurant reviews.

www.pataguide.co.uk
ASIA GUIDE

ORIGIN UK	Covering most of Indo-China including Japan, it's
SPEED ✓✓✓✓	aimed largely at the business traveller. You get help
INFO ✓✓✓✓	and tips on doing business in each country plus the
EASE ✓✓✓✓	usual travel information and booking service.

http://travel.excite.com
CITY GUIDES

ORIGIN US	Entertaining reviews of 14,000 of the world's cities
SPEED ✓✓✓✓	can be found here, you can also book a flight and
INFO ✓✓✓✓✓	get access to hundreds of travel links in Excite's
EASE ✓✓✓✓	directory.

Online maps and route finders

www.mappy.co.uk
START HERE

ORIGIN UK	Mappy has a great-looking site which is easy-to-use
SPEED ✓✓✓	and has lots of added features such as a personal
INFO ✓✓✓✓✓	mapping service where you can store the maps you
EASE ✓✓✓✓	use most. The route finder is OK, doesn't use post-
	codes but business users can fill in their mileage
	allowance and Mappy will calculate how much you
	should claim.

www.mapblast.com
IT'S A BLAST!

ORIGIN US	Get detailed maps and information on virtually
SPEED ✓✓✓	anywhere. It has a superb, probably the best, route
INFO ✓✓✓✓✓	finder.
EASE ✓✓✓✓	

See also:

www.easymap.co.uk – superb interactive map of the UK, easy-to-use and up-to-date.

http://maps.expedia.co.uk – limited to the US, France, Germany and the UK for detailed maps – modest route finder.

www.mapquest.com – find out the best way to get from a to b in Europe or America, not always as detailed as you'd like, but easy-to-use and you can customise your map or route plan.

www.mapsonus.com – it's notoriously difficult to find your way around America, but using the route planner you should minimise your risk of getting lost.

www.michelin-travel.com – a good all-round travel site with a built-in route finder service which is OK but not that detailed.

www.multimap.com – easy-to-use, excellent for the UK, you can search using postcodes, London street names, place names or Ordnance Survey Grid references.

www.ordsvy.gov.uk – free get-a-map service has potential but is actually very slow.

www.stanfords.co.uk – travel book and map specialists.

www.streetmap.co.uk – good UK map, easy-to-use.

www.theaa.co.uk
AUTOMOBILE ASSOCIATION

ORIGIN UK
SPEED ✓✓✓✓
INFO ✓✓✓✓✓
EASE ✓✓✓✓

A superb site that is divided into four key sections: breakdown cover, route planning and traffic information, hotel guide and booking and finally, help with buying a car. There is also information on insurance and other financial help.

www.rac.co.uk
GET AHEAD WITH THE RAC

ORIGIN UK	Great for UK traffic reports and has a very reliable
SPEED ✓✓✓	route planner, with live traffic reports. There's also a
INFO ✓✓✓✓✓	good section on finding the right place to stay, and
EASE ✓✓✓✓	lots of help if you want to buy a car.

Destinations

Here's a list to help you research your likely destinations and plan your holiday.

www.antor.com
ASSOCIATION OF NATIONAL TOURIST OFFICES

ORIGIN UK	A useful start point to find information about some
SPEED ✓✓✓✓	90 countries that are members of the association.
INFO ✓✓✓✓	Very good for links to key tourism sites. See also
EASE ✓✓✓✓	www.tourist-offices.org.uk

www.embassyworld.com
EMBASSIES AROUND THE GLOBE

ORIGIN US	Pick two countries one for 'whose embassy', one for
SPEED ✓✓✓✓	'in what location', press go and up pops the details
INFO ✓✓✓✓	on the embassy with contact and essential informa-
EASE ✓✓✓✓✓	tion.

A

www.africaonline.com
AFRICA

ORIGIN S AFRICA	Exhaustive site covering news, information and
SPEED ✓✓✓✓✓	travel in Africa, with very good features and articles.
INFO ✓✓✓✓✓	
EASE ✓✓✓✓	

See also:

www.africaguide.com – detailed country-by-country guides, discussion forums, shopping and a travelogue feature make this site a good first stop.

www.backpackafrica.com – excellent site for backpackers with over 400 links and advice on where to go and what to see.

www.ecoafrica.com – tailor-made safaris with the emphasis on eco-tourism.

www.onsafari.com – good advice on what sort of safari is right for you.

www.phakawe.demon.co.uk – safaris in Botswana and Namibia.

www.travelinafrica.co.za – budget travel in Southern Africa.

www.vintageafrica.com – awesome safaris and destinations from this specialist travel agent, who will tailor-make holidays if requested.

www.wildnetafrica.net – an excellent travel and information portal for safaris to south and south-east Africa.

www.australia.com

DISCOVER AUSTRALIA

ORIGIN AUSTRALIA	The Australian Tourist Commission offer a good
SPEED ✓✓✓✓	and informative site that gives lots of facts about the
INFO ✓✓✓✓✓	country, the people, lifestyle and what you can
EASE ✓✓✓✓	expect when you visit.

See also:

www.egoldcoast.com.au – find out all about the dynamic and entertaining Gold Coast, its resorts and sites of interest.

www.quantas.com.au – under construction when we visited but expect good things when back online.

www.ansett.com.au – one of the world's top rated
airlines with some good deals and flight prices
from Australia only.

B

www.indo.com
BALI ONLINE

ORIGIN INDONESIA	Concentrating on Bali and its top hotels, but there's
SPEED ✓✓✓	also plenty of information on the rest of Indonesia
INFO ✓✓✓✓	as well as links to other Asian sites.
EASE ✓✓✓	

www.trabel.com
BELGIUM

ORIGIN BELGIUM	The Belgium Travel Network offers a site packed
SPEED ✓✓✓✓	with information about the country and its key
INFO ✓✓✓✓	towns and cities. You can get information on hotels,
EASE ✓✓✓✓	travelling, an airport guide, flight information and
	there's also a good links page.

www.brazil.com
BRAZIL

ORIGIN US	A straightforward, no-nonsense guide, travelogue
SPEED ✓✓✓	and listing site for Brazil that also contains informa-
INFO ✓✓✓✓	tion on hotels and resorts.
EASE ✓✓✓✓	

C

www.travelcanada.ca
EXPLORE CANADA

ORIGIN CANADA
SPEED ✓✓✓✓
INFO ✓✓✓✓✓
EASE ✓✓✓✓

Did you know that the glass floor at the top of the world's tallest freestanding structure could support the weight of 14 large hippos? Find out much more at this wide-ranging and attractive site, from touring to city guides. See also **www.canadian-affair.com** who offer some excellent low cost flights and tours.

www.turq.com
CARIBBEAN

ORIGIN US
SPEED ✓✓✓
INFO ✓✓✓✓✓
EASE ✓✓✓✓

All you need to organise a great holiday in the Caribbean. There's information on flights, hotels, cruises, a travel guide and trip reports to the islands, all on a well presented and easy-to-use site.

See also:
www.caribtourism.com – for lots of information.
www.caribbeansupersite.com – good information.
www.nanana.com/caribbean.html – masses of links.
www.caribbeandreams.co.uk – UK travel agent
  specialising in the Caribbean.

www.chinatour.com
INFORMATION CHINA

ORIGIN CHINA
SPEED ✓✓✓✓
INFO ✓✓✓✓
EASE ✓✓✓✓

A comprehensive site stuffed with data on China: where to go and stay, how to get there and what to see, maps and visa application information. See also the China Travel System at **www.chinats.com** who have a good looking and very polite site where you can book hotels and tours, get travel information and chat to others who've experienced China.

D

www.visitdenmark.com
DENMARK

ORIGIN DENMARK	The official Danish tourist board site where you can
SPEED ✓✓✓✓	get links to book a holiday and all the advice and
INFO ✓✓✓✓	information you'd expect from a well-run and
EASE ✓✓✓✓	efficient looking site.

E

www.egyptvoyager.com
LAND OF THE PHARAOHS

ORIGIN EGYPT	A superb site with games, snippets of interesting
SPEED ✓✓✓✓	information, in-depth articles and a great photo
INFO ✓✓✓✓	gallery. You could be forgiven for forgetting that its
EASE ✓✓✓✓	primary function is to sell holidays – you can even

get a lesson on hieroglyphics. See also the more
conventional **http://touregypt.net** which is very
comprehensive.

www.eurotrip.com
BACKPACKING EUROPE

ORIGIN UK	Student and independent European travel with in-
SPEED ✓✓✓✓	depth information, facts, reviews, articles, discus-
INFO ✓✓✓✓✓	sion, live reports, links and travel advice on a good
EASE ✓✓✓✓	looking and well-designed site.

www.eurocamp.co.uk
SELF-CATERING EUROPE

ORIGIN	UK	The leading self-catering company with over 170
SPEED	✓✓✓✓	holiday parks in 9 countries. Here you can find
INFO	✓✓✓✓	details of the accommodation and book a holiday
EASE	✓✓✓✓	and there are some bargains too.

www.centraleurope.com
CENTRAL EUROPE ONLINE

ORIGIN	EUROPE	A news-based site with comprehensive information
SPEED	✓✓✓✓	on the region. You can get travel information and
INFO	✓✓✓✓✓	airline tickets via the links sections.
EASE	✓✓✓	

F

www.franceway.com
VOILA LA FRANCE!

ORIGIN	FRANCE	Excellent site giving an overview of French culture,
SPEED	✓✓✓✓	history, facts and figures, and of course, how to
INFO	✓✓✓✓✓	book a holiday. You can also sign up for the
EASE	✓✓✓✓	newsletter.

See also:
www.francetourism.com – the official French
Government Tourist Office site for the US; great
information for the UK too.
www.vive-la-france.org – very comprehensive and
good fun.
www.magicparis.com – good Paris guide with some
offers.
www.justparis.co.uk – details on how to get there
and hotels when you've arrived.

G

www.germany-tourism.de
GERMANY – WUNDERBAR

ORIGIN	GERMANY
SPEED	✓✓
INFO	✓✓✓✓✓
EASE	✓✓✓✓

As much information as you can handle with good features on the key destinations, excellent interactive mapping and links to related sites. For further information try **www.germany-info.org**

www.gnto.gr
GREEK NATIONAL TOURIST ORGANISATION

ORIGIN	GREECE
SPEED	✓✓✓✓
INFO	✓✓✓
EASE	✓✓✓✓

An attractive site with the official word on travelling in Greece, with a good travel guide and information for business travellers plus accommodation, advice and details on what you can get up to.

See also:

www.gogreece.com – a search engine devoted to all things Greek.

www.gtpnet.com – the Greek Travel Pages with the latest ferry schedules for island hoppers.

www.agn.gr – holidays, information and travel on the Aegean, the site has a good interactive map with lots of features. Aimed at US audience.

www.travel-greece.com – masses of links to everything about holidaying in Greece.

H

www.holland.com
HOLLAND IS FULL OF SURPRISES

ORIGIN	HOLLAND
SPEED	✓✓✓✓
INFO	✓✓✓✓✓
EASE	✓✓✓✓

Very professional site offering a mass of tourist information and advice on how to have a great time when you visit. There are sections on how to get there, what type of holiday will suit you and city guides.

I

www.iceland.org
ICELAND

ORIGIN ICELAND
SPEED ✓✓✓✓
INFO ✓✓✓✓
EASE ✓✓✓✓

Official site of the Icelandic Foreign Service with a wealth of information about the country, the people and its history. It's easy to navigate and there are good links to related sites. See also www.iceland.com

www.indiatouristoffice.org
INDIAN TOURIST OFFICE UK

ORIGIN UK
SPEED ✓✓✓✓
INFO ✓✓✓✓
EASE ✓✓✓✓

Essential tourist information and advice as well as cultural and historical background on the country and its diverse regions. It has a massive hotel database as well.

www.indiamart.com
INDIA TRAVEL PROMOTION NETWORK

ORIGIN UK
SPEED ✓✓✓✓
INFO ✓✓✓✓✓
EASE ✓✓✓✓

Basically a shopping site with diverse information including hotels, timetables, wildlife, worship, trekking, heritage and general tourism. It's well-organised and easy-to-use.

See also:
www.india-travel.com – a really strong travel site with lots of information and guidance as well as essential links.
www.rrindia.com – another good information site offering tour itineraries and hotel booking.
www.partnershiptravel.co.uk – specialist Indian travel agent.

www.shamrock.org
IRELAND

ORIGIN	IRELAND
SPEED	✓✓✓✓
INFO	✓✓✓✓
EASE	✓✓✓✓

Wide-ranging site giving you the best of Ireland. Aimed at the American market, it really sells the country well with good links to other related sites.

See also:

www.enjoy-ireland.co.uk – nice guide with lots of information, use the frames-free site though, it's much easier to navigate.

www.iol.ie/~discover – a good a–z travel guide with lots of links.

www.camping-ireland.ie – over 100 parks listed for caravanning and camping.

www.12travel.co.uk – Irish holiday specialists with lots of holiday options.

www.goisrael.com
ISRAEL

ORIGIN	ISRAEL
SPEED	✓✓✓
INFO	✓✓✓✓
EASE	✓✓✓✓

Excellent site with information on the country, its sights and sites, how to get there and how to organise a tour. There's also the latest information on 'the troubles' there from the official tourist board.

www.italytour.com
VIRTUAL TOUR OF ITALY

ORIGIN	ITALY
SPEED	✓✓✓
INFO	✓✓✓✓
EASE	✓✓✓✓

Good looking, stylish and cool, this site is essentially a search engine and directory but a very good one.

See also:

www.emmeti.it – slightly eccentric site with bags of good information, although it takes a while to find it. Very good for hotels, regional info and museums.

www.initaly.com – another eccentric site but generally well organised, informative and useful.

www.travel.it – a messy information site but you can book online.

J

www.jnto.go.jp

JAPAN

ORIGIN	JAPAN
SPEED	✓✓
INFO	✓✓✓✓✓
EASE	✓✓✓✓

This excellent site is the work of the Japanese Tourist Association. There's a guide to each region, the food, shopping and travel info with advice on how to get the best out of your visit.

See also:
www.embjapan.org.uk –Japanese Embassy site, useful but not that up-to-date.
www.jaltour.co.uk – travel agents specialising in Japan.

www.jiblondon.com

JORDAN

ORIGIN	JORDAN
SPEED	✓✓✓
INFO	✓✓✓✓
EASE	✓✓✓✓

This is the site of the Jordanian Information Bureau. It's upbeat, informative and there's a good magazine – Jordan Focus but the site is not tourist-oriented. Try **www.jordanembassyuk.gov.jo/** who offer guidance and some useful links from their site.

K

www.kenya.com

GATEWAY TO KENYA

ORIGIN	KENYA
SPEED	✓✓✓
INFO	✓✓✓✓
EASE	✓✓✓✓

A good directory site where you can get links and information on virtually any aspect of the country, from the latest news to organising a safari.

See also:
www.kenya-wildlife-service.org – dedicated to preserving the wildlife of Kenya.
www.passagetokenya.com – specialist safari company with personalised tours to Kenya.

L

www.lebanon.com
THE LEBANON

ORIGIN LEBANON
SPEED ✓✓✓
INFO ✓✓✓✓✓
EASE ✓✓✓✓

The Lebanon is going through a resurgence and is successfully rebuilding itself. Here you can find all the resources you need to organise a visit and see its many attractions.

M

www.malaysianet.net
MALAYSIA

ORIGIN MALAYSIA
SPEED ✓✓✓
INFO ✓✓✓✓
EASE ✓✓✓✓

Great for hotels in particular but you'll also find flight information and hidden away is a pretty good travel guide to the country. For air travel info see also www.malaysiaair.com and for more holiday details see www.tourism.gov/my

www.tourbymexico.com
MEXICO

ORIGIN US
SPEED ✓✓✓
INFO ✓✓✓✓
EASE ✓✓✓

A basic site, but there is a travel guide to Mexico plus information on tours, hotels, health, tips, links and sights to see. See also the bright and breezy www.mexicanwave.com/travel

www.mideasttravelnet.com
MIDDLE EAST TRAVEL NETWORK

ORIGIN US
SPEED ✓✓✓
INFO ✓✓✓✓✓
EASE ✓✓✓✓

A well-organised site concentrating on North Africa and the Middle East. It's easy-to-use, targeted slightly towards business users, but still very useful for holiday-makers or independent travellers.

N

www.nepal.com
NEPAL AND THE HIMALAYAS

ORIGIN US
SPEED ✓✓✓
INFO ✓✓✓✓
EASE ✓✓✓

A beautifully presented site showing Nepal in its best light. Business, sport, culture and travel all have sections and it's a good browse too. The travel section is not that comprehensive, it has a basic guide, lots about Everest and access to the useful *Sherpa* magazine. See also the specialist tour company **www.trans-himalaya.ndirect.co.uk** and also **www.rrindia.com/nepal.html**

www.purenz.com
NEW ZEALAND

ORIGIN NZ
SPEED ✓✓✓✓
INFO ✓✓✓✓
EASE ✓✓✓✓

A good looking and informative site about the country with a section devoted to recollections and recommendations from people who've visited. See also the comprehensive **www.nz.com**

www.visitnorway.com
NORWAY

ORIGIN NORWAY
SPEED ✓✓✓✓
INFO ✓✓✓✓
EASE ✓✓✓✓

The official site of the Norwegian Tourist Board offers a good overview of what you can get up to when you're there from adventure holidays to lounging around in the midnight sun to cruising the coast; it's all here. See also **www.norway.org** which is the Norwegian Embassy's site.

P

www.portugal-web.com

PORTUGAL

ORIGIN PORTUGAL
SPEED ✓✓✓
INFO ✓✓✓✓✓
EASE ✓✓✓

A complete overview of the country including business as well as tourism with good regional information, news and links to other related sites.

See also:
www.thealgarve.net – all you need to know about the Algarve.
http://nervo.com/pt – Portugal for travellers, with personal experiences.
www.portugal.com – a news and shopping site with a good travel section.

R

www.russia-tourism.com

RUSSIA

ORIGIN RUSSIA
SPEED ✓✓✓✓
INFO ✓✓✓✓✓
EASE ✓✓✓✓

A very good directory site with hundreds of useful links covering everything from tourist sites to the weather; there's even sections for children and eco-tourism.

S

www.sey.net

SEYCHELLES, PARADISE – PERIOD

ORIGIN US
SPEED ✓✓✓✓
INFO ✓✓✓✓
EASE ✓✓✓✓

A good all-round overview of the Seychelles with background information on the major islands and activities, there's also links to travel agents. The slower **www.seychelles.uk.com** is also informative and geared to a British audience.

www.southafrica.net
SOUTH AFRICA

ORIGIN S AFRICA	Official tourist site with masses of information
SPEED ✓✓✓✓	about the country and how you can set yourself up
INFO ✓✓✓✓	for the perfect visit with suggested itineraries. See
EASE ✓✓✓✓	also **www.gardenroute.org.za** which is excellent.

www.southamericanexperience.co.uk
SOUTH AMERICA

ORIGIN UK	Specialists on South America are hard to come
SPEED ✓✓✓	by, but at this site you can get tailor-made tours
INFO ✓✓✓✓	to suit you plus some scant information on the
EASE ✓✓✓	countries and special offers. See also
	www.americanadventures.com and
	www.adventure-life.com

www.tourspain.es
TOURIST OFFICE OF SPAIN

ORIGIN SPAIN	A colourful and award-winning web site that really
SPEED ✓✓✓✓	makes you want to visit Spain. Very good for an
INFO ✓✓✓✓	overview.
EASE ✓✓✓✓	

You could also try any of these listed below:
www.red2000.com – a colourful travel guide, with a
good search instrument!
www.costaguide.com – your Costa del Sol companion, lots of information.
www.iberia.com – Iberian airlines site, with helpful
advice and offers.
www.majorca.com - great site about the island.

www.lankadirectory.com
SRI LANKA

ORIGIN SRI LANKA
SPEED ✓✓✓
INFO ✓✓✓✓✓
EASE ✓✓✓✓

An excellent news and directory site with good links to specialist tour operators, the travel page is split into tourist guides, attractions, hotels and accommodation. There's also advice on the political troubles in the north of the island.

www.sverigeturism.se/smorgasbord
SWEDEN

ORIGIN SWEDEN
SPEED ✓✓✓✓
INFO ✓✓✓✓
EASE ✓✓✓✓

The largest source of information in English on Sweden. It's essentially a directory site but there are sections on culture, history and a tourist guide.

For more details of Sweden's cities see the very good http://cityguide.se

T

www.tanzania-web.com
TANZANIA

ORIGIN TANZANIA
SPEED ✓✓✓✓
INFO ✓✓✓✓
EASE ✓✓✓✓

Find your way round Tanzania with its wonderful scenery, Mount Kilimanjaro, safaris and resorts with this very good and comprehensive online guide from the official tourist board.

www.thailand.com
THAILAND

ORIGIN THAILAND
SPEED ✓✓✓✓
INFO ✓✓✓✓
EASE ✓✓✓✓

Another excellent portal site, which acts as a gateway to a mass of travel and tourism resources, it covers some of South East Asia too and it has a good search facility. www.tourismthailand.org is the official tourist board site and is very informative.

www.turkey.com

YOUR WINDOW ON TURKEY

ORIGIN TURKEY
SPEED ✓✓✓✓
INFO ✓✓✓✓
EASE ✓✓✓✓

A very well constructed site covering business, tourism, sport, culture and shopping. There's a great deal in terms of advice, tips, maps, but not much in-depth info. For that use the links or go to **www.exploreturkey.com** which is a good travel guide and **www.turkishembassy-london.com** for the official line.

U

www.go-unitedstates.com

A HIGHLIGHT IN EVERY STATE

ORIGIN US
SPEED ✓✓✓✓
INFO ✓✓✓✓
EASE ✓✓✓✓

Covers the USA by region, then State with key destinations noted. There are also recommendations on where to stay, books to read and where to eat.

See also:
www.amtrak.com – rail schedules and fares across America.
www.greyhound.com – coach and bus schedules, but you can't buy tickets online from outside the US.
www.disneyworld.com – all you need to know about the world's number one theme park.
www.gohawaii.com – great site for checking out Hawaii and it's many attractions.
www.usahotelguide.com – reserve your room in any one of 40,000 hotels across the USA.

Travel in Britain

www.visitbritain.com
HOME OF THE BRITISH TOURIST AUTHORITY

ORIGIN UK
SPEED ✓✓✓
INFO ✓✓✓✓✓
EASE ✓✓✓✓

Selling Britain using a holiday-ideas-led site with lots of help for the visitor, maps, background stories, images, entertainment, culture, activities and a planner. There's also a very helpful set of links.

www.informationbritain.co.uk
HOLIDAY INFORMATION

ORIGIN UK
SPEED ✓✓✓
INFO ✓✓✓✓✓
EASE ✓✓✓✓

Where to stay and where to go with an overview of all the UK's main tourist attractions, counties and regions, it has good cross-referencing and links to the major destinations.

www.atuk.co.uk
UK TRAVEL AND TOURIST GUIDE

ORIGIN UK
SPEED ✓✓✓
INFO ✓✓✓✓✓
EASE ✓✓✓

A good county-by-county guide-come-directory, with plenty of links and extras such as web cams, awards, weather, site of the day and competitions. It's very good if you want something unusual, but it's a bit unclear whether they rate the activity or the web site. For another good links directory see www.enjoybritain.com who concentrate solely on travel.

www.sightseeing.co.uk
SIGHT-SEEING MADE EASY

ORIGIN UK
SPEED ✓✓✓✓
INFO ✓✓✓✓
EASE ✓✓✓✓✓

A good looking and very useful site if you're stuck for an idea of what to do. Just type in what you want to see and where you are and up pops a listing giving basic information on each attraction, how far it is to get there, entrance fee and a map. One slight criticism is that there could be more background information on each attraction.

See also:

www.ukguide.org – well-organised directory with a UK and a London guide plus mapping.

www.aboutbritain.com – attractive, well laid out and comprehensive UK guide.

www.travelbritain.com – a modest directory site.

www.britain.co.uk – basic overview of tourist Britain with accommodation links thrown in, bizarrely the hotels are listed by their name rather than where they actually are located.

www.britainexpress.co.uk – very good travel site with lots of tourist information and links, it's easy-to-use and covers just about every aspect of Britain.

www.knowhere.co.uk
THE USER'S GUIDE TO BRITAIN

ORIGIN UK
SPEED ✓✓✓✓
INFO ✓✓✓✓✓
EASE ✓✓✓✓

An unconventional 'tourist guide' which gives a warts-and-all account of over 1,000 places in Britain; it's very irreverent and if you are squeamish or a bit sensitive then they have a good list of links to proper tourist sites.

www.a2btravel.co.uk
BOOKING BRITAIN

ORIGIN UK
SPEED ✓✓✓
INFO ✓✓✓✓✓
EASE ✓✓✓✓

Acknowledged as the best online travel information and booking service for the UK. The site offers the ability to book rooms in over 33,000 hotels, inns and guesthouses. There are other services such as travel tips, airport guides, ferry information and, if you need to go abroad after all, then there's everything on site for that too.

www.laterooms.co.uk
Hotel industry late availability database

ORIGIN UK
SPEED ✓✓✓
INFO ✓✓✓✓✓
EASE ✓✓✓✓

An attempt to fill empty beds, all you do is enter a destination and length of stay, and then a selection appears. Works about two weeks ahead. You can also search by hotel type as well as just look at the biggest savings or best deals. There are also sections for USA and European destinations.

See also:

www.travelengland.org.uk – nice online guide to everything English, places to visit and accommodation.

www.imagesofengland.com – 15,000 images of England, be part of the creation of an image bank of listed buildings.

www.aboutscotland.com – excellent site with information on a broad range of accommodation and sights to see, it's fast too.

www.scotland-info.co.uk – very good online guidebook, covering Scotland by area; it's quite slow but the information is very good.

www.holidays-in-wales.co.uk – holidays in the Welsh countryside with limited online booking, with a good overview of the country.

www.data-wales.co.uk – not so much a tourist site, but excellent for history and culture and quite funny too.

www.ni-tourism.com – Northern Ireland Tourist Board has an attractive site showing the best that the region has to offer, with a virtual tour, holiday planner, accommodation, guides and special offers.

www.jerseyhols.com – good looking site with lots of information and info on where to stay and what to do, see also **www.jersey.com** who have a very slick site.

www.guernseytouristboard.com – slightly dodgy site but there's all the information you need on Guernsey.

www.isle-of-man.com – learn all about this unique island with help on where to stay and, of course, background on the famous TT races.

www.isle-of-wight-tourism.gov.uk – hi-tech site with lots of information on the isle and details on breaks there, you can even have last minute breaks sent to your mobile.

www.londontown.com – very comprehensive survival and holiday guide rolled into one, with sections on restaurants, hotels, attractions and offers. It is quite slow.

www.londonhotelreservations.com – some good deals on London hotels.

Things to do in Britain

www.virgin.net/daysout
FIND A GOOD DAY OUT

ORIGIN UK
SPEED ✓✓
INFO ✓✓✓✓✓
EASE ✓✓✓✓✓

If you can put up with the adverts, Virgin's days out page is well worth a visit if you're stuck for something to do. There's plenty of information on the sights and there's a days out finder service for when you're really stuck. There are also links to related and useful sites. See also the exhaustive **www.daysoutuk.com** who list over 7,000 attractions and 10,000 events countrywide.

www.gardenvisit.com
GO TO A GARDEN

ORIGIN UK
SPEED ✓✓✓✓
INFO ✓✓✓✓
EASE ✓✓✓✓

A basic text-based site, which lists some 1,000 of the UK's gardens open to the public, giving details of each, how to get there and how they rate. It also covers the USA and Europe and there's also an excellent overview of garden history.

www.nationaltrust.org.uk
PLACES OF HISTORIC INTEREST AND BEAUTY

ORIGIN UK
SPEED ✓✓✓✓
INFO ✓✓✓✓✓
EASE ✓✓✓✓✓

The National Trust's site has an excellent overview of their activities and the properties they own. There is a very good search facility and up-to-date information to help with your visit. See also English Heritage site at www.english-heritage.org.uk which is excellent and building.

www.goodbeachguide.co.uk
THE BEST BEACHES

ORIGIN UK
SPEED ✓✓✓✓
INFO ✓✓✓✓
EASE ✓✓✓✓

From the Marine Conservation Society you can find out which are Britain's worst and best beaches. It's set out regionally and the site is updated regularly.

What to do with the kids

www.kidsnet.co.uk
WHAT'S ON AND WHERE?

ORIGIN UK
SPEED ✓✓✓✓
INFO ✓✓✓✓
EASE ✓✓✓✓

Strong design and ease-of-use make this site stand out aligned with a comprehensive database of places and attractions. Also has cinema listings, games and book search facilities which all add to the general excellence. Good links list too.

www.kidstravel.co.uk – nice design but comparatively little content, some good ideas and travelling tips for parents though.

www.planit4kids.com – covers seven major areas of the country centred on the major cites, the linked sites are excellent with plenty to see and do, on top of all the information you need for a great day out. There plans to rollout internationally.

www.xkeys.co.uk – specialist in residential camps for children of all ages, excellent web site with lots of information and references.

Cycling and touring

The following are mostly UK specialists, but some cover further afield too.

www.ctc.org.uk
WORKING FOR CYCLISTS

ORIGIN UK	
SPEED ✓✓✓	
INFO ✓✓✓✓✓	
EASE ✓✓✓✓	

The CTC have a great travel section with routes, tours, offers, links and directories, it's a great place to start your search for the perfect cycling holiday.

Also check out:

www.nationalcyclenetwork.co.uk – details of the National Cycle Network and how to make the best use of it.

www.bikemagic.com – go to the travel pages for an excellent section where Bike Magic have got partners who'll supply flight deals for cyclists or rail travel and holidays.

www.visitbritain.com/activities/cycling – pages from the excellent Visit Britain site with a route finder for rides from under 10 miles to over 100 miles all with detailed instructions and mapping.

www.bicycle-beano.co.uk – Bicycle Beano have a good site covering cycling holidays in Wales and the borders.

www.byways-breaks.co.uk – nice looking site, Byways Breaks arrange cycling and walking holidays in the Shropshire and Cheshire countryside.

www.scotcycle.co.uk Scottish Cycling Holidays are specialists in cycling holidays in Scotland obviously. Nice site too.

www.rough-tracks.co.uk – wide range of active adventure holidays from beginners to experts.

www.biketours.co.uk – a very good selection of biking tours through Europe and further afield.

Camping and Caravanning

Many of the sites listed specialise in Britain but some have information on camp sites abroad too.

www.camp-sites.co.uk
FIND A SITE

ORIGIN UK	Excellent regional listing of the UK's campsites with
SPEED ✓✓✓✓	comprehensive details on each site and links to other
INFO ✓✓✓✓	related directories.
EASE ✓✓✓✓	

See also:

www.camping-and-leisure.co.uk – lots of links and classified ads.

www.eurocampindependent.co.uk – excellent site if you want to go camping in Europe, some special offers and you can chat about your experiences too.

www.keycamp.co.uk – European specialist with a choice of 120 sites in eight countries.

www.pjcamping.co.uk – exhaustive selection of tents and camping equipment for sale, good info but no online ordering.

www.caravan.co.uk
THE CARAVAN CLUB

ORIGIN UK
SPEED ✓✓✓✓
INFO ✓✓✓✓
EASE ✓✓✓✓

Huge listing of sites, advice and practical help with details of over 200 sites and some 3,000 other certified locations where you can park up. There's also a European service featuring some 180 sites in 16 countries. You can join the club on site and request any of the 50 or so helps leaflets they publish.

See also:

http://camping.uk-directory.com – a good regional sites directory, with retailing links, caravans for sale and conservation information.

www.caravan-sitefinder.co.uk – listing of over 1,000 caravan sites, with background information on a wide range of topics.

Waterways

www.britishwaterways.co.uk
BRITISH WATERWAYS

ORIGIN UK
SPEED ✓✓✓✓
INFO ✓✓✓✓✓
EASE ✓✓✓✓

This organisation is responsible for maintaining a large part of Britain's waterways and this excellent site details their work and contains interactive mapping of the routes with a great deal of background information and events listings and history.

See also:

www.waterways.org.uk – Inland Waterways Association site, dedicated to keeping canals open and you can find out about their organised activities too.

www.canalroutes.com – a roots and routes history of Britain's canals in a regional directory, a labour of love.

www.canals.co.uk – the biggest canal-related shop
on the Internet, mainly videos, maps and books.

www.hoseasons.co.uk – great site from the specialists in boating holidays, you can book online too.

www.blakes.co.uk – another boating holiday
specialist.

Adventure and activity

www.activitiesonline.co.uk
ULTIMATE RESOURCE FOR LEISURE PURSUITS

ORIGIN UK
SPEED ✓✓✓✓
INFO ✓✓✓✓
EASE ✓✓✓

A directory of adventure and activity holiday
specialists covering everything from extreme sports
to gardening. You get a description of the activity,
then a list of relevant sites.

www.sportbreak.co.uk
SEARCH ENGINE FOR SPORTS HOLIDAYS

ORIGIN UK
SPEED ✓✓✓✓
INFO ✓✓✓✓
EASE ✓✓✓

Apart from sports it covers all activity holidays
including leisure breaks, health clubs, even stag and
hen parties. It's easy-to-use and the information is
well put over.

Other adventure holiday sites:

www.activityholsni.co.uk – Activity Holidays in
Northern Ireland have a great site and lots to do.

www.activitywales.co.uk – break out and discover
the real Wales with Activity Wales. Use this well-
constructed site to suss out what to have a go at.

www.activity-scotland.co.uk – lots of things to do in
here, nice regional guide as well.

www.adventure.uk.com – Adventure International
are experienced adventure holiday specialists
based in Bude, Cornwall.

www.adventureholiday.com – ProAdventure
specialise in activity holidays in North Wales.

www.leisurepursuits.com – one of the largest sports
tour operators and travel agents.

www.pgl.co.uk/holidays – adventure holidays for
kids – great site too.

www.mtn.co.uk – mountaineering, hillwalking and
trekking – excellent site with all the information
you're likely to need.

www.trailplus.com – the ultimate adventure, offering lifestyle experiences, adventure camps and
much more.

Walking and rambling

www.ramblers.org.uk
THE RAMBLERS' ASSOCIATION

ORIGIN UK
SPEED ✓✓
INFO ✓✓✓✓
EASE ✓✓✓✓

News, strong views and plenty of advice on offer
here, where you can find out about the Association's
activities and even join a campaign. There are
features on events and details of the *Rambler* magazine, though sadly archives aren't available.

www.walkingbritain.co.uk
BRITISH WALKS

ORIGIN UK
SPEED ✓✓
INFO ✓✓✓✓✓
EASE ✓✓✓✓

Over 1,000 pages of information about walking in
Britain, it mainly covers the national parks but it is
expanding to include less well-known areas. They
provide decent route maps and photos to guide you.
There's also a list of handy links and a good photo
gallery.

www.onedayhikes.com
WHERE DO YOU WANT TO HIKE TODAY?

ORIGIN US
SPEED ✓✓✓
INFO ✓✓✓✓✓
EASE ✓✓✓✓

A great site, which is basically a directory of hikes that you can complete in a day, it's not just for the UK either, it covers the whole world. There's excellent information on each hike plus pictures and you get the chance to win a digital camera if you send in a report of a hike you've done and it gets accepted.

For more sites for hikers try:

www.ramblersholidays.co.uk – Ramblers Holidays specialise in escorted rambling holidays.

www.bwf-ivv.org.uk – the British Walking Federation organise a wide range of activities and you can find out about them here.

www.gelert.com – equipment for sale, a new site is under construction but if it's half as good as the old one, then it'll be worth checking out.

www.sprayway.co.uk – excellent but slightly pretentious site from a supplier of clothing 'systems' for walking, running and mountaineering.

Train, coach and ferry journeys

www.pti.org.uk
PUBLIC TRANSPORT INFORMATION

ORIGIN UK
SPEED ✓✓✓
INFO ✓✓✓✓✓
EASE ✓✓✓✓

An incredibly useful site if you're a frequent user of public transport or if you're using it to go somewhere you're not familiar with. It categorises all the major forms of public transport and lists for each area useful numbers, timetables, web sites and interactive mapping to help you. It also includes routes to Europe and Ireland.

www.kizoom.co.uk
TRAVEL SERVICE TO YOUR PHONE

ORIGIN UK
SPEED ✓✓✓
INFO ✓✓✓
EASE ✓✓✓

Good quality travel information to your mobile phone sounds great and this is a very well set up and easy-to-use site. Unfortunately, it only works with a limited number of WAP phones, so if you've one of those you're in luck.

www.travelfusion.com
THE TRAVEL COMPARISON PORTAL

ORIGIN UK
SPEED ✓✓✓
INFO ✓✓✓✓✓
EASE ✓✓✓✓

A brilliant idea – pick a journey then compare whether it would be best to go by coach, car, ferry or by air. It's simple to use and you can compare by price or speed. It then connects you with the right operator if you want to book.

Railways

www.railtrack.co.uk
FOR TRAIN TIMES

ORIGIN UK
SPEED ✓✓✓
INFO ✓✓✓✓✓
EASE ✓✓✓

Go to the travel section and type in the start point and destination then Railtrack will tell you the time of the next train. It's very easy-to-use and a must for all rail travellers. You can also get travel news and information about Railtrack; there are no details of rail fares.

www.nationalrail.co.uk
NATIONAL RAIL

ORIGIN UK
SPEED ✓✓✓
INFO ✓✓✓✓✓
EASE ✓✓✓✓

National Rail's site has all the latest information, timetables and links you need to plan a rail journey. It's very comprehensive with up-to-the-minute information on what's going on.

www.thetrainline.com
BUY TRAIN TICKETS

ORIGIN	UK
SPEED	✓✓✓
INFO	✓✓✓✓✓
VALUE	✓✓✓✓
EASE	✓✓✓✓

You can book a ticket for train travel, whether business or leisure, (except sleeper, Motorail, Eurostar and ferry services) they have an up-to-date timetable and the tickets will be sent or you can collect.

See also:
www.eurail.com – details of the Eurailticket, information and prices, but you can't buy online.
www.eurostar.co.uk – online booking plus timetables and offers.

www.thetube.com
LONDON UNDERGROUND

ORIGIN	UK
SPEED	✓✓✓
INFO	✓✓✓✓✓
EASE	✓✓✓✓

An excellent and informative site from London Underground with lots of features, articles on visiting London and links to related sites. There's a good journey planner and tube maps too.
You buy your tickets from a different site – **www.ticket-online.co.uk** See also the Tube Planner at **www.tubeplanner.com** which is a straightforward, easy-to-use journey planner.

Coaches

www.gobycoach.com
BOOK COACH TICKETS

ORIGIN	UK
SPEED	✓✓✓
INFO	✓✓✓✓✓
EASE	✓✓✓

Organise your journey with this easy-to-use web site from National Express, and then book the tickets. Also offers an airport service, transport to events and tours.

Ferries

www.ferrybooker.com
BOOK YOUR CROSSING

ORIGIN	UK
SPEED	✓✓✓
INFO	✓✓✓✓✓
VALUE	✓✓✓
EASE	✓✓✓✓

The best ferry site for a wide range of information on crossing times featuring a large number of routes. There is help with planning, special offers, channel tunnel ticket booking and they offer holiday breaks too.

See also:

www.brittany-ferries.co.uk – crossings to France and Spain with online booking and special offers, also cruises and holidays.

www.dfdsseaways.co.uk – details and offers on Scandinavian routes.

www.drive-alive.com – motoring holiday specialists who get good rates on channel crossings as part of their package.

www.ferry.co.uk – great offers on selected crossings from Dover to Calais.

www.ferrysavers.co.uk – wide range of offers and much improved selection of crossings at good prices, you can book online and they offer a price promise too.

www.hoverspeed.com – online booking and all the information you need to make the fastest channel and Irish sea crossings.

www.irishferries.ie – excellent magazine-style site where amongst all the features you can find timetables and book tickets.

www.posl.com – P&O Stena Line with online booking, details of sailings and offers.

www.seafrance.co.uk – bookings and information on their Calais-Dover service plus some special offers.

Car hire

It's probably best to go to a price comparison site before going to one of the car hire companies, that way you should get the best prices. One of the best is to be found at www.priceline.co.uk

www.holidaycars.co.uk
WORLD-WIDE CAR HIRE

ORIGIN	UK	Over 3,000 car hire locations throughout the world
SPEED	✓✓✓	means that this site is well worth a visit on your
INFO	✓✓✓✓	quest, you can get an instant online quote and you
VALUE	✓✓✓	can book too. Very good for the USA. See also
EASE	✓✓✓✓	Holiday Autos who have a similar site at

www.holidayautos.co.uk and also the competitive
www.pelicancarhire.co.uk

Cruises

www.whatcruise.co.uk
WHAT CRUISE?

ORIGIN	UK	Check out the best cruises, look for the best prices
SPEED	✓✓✓✓	and get information on what to do on board. You
INFO	✓✓✓✓✓	can browse the site by region, by line and by ship
VALUE	✓✓✓	and there's lots of tips and advice.
EASE	✓✓✓✓	

www.cruiseinformationservice.co.uk
CRUISE INFO

ORIGIN	UK	A trade site put together to encourage people to take
SPEED	✓✓✓✓	cruise holidays. There's an introduction to cruising
INFO	✓✓✓✓	and information on the lines, a magazine and links
EASE	✓✓✓✓	to useful sites. There's also information on how to

book and what sort of cruise is right for you.

Utilities

Get the best prices on your gas, electricity and water and find out what the big suppliers are up to as well.

www.ofgem.gov.uk
GAS AND ELECTRICITY SUPPLIER WATCHDOG

ORIGIN UK
SPEED ✓✓✓✓
INFO ✓✓✓✓✓
EASE ✓✓✓✓✓

Data on the suppliers and companies providing comparison information makes for interesting reading. There's also background on how bills are made up, complaints and how energy reaches your home. Excellent.

www.buy.co.uk
CUT YOUR BILLS – COMPARE PRICES

ORIGIN UK
SPEED ✓✓✓✓✓
INFO ✓✓✓✓
VALUE ✓✓✓✓✓
EASE ✓✓✓✓✓

Take a few minutes to check the prices of the key utilities and see whether you can save on your current bills, its easy and quick. It also covers phones and loans, and there's also access to *Which?* magazine's energy reports. See also **www.servista.com** which is easy-to-use and well designed, while **www.uswitch.com** and **www.unravelit.com** have signed up to OFGEM's code of conduct on price comparison information.

Electricity and gas

Here are the main energy sites, who owns them at time of writing and the highlights of the site.

www.amerada.co.uk – one of the best value suppliers with an excellent site, you can even switch to them online.

www.british-energy.com – one of the largest electricity providers with a good looking but not very useful site.

www.centrica.co.uk – owners of British Gas and the AA, this site aims to give information about the group.

www.easternenergy.co.uk – good service, helpful, much improved.

www.esb.ie – good looking site from an Irish supplier with online sign-up available.

www.gas.co.uk – comprehensive service from British Gas with account viewing.

www.hydro.co.uk – Scottish Hydro Electric has one of the sites most oriented to its customers.

www.innogy.com – good looking site from this new company with useful features and not much help in the customer care centre.

www.london-electricity.co.uk – straightforward but slow.

www.mep.co.uk – the old Midland supplier, really a corporate site.

www.nationalgrid.com/uk – the National Grid, the Railtrack of power.

www.nie.co.uk – Northern Ireland Electricity with customer information on their service the rest is fairly corporate.

www.npower.com – nicely designed site with online application.

www.powergen.co.uk – Powergen has a neat site with calculators and a switching service.

www.scottish-southern.co.uk – owner of Swalec, site aimed at shareholders.

www.swalec.co.uk – Swalec, good house move planner.

www.yeg.co.uk – Yorkshire Electric has a nice, helpful site – soon to be part of Innogy.

www.transco.uk.com
FOR GAS LEAKS

ORIGIN UK	Transco doesn't sell gas, but maintains the 24-hour
SPEED ✓✓✓✓	emergency service for stopping gas leaks –
INFO ✓✓✓	call 0800 111 999 to report one.
EASE ✓✓✓✓	

www.corgi-gas.co.uk
COUNCIL OF REGISTERED GAS INSTALLERS

ORIGIN UK	CORGI is the gas industry watchdog; the site has
SPEED ✓✓✓✓	advice on gas installation and where to find a fitter
INFO ✓✓✓✓	or repairman.
EASE ✓✓✓✓	

www.calorgas.co.uk
CALOR GAS

ORIGIN UK	Information on your nearest stockists, how best to
SPEED ✓✓✓✓	use Calor gas and Autogas, there's also corporate
INFO ✓✓✓✓	background and customer services too. You can also
VALUE ✓✓✓	order it online with payment collected on delivery.
EASE ✓✓✓✓	

Water

www.open.gov.uk/ofwat/index.htm
OFFICE OF WATER SERVICES

ORIGIN UK	A very poor effort, especially when compared to the
SPEED ✓✓✓✓	OFGEM counterpart's site, however, you can find
INFO ✓✓✓✓	out about what they do and you can contact them
VALUE ✓✓✓	for advice.
EASE ✓✓✓✓	

The following are the main water company sites:
www.nww.co.uk – North West Water has a well-
    designed site with help, information and good
    advice for consumers, with online access to your
    account.

www.severntrent.co.uk – well it's got the share price, which is nice.

www.swwater.co.uk – lots of information and good advice, bill paying online.

www.wessexwater.plc.uk – good site with bill paying facilities and information, even which reservoirs you can fish in.

www.nwl.co.uk – nice lifestyle site with leisure information and bill paying.

www.thameswater.co.uk – good information and advice.

The Weather

www.met-office.gov.uk

EXCELLING IN WEATHER SERVICES

ORIGIN UK
SPEED ✓✓✓
INFO ✓✓✓✓
EASE ✓✓✓✓

Comprehensive information on Britain's favourite topic of conversation, easy-to-use in 4 sections with interactive maps – world weather and world weather news, UK weather headlines and flash weather warnings. There's also a good selection of links and a mobile phone service.

www.bbc.co.uk/weather

ANOTHER WINNER FROM THE BBC

ORIGIN UK
SPEED ✓✓✓✓
INFO ✓✓✓✓✓
EASE ✓✓✓✓

Another page from the BBC site, it gives up-to-the-minute forecasts, and is very clear and concise. It features: 5-day forecasts by town, city or post code; specialist reports such as ski resorts; pollution; sun index; world weather and the shipping forecast. A section dedicated to articles on various aspects of the weather and details on making the weather forecast programme.

For more information about the weather, the Weather Channel has a very good site on www.weather.com this is geared to the USA, but has some really good articles and features. For regional UK links try the very basic but informative UK weather information site www.weather.org.uk and www.uk-weather.co.uk which is good for links.

www.weatherimages.org
SEE THE WORLD'S WEATHER – LIVE

ORIGIN	US	Weatherimages is compiled by a true weather fan.
SPEED	✓✓✓	Split into twenty or so areas of interest, there is
INFO	✓✓✓✓	plenty of information and there's loads to see. The
EASE	✓✓✓✓	best feature is the network of weather cams, from which you can see the best and worst of the world's weather.

Web cameras

One of the most fascinating aspects of the Internet is the ability to tap into some CCTV or specially set up web cameras from all around the world.

www.camcity.com
WEB CAM SEARCH ENGINE

ORIGIN	US	A search facility with a database of thousands of
SPEED	✓✓✓	CCTV city based cameras from around the world, if
INFO	✓✓✓✓	you're in browsing mood you can also use the inter-
EASE	✓✓✓✓	active city map to find what you're interested in.

See also:

www.allcam.com – small directory of web cameras on a well laid out site, some interesting categories too.

www.camcentral.com – excellent selection of cameras, chosen for quality rather than quantity; the wildlife ones are very good.

www.webcamworld.com – big directory with a useful top 100 feature.

www.cammunity.com – good-looking site with a massive directory of sites and web cams.

Web Site Guides and Directories

If you can't find the site you're looking for in this book then rather than use a search engine, check out one of these web site directories.

www.uk250.co.uk
OVER 10,000 SITES IN 250 CATEGORIES

ORIGIN UK
SPEED ✓✓✓
INFO ✓✓✓✓✓
EASE ✓✓✓

Heavily advertised and hyped though this site has been, many people seem to think that it consists of just the top 250 sites, but it's actually a very comprehensive database of Britain's most important and useful '.co.uks' and '.coms'. The sites listed are not reviewed but a one-liner gives a brief description of what they are about. Desperately needs a good search facility.

www.thegoodwebguide.co.uk
GOOD WEB GUIDE

ORIGIN UK
SPEED ✓✓✓✓
INFO ✓✓✓✓
VALUE ✓✓
EASE ✓✓✓✓

The best web sites in several key categories are comprehensively reviewed but you have to subscribe (£30 per annum) or buy the related book (subscription then free to that subject area) to get the best out of it. It's a good site and the books are good (if a little expensive), but the problem for the good web guide team is that you can get all the information at reduced cost elsewhere.

http://cool.infi.net
THE COOLEST SITES

ORIGIN US
SPEED ✓✓✓
INFO ✓✓✓✓
EASE ✓✓✓

Vote for the coolest sites, and find out which are considered the best. This has got very commercial now, so lots of deals and adverts get in the way.

www.ukdirectory.co.uk
DEFINITIVE GUIDES TO BRITISH SITES

ORIGIN UK
SPEED ✓✓
INFO ✓✓✓✓✓
EASE ✓✓✓

A massive database of web sites conveniently categorised into fourteen sections, it is mainly geared to business, but there's leisure too. They don't review, but there are brief explanations provided by the site owners. It's also slow.

Weddings

www.confetti.co.uk
YOUR INTERACTIVE WEDDING GUIDE

ORIGIN UK
SPEED ✓✓✓✓
INFO ✓✓✓✓✓
VALUE ✓✓✓
EASE ✓✓✓✓

A good looking and busy site, designed to help you through every stage of your wedding with information for all participants. There are gift guides, planning tools, advice, a supplier directory and a shop. They don't miss much.

www.wedding-service.co.uk
UK's LARGEST WEDDING AND BRIDE DIRECTORY

ORIGIN UK
SPEED ✓✓✓
INFO ✓✓✓✓✓
EASE ✓✓✓

A huge list of suppliers, service providers and information by region, everything from balloons to speechwriters are listed. The site is not that easy on the eye and it takes a little while to find what you want.

www.all-about-weddings.co.uk
INFORMATION ABOUT GETTING MARRIED IN THE UK

ORIGIN UK
SPEED ✓✓✓
INFO ✓✓✓✓✓
VALUE ✓✓✓
EASE ✓✓✓✓

Excellent for basic information about planning weddings from the ceremony to the reception; it also has a good set of links to related and specialist supplier sites, a travel section and a shop. It's all wrapped up in suitably matrimonial design with love hearts flowing across the screen as you browse.

Other good sites for weddings:
www.bridalplanner.com – well designed and wide ranging, including advice and real life stories plus print off checklists and planners.
www.bridesuk.net – excellent site from *Brides* magazine; get all the latest in bridal fashion.

www.ebonyweddings.co.uk – the first online wedding directory for people of Afro-Caribbean origin within the United Kingdom.

www.hitched.co.uk – another good all-rounder with the added feature of a discussion forum where you can swap wedding stories.

www.planmyperfectwedding.co.uk – excellent selection of links to suppliers and services.

www.pronuptia.co.uk – details of the range and stores, not much else.

www.webwedding.co.uk – lots of expert advice and inspiration, a bit slow though.

www.weddingguide.co.uk – clean-looking site with shop, directory and advice plus a good search facility.

www.weddings.co.uk – another good site with free wedding planning software, follow a bride-to-be as she keeps a diary of the countdown to the big day.

www.weddingstationery.co.uk – select your stationery from the comfort of your own home.

Women

The following are a few sites of particular interest to women.

www.cabinet-office.gov.uk/womens-unit
THE WOMEN'S UNIT AT No 10

ORIGIN UK
SPEED ✓✓✓
INFO ✓✓✓✓
EASE ✓✓✓✓

The Government's Women's Unit 'provides a two-way voice between Government and the women of the UK'. Politics aside, the site provides useful information on how government policies impact on women's lives, covering hot topics such as balancing work and family, domestic violence, money, health and learning. Worth visiting for the useful links. For the UN go to **www.un.org/womenwatch**

www.working-options.co.uk
PART-TIME RECRUITMENT

ORIGIN UK
SPEED ✓✓✓
INFO ✓✓✓
EASE ✓✓✓✓

Founded by two professional mothers unable to find stimulating part-time work, this site is devoted to finding such jobs for others. Register and they will try to match your skills with employers looking for part-time workers. For a similar site send your cv to **www.resourceconnection.co.uk**

Magazines

www.flametree.co.uk
INSPIRING SOLUTIONS TO BALANCE YOUR LIFE

ORIGIN UK
SPEED ✓✓✓✓
INFO ✓✓✓✓
EASE ✓✓✓✓

A sensible magazine-style site aimed at putting the balance back into women's lives. Informative articles on flexible work, parenting and good links for legal and health advice. Register to make the most of the site.

www.women.com
THE SMART WAY TO GET THINGS DONE

ORIGIN US
SPEED ✓✓✓
INFO ✓✓✓✓✓
EASE ✓✓✓✓

Aimed at the professional American woman, this is a no-nonsense site offering a great deal of news, information and recommendation on a wide variety of topics such as careers, pregnancy, family, technology, stocks, home and garden and so on.

See also **www.womenswire.com** and **www.webgrrls.com** both of which offer similar information but in differing styles.

www.handbag.com
THE ISP FOR WOMEN

ORIGIN UK
SPEED ✓✓✓✓
INFO ✓✓✓✓✓
VALUE ✓✓✓
EASE ✓✓✓✓

Described as the most useful place on the Internet for British women, Handbag lives up to that with a mass of information written in an informal style and aimed helping you get through life. There's shopping and competitions too. For some it's a little too commercial though. For another magazine-style approach try **www.icircle.co.uk** which is part of the Freeserve network calling itself the Women's Channel.

www.beme.com
FOR THE CHIC WITHIN

ORIGIN UK
SPEED ✓✓
INFO ✓✓✓✓
EASE ✓✓✓✓

Everything you'd expect from a magazine site aimed at the young women: beauty, fashion, travel, stories, advice, horoscopes competitions and, oh yes, sex, packaged on a elegantly designed, simple site. Under construction is beme shop which promises to be an upmarket emporium. Could do with speeding up.

e-women.com
THE INTERNATIONAL WOMEN'S PORTAL

ORIGIN UK
SPEED ✓✓✓
INFO ✓✓✓✓
EASE ✓✓✓✓

E-women aims to provide women world-wide with features and links which are relevant to their lives. There are lots of women's magazine-type features combined with serious comment on human rights, cultural and workplace issues along with a shopping directory.

www.winmagazine.org
WOMEN'S INTERNATIONAL NET

ORIGIN US
SPEED ✓✓✓
INFO ✓✓✓✓
EASE ✓✓✓✓

This is an online magazine devoted to bringing together women from all over the world for dialogue and mutual understanding, furthering the knowledge of women's issues and featuring new writing talent. Some of the writing is excellent, but it can be a little earnest.

Women's health

www.healthywomen.org
EDUCATING WOMEN ABOUT THEMSELVES

ORIGIN US
SPEED ✓✓✓✓
INFO ✓✓✓✓✓
EASE ✓✓

The layout doesn't do justice to the quality of information on the site provided by the American-based National Women's Health Resource Center. Go to the 'health center' and use the pull-down menu to select a topic such as breast cancer, acupuncture or menopause. The aim is to provide women with good information to help them make informed decisions about their health.

www.womens-health.co.uk
OBS AND GYNAE EXPLAINED

ORIGIN UK
SPEED ✓✓✓✓
INFO ✓✓✓✓
EASE ✓✓✓

A good starting point for information on obstetrics and gynaecology including pregnancy, infertility, complications and investigations. Has a good search facility and useful links.

www.fpa.org.uk
FAMILY PLANNING

ORIGIN UK
SPEED ✓✓✓✓
INFO ✓✓✓✓✓
EASE ✓✓✓✓

A really comprehensive web site from the Family Planning Association with information on all aspects of birth control written in an easy-to-use and helpful style. There is a useful page entitled 'I need help now' plus good links. For a more campaigning approach, try **www.mariestopes.org.uk** for a rundown on contraception choices and information on related topics such as health screening. You can even arrange for him to have a vasectomy online.

Leisure

www.journeywoman.com
PREMIER TRAVEL RESOURCE FOR WOMEN

ORIGIN US
SPEED ✓✓✓
INFO ✓✓✓✓✓
VALUE ✓✓✓
EASE ✓✓✓✓

Dedicated to ensuring safe travel for women, registering gets you access to the free newsletter plus lots of advice, guidance and tips from women who've travelled, traveller's tales and health warnings. For another good but US-biased site try **www.women-traveling.com**

www.womengamers.com

BECAUSE WOMEN DO PLAY

ORIGIN US	The aim is to provide a selection of reviews and games
SPEED ✓✓✓✓	geared specifically to a female audience (although it
INFO ✓✓✓✓	doesn't stop this being an enjoyable site for men to
EASE ✓✓✓✓	visit). It has up-to-the-minute reviews, really well-written articles, lots of content and high quality design.

www.wsf.org.uk

WOMEN'S SPORT FOUNDATION

ORIGIN UK	The voice of women's sport is committed to improving
SPEED ✓✓✓✓	and promoting opportunities for women and girls in
INFO ✓✓✓✓	sport at every level. It does this by lobbying and raising
EASE ✓✓✓✓	the awareness of the importance of women in sport to the organisers and governing bodies. Here you can find out how to get involved or get help.

Index

accessories 114
ADSL 17
adult education 102–3
adventure 433
advertisements 43–4
aircraft 17–20
airlines 401–3
alternative medicine
    207–8
American football 341
animals 261–7, 283–9
antiques 21–23
anti-virus software 169
Apple Mac 24–6, 81–3,
    333–5
appliances 103–6
archery 342
architecture 27
art 28–39
    materials 214–5
astrology 39–40
astronomy 336–8
athletics 342
auctions 41–2, 398
Australian rules football
    343
aviation 17–20
babies 274–8
banks 125–8
baseball 344
basketball 344
BBC 384–6
beauty products 115–7
betting 166–9
biography 211–4

birds 265, 286
boats 317–9, 438–9
books 44–51
bowls 344
boxing 345
Britain
    food 139–40
    shops 330
    travel 425–37
buses 435, 437
business 128–29
cameras 103–6, 292
camping 431–2
caravans 431–2
cars 52–62
    registrations 59
    insurance 59
    repair 59–60
    sport 357–8
car hire 439
careers 222–6, 449
cartoons 37
CDs 246–8
celebrities 63
ceramics 23–4
charities 64–5, 261–7,
    278, 285
chat 65–8
chefs 140–1
children 68–80
    chat 68
    childcare 277
    days out 429–30
    education 97–102
    entertainment 72–5, 80

competitions 81
computers 279
holidays with 429–30, 434
parenting 274–83
problems 278–83
search engines for 80
shopping 69–72, 277–8
toys 69–72
TV 75–8
web sites for 72–5, 129
chocolate 143
cinemas 238
classified ads 43-4
clay shooting 346
clip art 36
clothes 107–14, 321–33
sports clothes 369
coaches 435, 437
coins 215
collecting 21–3, 215–6
computers 24–6, 81–3, 333–5
concerts 259–60
cosmetics 115–7, 321–33
costume 213
cricket 346–7
cruises 439
cycling 83–4, 348, 430
darts 349
dating 85–6
days out 80, 429–30
design 29, 93–7
diaries 271
DIY 86–97
dictionaries 307–8
diet 144–5, 205–6
dinosaurs 266
drink 156–61

drugs 279
DVD 240–1, 246–8
education 97–102
adult 102–3
electrical goods 103–6
electricity 440–1
e-mail addresses 130–1
employment 222–6
encyclopaedias 305–6
environment 261–6
equestrian 349
estate agents 294–8
extreme sports 350
fashion 107–14, 321–33
ferries 435, 438
films 234–42
finance 118–29
finding someone 130–1
fishing 350
fitness 205–6
flowers 132–3
food and drink 133–63
football 350–2
free stuff 163–4
furniture 93–7, 164–6
gambling 166–9
games 169–85
gardening 185–93
gardens 193–94, 429
gas 440–2
gay 194–5
genealogy 195–8
general knowledge 184–5
gifts 106, 149–50, 328
gigs 259–60
gliding 20
golf 353–4
government 198, 449

greetings cards 199–200
health 200–11, 231–2,
    280, 283, 451–2
history 211–4
hobbies 214–6
hockey 354
holidays 274, 392–439
homework 97–101, 301–5
horology 215
horoscopes 39–40
horse
    racing 168–9, 351,
    354–5
    equestrian 288, 349
hotels 403–4, 427
humour 217–21
hygiene 146–7
ice hockey 355
insurance 59, 122, 396
interior design 93–7
internet filtering software
    279
internet service providers
    222
jewellery 114–5
jobs 222–6, 449
kitchen equipment 148
law 226–9
lesbian 195
lingerie 114
magazines 229
maps 305, 407–8
martial arts 356
maternity wear 71, 113
men 230–2
mobiles 379–81
modelling 216
monarchy 198
mortgages 121–2

motor sport 357–8
motorcycles 233–4,
    sport 359
motoring organisations
    52–3
mountaineering 360
movies 234–42
MP3 242–5, 253, 300
museums 32–6
music 242–60
nature 190–1, 262–7, 309,
    312–3
needlework 214–5
news 267–70
nutrition 144–5
Olympics 361
organics 154
organiser 271
over 50s 271–4
parenting 274–83
party goods 71
pensions 124
pets 283–9
phone numbers 130–2
phones 379–81
photography 289–93
Potter, Harry 75, 79–80
pottery 23–4
pre-school 101–2, 274–7
price checkers 293–4
property 294–8
public transport 435–8
pubs 161
quizzes 184–5
radio 298–300
railways 300–1, 435–7
recipes 151–3
reference 51, 301–5
restaurants 161–3

rowing 361
royalty 198
rugby 362
sailing 363
science 309–13
scuba diving 369
search engines 313–6
senior citizens 271–4
Shakespeare 49
shares 123–4
ships 317–9
shoes 113
shopping 319–33
skiing 363–4
snooker 365
soaps 388–91
software 129, 169, 333–5
space 336–8
special needs 146, 194, 210
sport 339–70
stamp collecting 215–6
stationery 370–1
students 371–3
supermarkets 134–6, 330
swimming 368–9
tax 127–8
teachers 97–102
teenagers 373–8
telecommunications 379–81

television 384–91
tennis and racquet sports 366–67
theatre 382–3
tickets 238, 259–60, 382–3
toys 69–72
trains 300–1, 435–7
travel 274, 392–439
  in Britain 425–37
  overseas destinations 409–24
utilities 440–3
vegetarian 154–6
virus software 169
walking 434–5
water 442–3
water sports 368
waterways 432
weather 443–4
web cameras 265–6, 444–5,
web site guides 445–6
weddings 447–8
white goods 103–6
wildflowers 190–1
wine 157–61
women 449–53
yellow pages 130–1
zoos 266–7

Notes

Here are a few free pages for you to use to note down sites that you have found useful and links not mentioned in this book. Don't forget to send us any that you think have that 'wow' factor at the **goodwebsiteguide@hotmail.com**